AIMR Annual Report Supplement

to accompany

THE ANALYSIS AND USE OF FINANCIAL STATEMENTS

THIRD EDITION

Gerald I. White, CFA
Grace & White, Inc.

Ashwinpaul C. Sondhi, Ph.D.
A.C. Sondhi & Associates, LLC.

Dov Fried, Ph.D.
Stern School of Business
New York University

WILEY

JOHN WILEY & SONS, INC.

To order books or for customer service call 1-800-CALL-WILEY (225-5945).

ISBN 0-555-01230-1

Printed in the United States of America

10 9 8 7 6 5 4 3 2

Printed and bound by Courier Kendallville, Inc.

Contents

Aracruz Celulose S. A.

**Consolidated Financial Statements at
December 31, 1999 and 2000 and
Report of Independent Accountants**

Report of Independent Accountants

To the Board of Directors and Stockholders of
Aracruz Celulose S.A.

In our opinion, the accompanying consolidated balance sheets and the related consolidated statements of income, of cash flows and of changes in stockholders' equity, expressed in United States dollars, present fairly, in all material respects, the financial position of Aracruz Celulose S.A. and its subsidiaries at December 31, 1999 and 2000 and the results of their operations and their cash flows for each of the three years in the period ended December 31, 2000, in conformity with accounting principles generally accepted in the United States of America. These consolidated financial statements are the responsibility of the management of Aracruz Celulose S.A.; our responsibility is to express an opinion on these consolidated financial statements based on our audits. We conducted our audits of these statements in accordance with auditing standards generally accepted in the United States of America which require that we plan and perform the audit to obtain reasonable assurance about whether the financial statements are free of material misstatement. An audit includes examining, on a test basis, evidence supporting the amounts and disclosures in the financial statements, assessing the accounting principles used and significant estimates made by management, and evaluating the overall financial statement presentation. We believe that our audits provide a reasonable basis for the opinion expressed above.

PricewaterhouseCoopers
Auditores Independentes

Vitória, Brazil
January 12, 2001

Aracruz Celulose S.A.

Consolidated Balance Sheets

Expressed in thousands of United States dollars
(except number of shares)

Assets	December 31	
	1999	2000
Current assets		
Cash and cash equivalents	312.590	18.091
Debt securities available-for-sale	189.480	323.032
Accounts receivable. net		
Related party	5.892	9.530
Other	78.085	84.536
Inventories. net	69.639	80.976
Deferred income tax. net	6.488	6.736
Recoverable income and other taxes	22.323	72.081
Prepaid expenses and other current assets	8.462	7.956
	692.959	602.938
Property. plant and equipment. net	1.702.747	1.664.322
Investment in affiliated company		79.698
Other assets		
Advances to suppliers	15.993	16.659
Deposits for tax assessments	21.181	20.329
Deferred income tax. net	49.473	7.163
Recoverable income taxes	114.430	54.868
Other	4.270	8.481
	205.297	100.673

Liabilities and stockholders' equity	December 31	
	1999	2000
Current liabilities		
Suppliers	21.158	29.310
Payroll and related charges	8.753	11.036
Income and other taxes	7.356	13.416
Current portion of long-term debt		
Related party	65.044	60.251
Other	288.572	45.035
Short-term borrowings - export financing and	102.368	157.693
Accrued finance charges	17.668	9.063
Other accruals	2.907	1.273
	513.826	327.077
Long-term liabilities		
Long-term debt		
Related party	175.593	109.367
Other	216.761	169.506
Tax assessments and litigation contingencies	36.883	68.910
Other	4.255	6.115
	433.492	353.898
Commitments and contingencies (Note 16)		
Minority interest	373	362

Aracruz Celulose S.A.

Consolidated Balance Sheets

Expressed in thousands of United States dollars
(except number of shares)

(Continued)

Stockholders' equity		
Share capital - no-par-value shares authorized and issued		
Preferred stock		
Class A - 1999 - 40.941.849 shares: 2000 - 40.929.550 shares	33.465	33.455
Class B - 1999 - 581.587.165 shares: 2000 - 581.599.464 shares	581.031	581.041
Common stock - 1999 and 2000 - 455.390.699 shares	297.265	297.265
Treasury stock		
Class A preferred stock - 1999 and 2000 – 35.301 shares: Class B preferred stock - 1999 - 28.235.292 shares: 2000 - 45.330.292 shares: and common stock - 1999 and 2000 - 483.114 shares	(35.089)	(57.807)
Total share capital	876.672	853.954
Other cumulative comprehensive income		
Net unrealized gain (loss) on available-for-sale securities	514	1.095
Appropriated retained earnings	203.425	340.250
Unappropriated retained earnings	572.701	577.822
	1.653.312	1.773.121
	2.601.003	2.454.458

2.601.003   2.454.458

The accompanying notes are an integral part of these consolidated financial statements.

5

Aracruz Celulose S.A.

Consolidated Statements of Income

Expressed in thousands of United States dollars
(except number of shares and per-share amounts)

	Year ended December 31.		
	1998 **Reclassified** **Note 1**	**1999**	**2000**
Operating revenues			
Sales of eucalyptus pulp			
Domestic	38,449	33,796	43,601
Export	462,163	550,729	751,900
	500,612	584,525	795,501
Sales taxes and other deductions	(39,490)	(43,459)	(63,240)
Net operating revenues	461,122	541,066	732,261
Operating costs and expenses			
Cost of sales	349,621	311,190	344,515
Selling	34,231	32,626	28,390
Administrative	47,238	29,849	34,620
Other, net	28,188	33,060	11,978
	459,278	406,725	419,503
Operating income	1,844	134,341	312,758
Non-operating (income) expenses			
Equity in results of affiliated company			1,313
Financial income	(104,840)	(100,692)	(64,849)
Financial expenses	120,955	120,336	101,461
Loss (gain) on currency remeasurement, net	7,780	7,454	(8,812)
Other, net	65	(146)	(120)
	23,960	26,952	28,993
Income (loss) before income taxes and minority interest and	(22,116)	107,389	283,765
Income tax expense (benefit)			
Current	(9,573)	8,980	40,461
Deferred	(15,733)	7,699	41,604
	(25,306)	16,679	82,065
Minority interest in losses of subsidiary	257	63	11
Net income for the year	3,447	90,773	201,711

Aracruz Celulose S.A.

Consolidated Statements of Income
Expressed in thousands of United States dollars
(except number of shares and per-share amounts)

(Continued)

	Year ended December 31,		
	1998	**1999**	**2000**
Basic and diluted earnings per share			
Class A preferred stock	0.09	0.09	0.20
Class B preferred stock	0.00	0.09	0.20
Common stock	0.00	0.08	0.18
Weighted-average number of shares outstanding (thousands)			
Class A preferred stock	41,007	40,979	40,903
Class B preferred stock	564,374	553,279	552,889
Common stock	454,908	454,908	454,908

The accompanying notes are an integral part of these consolidated financial statements.

Aracruz Celulose S.A.

Consolidated Statements of Cash Flows

Expressed in thousands of United States dollars

	Year ended December 31,		
	1998	1999	2000
Cash flows from operating activities			
Net income	3,447	90,773	201,711
Adjustments to reconcile net income to cash provided by operating activities:			
Non-cash items			
Depreciation and depletion	152,803	158,829	167,960
Equity in results of affiliated company			1,313
Provision for impairment of property, plant and equipment	12,098	1,573	
Deferred income tax	(15,733)	7,699	41,604
Loss (gain) on currency remeasurement	7,780	7,454	(8,812)
Provision for contingencies	700		
Loss on sale of equipment	3,775	23,864	1,643
Other		648	
Decrease (increase) in assets			
Accounts receivable, net	4,943	(16,000)	(11,226)
Inventories, net	(580)	13,303	(11,337)
Interest receivable on debt securities	(14,685)	11,606	(36,398)
Recoverable income taxes	(54,488)	(14,015)	(1,047)
Other	12,821	(2,734)	(890)
Increase (decrease) in liabilities			
Suppliers	(19,145)	4,429	7,788
Payroll and related charges	272	(4,021)	3,458
Income and other taxes and litigation contingencies	(4,747)	18,888	45,323
Accrued finance charges	1,244	(11,739)	(8,381)
Other	(1,993)	(1,898)	407
Net cash provided by operating activities	88,512	288,659	393,116
Cash flows from investing activities			
Debt securities		509,108	(96,165)
Proceeds from sale of equipment	2,420	61,871	677
Acquisition of Terra Plana Agropecuária Ltda and Veracel Celulose S.A.			(101,215)
Additions to property, plant and equipment	(88,306)	(56,467)	(118,152)
Net cash provided by (used in) investing activities	(85,886)	514,512	(314,855)

Aracruz Celulose S.A.

Consolidated Statements of Cash Flows
Expressed in thousands of United States dollars

(Continued)

	Year ended December 31,		
	1998	**1999**	**2000**
Cash flows from financing activities			
Short-term debt, net	171,832	(403,105)	57,134
Long-term debt			
Issuances			
Related parties	59,939	2,703	
Other	209,216	78,400	
Repayments			
Related parties	(41,564)	(52,020)	(62,699)
Other	(229,595)	(231,654)	(289,085)
Bank deposits, as compensating balances	4,442	1,195	2,589
Treasury stock acquired	(26,400)		(22,718)
Dividends paid	(24,388)	(18,196)	(57,963)
Net cash provided by (used in) financing activities	123,482	(622,677)	(372,742)
Effect of changes in exchange rates on cash and cash equivalents	(1,960)	(19,790)	(18)
Increase (decrease) in cash and cash equivalents	124,148	160,704	(294,499)
Cash and cash equivalents, beginning of year	27,738	151,886	312,590
Cash and cash equivalents, end of year	151,886	312,590	18,091
Supplementary cash flow information			
Financial charges paid	117,014	138,309	69,303
Income taxes paid, including escrow deposits for tax assessments	329	19	20
Withholding income tax on financial income	99,629	64,909	25,825

The accompanying notes are an integral part of these consolidated financial statements.

Aracruz Celulose S.A.

Consolidated Statements of Changes in Stockholders' Equity

Expressed in thousands of United States dollars
(except number of shares and per-share amounts)

	1998		1999		2000	
	Shares	U.S.$	Shares	U.S.$	Shares	U.S.$
Share Capital						
Preferred stock - Class A						
Balance, January 1	41.042.246	33.547	41.042.246	33.547	40.941.849	33.465
Conversion to Class B stock			(100.397)	(82)	(12.299)	(10)
Balance, December 31	41.042.246	33.547	40.941.849	33.465	40.929.550	33.455
Preferred stock - Class B						
Balance, January 1	581.486.768	580.949	581.486.768	580.949	581.587.165	581.031
Conversion from Class A stock			100.397	82	12.299	10
Balance, December 31	581.486.768	580.949	581.587.165	581.031	581.599.464	581.041
Common stock						
Balance, January 1 and December 31	455.390.699	297.265	455.390.699	297.265	455.390.699	297.265
Treasury stock						
Balance, January 1	(6.921.707)	(8.689)	(28.753.707)	(35.089)	(28.753.707)	(35.089)
Treasury stock acquired	(21.832.000)	(26.400)			(17.095.000)	(22.718)
Balance, December 31	(28.753.707)	(35.089)	(28.753.707)	(35.089)	(45.848.707)	(57.802)
Total share capital	1.049.166.006	876.672	1.049.166.006	876.672	1.032.071.006	853.954

Aracruz Celulose S.A.

Consolidated Statements of Changes in Stockholders' Equity
Expressed in thousands of United States dollars
(except number of shares and per-share amounts)

(Continued)

	Year ended December 31					
	1998		**1999**		**2000**	
	Shares	**U.S.$**	**Shares**	**U.S.$**	**Shares**	**U.S.$**
Balance brought forward	1,049,166,006	876,672	1,049,166,006	876,672	1,032,071,006	853,954
Net unrealized gain (loss) on available-for-sale securities						
Balance January 1				(11,177)		514
Unrealized gain (loss) on available-for-sale securities net of reclassification adjustments		(16,420)		17,236		988
Tax effect on above		5,243		(5,545)		(407)
Balance December 31		(11,177)		514		1,095
Appropriated retained earnings						
Unrealized income reserve						
Balance January 1		19,687		8,572		9,016
Transfer from (to) unappropriated retained earnings		(11,115)		444		(9,016)
Balance December 31		8,572		9,016		
Investments reserve						
Balance January 1		376,362		313,942		143,917
Transfer from (to) unappropriated retained earnings		(62,420)		(170,025)		138,558
Balance December 31		313,942		143,917		282,475
Fiscal incentive reserve						
Balance January 1		97				
Transfer to share capital		(97)				
Balance December 31						
Legal reserve						
Balance January 1		66,801		66,801		50,492
Transfer from (to) unappropriated retained earnings				(16,309)		7,283
Balance December 31		66,801		50,492		57,775
Total appropriated retained earnings		389,315		203,425		340,250
Balance carried forward	1,049,166,006	1,254,810	1,049,166,006	1,080,611	1,032,071,006	1,195,299

Aracruz Celulose S.A.

Consolidated Statements of Changes in Stockholders' Equity
Expressed in thousands of United States dollars
(except number of shares and per-share amounts)

| | Year ended December 31, | | | | | |
| | 1998 | | 1999 | | 2000 | |
	Shares	U.S.$	Shares	U.S.$	Shares	U.S.$
Balance brought forward	1,049,166,006	1,254,810	1,049,166,006	1,080,611	1,032,071,006	1,195,299
Unappropriated retained earnings						
Balance, January 1		259,822		312,354		572,701
Net income for the year		3,447		90,773		201,711
Cash dividends (per share: 1998 - U.S.$ 0.09 to Class A preferred stock and U.S.$ 0.02 to both Class B preferred stock and common stock; 1999 - U.S.$ 0.06 to Class A preferred stock and U.S.$ 0.01 to both Class B preferred and common stock; 2000 - U.S.$ 0.06 to both Class A preferred and Class B preferred stock and U.S.$ 0.05 to common stock)		(24,450)		(16,316)		(59,765)
Transfer from (to) reserves		73,535		185,890		(136,825)
Balance, December 31		312,354		572,701		577,822
Total stockholders' equity	1,049,166,006	1,567,164	1,049,166,006	1,653,312	1,032,071,006	1,773,121
Comprehensive income (loss) is comprised as follows:						
Net income for the year		3,447		90,773		201,711
Net unrealized gain (loss) on available-for-sale securities						
Unrealized gain (loss) arising during the year		(11,177)		12,340		581
Less: reclassification adjustments for losses included in net income				(649)		
		(11,177)		11,691		581
Total comprehensive income (loss)		(7,730)		102,464		202,292

(Continued)

The accompanying notes are an integral part of these consolidated financial statements.

12

Aracruz Celulose S.A.

Notes to Consolidated Financial Statements
Expressed in thousands of United States dollars
(unless otherwise stated)

---

1   **Summary of significant accounting policies**

The consolidated financial statements of Aracruz Celulose S.A. and its subsidiaries (the Company) have been prepared in conformity with accounting principles generally accepted in the United States of America ("US GAAP"), which require management to make estimates and assumptions that affect the reported amounts of assets, liabilities, revenue and expenses during the reporting periods and require the disclosure of contingent assets and liabilities as of the date of the financial statements. The Company's consolidated financial statements therefore include estimates concerning such matters as the selection of useful lives of property, plant and equipment, provisions necessary for asset impairments, contingent liabilities, employee postretirement benefits and other similar evaluations; actual results may vary from estimates.

(a)   **Basis of presentation**

The consolidated financial statements have been prepared in accordance with US GAAP, which differ in certain respects from the Brazilian accounting principles applied by the Company in its statutory financial statements prepared in accordance with Brazilian corporate legislation.

The Company has reported in U.S. dollars since 1994 when the U.S. Securities and Exchange Commission permitted foreign registrants to report in U.S. dollars rather than in the currency of the country in which they are incorporated. The U.S. dollar amounts have been remeasured from Brazilian reais (R$) in accordance with the criteria set forth in Statement of Financial Accounting Standards Nº 52 - "Foreign Currency Translation" ("SFAS 52"). The Board of Directors and management have historically considered the U.S. dollar as the Company's functional currency as this has been, and remains in their opinion, the currency in which it principally operates as well as being the Company's primary unit of economic measure. Accordingly, the Company's management has concluded that the Company's functional currency is and will continue to be the U.S. dollar.

On January 13 and 15, 1999, certain significant changes occurred in the exchange rate policy until then adopted by the Brazilian government, which resulted in the elimination of certain exchange controls, previously carried out by means of a system of trading bands, when the Central Bank decided to no longer intervene in the foreign exchange markets. Following this decision and the markets' reaction, the Real devalued to U.S.$ 1: R$ 1.7890 at December 31, 1999 from U.S.$ 1: R$ 1.2087 at December 31, 1998 (U.S.$ 1: R$ 1.9554 at December 31, 2000).

Gains and losses resulting from the remeasurement of the financial statements, as well as those resulting from foreign currency transactions, have been recognized in the statements of income. The impact of the devaluation of the Real on the Company's monetary assets and liabilities in

Aracruz Celulose S.A.

Notes to Consolidated Financial Statements
Expressed in thousands of United States dollars
(unless otherwise stated)

2000 was a net gain of U.S.$ 8.8 million (U.S.$ 7.5 million loss in 1999 and U.S.$ 7.8 million loss in 1998).

Stockholders' equity included in the consolidated financial statements presented herein differs from that included in the Company's statutory accounting records as a result of the variations in the U.S. dollar exchange rate, the indexation mandated over the years up to December 31, 1995 for statutory financial statements and adjustments made to reflect the requirements of US GAAP.

(b)   Basis of consolidation

The financial statements of majority-owned subsidiaries have been consolidated, and all significant intercompany accounts and transactions have been eliminated.   Accordingly, the following companies were consolidated: Aracruz Trading S.A., Aracruz Celulose (USA) Inc., Portocel – Terminal Especializado de Barra do Riacho S.A., Mucuri Agroflorestal S.A., Aracruz Produtos de Madeira S.A., Aracruz Empreendimentos S/C Ltda. and Terra Plana Agropecuária Ltda..

(c)   Cash and cash equivalents

Cash and cash equivalents represent cash, bank accounts and short-term financial investments with a ready market and maturities when purchased of 90 days or less, and are stated at the lower of cost plus accrued interest or market value.

(d)   Concentration of risk

Financial instruments which potentially subject the Company to concentrations of credit and performance risk are cash and cash equivalents, debt securities and trade accounts receivable. The Company limits its credit and performance risk associated with cash and cash equivalents by placing its investments with highly rated financial institutions and in very short-term securities, and the Company's debt securities are principally comprised of U.S. dollar denominated notes which are issued and guaranteed as to principal and interest by the Brazilian government.   An allowance for doubtful accounts is established to the extent the Company's trade receivables are estimated not to be fully collectible.

The Company's pulp sales are made substantially to the paper industry; consequently, its performance is dependent upon that industry's worldwide demand for pulp and the related supply, as well as fluctuations in the market price for pulp which can be significant.

Aracruz Celulose S.A.

Notes to Consolidated Financial Statements
Expressed in thousands of United States dollars
(unless otherwise stated)

(e)   Inventories

Inventories are stated at the lower of the average cost of purchase or production, and replacement or realizable values.   Cost is determined principally on the average-cost method.

(f)   Investments in affiliated companies and debt securities available-for-sale

(i)   Investments in affiliated companies

The Company uses the equity method of accounting for all long-term investments for which it owns between 20% and 50% of the investee's voting stock and/or has the ability to exercise significant influence over operating and financial policies of the investee. The equity method requires periodic adjustments to the investment account to recognize the Company's proportionate share in the investee's results, reduced by receipt of investee dividends and amortization of goodwill.

(ii)   Debt securities available-for-sale

In accordance with SFAS 115 - "Accounting for Certain Investments in Debt and Equity Securities", the Company's investments in securities are classified in accordance with their nature and management's intentions. Available-for-sale debt securities are carried at cost plus accrued interest, adjusted to market value. Any unrealized gains or losses, net of taxes, are excluded from income and recognized as a separate component of stockholders' equity until realized.

(g)   Property, plant and equipment

Timber resources are stated at cost, less accumulated depletion.   Tree development costs and forest maintenance costs are capitalized.   Depletion is determined on the unit-of-production basis, excluding from the amount to be depleted the portion of tree-development costs that benefits future harvests; such costs are deferred and included in the cost of those harvests.

Other property, plant and equipment are recorded at cost, including interest incurred on financing during the construction period of major new facilities.   Interest on local currency borrowings is determined as that part of the total finance cost incurred on borrowings net of the foreign currency translation adjustments arising on such borrowings, and, on foreign currency borrowings (including those denominated in U.S. dollars), at the contractual interest rates. Depreciation is computed on the straight-line basis at rates which take into consideration the useful lives of the assets, principally an average of 25 years for buildings, 10 years for

Aracruz Celulose S.A.

Notes to Consolidated Financial Statements
Expressed in thousands of United States dollars
(unless otherwise stated)

---

improvements and installations, and 4 to 25 years for machinery and equipment and other assets.

(h) Environmental costs

Expenditures relating to ongoing programs for compliance with environmental regulations are generally expensed but may be capitalized under certain circumstances. Capitalization is considered appropriate when the expenditures relate to the acquisition and installation of pollution control equipment. These ongoing programs are designed to minimize the environmental impact of the Company's pulp-producing activities.

(i) Recoverability of long-lived assets

In accordance with SFAS 121 – "Accounting for the Impairment of Long-Lived Assets and for Long-Lived Assets to be Disposed of", management reviews long-lived assets, primarily property, plant and equipment to be held and used in the business, for the purposes of determining and measuring impairment on a recurring basis or when events or changes in circumstances indicate that the carrying value of an asset or group of assets may not be recoverable. At December 31, 1998 and 1999 the Company recorded provisions of U.S.$ 12.1 million and U.S.$ 1.6 million, respectively, for impairment related to plant and equipment expected to be discontinued. The Company did not record a provision for impairment in 2000.

(j) Employee retirement and postemployment benefits

The cost of the retirement benefits plans is accrued currently. Employee postretirement and postemployment benefits as defined by SFAS 106 - "Employers' Accounting for Postretirement Benefits other than Pensions" and SFAS 112 - "Employers' Accounting for Postemployment Benefits", respectively, are not significant. The Company is required by law to provide severance benefits to employees terminated without just cause. No significant amounts were accrued at December 31, 1999 and 2000, since future severance costs are not reasonably estimable.

(k) Compensated absences

The liability for employees' future vacation compensation is accrued as vacation vests during the year.

Aracruz Celulose S.A.

Notes to Consolidated Financial Statements
Expressed in thousands of United States dollars
(unless otherwise stated)

(l) **Revenues and expenses**

Revenues arise from annual and long-term contracts and from spot sales and are recognized when products are invoiced. Expenses and costs are accrued as incurred.

(m) **Accounting for derivatives and hedging activities**

The Company maintains an overall risk management strategy to minimize significant unplanned fluctuations caused by foreign exchange rate volatility. The Company may enter into forward foreign exchange contracts to protect against exchange-rate movements affecting its non-US dollar denominated export accounts receivable. Additionally, the Company may enter into foreign currency swaps and foreign currency options to manage risk in administering the Company's cash and cash equivalents portfolio. Finally, the Company may enter into contracts to protect against exchange-rate movements affecting its non-US dollar denominated export accounts payable and indebtedness. Market-value gains and losses on these contracts are recognized in income currently, offsetting foreign exchange gains and losses arising on the accounts receivable and cash equivalent balances.

In June 1998, the Financial Accounting Standards Board (FASB) issued Statement of Financial Accounting Standards No. 133 - Accounting for Derivative Financial Instruments and Hedging Activities (SFAS 133), as amended by SFAS 137 and SFAS 138. These standards are effective for the Company as from January 1, 2001. FAS 133, as amended, requires that all derivative instruments be recorded on the balance sheet at fair value. Changes in fair value of derivatives are recorded each period in current earnings or other comprehensive income, depending on whether the derivative is designated as part of a hedge transaction and, if it is, depending on the type of hedge transaction. For fair value hedge transactions, in which the Company is hedging changes in the fair value of an asset, liability or firm commitment, changes in the fair value of the derivative instrument will generally be offset in the income statement by changes in the hedged item's fair value. For cash-flow hedge transactions in which the Company is hedging the variability of cash flows related to a variable-rate asset, liability, or a forecasted transaction, changes in the fair value of the derivative instrument will be reported in other comprehensive income. The gains and losses on the derivative instrument that are reported in other comprehensive income will be reclassified as earnings in the periods in which earnings are impacted by the variability of the cash flows of the hedged item. The ineffective portion of all hedges will be recognized in current period earnings.

Aracruz Celulose S.A.

Notes to Consolidated Financial Statements
Expressed in thousands of United States dollars
(unless otherwise stated)

Management estimates that, due to the limited number of unsettled derivative instruments as of December 31, 2000, the adoption of FAS 133, as amended, as of January 1, 2001 will not have a significant effect on the Company's results of operations or its financial position.

(n)   Income taxes

The Company has adopted SFAS 109 - "Accounting for Income Taxes" for all years presented. Accordingly, the Company recognizes (i) the benefits of tax loss carryforwards available to be offset against future taxable income and (ii) deferred tax assets and liabilities for the expected future tax consequences of temporary differences between the tax bases and financial reporting bases of assets and liabilities, as well as on the effects of adjustments made to reflect the requirements of US GAAP. A valuation allowance is provided to reduce deferred tax assets when management considers that realization is not reasonably assured.

(o)   Basic and diluted earnings per share

Basic and diluted earnings per share are computed by dividing net income by the weighted average number of all classes of shares outstanding during the year, net of treasury stock, after taking into consideration the dividend provisions applicable to Class A preferred and Class B preferred stocks, assuming that all earnings for the year are fully distributed. There were no dilutive securities outstanding in 1998, 1999 and 2000.

(p)   Comprehensive income

The Company has disclosed comprehensive income as part of the Statement of Changes in Stockholders´ Equity, in compliance with SFAS 130 - "Reporting Comprehensive Income".

2   Sale of the "Electrochemical Plant"

On September 27, 1999, the Company formed Aracruz Eletroquímica Ltda., a wholly-owned subsidiary, and transferred to the subsidiary certain equipment comprising an "electrochemical plant", at its net book value of U.S.$ 82.6   million, as payment of capital subscribed.

On December 17, 1999, Aracruz Eletroquímica Ltda. issued debt securities in the international market ("Fixed rate notes") in the amount of U.S.$ 58 million. In addition, at that date, the subsidiary was split and cash in the amount of U.S.$ 54.9 million was retained by the twin subsidiary Aracruz Empreendimentos S/C Ltda., also wholly-owned, incorporated on December 6, 1999.

Aracruz Celulose S.A.

Notes to Consolidated Financial Statements
Expressed in thousands of United States dollars
(unless otherwise stated)

Aracruz Eletroquímica Ltda., which retained the electrochemical plant assets and the liability for the notes, with a net equity of U.S.$ 27.7 million, was then sold for U.S.$ 6.1 million, on December 17, 1999, to CanadianOxy Chemicals Holding Ltd., a Canadian group. The loss on sale of the plant of U.S.$ 21.6 million (U.S.$ 13.6 million net of taxes), was recorded in "Other operating costs and expenses".

Pursuant to a contract signed by the Company and the acquirors of the electrochemical plant, the Company will purchase future production from the plant. See discussion of "take-or-pay" contract in Note 16 (b).

3   Acquisition of Terra Plana Agropecuária Ltda

On June 1, 2000 the Company acquired Terra Plana Agropecuária Ltda ("Terra") for U.S.$ 20,204. The acquisition has been accounted for using the purchase method of accounting. The net assets of Terra are comprised solely of land, and at September 30, 2000 the Company has allocated the purchase price to land (U.S.$ 13,169) and goodwill (U.S.$ 7,035), based upon estimates of the fair value of the land. Goodwill will be amortized on a straight-line basis over 7 years, which the Company believes is the estimated benefit period.

4   Investment in Veracel Celulose S.A.

On October 10, 2000, the Company acquired a 45% interest in Veracel Celulose S.A. (Veracel) for U.S.$ 81,011. Veracel is currently in the pre-operational stage, growing eucalyptus plantations in the state of Bahia in Brazil. Stora Enso OYJ and Odebrecht S.A. own the remaining 45% and 10%, respectively. At the end of 2002, the Company and Stor Enso will jointly decide, based upon prevailing market conditions, whether to proceed with a planned construction of Veracel´s own green field.

Upon closing of the purchase agreement, the Company andVeracel entered into a three-year wood supply contract to provide wood for the Company´s mill expansion currently in progress. Under terms of the contract, beginning in 2002 Veracel will supply up to 3.85 million cubic meters of wood at U.S.$ 40.50 per cubic meter.

The Company accounts for its investment in Veracel using the equity method of accounting. At December 31, 2000 the Company's investment in Veracel included goodwill of U.S.$ 15,583, which will be amortized over a period up to 7 years. Amortization is expected to commence in 2002, which corresponds to the estimated beginning of the period the Company believes it will benefit from its investment. For the year ended December 31, 2000, the Company recognized equity earnings of U.S.$ 1,313.

Aracruz Celulose S.A.

Notes to Consolidated Financial Statements
Expressed in thousands of United States dollars
(unless otherwise stated)

---

5   Income taxes

Income taxes in Brazil comprise federal income tax and social contribution (which is an additional federal income tax).   The statutory rates applicable for federal income tax and social contribution are presented as follows:

	Year ended December 31 - %		
	1998	**1999**	**2000**
Federal income tax rate	25.0	25.0	25.0
Social contribution (*)	8.0	8.0 to 12.0	9.0 to 12.0
Composite tax rate	33.0	33.0 to 37.0	34.0 to 37.0

(*) Pursuant to a provisional measure, the social contribution rate was increased to 12% for the period May 1, 1999 to January 31, 2000 and was reduced to 9% for the period February 1, 2000 to December 31, 2000. The social contribution rate will continue to be 9% until December 31, 2002 and will be reduced to 8% again effective January 1, 2003. Because provisional measures are valid only for 30 days unless approved by the Congress, the enacted rate continues to be 8% in accordance with the provisions of SFAS 109. Therefore, this rate was used to calculate deferred taxes at December 31, 2000 and 1999.

Aracruz Celulose S.A.

Notes to Consolidated Financial Statements
Expressed in thousands of United States dollars
(unless otherwise stated)

The amounts reported as income tax expense (benefit) in the consolidated statements of income are reconciled to the statutory rates as follows:

	Year ended December 31,		
	1998	**1999**	**2000**
Income (loss) before income taxes and minority interest	(22,116)	107,389	283,765
Federal income tax and social contribution at statutory rates	(7,298)	39,734	93,642
Adjustments to derive effective tax rate:			
Effects of differences in remeasurement from reais to U.S. dollars, using historical exchange rates and indexing for tax purposes:			
Translation effect for the period	(5,716)	(14,797)	(4,688)
Depreciation on difference in asset basis	1,074	29,025	22,406
Valuation allowance (reversal)			
Operations in Brazil	(4,168)	(38,924)	(5,394)
Operations outside Brazil	(4,389)	2,617	(29,737)
Effects of changes in tax rates for 1999		(1,116)	
Social contribution recovered, net of federal income tax effect of U.S.$ 2,601 (see Note 16 (a) (iv))	(7,806)		
Other permanent items	2,997	140	5,836
Income tax expense (benefit) per consolidated statement of income	(25,306)	16,679	82,065

Aracruz Celulose S.A.

Notes to Consolidated Financial Statements
Expressed in thousands of United States dollars
(unless otherwise stated)

The major components of the deferred tax accounts in the balance sheet are as follows:

	December 31,	
	1999	**2000**
Assets		
Tax loss carryforwards		
Operations in Brazil	22,777	63
Operations outside Brazil	32,211	2,474
Depreciation - book over tax	10,961	
Expenses not currently deductible	22,235	7,100
Others	6,488	6,736
Valuation allowance	(38,761)	(2,474)
	55,911	13,899
Current assets	6,488	6,736
Long-term assets	49,423	7,163

Although realization of net deferred tax assets is not assured, management believes that, except where a valuation allowance has been provided, such realization is more likely than not to occur. The amount of the deferred tax asset considered realizable could, however, be reduced if estimates of future taxable income during the tax loss carryforwards period are reduced. Tax loss carryforwards do not expire and are available to offset against future taxable income limited to 30% of taxable income in any individual year.

In addition, at December 31, 2000, the Company had recoverable taxes in the total amount of U.S.$ 126,949, relating mainly to the withholding income tax on financial income (U.S.$ 63,974), which can be offset with future income tax payable, and to the value-added tax credits (U.S.$ 41,056) for which management is studying alternatives of recovery with the Government of the Espírito Santo State.

Aracruz Celulose S.A.

Notes to Consolidated Financial Statements
Expressed in thousands of United States dollars
(unless otherwise stated)

---

6   Cash and cash equivalents

	December 31,	
	1999	**2000**
Brazilian reais	13,934	704
United States dollars	288,743	15,768
Other European currencies	9,913	1,619
	312,590	18,091

Cash equivalents in Reais represent principally short-term investments in certificates of deposit placed with major financial institutions in Brazil. The amount invested in United States dollars at December 31, 1999 consists of participations in an investment fund whose assets are basically denominated in U.S. dollar. The amount invested in United States dollars at December 31, 2000 consist primarily of time deposits with prime financial institutions.

7   Debt securities available-for-sale

The Company's debt securities available-for-sale are comprised of Notas do Tesouro Nacional ("National Treasury Notes") Series D, and Notas do Banco Central ("Central Bank Bonds") Series E, which are issued and guaranteed by the Brazilian Federal Government. These securities have maturity dates ranging from May 2001 to June 2004.

During the first half of 1999 the Company sold National Treasury Notes for an amount of U.S. $ 80,313, realizing losses of U.S. $648, net of taxes, calculated on an identified security basis. The realized loss that had been previously recorded as a component of other cumulative comprehensive income in stockholders' equity was classified as financial expense in the statement of income. Additionally, in accordance with the maturity schedule of the National Treasury Notes, U.S. $94,398 were redeemed in September 1999 and partially reinvested.

During October and November of 2000, National Treasury Notes with a value of U.S. $ 119,768 matured and the Company partially reinvested proceeds of U.S. $34,924 into Central Bank Bonds, Series E with a maturity date in June 2004.

Aracruz Celulose S.A.

Notes to Consolidated Financial Statements
Expressed in thousands of United States dollars
(unless otherwise stated)

At December 31, 2000, the fair value of the Company's debt securities available for sale amounted to U.S. $323,032 (1999 – U.S. $189,480), with an unrealized gain, net of tax, of U.S. $1,095 recorded as a component of other cumulative comprehensive income.

8   Accounts receivable, net

	December 31,	
	1999	**2000**
Customers - pulp sales		
Domestic	6,999	8,149
Export	71,074	80,887
Advances to suppliers	1,223	3,432
Other	5,171	2,044
	84,467	95,512
Allowance for doubtful accounts	(490)	(446)
Total, net	83,977	94,066

At December 31, 2000, one customer accounted for 30% of total customer receivables (1999 - two customers accounted for 37%) and no other accounted for more than 10%.

Export receivables are denominated in the following currencies:

	December 31,	
	1999	**2000**
United States dollars	41,416	77,439
European currency units - EURO	29,399	3,448
British pounds	259	
	71,074	80,887

Export receivables in currencies other than U.S. dollars are swapped into U.S. dollars through forward foreign exchange contracts as discussed in Note 17.

Aracruz Celulose S.A.

Notes to Consolidated Financial Statements
Expressed in thousands of United States dollars
(unless otherwise stated)

9   Inventories, net

	December 31,	
	1999	**2000**
Finished products	24,054	34,151
Work in process	853	824
Timber	3,181	5,737
Raw materials	7,694	10,731
Spare parts and maintenance supplies, less allowance for loss of U.S.$ 4,841 (1999 – U.S.$ 3,522)	33,857	29,533
	69,639	80,976

Spare parts include parts which, when utilized, are expected to extend the useful lives of plant and equipment and will be capitalized.

10   Property, plant and equipment

	December 31, 1999			December 31, 2000		
	Cost	Accumulated depreciation	Net	Cost	Accumulated depreciation	Net
Land	134,581		134,581	178,192		178,192
Timber resources	454,491	296,038	158,453	482,164	327,680	154,484
Buildings, improvements, and installations	462,092	244,295	217,797	467,231	264,275	202,959
Equipment	1,842,545	759,931	1,082,614	1,831,744	830,576	1,001,168
Information tecnology equipment	41,572	24,635	16,937	41,898	28,082	13,816
Other	135,444	76,620	58,824	144,617	95,331	49,287

Aracruz Celulose S.A.

Notes to Consolidated Financial Statements
Expressed in thousands of United States dollars
(unless otherwise stated)

	3,070,725	1,401,519	1,669,206	3,145,849	1,545,943	1,599,906
Construction in progress	33,541		33,541	64,416		64,416
Total	3,104,266	1,401,519	1,702,747	3,210,265	1,545,943	1,664,322

During the second quarter of 2000, the Company commissioned a technical report from engineering experts in order to align, for accounting purposes, the remaining useful life of the plant assets to their prospective economical use. Based on that report, which considered aspects such as the useful economic life established by the assets' manufacturers, the Company's maintenance standards and the general conditions of use and conservation, management concluded that the Company should depreciate its industrial assets at higher annual rates to reflect the actual wear of the assets by their use. Accordingly, as a result of this change, which was effective April 1, 2000, the depreciation charge for the year ended December 31, 2000 increased by U.S.$ 17.8 million. For the year ended December 31, 2000 U.S.$ 15.6 million, respectively, was charged against cost of sales, net income was reduced by U.S.$ 10.5 million, respectively, and earnings per share were reduced by U.S.$ .02 per Class A and B shares U.S.$ .02 per common share for the year ended December 31, 2000. Assets acquired in the future will be depreciated at the same rates as those determined in the technical report, taking into consideration the nature of the assets.

11 Short-term borrowings

The Company's short-term borrowings are principally from commercial banks for export financing and are substantially denominated in U.S. dollars. Average annual interest rates at December 31, 1999 and 2000 were, respectively, 8.2% and 7.4%.

At December 31, 2000, U.S.$ 125,203 of short-term borrowings fall due within 90 days, U.S.$ 29,440 from 91 to 180 days and U.S.$ 3,050 from 181 to 365 days.

Aracruz Celulose S.A.

Notes to Consolidated Financial Statements
Expressed in thousands of United States dollars
(unless otherwise stated)

12   Long-term debt

	December 31,	
	1999	**2000**
Denominated in Brazilian currency - term loans with varying interest rates: principally the "Long-term Interest Rate" (TJLP) plus 5.5% to 11.5% (1999 - 5.5% to 11.5%), due 2000 to 2006	162,330	117,464
Denominated in foreign currencies		
Term loans - 9.26% to 12.37% (1999 - 8.45% to 12.23%), due 2001 to 2004	193,354	136,640
Securitization of receivables - 7.98% (1999 - 7.98% to 9.89%) due 2001 to 2002	69,572	39,547
Import financing - 6.56% to 7.31% (1999 - 5.55% to 7.08%), due 2001 to 2007	40,197	34,227
Import financing - LIBOR plus 1.4%, due 2001 to 2004	73,167	56,281
Pre-export financing - 1999 - 5.54% to 10.7%, due 2000	207,350	
	583,640	266,695
Total	745,970	384,159
Less current maturities	353,616	105,286
	392,354	278,873

In January 1994, the Company issued U.S.$ 120 million of 10.375% unsecured notes (the "Notes") maturing 2002. The Notes were redeemable on January 31, 1997 at 94.527% of face value if redeemed at the option of the Company, or at 93.710% of face value if redeemed at the option of the bondholder. On January 31, 1997, the terms of the Notes were remarketed and amended, through a purchase and resale operation under which they were redeemed at 94.527% of their face value and reissued at 104.75% of face value on the same date. The gain on the redemption was recognized currently in financial income in 1997 while the premium on reissuance is being amortized over the remaining term of the Notes.   Interest, fees and commissions on the Notes are exempt from Brazilian withholding tax. However, should the instruments be redeemed prior to their original final maturities, the Company will be obligated to pay such tax on both past and future payments at rates from 12.5% through 15%, depending upon the country to which such payments are remitted.

In November 1994, the Company, through Aracruz Trading S.A. entered into a U.S.$ 100 million Euro-Commercial Paper program, guaranteed by the Company, with maturities through 1997 and with interest negotiated as each tranche is released. The Company has drawn down and repaid several tranches under this program. On September 2, 1998, renewal of this

Aracruz Celulose S.A.

Notes to Consolidated Financial Statements
Expressed in thousands of United States dollars
(unless otherwise stated)

program was approved by the Brazilian Central Bank for a 3-year term, in conjunction with an increase in the amount from U.S.$ 100 million to U.S.$ 200 million. The Company did not draw down on this facility during 2000.

In February 1995, the Company, through Aracruz Trading S.A., signed a financing agreement with a special-purpose entity (SPE) under which such entity received from a trust and advanced to the Company, as a first phase of a U.S.$ 200 million program, U.S.$ 50 million, representing funds received by the trust through the private placement of trust certificates. In return, the Company securitizes the financing by selling to the SPE its current and future accounts receivable from designated customers. Concurrently, the SPE has assigned its right, title and interest on the certificates to the trust. Each month such collections in excess of contractual funding requirements are transferred to the Company. The financing bears fixed annual interest of 9.89% and has been fully repaid. The net proceeds were transferred to Aracruz Celulose S.A. as advances for future purchases of pulp. In July 1995, the Company completed the remaining U.S.$ 150 million phase of the securitization program, which has been structured similarly to the first phase described above. This second phase comprehends U.S.$ 38 million of five-year certificates with interest equal to one-month LIBOR plus 1.75%, which were fully redeemed during 1997, and U.S.$ 112 million of seven-year certificates, with interest of 7.98%, and repayments beginning, respectively, in December 1996 and June 1999, with monthly interest payments which began in July 1995. In August 1995, Aracruz Trading S.A., a wholly-owned subsidiary of the Company, used the funds to purchase the full amount of an issue of US$ 150 million of Aracruz Celulose S.A.'s unsecured 9% notes, due August 2003; accordingly these amounts have been offset against each other in the consolidated financial statements.

During 1998, the Company, through Aracruz Trading S.A., entered into a U.S.$ 65 million long-term debt, with maturities from September 2000 to November 2000. This debt was fully paid at each maturity date during the year 2000.

At December 31, 2000, the Company had outstanding debt with the Banco Nacional de Desenvolvimento Econômico e Social - BNDES, a stockholder, in an amount equivalent to U.S.$ 170 million (1999 - U.S.$ 241 million) maturing up to 2006; local currency loans bear interest at varying rates based on the TJLP plus 5.5% to 11.5% and foreign currency loans are linked to a basket of foreign currencies. The loans are secured by liens on the Company's property, plant and equipment and on its timber resources.

At December 31, 2000, the Company had in treasury and available for resale all of its debentures (approximately U.S.$ 140 million at December 31, 2000 values) issued in 1982 and 1990, which were repurchased in the market in 1992.

Aracruz Celulose S.A.

Notes to Consolidated Financial Statements
Expressed in thousands of United States dollars
(unless otherwise stated)

The long-term portion of the Company's debt at December 31, 2000 becomes due in the following years:

2002	196,045
2003	46,363
2004	17,935
2005	7,274
2006 and thereafter	11,256
Total	278,873

13 Stockholders' equity

The Company's principal common stockholders and their common stock ownership interests, either direct or indirect, are as follows: Arapar S.A. (a Company associated with the Chairman of the Board of the Company), S.O.D.E.P.A. - Sociedade de Empreendimentos, Publicidade e Participação S.A. (SODEPA) (an affiliate of Banco Safra S.A.), and Mondi International for 28% each; Banco Nacional de Desenvolvimento Econômico e Social - BNDES for 12.5%. At December 31, 1999 and 2000, SODEPA and the Banco Nacional de Desenvolvimento Econômico e Social - BNDES also owned preferred stocks which in total amounted to 16.4% and 23.5%, respectively, of the total preferred stocks.

Class A preferred stock may be converted into Class B preferred stock at any time at the option of the stockholder. Preferred stock does not have voting rights but has priority in the return of capital in the event the Company is liquidated. Stock dividends payable to Class A preferred stockholders are effected through issuance of Class B preferred stock. Class A preferred stock has priority in the distribution of a minimum annual cash dividend equivalent to 6% of the related capital. Additionally, in order to comply with Law 9457/97, the Company's By-laws were changed to grant Class B preferred stock the right to receive an annual dividend in an amount that is 10% greater than dividends paid to common stockholders ("Dividend Ratio"); earnings, if any, in excess of the Class A preferred stock minimum dividend will be distributed as dividends to Class B preferred stock and common stock, up to the equivalent on a per-share basis to those paid to Class A preferred stock, while maintaining the Dividend Ratio between Class B preferred stock and common stock. Any earnings remaining for distribution thereafter are shared ratably among Class A preferred, Class B preferred and common stocks while maintaining the Dividend Ratio between Class A and Class B preferred stock and common stock . In the event that Class A preferred stock is not paid dividends for three consecutive years, holders of that stock are entitled to voting rights until the dividends in arrears for those three years are paid.

Aracruz Celulose S.A.

Notes to Consolidated Financial Statements
Expressed in thousands of United States dollars
(unless otherwise stated)

Basic and diluted earnings per share ("EPS") as of December 31, 1998, 1999 and 2000, as presented in the Company's statement of income, have been calculated on the above basis taking into consideration the Dividend Ratio between Class A and Class B preferred stock and common stock. However, the per share amounts have been rounded to two decimal places. The following presents the earnings per share calculations:

	1998	1999	2000
Net income	3,447	90,773	201,711
Less priority Class A preferred stock dividends	(3,561)	(2,429)	(2,219)
Less Class B preferred stock and common stock dividends up to the Class A preferred stock dividends on a per-share basis while maintaining the Dividend Ratio	114	(57,308)	(52,429)
Remaining net income to be equally allocated to Class A and Class B preferred stock and common stock while maintaining the Dividend Ratio		31,036	147,063
Weighted average number of shares outstanding (thousands)			
Class A preferred	41,007	40,979	40,903
Class B preferred	564,374	553,279	552,889
Common	454,908	454,908	454,908
Basic and diluted earnings per share			
Class A preferred	0.09	0.09	0.20
Class B preferred	0.00	0.09	0.20
Common	0.00	0.08	0.18

Brazilian law permits the payment of cash dividends only from retained earnings and certain reserves registered in the Company's statutory accounting records. At December 31, 2000, after considering appropriated retained earnings which can be transferred to unappropriated retained earnings, the earnings and reserves available for distribution as dividends, upon approval by the Company's stockholders, amounted to the equivalent of U.S.$ 239 million.

Aracruz Celulose S.A.

Notes to Consolidated Financial Statements
Expressed in thousands of United States dollars
(unless otherwise stated)

Retained earnings that represent unrealized income (principally inflationary income recognized up to December 31, 1995 in the Company's statutory financial statements) are transferred to unrealized income reserve and are transferred back to retained earnings as financial resources become available for dividend distribution.

The investments reserve represents discretionary appropriations, ratified by the stockholders, for plant expansion and other capital projects, the amount of which is based on an approved capital budget presented by management. After completion of the projects, the Company may elect to retain the appropriations until the stockholders vote to transfer all or a portion of the reserve to capital or to retained earnings, from which a cash dividend may then be paid.

The fiscal incentive reserve results from an option to invest a portion of income tax otherwise payable in the acquisition of capital stock of companies undertaking specified government-approved projects. The amount so applied is credited to non-operating income and subsequently appropriated from retained earnings to this reserve.

The legal reserve results from appropriations from retained earnings of 5% of annual net income recorded in the statutory accounting records. Such appropriations are required until the balance reaches 20% of the balance of capital stock, based on the statutory accounting records. At December 31, 2000, such capital stock was R$ 1,855 million and the balance in the legal reserve was R$ 113 million.

The fiscal incentive and legal reserves may be used to increase capital and to absorb losses, but are not available for distribution as cash dividends.

14   Pension plans

The Company sponsors a retirement plan covering substantially all of its employees. Prior to May 1, 1992, the program ("Plan 1") consisted of a final-pay, defined-benefit pension plan with benefits based on years of service and salary so as to complement the government social security benefits. As of May 1, 1992, a new program ("Plan 2") was created under which the retirement benefits were based principally on defined-contribution accumulations and the disability and death benefits were based on a defined-benefits formula. On attaining retirement, participants could either opt for a defined monthly retirement benefit or withdraw a capital sum, both determined on the basis of the contributions accumulated relating to the participant. Substantially, all active employees elected to transfer to Plan 2 while the retired employees remained in Plan 1.

In September 1998, the Company implemented another plan ("Plan ARUS"), which automatically replaced Plan 2, with retirement benefits based solely on defined contribution accumulations. Upon implementation of Plan ARUS, each participant was assigned an

Aracruz Celulose S.A.

Notes to Consolidated Financial Statements
Expressed in thousands of United States dollars
(unless otherwise stated)

individual account with his/her accumulated benefit at the date of implementation; also, the option for a defined monthly retirement benefit provided under Plan 2 was eliminated.

The net effect of U.S.$ 1,395 resulting from the transfer of the benefit obligation and related assets from Plan 2 to Plan ARUS was accounted for as a settlement gain in accordance with SFAS 88 - "Employers' Accounting for Settlements and Curtailments of Defined Benefit Pension Plans and for Termination Benefits", and credited to income for the year ended December 31, 1998.

The Company and eligible employees make monthly contributions under the plan to a private, government-approved pension fund, whose sponsors are Aracruz Celulose S.A. and its subsidiary companies and whose board of administrators is composed principally of officers of Aracruz Celulose S.A. Contributions by employees to the new plan are optional. The fund owns and administers (or places with a trustee) its investments and other assets, which comprise, principally, bank certificates of deposit, investments funds, marketable equity securities and real estate.

Contributions made by the Company to the plan amounted to U.S.$ 1,211, U.S.$ 1,266 and U.S.$ 1,183 in 1998, 1999 and 2000, respectively, and represented the annual pension expense of the Company for this plan.

After the implementation of Plan 2, and its subsequent substitution by Plan ARUS, few participants remained in the defined-benefit plan (Plan 1), and it no longer represents a significant liability for the Fund. Accordingly, the Company's management considers that it is no longer necessary to disclose the plan's funded status and other information required by SFAS 132 – "Employers' Disclosures about Pensions and Other Posretirement Benefits".

15   Employee benefits

In addition to the pension plans, the Company makes monthly contributions, based on total payroll, to government pension, social security and severance indemnity plans and such payments are expensed as incurred. Also, certain severance payments are due on dismissal of employees, principally notice of one month's salary and a severance payment calculated at 40% of the accumulated contributions made to the government severance indemnity plan on behalf of the employee. Based on current operating plans management does not expect that amounts of future severance indemnities will be material.

Aracruz Celulose S.A.

Notes to Consolidated Financial Statements
Expressed in thousands of United States dollars
(unless otherwise stated)

16   Commitments and contingencies

(a)   Contingencies

(i)   Labor Proceedings

The Company has been involved in legal proceedings with labor unions in respect of wage adjustments to incorporate inflation for the period February 16, 1990 through March 15, 1990. Such suits, however, have been denied by the Superior Labor Court, based on rulings by the Federal Supreme Court.

The Company has received an unfavorable judgment in respect of a suit brought by certain industrial employees represented by their union, claiming additional compensation for alleged hazardous conditions at the mill. The Court's decision established a framework for computing the amount of liability. Five other collective suits of the same nature have their respective technical expertise proceedings concluded although not yet decided by the local court. At December 31, 2000, the Company had recorded a provision for eventual losses, based on the Court's computation framework and existing labor jurisprudence, in the amount of U.S.$ 16,849 regarding these claims, and deposited U.S.$ 4,180 in an escrow account.

(ii)   Administrative Proceedings

The Company has been involved in an administrative claim regarding the enlargement of Indian reservations in an area owned by the Company. In April 1998, the Indian communities signed two Terms of Settlement recognizing the legitimacy of the Ministry of Justice Edicts 193, 194 and 195, dated March 6, 1998, that restricted expansion of the reservation to 2,571 hectares of land belonging to the Company. Additionally, the Company committed itself to a financial aid program to be implemented through social, agricultural, educational, shelter and health projects, up to an amount of approximately R$ 13.5 million (equivalent to U.S.$ 6.9 million at December 31, 2000), to be disbursed within a twenty-year period, conditioned to the accomplishment of certain obligations by the Indian communities.

If the Indian communities breach any of their obligations, Aracruz will be released from the obligations defined by the Terms of Settlement. Decrees approving the enlargement of the Indian reservations have extinguished the aforementioned administrative claim. As of December 31, 2000, the Company had donated to the Indian Associations approximately R$ 2.6 million (U.S.$ 1.8 million) (U.S. $ 445 in 2000) under the Terms of Settlement.

Aracruz Celulose S.A.

Notes to Consolidated Financial Statements
Expressed in thousands of United States dollars
(unless otherwise stated)

(iii) Fiscal Proceedings

In March 1997, the Company received notification from the INSS (the Brazilian Social Security System) relating to the value of housing allowances paid to certain employees over a period of several years. At December 31, 2000, the Company is contesting this notification and has placed approximately U.S.$ 9,942 in an escrow account to cover this claim. Based on the opinion of its legal advisors, the Company's management does not believe that the ultimate resolution of this matter will have a material adverse impact on the Company, and accordingly, no provision has been made therefor.

(iv) Income tax and social contribution related to the Plano Verão

In December 1994, the Company petitioned the Tribunal Regional Federal da 2ª região (the "Tribunal") to include in the determination of income tax and social contribution the IPC difference in January 1989 of 70.28%. The Tribunal subsequently accepted the use of 42.72%. Beginning in the third quarter of 2000 with the substantial utilization of the Company's net operating losses in Brazil, the Company began remitting income tax using the 42.72% deduction and has included a provision for contingencies of U.S.$ 20,362.

(v) PIS and COFINS contributions

The Company is questioning in Court certain changes in the rates and rules for the calculation of the PIS and COFINS contributions determined by Law 9718/98. The Company recorded a provision in the amount of U.S.$ 26,981 in relation to these contributions, which it believes is sufficient to cover any possible loss which could arise from this case.

(vi) Others

The Company has, based on the advice of its legal counsel, recorded additional provisions in the amount of U.S.$ 4,690 relating to several other legal disputes and has also made deposits in the amount of U.S.$ 6,003 in escrow accounts.

(b) "Take-or-pay" contract

In connection with the sale of the electrochemical plant (see Note 2), the Company and CanadianOxy Chemicals Holding Ltd. (CXY) entered into a long-term contract for chemical products supply. The contract includes clauses of performance incentives such as sharing of productivity gains, preference prices and "take-or-pay", by which the Company is committed to acquire from the electrochemical plant purchased by CXY a volume of chemical products conservatively projected for the next 6 years. Volumes purchased by the Company in addition to the minimum agreed for a given year may be compensated with lower volumes acquired in subsequent years. For the take-or-pay quantities, the Company will pay unit prices which equal cost plus margin as determined in the contract.

Aracruz Celulose S.A.

Notes to Consolidated Financial Statements
Expressed in thousands of United States dollars
(unless otherwise stated)

(c)   **Compliance with Regulations**

The Company's forestry and manufacturing operations are subject to both Federal and State government environmental regulations. The Company's management believes that it is in compliance, in all material respects, with all applicable environmental regulations.

17   **Derivative Instruments, Hedging and Risk Management Activities**

The Company is engaged in the exportation of market pulp to various markets throughout the world. Management considers the Company's functional currency to be the U.S. dollar and approximately 22% of the Company's indebtedness was Real-denominated, consisting of loans bearing interest at variable rates. These activities expose the Company to credit and foreign currency fluctuation risks, as well as risks associated with the effects of changes in floating interest rates. The Company maintains an overall risk management strategy to minimize significant unplanned fluctuations caused by foreign exchange rate volatility.

The Company's Treasury assesses, at least on a weekly basis, macroeconomic issues and the implications of these issues on the Company's financial performance. The Treasury reports to the Chief Financial Officer. The responsibilities of the Treasury includes the proposal of the Company's corporate risk management policy and its implementation, and the evaluation of the effectiveness of the Company's overall risk management strategy.

The Company may use derivative and non-derivative instruments to implement its overall risk management strategy. However, by using derivative instruments, the Company exposes itself to credit and market risk. Credit risk is the failure of a counterparty to perform under the terms of the derivative contract. Market risk is the adverse effect on the value of a financial instrument that results from a change in interest rates, currency exchange rates, or commodity prices. The Company addresses credit risk by restricting the counterparties to such derivative financial instruments to major financial institutions. Market risk is managed by the Treasury. The Company does not hold or issue financial instruments for trading purposes.

(a)   **Foreign Currency Risk Management**

The Company's foreign currency risk management strategy may use derivative instruments to protect against foreign exchange rate volatility, which may impair the value of certain of the Company's assets. The Company may use foreign currency forward-exchange contracts, foreign currency swaps and forward currency options contracts to implement this strategy.

35

Aracruz Celulose S.A.

Notes to Consolidated Financial Statements
Expressed in thousands of United States dollars
(unless otherwise stated)

At December 31, 2000, the Company had entered into five forward foreign-exchange contracts to protect its foreign currency denominated accounts receivable and bank balances against exchange rate movements in the aggregate amount of EUR 3,103 thousand (1999 – EUR 23,840 thousand), equivalent in aggregate to U.S.$ 2,885 (1999 – U.S.$ 24,173). The contracts expire in January, February and March 2001. The Company realized a net loss in 2000 associated with its forward foreign exchange contracts of U.S.$ 227 (1999 – U.S.$ 144).

Additionally, the Company has been investing substantially all of its financial resources in long-term U.S. dollar denominated or U.S. dollar indexed available-for-sale debt securities to protect against the exchange risk of a devaluation of the Brazilian real in relation to the U.S. dollar.

(b) Interest Rate Risk Management

The Company´s strategy for interest rate management has been to maintain a diversified portfolio of interest rates in order to optimize cost and volatility. The Company's interest rate risk management strategy may use derivative instruments to reduce earnings fluctuations attributable to interest rate volatility. The Company may use interest rate swaps to implement this strategy. At December 31, 2000 the Company had no outstanding interest rate swap contracts.

(c) Commodity Price Risk Management

The Company is exposed to commodity price risks through the fluctuation of pulp prices. The Company currently does not utilize derivative financial instruments to manage its exposure to fluctuations in commodity prices, but may utilize them in the future.

18 Nonderivative financial instruments

Fair value - the Company considers that the carrying amount of its financial instruments generally approximates fair market value. Fair value have been determined as follows:

Cash - the carrying amount of cash is a reasonable estimate of its fair value.

Cash equivalents and short-term investments and bank deposits - cash equivalents are represented, principally, by short-term investments. Their fair value, and that of other bank deposits not meeting the definition of cash equivalents, were estimated using the rates currently offered for deposits of similar remaining maturities.

Aracruz Celulose S.A.

Notes to Consolidated Financial Statements
Expressed in thousands of United States dollars
(unless otherwise stated)

Debt securities - the fair value of the Company's debt securities was estimated by obtaining quotes from major financial institutions and brokers.

Short-term debt and long-term debt - interest rates that are currently available to the Company for issuance of debt with similar terms and remaining maturities are used to estimate fair value. The Company´s financial structure does not require any substitution of such financing or the contracting of similar fundings.

The estimated fair value amounts have been determined by the Company using available market information and appropriate valuation methodologies. However, considerable judgment is necessarily required in interpreting market data to develop the estimates of fair value.

19 Geographical information

The Company's exports from Brazil, classified by geographic destination, are as follows:

	Year ended December 31,		
	1998	**1999**	**2000**
North America	181,439	252,078	267,859
Europe	193,608	194,640	368,992
Asia	83,472	94,847	109,122
Other	3,644	9,164	5,927
Total	462,163	550,729	751,900

Sales to one unaffiliated customer represented 25% of net sales in 2000, sales to one unaffiliated customer represented 26% in 1999 and 2 unaffiliated customers represented 30% in 1998. Sales to no other individual customers represented more than 10% of net sales.

Aracruz Celulose S.A.

Notes to Consolidated Financial Statements
Expressed in thousands of United States dollars
(unless otherwise stated)

20   Related parties

Transactions with related parties resulted in the following balance sheet and income statement balances:

			December 31,	
	1999		2000	
	Assets	Liabilities	Assets	Liabilities
Balance sheet				
Current assets				
Cash and cash equivalents	35		2	
Accounts receivable	5,892		9,530	
Current liabilities – suppliers				
Long-term debt (including current portion and accrued finance charges)		242,847		171,133
	5,927	242,847	9,532	171,133

				Year ended December 31,		
	1998		1999		2000	
	Income	Expense	Income	Expense	Income	Expense
Income statement						
Operating revenues	34,108		36,855		44,555	
Financial expenses		25,304		78,168		14,152
	34,108	25,304	36,855	78,168	44,555	14,152

38

Aracruz Celulose S.A.

Notes to Consolidated Financial Statements
Expressed in thousands of United States dollars
(unless otherwise stated)

21 **Supplementary information –**
Valuation and qualifying accounts

Description	Balance at beginning of year	Additions Charged to Costs and Expenses	Deductions credited to costs and expenses	Balance at end of year
2000				
Allowances deducted from related balance sheet accounts:				
Accounts receivable	490		44	446
Inventories	3.522	1.319		4.841
Investments (other assets - other)	801			801
Property, plant and equipment, net	20.164		20.164	
Deferred income tax	38.761		36.287	2.474
1999				
Allowances deducted from related balance sheet accounts:				
Accounts receivable	112	400	22	490
Inventories	3.522			3.522
Investments (other assets - other)	802		1	801
Property, plant and equipment, net	18.591	1.573		20.164
Deferred income tax	75.068		36.307	38.761
1998				
Allowances deducted from related balance sheet accounts:				
Accounts receivable	122		10	112
Inventories	3.485	1.664	1.627	3.522
Investments (other assets - other)	802			802
Property, plant and equipment, net	6.500	12.098	7	18.591
Deferred income tax	83,625		8,557	75,068

*   *   *

Holmen
Annual Report 1999

Annual General Meeting

The Annual General Meeting of Holmen AB will be held at Grand Hotel Stockholm, at 4 p.m. on Wednesday, April 12, 2000.

PARTICIPATION IN ANNUAL GENERAL MEETING. Shareholders who wish to take part in the Annual General Meeting shall be entered in the register of shareholders maintained by VPC AB by no later than Friday, March 31, 2000 and shall notify the company by no later than 5 p.m. on Wednesday, April 5, 2000 at: Holmen AB, Group Legal Affairs, P.O. Box 5407, SE-114 84 Stockholm, Sweden.

Notification may also be made by telephone: +46 8 666 21 11 or by fax +46 660 759 78.

Shareholders whose shares are registered in a nominee name should temporarily re-register their shares in their own name with VPC by no later than March 31, 2000 to be entitled to take part in the Annual General Meeting.

DIVIDEND.* The Board has proposed that a dividend of SKr 11 per share be paid to shareholders.

The Board has proposed Monday, April 17, 2000 as the date of record for entitlement to the dividend.

Provided the Annual General Meeting resolves in favour of the proposal, the dividend is expected to be distributed by VPC on Thursday, April 20, 2000. Shareholders are requested to inform their account operator of any change of name and/or address.

Financial information

Holmen publishes the following financial reports in 2000.

JANUARY 31: Year-end communiqué for 1999
MID MARCH: Annual Report 1999
APRIL 28: Interim report for January–March
AUGUST 15: Interim report for January–June
OCTOBER 27: Interim report for January–September

The year-end communiqué and the interim reports are included in *Holmen Business Report* which is published four times a year.

The annual report is sent by VPC AB to shareholders who have indicated their wish to receive it. Holmen Business Report is sent to all shareholders who are registered with VPC.

Holmen's financial information in Swedish and English may be obtained from:

Holmen AB, Group Public Relations, P.O. Box 5407, SE-114 84 Stockholm, Sweden
Telephone: +46 8 666 21 00
Fax: +46 8 666 21 30
E-mail: info@holmen.com

---

*Modo Paper´s stock market flotation off

On March 8, SCA and Holmen announced their joint decision to discontinue the efforts to float Modo Paper on the stock market and broaden the ownership, planned for the spring of 2000. The decision means that the public offering of shares in Modo Paper announced by SCA will not take place. As a consequence of this, Holmen´s Board has decided to withdraw the proposal in the Report of the Directors on page 27 regarding the distribution of shares in Modo Paper.

Contents

43

The year in brief

- Profit after financial items was SKr 2,409 million.

- Profit for the year after tax amounted to SKr 1,814 million corresponding to earnings per share of SKr 20.40.

- Return on equity was 10.6 per cent.

- The Board proposes that an ordinary dividend of SKr 11 per share be paid together with an extra dividend in the form of shares in Modo Paper, provided that the company obtains a stock market listing.

- In accordance with the strategic orientation the new fine paper company Modo Paper was founded, of which Holmen and SCA each own 50 per cent.

- Domsjö sulphite mill was divested at the end of the year.

- In February 2000, the Group's name was changed to Holmen.

The Group has changed its name to Holmen

AN EXTRAORDINARY GENERAL MEETING held on February 10, 2000 made a decision to change the Group's name to Holmen. This decision was a consequence of the strategy that was laid down in January 1999, and the changes the Group has undergone since then.

THE CHANGE OF NAME means that the MoDo name disappeared from the OM Stockholm Exchange after 64 years. However, the name will live on with the new fine paper group, Modo Paper, which is planned to be floated on the stock market in 2000.

HOLMEN is a company name whose roots go back a long way. The name originates from an arms factory that was established in 1609 on a small island (a holm) in the fast flowing waters of the river Motala in Norrköping. It is this holm that has given Holmen its name.

Holmen was listed on the stock market until 1989, when, together with Iggesund, it was acquired by MoDo.

Holmen in 1999

Highlights	1999	1998
Net turnover, SKr million	20,508	22,676
Operating profit, SKr million	2,615	2,475
Profit after financial items, SKr million	2,409	2,338
Profit for the year, SKr million	1,814	2,504
Earnings per share, SKr	20.40	28.20
Ordinary dividend, SKr	11.00*	10.00
Extra dividend, SKr	**	35.00
Debt/equity ratio	0.13	0.17
Capital expenditure, SKr million	1,988	2,557
Average No. of employees	8,433	9,586
of which in Sweden	6,176	6,754
of which outside Sweden	2,257	2,832

* Proposal of the Board.
** Proposed distribution of shares in Modo Paper.

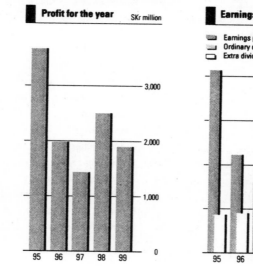

Profit for the year SKr million

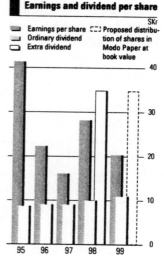

Earnings and dividend per share SKr

Earnings per share Proposed distribution of shares in Modo Paper at book value
Ordinary dividend
Extra dividend

This is Holmen

Holmen is a financially strong and internationally oriented Group. Operations are primarily directed at newsprint and magazine paper as well as paperboard.

The Group was known as MoDo until mid February 2000, when the name was changed to Holmen. The change of name was a result of the strategy determined by the Board in January 1999, and which implies a clear focus on the business areas Holmen Paper and Iggesund Paperboard. In accordance with this strategy, the new fine paper company Modo Paper, which is half-owned by Holmen, was formed in October 1999.

The Holmen Group also includes the business areas Iggesund Timber and Holmen Skog (formerly MoDo Skog).

▮ Business areas

HOLMEN PAPER produces newsprint, MF Special, SC paper and coated printing paper. Mills in Norrköping, Hallstavik and Vargön. Holmen Kraft is part of Holmen Paper and has responsibility for procuring electricity for all the Group's Swedish units.

IGGESUND PAPERBOARD produces paperboard and is focused on the customer segments that place the highest demands on quality and service. Mills in Iggesund, Workington and Strömsbruk.

IGGESUND TIMBER produces and distributes sawn timber. Sawmills in Iggesund and Domsjö.

HOLMEN SKOG procures wood for the Group's Swedish mills, trades in wood and manages the Group's forest holdings. Its activities are carried out through four regions, a central wood department and a subsidiary in Estonia.

▮ External net turnover by business area in 1999

Share of Group, per cent, excl. divested activities

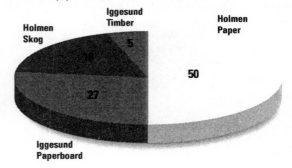

Associate company

MODO PAPER produces office paper, graphic paper and runs merchanting operations.

Financial targets

▪ Holmen shall have a strong financial position with a target debt/equity ratio of 0.5–0.7.

▪ It is intended to keep the capital structure in line with the established target by special capital structure decisions when required.

▪ Each year the dividend shall correspond to 5–7 per cent of the equity.

Strategic direction

CORE BUSINESS AREAS. Holmen focuses on growth and development within newsprint and magazine paper (Holmen Paper) and paperboard (Iggesund Paperboard). Within these areas Holmen is highly competitive, and is well placed to further strengthen its positions. The growth can be organic as well as via acquisition.

OTHER BUSINESS AREAS. The business activities conducted through Iggesund Timber and Holmen Skog will continue with the same direction.

Holmen in 1999, SKr million

The net turnover of Holmen's current business activities amounted to SKr 14,565 million. Its breakdown by business area is shown below.

	Net turnover*	Operating profit/loss
Holmen Paper	7,261	1,494
Iggesund Paperboard	3,898	318
Iggesund Timber	767	−66
Holmen Skog	2,639	521

* excl deliveries to other business areas

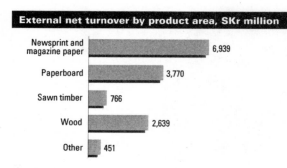

External net turnover by product area, SKr million

Excl divested activities

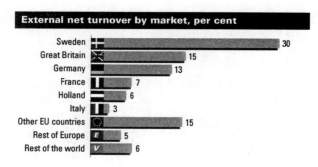

External net turnover by market, per cent

Excl divested activities

46

Comments by the President and CEO

In 1999 MoDo underwent far-reaching changes. The Holmen Group, as it is now perceived by our stakeholders, is in many ways a new company. The changes are based on the strategy laid down by the Board in January 1999. This strategy was presented in detail in last year's annual report and is reproduced in summary form on page 3 in this annual report.

Important steps were taken in 1999 to realise both the financial targets and the operative direction laid down in the strategy.

Within the limits of the financial targets, an extra dividend of SKr 35 per share was paid in addition to the ordinary dividend of SKr 10. The total dividend paid to the shareholders amounted to some SKr 4 billion, and brought the consolidated capital structure into line with the targets established in the strategy.

The strategic direction of finding a partner in the fine paper field was achieved in the autumn, when, on October 1, Modo Paper, a new fine paper and merchanting company, in which Holmen and SCA each have a 50 per cent interest, was set up. Modo Paper is expected to have a turnover of some SKr 20 billion per year, and is the third largest fine paper company in Europe. The units from SCA and the former MoDo complement each other particularly well in product terms as well as geographically. This creates a foundation for extensive synergies in a strong company with considerable development potential.

The sale of the Domsjö sulphite mill at the turn of 2000 completed the strategy of reducing exposure to the highly cyclical market pulp. This divestment means that Holmen is now a net purchaser of pulp.

Holmen retained all of its forest assets when Modo Paper was formed and Domsjö divested. This gives the Group a higher degree of wood self-sufficiency, and reduces its exposure to changes in the price of wood.

Flotation of Modo Paper

The intention is to have Modo Paper listed on the OM Stockholm Exchange this spring, assuming market conditions are prevailing. This will be effected by Holmen distributing shares equivalent to 35 per cent of the total number of shares in Modo Paper to its shareholders. SCA intends to sell a corresponding interest by means of a public offering. As Holmen does not intend to retain a significant long-term equity interest in Modo Paper, it is planned to reduce the remaining holding at a later stage.

A new group with a new name

In many respects, a new company is evolving from these radical changes to the Group's structure. The company is now sharply focused on newsprint and magazine paper as well as paperboard, it has a very strong financial position, and it is relatively insensitive to cyclical fluctuations. Compared with the situation in 1994, the product palette has been concentrated on fewer products with, on average, higher and more sustainable profitability (see diagram).

Now that these changes to the Group structure have been completed, it was both appropriate and timely for the company to change its

name. The company's registered name is now Holmen Aktiebolag, following the decision of the Extraordinary General Meeting held on February 10 this year.

1999 pro forma — Other, Paperboard, Sawn timber, Newsprint and magazine paper, Wood

1994 — Fine paper, Newsprint and magazine paper, Wood, Paperboard, Packaging paper, Pulp, Sawn timber, Other

Continuous improvement and development

The process of continuously improving efficiency, profitability and competitiveness continued in 1999 in the business areas of the Holmen Group.

As one aspect of the policy of raising quality and improving the product range, Iggesund Paperboard rebuilt the larger of the two paperboard machines at Workington during the autumn. After certain running-in problems, the machine is back in operation and the quality goals have been reached. Iggesund Paperboard also restructured its marketing organisation in 1999. Resources for marketing paperboard were concentrated in Amsterdam and the sales organisation was product- and end user-orientated instead of the traditional

country-orientation. The relocation and re-orientation reflect the increasingly cross-border structure and purchasing policy that typifies European paperboard customers.

Holmen Paper is continuing to develop its wood-containing printing paper, in particular its improved newsprint, a product area experiencing steadily growing demand and in which Holmen Paper has a strong market position. Product development activities were intensified and various options are currently being examined for the development of improved newsprint at the Hallsta paper mill.

The Iggesund Sawmill began the process of expanding its drying capacity for sawn timber. This will bring substantial cost reductions, as well as raising the product value and strengthening the mix of sawn timber. The intention is to improve the profitability of the Iggesund Sawmill by raising the relative output of value added products.

At the beginning of 1999, the Group completed a major land exchange transaction (approx. 80,000 hectares) with AssiDomän. This will consolidate the Holmen Group's forest holdings in northern Sweden, and enable it to raise operational efficiency.

A couple of years ago, Holmen introduced a new organisation for product and process development with the object of strengthening the links between R&D and the commercial side of the company. The new organisation is now fully established and a number of valuable ideas for further product development are being explored at business area level.

Making our products and production processes more environmentally adapted is an important aspect of the business. These activities are described in more detail in our environmental report, which is now being published for the seventh consecutive year.

Results

The consolidated profit after financial items increased to SKr 2,409 million, which represents a return on equity of 10.6 per cent, and earnings per share of SKr 20.40. The average return on equity over the six-year period beginning in 1994 is 15 per cent. During the same period, the total return, defined as change in share price including reinvested dividends, averaged 20 per cent per year (see figure on page 6).

The market for newsprint and magazine paper was strong. Holmen Paper reports another very good result, with a 22 per cent return on operating capital. During the 1994–1999 period, Holmen Paper earned an average return on operating capital of 24 per cent.

Conditions on the market for paperboard were weak at the beginning of the year, although they then gradually improved. Iggesund Paperboard's result was lowered by more than SKr 100 million on account of the production disturbances at Workington during the fourth quarter following a major rebuild. It is estimated that production will be back to normal during the first quarter of 2000. Iggesund Paperboard earned a return of 7.5 per cent on operating capital for 1999, and an average of 16 per cent during the 1994–1999 period.

Like in 1998, the market for sawn timber was characterised by excess supply and depressed prices despite buoyant demand. Iggesund Timber incurred a further loss. On average, the sawn timber business broke even during the 1994–1999 period.

The state of the market for products marketed by Modo Paper, the associate company, improved steadily during the year. The integration of the units is proceeding satisfactorily.

Market prospects for 2000

At the beginning of 2000, conditions on the markets for Holmen's main products – newsprint and magazine paper as well as paperboard – are strong. Newsprint and magazine paper prices are more or less unchanged, whereas, paperboard prices are being increased. In the case of sawn timber, markets are still depressed, although it looks as if some price increases might be possible in the case of whitewood products.

Ready for a more expansive direction

The conditions for further developing the Holmen Group are particularly good. After some years of consolidation and concentration, the ground has now been prepared for a more expansive direction. Holmen has a well-concentrated product portfolio, good products, a strong market position and an efficient, effective and environmentally adapted production system. The strategic direction is to grow within newsprint and magazine paper as well as paperboard, product areas where we are earning a good return and are highly competitive. Growth shall be organic as well as via acquisition, and the Group's robust financial position means that the chances of success are very good.

Now that I am retiring and handing over operative responsibility for Holmen, it feels very satisfying to have had the privilege of being involved in bringing the company to this position.

Stockholm, February 14, 2000

Bengt Pettersson
President and CEO

Per Ericson, new President

Per Ericson took up his position as President and CEO on February 15, 2000. He was previously President of AB Sandvik Steel.

The Holmen share

The company's two series of share are listed on the OM Stockholm Exchange's list of most heavily traded shares. In the middle of February 2000, the Series' names were changed to Holmen "A" and Holmen "B" as a consequence of the Group's change of name. In 1999 the highest turnover was in the Holmen "B" shares, for which the average turnover amounted to 236,000 shares per day, which corresponds to a value of SKr 51 million.

Convertibles and warrants issued by Holmen are also listed on the OM Stockholm Exchange. Standardised put and call options in Holmen "B" shares are traded on OM in Stockholm. At the turn of the year, Holmen's weighting in the Affärsvärlden General Index was 0.7 per cent and in the Forestry Index 17 per cent.

Share capital

Holmen has 88.8 million shares in issue, which are divided into 22.6 million Series "A" shares and 66.2 million Series "B" shares. Each Series "A" share entitles the owner to 10 votes, while each Series "B" share carries one vote. Otherwise, there is no difference between the two series of shares.

In 1998, a convertible loan and warrants were issued to the Group's employees. In the event of full conversion and subscription, these would correspond to a total of 3.2 million new Series "B" shares, which would dilute the capital by 3.5 per cent and the voting rights in Holmen by 1.1 per cent.

Per share information

Earnings per share amounted to SKr 20.40 (28.20), or SKr 19.90 (27.40) after full dilution. It is proposed to pay an ordinary dividend of SKr 11 (10) per share. Provided the floating of the associate company Modo Paper is carried through, the Board also intends to propose that the ordinary Annual General Meeting resolves to distribute shares in Modo Paper to the shareholders. The ordinary dividend corresponds to a direct yield of 4 per cent (6) on the basis of the closing share price on the stock market. Equity per share amounted to SKr 179 (207) at the year-end.

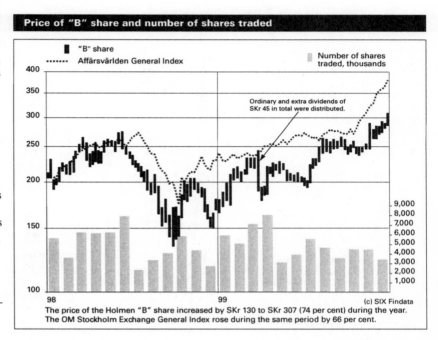

Price of "B" share and number of shares traded

"B" share
Affärsvärlden General Index
Number of shares traded, thousands

Ordinary and extra dividends of SKr 45 in total were distributed.

(c) SIX Findata

The price of the Holmen "B" share increased by SKr 130 to SKr 307 (74 per cent) during the year. The OM Stockholm Exchange General Index rose during the same period by 66 per cent.

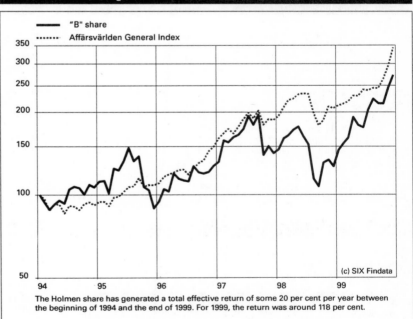

Total return including reinvested dividends, no tax deducted

"B" share
Affärsvärlden General Index

(c) SIX Findata

The Holmen share has generated a total effective return of some 20 per cent per year between the beginning of 1994 and the end of 1999. For 1999, the return was around 118 per cent.

Share data

Share data		1999	1998	1997	1996	1995	1994	1993	1992	1991	1990
Earnings per share [1]											
Before dilution	SKr	20.40	28.20	16.10	22.30	41.30	14.90	−3.60	−13.90	1.70	19.–
After dilution	SKr	19.90	27.40	16.10	22.30	41.30	14.90	−3.60	−13.90	1.70	19.–
Dividend per share											
Ordinary dividend	SKr	11[6]	10	9.–	9.–	8.50	5.50	0	0	3.–	5.50
Extra dividend	SKr	[7]	35								
Ordinary dividend as % of:											
Equity	%	6	5	5	5	5	4	–	–	2	4
Closing listed share price	%	4	6	4	5	6	3	–	–	4	6
Earnings per share	%	54	35	56	40	21	37	–	–	179	30
P/E ratio [2]		15	6	13	9	3	12	Neg	Neg	47	5
EV/EBITDA [3]		8	5	6	5	3	6	11	25	8	5
Return on [1]											
Equity	%	11	14	9	13	29	12	−3	−10	1	13
Operating capital	%	12	10	10	14	26	12	3	−2	3	10
Equity per share	SKr	179	207	184	176	163	127	118	129	146	150
Closing listed share price, "B"	SKr	307	176.5	205	192	142	173	128	87	80	95
Holmen's closing market value	SKr billion	27.3	15.7	18.1	17.1	12.7	15.4	11.0	6.4	5.8	6.2
Highest share price quoted during the year, "B"	SKr	309	275	304	200	243	186	141	118	149	147
Lowest share price quoted during the year, "B"	SKr	165	134	188	140	135	122	84	36	73	64
Beta value (48 months) "B", at year end [4]		1.1	1.5	1.5	1.4	1.8	1.6	1.6	1.6	1.1	1.3
Volatility (250 days) "B", at year end [5]	%	38	44	37	27	26	28	38	77	60	58

1) See definitions on page 41.
2) Closing share price divided by earnings per share.
3) Market value plus net financial debt (EV) at the end of the year divided by profit before depreciation (EBITDA).
4) Measures the sensitivity of the yield on the "B" share in relation to the yield on the Affärsvärlden General Index over a period of 48 months.

5) Measures changes in the price of the "B" share, expressed in percentage terms, over 250 days.
6) Proposal of the Board.
7) At a floating of Modo Paper the Board intends to propose distribution of shares in Modo Paper.

Changes in share capital

		Increase in No. of shares	Total No. of shares	Increase in share capital, SKr million	Total share capital, SKr million
1990	Conversion of convertible subordinated loan	1	15,681,288	0.0	1,568.1
	Conversion of KVBs	61,087	15,742,375	6.1	1,574.2
1991	Conversion of KVBs	551	15,742,926	0.1	1,574.3
1992	Conversion of KVBs	6,331	15,749,257	0.6	1,574.9
1993	Rights issue	14,469,139	30,218,396	1,446.9	3,021.8
	Conversion of KVBs	204,285	30,422,681	20.4	3,042.2
1994	Conversion of KVBs	3,978,257	34,400,938	397.8	3,440.1
1995	Conversion of KVBs	10,028,201	44,429,139	1,002.8	4,442.9
1996	Share split	44,429,139	88,858,278		4,442.9
1997			88,858,278		4,442.9
1998			88,858,278		4,442.9
1999			88,858,278		4,442.9

Shareholders at December 31, 1999

	% of shares	% of votes
L E Lundbergföretagen	22.9	49.5
Kempe Foundations	5.0	14.6
Handelsbanken incl. pension fund	2.8	8.4
Robur Funds	12.7	3.9
Fourth AP Fund	4.3	3.3
SPP	2.3	0.8
Nordbanken Funds	2.4	0.7
AMF Pension	2.3	0.7
Zenit Fund	1.8	0.5
Other*	43.5	17.6
Total	100.0	100.0
* of which non-Swedish shareholders	22.3	7.0

Share structure

Share	Votes	No. of shares	No. of votes	Par value	SKr million
"A"	10	22,623,234	226,232,340	50	1,131.2
"B"	1	66,235,044	66,235,044	50	3,311.7
Shares in total		88,858,278	292,467,384		4,442.9
Convertibles, Series "B" *	1	2,436,191	2,436,191	50	121.8
Warrants, Series "B" *	1	773,500	773,500	50	38.7
Total number of shares after dilution		92,067,969	295,677,075		4,603.4

* After full conversion and subscription

Ownership structure

No. of shares	No. of shareholders	Percentage of total no. of shares
1– 1,000	23,031	5
1,001– 5,000	1,469	4
5,001– 10,000	155	1
10,001– 50,000	155	4
50,001–100,000	34	3
100,001–	65	83
Total	24,909	100

Ten-year review of the Group

		1999	1998	1997	1996	1995	1994	1993	1992	1991	1990
Profit and loss accounts, SKr million											
Net turnover*		20,508	22,676	21,878	21,495	24,024	21,320	18,020	15,759	17,414	18,435
Operating costs		−16,669	−18,700	−18,244	−16,981	−17,397	−17,331	−15,990	−15,063	−15,385	−15,628
Items affecting comparability		–	–	–	11	282	−51	–	85	−280	418
Interest in earnings of associate companies		163	6	5	4	73	−32	−82	−22	−8	34
Depreciation according to plan		−1,387	−1,507	−1,409	−1,239	−1,151	−1,222	−1,261	−1,166	−992	−887
Operating profit/loss after depreciation		**2,615**	**2,475**	**2,230**	**3,290**	**5,831**	**2,684**	**687**	**−407**	**749**	**2,372**
Net financial items		−206	−137	−204	−371	−615	−859	−1,136	−1,104	−748	−715
Profit/loss after financial items		**2,409**	**2,338**	**2,026**	**2,919**	**5,216**	**1,825**	**−449**	**−1,511**	**1**	**1,657**
Tax		−595	166	−592	−940	−1,545	−497	193	568	112	−366
Less minority interests (after tax)		–	–	–	–	–	–	–	–	1	−4
Profit/loss for the year		**1,814**	**2,504**	**1,434**	**1,979**	**3,671**	**1,328**	**−256**	**−943**	**114**	**1,287**
Interest on KVBs		–	–	–	–	–	−37	–	–	−107	−199
Stated net profit/loss		**1,814**	**2,504**	**1,434**	**1,979**	**3,671**	**1,291**	**−256**	**−943**	**7**	**1,088**

* Holmen Skog's wood sales are stated as net turnover for the period 1993–1999.

		1999	1998	1997	1996	1995	1994	1993	1992	1991	1990
Balance sheets, SKr million											
Fixed assets		14,861	20,783	19,669	19,148	18,099	17,721	18,010	18,113	18,686	14,739
Shares and participations		4,392	148	177	190	641	695	809	809	1,011	973
Restricted accounts at Sveriges Riksbank		–	–	–	–	–	–	–	8	343	146
Current assets		5,068	8,262	8,220	7,805	8,707	8,207	6,774	6,696	6,817	7,742
Financial receivables		3,395	–	–	–	–	–	–	–	–	–
Liquid funds		1,456	1,241	1,636	2,133	1,296	1,140	3,996	4,423	2,682	3,542
Total assets		**29,172**	**30,434**	**29,702**	**29,276**	**28,743**	**27,763**	**29,589**	**30,049**	**29,539**	**27,142**
Equity		15,883	18,377	16,375	15,670	14,471	11,285	10,281	8,786	9,878	10,159
Minority interests		–	5	5	5	5	5	5	5	46	53
Deferred tax liability		2,408	2,920	3,419	2,862	2,421	1,938	1,394	1,724	2,514	2,540
Financial liabilities and interest-bearing provisions		6,905	4,384	5,505	6,229	7,180	10,247	14,446	15,517	13,261	10,424
Operating liabilities		3,976	4,748	4,398	4,510	4,666	4,288	3,463	4,017	3,840	3,966
Total equity and liabilities		**29,172**	**30,434**	**29,702**	**29,276**	**28,743**	**27,763**	**29,589**	**30,049**	**29,539**	**27,142**

		1999	1998	1997	1996	1995	1994	1993	1992	1991	1990
Ratios (see page 41 for definitions)											
Debt/equity ratio		0.13	0.17	0.24	0.26	0.41	0.81	1.02	1.26	1.07	0.67
Equity ratio	%	54.4	60.4	55.2	53.5	50.4	40.7	34.8	29.3	33.6	37.6
Interest coverage		12.7	18.1	10.9	8.9	9.5	3.1	0.6	−0.4	1.0	3.3
Return on operating capital	%	11.7	10.3	9.6	14.5	25.8	12.1	3.1	−1.8	3.5	12.5
Return on equity	%	10.6	14.4	9.0	13.1	28.5	12.3	−2.7	−10.1	1.1	13.4
Operating margin	%	12.0	10.9	10.2	15.2	22.8	13.0	4.3	−3.0	6.0	10.4
Net margin	%	8.8	11.0	6.6	9.2	15.3	6.2	−1.4	−6.0	0.7	7.0
Capital turnover rate		0.9	0.9	0.9	0.9	1.0	0.9	0.8	0.7	0.8	1.0
Capital expenditure, SKr million											
Shares and participations		–	–	–	35	29	51	31	5	95	79
Other fixed assets excl. company acquisitions		1,988	1,642	1,856	2,257	2,625	1,080	563	937	1,614	1,582
Company acquisitions, etc.		–	915	–	123	–	–	–	–	3,581	–
Employees											
Average number of employees		8,433	9,586	9,849	9,899	9,707	11,122	11,414	12,266	12,872	12,961
Wages and salaries	SKr million	2,410	2,659	2,573	2,497	2,400	2,648	2,628	2,617	2,635	2,498
Social security charges	SKr million	934	933	985	954	889	942	908	1,018	1,101	1,011

Operations by country

	Net turnover SKr million		Operating profit/loss SKr million		Capital expenditure SKr million		Employees Average number	
	1999	1998	**1999**	1998	**1999**	1998	**1999**	1998
Sweden	16,387	17,612	2,785	2,577	1,415	1,346	6,176	6,754
Australia	–	–	1	–	–	–	2	2
Belarus	10	28	–	–	–	–	22	32
Belgium	110	150	1	1	1	–	20	27
Denmark	5	6	–	1	–	2	6	8
Estonia	28	44	6	3	2	4	50	58
France	1,839	2,284	−58	−98	101	79	720	982
Germany	47	47	19	18	2	3	52	69
Great Britain	2,066	2,622	−193	−18	421	154	910	1,008
Holland	700	834	33	46	17	7	225	234
Ireland	3	4	−1	−2	–	–	–	–
Italy	14	15	1	1	–	–	6	8
Latvia	47	80	3	8	23	35	60	64
Lithuania	55	84	3	1	2	7	51	58
Norway	254	325	11	6	–	1	30	40
Poland	2	1	–	–	–	–	–	–
Russia	42	115	5	−72	1	3	54	167
Singapore	–	–	–	–	1	–	6	5
Spain	178	213	3	1	–	–	31	44
Switzerland	5	9	1	–	1	1	8	20
Ukraine	–	–	–	–	–	–	–	4
USA	1	1	−2	−1	1	–	4	2
Non-allocated	12	14	−3	3	–	–	–	–
Intra-Group sales	−1,297	−1,812	–	–	–	–	–	–
Total	**20,508**	**22,676**	**2,615**	**2,475**	**1,988**	**1,642**	**8,433**	**9,586**

The fine paper operations are included for the period January–September 1999.

Holmen Paper

HOLMEN PAPER produces newsprint, MF Special (MF Magazine i.e. improved newsprint, telephone directory paper and coloured newsprint), SC paper and coated printing paper (MWC medium weight coated).

PRESIDENT: Göran Lundin

HEAD OFFICE: Norrköping

MILLS: Braviken, Hallsta and Wargön.

HOLMEN PAPER has a strong market position, mainly for MF Magazine (improved newsprint) and telephone directory paper.

HOLMEN KRAFT is included in Holmen Paper and is responsible for the supply of electric power to the Group's Swedish mills and for the hydro-electric power stations.

Operations in 1999

HOLMEN PAPER'S net turnover amounted to SKr 7,327 million compared with SKr 7,432 million for 1998. The operating profit was SKr 1,494 million (1,511). Holmen Kraft's profit amounted to SKr 76 million (56).

The result was affected by slightly lower prices in Swedish kronor, which were largely offset by higher delivery volumes and lower costs.

THE MARKET for newsprint and magazine paper was strengthened. Newsprint deliveries to Western Europe increased by 2.5 per cent. There was a 5 per cent increase in deliveries to Germany. Deliveries of MF Magazine of higher brightness grades increased by a full 19 per cent. Over a period of 3 years, deliveries of this grade have almost doubled. A positive growth of 5 per cent was also seen for deliveries of SC paper, while for coated paper, the increase was just under 2 per cent.

PRICES in local currencies fell at the start of the year by between 1 and 3 per cent, but then remained stable.

CAPACITY UTILISATION at Holmen Paper's mills reached 97 per cent, which in practice means an almost maximum utilisation of the available production capacity.

Newsprint

CAPITAL EXPENDITURE amounted to SKr 606 million (682). This was put primarily into enhancing quality and to improving printability of improved newsprint. A new wood line started up in Hallsta, giving a more rational wood handling. Capital expenditure was made also to increase capacity and to reduce energy consumption.

Summary	1999	1998
Net turnover, SKr million	7,327	7,432
of which to external customers, SKr million	6,987	7,012
Operating profit, SKr million	1,494	1,511
Operating capital (average)*, SKr million	6,435	6,269
Return on operating capital*, %	22.0	23.2
Capital expenditure, SKr million	606	682
Average number of employees	2,322	2,344

* Excluding Holmen Kraft.

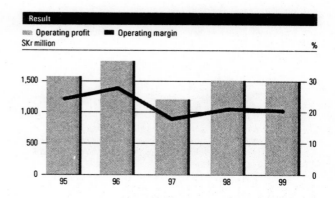

Result

■ Operating profit   ■ Operating margin
SKr million   %

53

Most of the deliveries from Braviken and Hallsta go to newspaper printing works and publishers. Wargön's products are delivered mainly to commercial printers and merchants.

MARKET POSITION. The strong position held by Holmen Paper with the European daily newspaper publishers is one of the most important assets of the company. In Sweden, Germany, Great Britain, Spain, France and Benelux, Holmen Paper is the largest, or second largest, supplier to the leading publishers.

MF SPECIAL PAPER. Holmen Paper is one of the larger European producers of MF Special Paper, i.e. *MF Magazine (improved newsprint), telephone directory paper* and *coloured newsprint.*

MF Magazine is an expanding product area. The primary product applications are supplements and advertising print-outs in both offset-coldset and heatset. The trend is towards an increased share of highly bleached products.

Holmen Paper is one of the leading suppliers in terms of quality and quantity. The strength lies in its wide product palette with speciality products such as Ultra Bright Plus, a paper of very high brightness. Other significant factors are the long experience within this product area, the well-established customer base and the high capacity.

However, competition is stiffening as many manufacturers are extending their capacity and developing their products.

Sales of *telephone directory paper* are rising, particularly in Eastern Europe. Holmen Paper is currently the leading European supplier of telephone directory paper.

Coloured newsprint, especially pink newsprint, has become something of a standard hallmark of financial newspapers and supplements. Within this market segment, Holmen Paper also holds a strong position.

Holmen Paper has established its leading position within the MF Special Paper product area over the last 15 years. Entirely new products have been developed, existing ones have been improved while considerable capital expenditure has been made to refine the manufacturing process. During the forthcoming years, work will continue to develop products within the area even further.

Market conditions

Holmen Paper's main market is Western Europe, which accounts for almost 90 per cent of deliveries. The largest single markets are Great Britain, Sweden and Germany. New and interesting growth markets are Poland and the Baltic States.

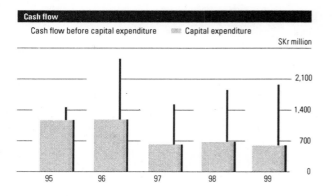

Cash flow

Cash flow before capital expenditure   Capital expenditure

SKr million

| | 2,100 |
| 1,400 |
| 700 |
| 0 |
| 95 | 96 | 97 | 98 | 99 |

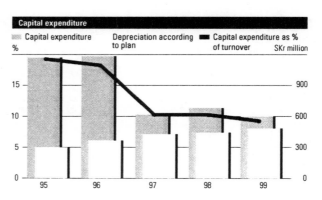

Capital expenditure

Capital expenditure   Depreciation according to plan   Capital expenditure as % of turnover

%   SKr million

15		900
10		600
5		300
0		0
95	96	97	98	99

NEWSPRINT. Following major capital expenditure at Braviken in 1996, when a new paper machine was started up, Holmen Paper has been able to increase its market share within this product area.

Newsprint, in terms of volume, is the largest product for the majority of Holmen Paper's customers. Most customers also purchase additional products, which makes a first-class newsprint something of a basis for many customer relationships and allows the successful sale of further products, such as MF Magazine.

The development of newsprint is tending towards lightweight paper, from the present 45 grams down to 42 grams per square meter.

SC AND MWC PAPER. Holmen Paper is concentrating on quality within these product areas and on the optimal utilisation of production equipment. SC paper is produced in Hallsta and MWC paper in Wargön.

Research & Development

Holmen Paper prioritises research and development within highly bleached MF Magazine paper and low-weight wood-containing paper.

The R&D work is based at the development departments at Braviken, Hallsta and Wargön. A central unit, the Competence Centre for Mechanical Pulp is engaged in larger and more time consuming projects.

Strategy

Holmen Paper shall be an *important supplier* of newsprint and a *leading supplier* of MF Special Paper, i.e. MF Magazine (improved newsprint), telephone directory paper and coloured newsprint, as well as a *supplier* of the important range supplements SC paper and coated printing paper (MWC).

Since the mid-1980s, Holmen Paper's strategy has been to increase the number of processed products in its product range, with special attention given to MF Special Paper. This has meant

that the production share of standard newsprint has dropped from approximately 70 per cent to 47 per cent today. At the same time, the total sales volume almost doubled. This strategy has had a decisive role in the good economic results of the last five years. On average, return on operating capital during this period was 24 per cent.

Long-term capital expenditure

In 1995–99, Holmen Paper carried out an extensive investment programme totalling about SKr 4,200 million. Most of this was put into expansionary capital expenditure within the sectors of newsprint and MF Special Paper. The largest single project, in the region of SKr 2,000 million, was the paper machine PM 53 at Braviken.

These investments made possible an increase in deliveries during the period from 1.1 million tonnes per year up to 1.5 million tonnes. Quality was improved and several newly developed products with interesting potential were introduced.

During the coming years, Holmen Paper will concentrate on strengthening its leading position within the MF Special paper product area. At Hallsta an extensive programme for quality and product development is planned. This has a dual purpose, to increase mill profitability and to reinforce product competitiveness.

Holmen Kraft

Holmen Kraft is responsible for the supply of electric power to the Holmen Group's units in Sweden and for the Group's hydro-electric power stations.

Holmen's turnover of electric power in 1999 amounted to 3,937 GWh.

The Group's short-term and long-term needs of electric power are covered by purchases, selfgenerated hydro-electric power and by the industries' back pressure plants. See the table below.

Production and deliveries*	1999	1998	1999	1998
1,000 tonnes	Production		Deliveries	
Newsprint, standard	652	685	662	682
Newsprint, MF Special	513	484	509	478
SC paper	127	127	125	123
Coated printing paper	119	121	117	112
Sulphite pulp	38	40	–	1
	1,449	1,457	1,413	1,396

* Including deliveries to other business areas in the Group.

Electric power	1999	1998
The Group's turnover of electric power in Sweden* Production/purchases GWh		
Company-owned and associate hydro-electric power stations	1,135	1,384
Back pressure turbines at mills	338	400
Purchased electric power	2,464	2,141
Total	3,937	3,925

* Excluding divested activities.

Printed media maintains its position

The consumption of newsprint and magazine paper increases yearly. In 1999, deliveries of newsprint to Western Europe increased by 2 per cent while deliveries of improved newsprint with a high brightness reached a full 19 per cent. All forecasts also indicate a continuing high rate of increase during coming years.

Developments in IT, however, are about to change established consumer patterns. The traditional daily newspapers – both quality broadsheets and tabloids – are facing falling circulation figures while various types of speciality newspapers and free papers are increasing. This trend is very apparent, with the range of niche newspapers growing daily, forcing the local newsagents to extend their shelving to hold an ever increasing and wider range of speciality newspapers and magazines.

There are several factors behind this development. Techniques for producing newspapers with advanced layout have become more accessible with PC's and software opening up new opportunities for magazine production. In addition to this, the market for speciality newspapers has increased due partly to the fact that increased use of computers and advanced electronics leads to a greater need to read *about* them.

The same principle applies to the increased range of TV channels available, which creates a large and entirely new market for different TV magazines, the latest trend being for newspapers based upon popular TV series. These newspapers can be seen as an enhancement of the series. They give readers ideas and information that can only be conveyed by means of the printed word.

The free newspapers which are distributed on public transport systems in towns and cities are yet another example of the shift taking place between different types of printed media. These newspapers, which are entirely financed by advertising show an interesting development.

The content of advertisements, which are the back-bone of all newspaper and magazine production, is also changing with certain types of advertisements becoming less frequent - such as

MF Magazine paper

those for housing, cars and other capital goods, which have given way to electronic advertising domains. The same applies to traditional "situations vacant" columns, as it is both simple and cheap for companies to place their advertisements in different electronic market places.

One consequence of this development is the need for companies to advertise *that* they exist and, above all, *where* they can be contacted. "Institutional advertising", starting off at an electronic address, has quickly become extremely popular and will be even more common in the future.

A survey recently conducted by Swedish newspaper publishers clearly shows that people want to increase their newspaper reading in the future; however, it was also recognised that the time available for media consumption is shrinking. This trend is particularly strong among the younger generation and city dwellers.

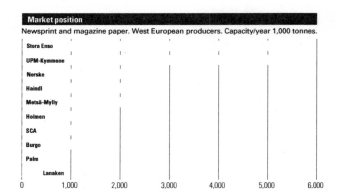

Market position

Newsprint and magazine paper. West European producers. Capacity/year 1,000 tonnes.

Stora Enso
UPM-Kymmene
Norske
Haindl
Metsä-Mylly
Holmen
SCA
Burgo
Palm
Lanaken

0   1,000   2,000   3,000   4,000   5,000   6,000

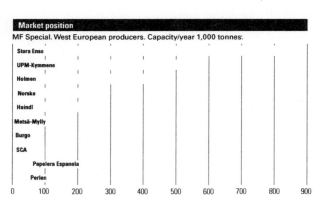

Market position

MF Special. West European producers. Capacity/year 1,000 tonnes.

Stora Enso
UPM-Kymmene
Holmen
Norske
Haindl
Metsä-Mylly
Burgo
SCA
Papelera Espanola
Perlen

0   100   200   300   400   500   600   700   800   900

Iggesund Paperboard

IGGESUND PAPERBOARD produces solid bleached board (SBB) and folding boxboard (FBB) using only virgin fibre as raw material. Paperboard with barrier functions is also produced.

Iggesund Paperboard is Europe's leading paperboard producer for customers with highest demands on product quality and service. The paperboard is used as packaging for food, cosmetics, pharmaceuticals, tobacco and chocolates as well as for graphic purposes.

PRESIDENT: Erik Sjölund

HEAD OFFICE: Iggesund

MILLS: Iggesunds Bruk, Workington and Ströms Bruk.

Operations in 1999

IGGESUND PAPERBOARD'S net turnover fell to SKr 3,913 million compared with SKr 4,051 million for 1998. The operating profit fell to SKr 318 million (590), primarily due to the unfavourable developments of the English and Swedish currencies against the euro. The result was also hit by the start-up problems with the rebuilt paperboard machine at Workington. Production stability improved at the beginning of the year, and normal production conditions are expected to be restored during the first quarter of 2000.

THE MARKET. Following a weak start, the paperboard market gradually improved during the year. Demand increased strongly in both Western Europe and USA. The important Asian export markets started to recover following several years of subdued demand in the aftermath of the financial crisis.

Product sales from Iggesunds Bruk and Ströms Bruk reached a record high, while deliveries from Workington were hit by limitations imposed by the ongoing rebuild.

PRICES in local currencies remained largely unchanged. The strong demand during the last six months of the year meant that price increases were announced in the fourth quarter with full effect from the beginning of 2000.

NEW SALES ORGANISATION. Iggesund Paperboard's central sales management was relocated to Amsterdam. At the same time, the previously geographically-based sales organisation was adapted to area of application and to international customers. All customer services and marketing resources have been transferred to the new Amsterdam office. However, sales and technical-based customer service will remain in the local countries.

Central and Eastern European sales resources were strengthened. In addition to sales functions located in Europe, Iggesund Paperboard also has sales companies in North America and South East Asia.

CAPACITY UTILISATION at Iggesund Paperboard's mills remained at 82 per cent. For solid bleached board (SBB) capacity was utilised to the full during the second half of the year, while capacity utilisation for folding boxboard decreased very much during the last quarter in connection with the Workington rebuild.

CAPITAL EXPENDITURE amounted to SKr 752 million (302). The major portion of this went towards the "Workington Millennium Project" which will give a higher paperboard quality and will increase the mill's delivery capacity.

Market conditions

AN EXPANDING AND INCREASINGLY GLOBAL MARKET. The annual global paperboard consumption is about 27 million tonnes, of which just under half consists of virgin fibre-based paperboard. The market for this kind of virgin fibre-based paperboard produced by Iggesund Paperboard – solid bleached board (SBB) and folding boxboard (FBB) – amounts to approximately 8 million tonnes. About 2 million tonnes of this is consumed in Europe. This market growth is around 2 per cent per year and within certain segments in the highest quality class, 3 to 5 per cent.

Asia is the most rapidly expanding market. Currently, consumption in Asia is on a par with Western European consumption but market growth is on the whole considerably greater. The

Summary	1999	1998
Net turnover, SKr million	3,913	4,051
of which to external customers, SKr million	3,819	3,915
Operating profit, SKr million	318	590
Operating capital (average), SKr million	4,239	4,065
Return on operating capital, %	7.5	14.5
Capital expenditure, SKr million	752	302
Average number of employees	2,011	2,023

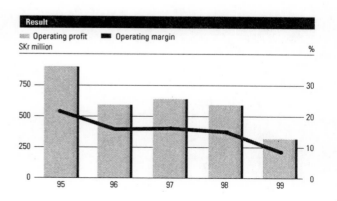

Result

Operating profit · Operating margin
SKr million · %

Central and East European markets are also expanding at a greater rate than the West European markets.

Mergers are taking place among both producers and customers and their corporate strategies are becoming increasingly global. Fewer yet larger customers means more intense competition. However, as yet there has been no notification of new paperboard production capacity. In this respect, the Asian crisis had a long-term positive effect on the paperboard industry as the lack of risk capital put a stop to a considerable number of expansion projects. It is predicted that the balance between supply and demand on the paperboard market will therefore improve.

MARKET POSITION. Iggesund Paperboard is since long a European market leader for paperboard of the highest quality, and has a total share of about 20 per cent of the market for virgin fibre-based paperboard.

Countries in South East Asia, Eastern and Central Europe, and the USA are gaining ground and now account for almost 10 per cent of Iggesund Paperboard's deliveries. This market share is expected to increase not only as a result of the company's own efforts but also because of the high growth rate of these markets.

Paperboard for perfume packaging

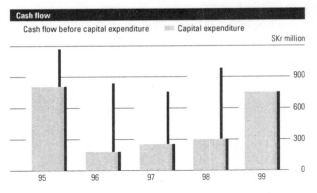

Cash flow

Cash flow before capital expenditure   Capital expenditure

SKr million

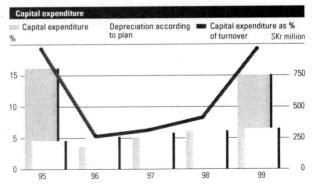

Capital expenditure

Capital expenditure   Depreciation according to plan   Capital expenditure as % of turnover

%   SKr million

Research & Development

Iggesund Paperboard is increasing its investments into research and development. Work is directed towards product and process development and, increasingly, to technical customer service.

R&D work is decentralised and conducted at each mill within the framework of commercially defined projects. The work also involves other sections of the Group, research institutions and suppliers of process equipment.

At Workington new high-grammage products designed for whisky packaging, for example, have been launched. The largest R&D project at Workington involves an entirely new generation of paperboard products, mainly products with a more even quality and a higher rigidity and whiteness, which will be introduced onto the market in 2001.

A "pilot coater" has been installed at Iggesunds Bruk. This creates a greater potential to develop new products and to improve quality within the important surface treatment area.

A new generation paperboard for hard cigarette packs is being developed, which will help to consolidate Iggesund Paperboard's market position even more.

Within the process technique area, development work is predominantly focused on measures to improve paperboard quality and reduce the costs of pulp production.

At Ströms Bruk, work is focused on improving barrier functions, which will also contribute towards broadening the field of application for paperboard.

Paperboard for graphic purposes

Strategy

Iggesund Paperboard shall consolidate its market position by concentrating on high quality products and fulfilling the customers' high demands on service.

Iggesund Paperboard shall hold a leading position within the prioritised end-user areas of tobacco, graphic paperboard and packaging.

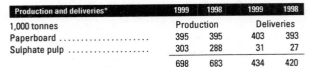

Production and deliveries*	1999	1998	1999	1998
1,000 tonnes	Production		Deliveries	
Paperboard	395	395	403	393
Sulphate pulp	303	288	31	27
	698	683	434	420

* Including deliveries to other business areas in the Group.

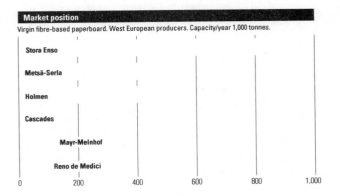

Market position

Virgin fibre-based paperboard. West European producers. Capacity/year 1,000 tonnes.

Stora Enso

Metsä-Serla

Holmen

Cascades

Mayr-Melnhof

Reno de Medici

0   200   400   600   800   1,000

Long-term capital expenditure

As of mid 1999, a major project, entitled "The Millennium Project", has been underway at Workington. This project involves the upgrading of the factory in line with the Iggesund Paperboard strategy, which, by making full use of the mill's capacity and profitability potential, will optimise production. The competitiveness of paperboard products will be raised by an increase in quality, evenness and improved optical properties. Marketing activities are focused on the end-users with the highest demands on quality and service.

Parallel with this capital expenditure is a lengthy series of measures to reduce costs and increase efficiency.

Workington's annual delivery capacity will increase from 190,000 tonnes to 235,000 tonnes.

Some years ago, a large investment programme was also carried out at Iggesunds Bruk. This enabled the development of several new products, such as two-sided coated paperboard and high gloss paperboard.

This has helped to strengthen Iggesund Paperboard's market position, not least as the company has increased its quality lead even more.

Paperboard packaging in society

Iggesund Paperboard's production of virgin fibre-based paperboard is largely focused on the packaging industry. Today, packaging is a way of life in western society. It is necessary for the distribution of both foodstuffs and other goods. The amount of packaged goods has been steadily increasing, driven up by the need for rational handling and people's willingness, and ability, to pay for convenience, which is reflected in the steadily growing consumption of ready-to-eat, pre-packed foods.

Packaging also helps to save on resources, a fact which is frequently overlooked; a comparison between the packaging-intensive western world and developing countries makes this all too clear. In the developing countries, where pre-packed foodstuffs are rare, up to about half the number of goods are lost before they reach the consumer, while in Western Europe only a small percentage of foodstuffs is lost en route between the producer and the consumer.

The resources required for the manufacture of packaging must always be seen in relation to their value and to how well they protect the goods they contain. This means that packaging must always save more resources than are required in their production.

Over the past few decades, the packaging industry and the distribution systems have developed in such a way that it cuts the use of material by around two per cent a year, a development which has been fuelled by society's attention to resource utilisation and environmental impact. This has favoured the use of paperboard as a packaging material, not least as paperboard is

Paperboard for food packaging

produced using a renewable raw material and as it can be recycled. In this respect, paperboard is unique among all packaging materials available.

However, there are also problems. EU legislation prioritised materials recovery over energy recovery during the 1980s-90s, which resulted in the construction of large and resource-intensive recovery systems. This has been costly for consumers and has not helped to improve the environment. However, a new approach has become evident which has started to question the value of producer responsibility. It's important that the issue is highlighted so that used paper- and paperboard products can be handled in an economical and environmentally balanced way.

Iggesund Timber

Customised sawn timber

IGGESUND TIMBER manufactures and distributes sawn timber.

PRESIDENT: Per Erik Frick

HEAD OFFICE: Iggesund

SAWMILLS: Iggesund and Domsjö.

Around half of the output consists of customised speciality products for wood working industries, while the remainder consists of standard products for the sawn timber trade.

◼ Operations in 1999

IGGESUND TIMBER'S net turnover increased to SKr 767 million, which may be compared with SKr 727 million in 1998. The operating loss deteriorated further to SKr 66 million (loss 59), mainly due to the persistence of low delivery prices and high raw material prices.

THE MARKET for sawn timber was characterised by excess supply and depressed prices. Whitewood products enjoyed firm demand, mainly due to a higher level of building activity in the Netherlands and France and increased exports to Japan.

The supply of standard redwood products was in excess of demand. Several small sawmills in Sweden were closed down, while new capacity was added mainly in the form of large, new sawmills or expansions of large sawmills.

Competition intensified, mainly from Finnish, Baltic and German producers.

PRICES. The prices in local currencies of whitewood products increased by 10 per cent. The effect in Swedish kronor was, however, far less on account of a deterioration in the exchange rate. Redwood prices weakened steadily and the average price was 4 per cent lower than in the previous year.

CAPACITY UTILISATION at Iggesund Timber's sawmills amounted to 91 (91) per cent.

CAPITAL EXPENDITURE amounted to SKr 39 million. The main capital expenditure was in the newly started project to raise drying capacity at the Iggesund Sawmill. This project involves the installation of 22 chamber kilns at the sawmill in conjunction with the closure of the drying unit at Håstaholmen in Hudiksvall.

The cost of this is SKr 90 million and it will make the Iggesund Sawmill the largest producer of specially dried sawn timber in the Nordic countries.

Summary	1999	1998
Net turnover, SKr million	767	727
of which to external customers, SKr million	767	727
Operating profit/loss*, SKr million	−66	−59
Operating capital (average), SKr million	429	430
Return on operating capital, %	−15.3	−13.8
Capital expenditure, SKr million	39	54
Average number of employees	287	298

* Including interest in earnings of associate companies.

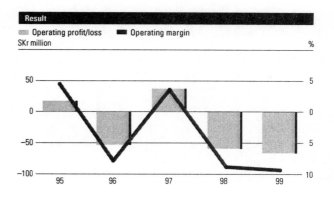

Result

▨ Operating profit/loss   ▬ Operating margin

SKr million   %

Photo: Michael Perlmutter/rupertgardnerdesignab

Market conditions

Western Europe is the main market for Swedish sawn timber. Exports from Sweden amounted to some 11 million m³ in 1999, which corresponds to 75 per cent of total production.

Consumption of sawn timber increased by about 1 per cent in Europe in 1999. The level of building activity increased by 2.3 per cent, which indicates that other materials are replacing sawn timber in certain building structures.

Japan has once again become a significant market for Nordic and European whitewood products since the level of building activity there has taken off again after the crisis in Asia. In 1999, some 1.5 million m³ of Nordic whitewood products were exported to Japan.

Research and Development

The moisture content of the wood is a very important quality factor. Advanced technology is needed to achieve the precise moisture content specified by many customers. Iggesund Timber has therefore invested in developing methods for timber drying. The experiences and results of this developmental work now provide an important foundation for the timber drying plant that is now being installed at the Iggesund Sawmill.

Strategy and long-term capital expenditure

Iggesund Timber has concentrated for some years on processed sawn timber that are marketed under the collective name of INDUSTRY TIMBER. These are input products for wood working industries with high demands with regard to service and quality. Product development takes place in close co-operation with customers - manufacturers of furniture, windows, doors, kitchen cabinets, floors and staircases. In 1999, INDUSTRY TIMBER accounted for some 50 per cent of total deliveries.

The new timber-drying plant will enable the entire production of the Iggesund Sawmill to be specially dried as of the second half of 2000.

Coming capital expenditure is related to a finishing and packaging unit at Iggesund.

Production and deliveries*	1999	1998	1999	1998
1,000 m³	Production		Deliveries	
Company sawmills, sawn timber redwood	213	215	220	207
Company sawmills, sawn timber whitewood	141	139	146	142
Purchased sawn timber	–	–	100	93
	354	354	466	442

* Including deliveries to other business areas in the Group.

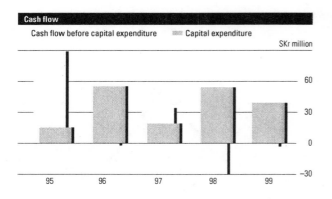

Cash flow

Cash flow before capital expenditure ▨ Capital expenditure

SKr million

95 96 97 98 99

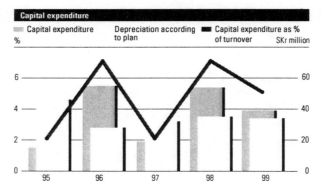

Capital expenditure

▨ Capital expenditure Depreciation according to plan ■ Capital expenditure as % of turnover

% SKr million

95 96 97 98 99

Holmen Skog

HOLMEN SKOG is responsible for wood procurement for the Group's Swedish mills as well as for managing the Group's forest holdings of some one million hectares of productive forestland. Operations are conducted through the harvesting of Holmen's own forests and through wood trade, whereby wood is purchased from private forest owners, forest-owners' co-operatives, other companies and sawmills and sold to Holmen's and other forest company's industries. After the divestment of the Husum and Domsjö mills, more than half of Holmen Skog's net turnover will consist of external sales.

PRESIDENT: Björn Andrén

HEAD OFFICE: Örnsköldsvik

THE ORGANISATION includes four regions: Lycksele, Örnsköldsvik, Iggesund and Norrköping, a central wood department and a subsidiary company in Estonia.

■ Operations in 1999

HOLMEN SKOG'S operating profit fell to SKr 521 million compared with SKr 548 million for 1998. The decline is mainly due to lower wood prices.

WOOD PROCUREMENT. Consumption of pulpwood and saw logs amounted to 4.3 million m^3 excl. divested mills and to 8.1 million m^3 incl. divested mills. Harvesting in the Group's forests amounted to 2.4 (2.4) million m^3. External procurement of Swedish wood remained largely the same as for the previous year. Imports from the Baltic states and Russia increased to 2.3 (2.2) million m^3.

PRICES for pulpwood in Sweden were reduced at the end of 1998. The mills' costs for pulpwood were on average 5 per cent lower in 1999 compared to the previous year. Saw log prices also fell and the sawmills' wood costs were almost 2 per cent lower.

Forestry, wood trade and procurement of wood

FOREST EXCHANGE. A large land exchange, involving about 80,000 hectares of productive forest land in northern Sweden, was carried out between Holmen and AssiDomän in order to help cut the distance between Holmen's forests and its industries.

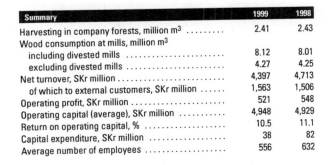

Summary	1999	1998
Harvesting in company forests, million m^3	2.41	2.43
Wood consumption at mills, million m^3		
including divested mills	8.12	8.01
excluding divested mills	4.27	4.25
Net turnover, SKr million	4,397	4,713
of which to external customers, SKr million	1,563	1,506
Operating profit, SKr million	521	548
Operating capital (average), SKr million	4,948	4,929
Return on operating capital, %	10.5	11.1
Capital expenditure, SKr million	38	82
Average number of employees	556	632

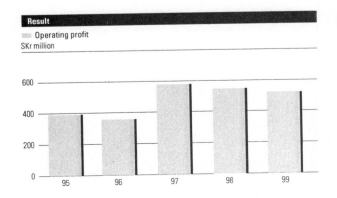

Result

Operating profit
SKr million

between Holmen, Stora Enso and Korsnäs through the purchasing company Industriskog was also phased out. Holmen left Sydved and is now an independent player on the market and Holmen Skog took over some staff from Sydved. Industriskog's operations were adjusted to concentrate mainly on transportation optimisation.

NEW ROLE IN NORTHERN SWEDEN. Holmen Skog took on a somewhat different role in northern Sweden following the establishment of the new Modo Paper and the divestment of the Domsjö sulphite mill. Holmen Skog has no internal buyer in the area now besides Iggesund Timber's sawmill in Domsjö and will procure and sell wood under market conditions. Holmen Skog has long-term agreements for wood deliveries to Husum and Domsjö mills.

NEW ORGANISATION. The reorganisation that was decided upon at the end of 1998 was carried out during the year and is expected to reduce administration costs by about 10 per cent.

CHANGED IMPORT ORGANISATION. The establishment of new Modo Paper also led to changes in the purchasing organisations in the Baltics and Russia. Holmen Skog's previously wholly-owned purchasing companies in Latvia, Lithuania, and Russia are now, as of 2000, part of Modo Paper. The Estonian purchasing company, however, will remain part of Holmen Skog as the quantities procured in Estonia generally satisfy the import requirements of the new Holmen Group.

Market conditions

SWEDEN. The terminated wood purchasing co-operation through the purchasing companies Sydved and Industriskog has changed competition in the southern and middle parts of Sweden, which has created new supply conditions for the industries.

In order to deal with this situation, Holmen Skog has changed the organisation and launched an extensive project aimed to make wood purchasing more efficient. The project also includes measures to stimulate supply from private forest owners.

Organisational changes

TERMINATED PURCHASING CO-OPERATION. The joint purchase of wood between Holmen, Stora Enso and Munksjö through the purchasing company Sydved was forbidden following the decision of the Swedish Market Court. A corresponding co-operation

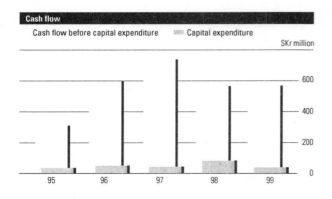

Cash flow

Cash flow before capital expenditure   Capital expenditure

SKr million

Capital expenditure

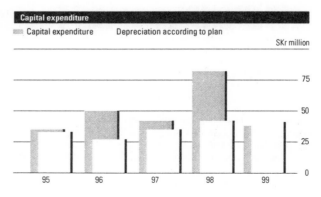

Capital expenditure   Depreciation according to plan

SKr million

Associate company

◼ Modo Paper

MODO PAPER, in which Holmen and SCA each have a 50 per cent interest, produces office paper, graphic paper and runs merchanting operations.

PRESIDENT: Jan Åström

HEAD OFFICE: Stockholm

MILLS: Husum, Stockstadt, Alizay, Hallein, Wifsta, Pont Sainte Maxence, and Silverdalen.

Modo Paper Trade, a fine paper merchant active in 22 countries.

◼ New fine paper group

Holmen's and SCA's units within fine paper and merchanting were merged in a new, jointly owned company, Modo Paper, on October 1, 1999. The new group has an annual production capacity of some 1.8 million tonnes of paper, and is thus Europe's third largest fine paper company with a market share of almost 15 per cent. Modo Paper concentrates on office paper and graphic paper.

◼ Operations in 1999

MODO PAPER'S net turnover, pro forma for the whole year, amounted to SKr 18,880 million, and its operating profit to SKr 902 million.

THE MARKET for fine paper in Western Europe improved. Demand for coated fine paper rose by close to 10 per cent and for uncoated grades by some 5 per cent. Office paper, one of Modo Paper's main products, is estimated to have increased by almost 6 per cent. Fine paper imports to Western Europe from e.g. South East Asia increased to a lesser degree than expected.

PRICES rose by approximately 10 per cent.

CAPACITY UTILISATION at Modo Paper's mills averaged some 92 per cent.

CAPITAL EXPENDITURE amounted to SKr 1,085 million.

◼ Market conditions

THE MARKET for fine paper is relatively fragmented, despite several mergers during the 1990s. Recurring problems due to excess supply and low capacity utilisation have put pressure on margins in the industry, and further concentration can therefore be expected.

The consumption of fine paper in Western Europe amounted to almost 14 million tonnes in 1999, of which approximately 7.5 million tonnes consisted of uncoated paper and 6.5 million tonnes of coated paper. Consumption is growing at a rate of some 4 per cent per year. The growth rate is fastest within the coated reels and sheet segments and in office paper (A4).

Modo Paper focuses on a number of strategic products: coated paper in large sheets and on reel, office paper in small format (A4) and uncoated large sheets. Investments within these segments will be made to improve the market position. Exposure to the competitive market for uncoated paper on reel will be significantly reduced.

Modo Paper's aim is to make greater use of internally produced pulp in order to enable a higher capacity utilisation at the own pulp mills.

Modo Paper's customers consist primarily of commercial printers, fine paper merchants/distributors, users of office paper and paper converters.

The most important markets are Germany, France, Great Britain and Scandinavia.

The extensive merchanting organisation is one of Modo Paper's strengths. The company is the third largest paper merchant in Europe.

◼ Strategic direction

In February 2000 the Board of Modo Paper approved the strategic direction for the Group. It is based on the Group's existing mills and its paper merchanting operations, and an assessment of the life cycles of the various fine paper products. The strategy is based on the following keystones:

- ◾ To concentrate on growth segments, namely coated paper and office paper in small formats.
- ◾ To strengthen market position within priority segments that are supported by the company's own merchanting operations.
- ◾ To improve efficiency and increase utilisation of machinery by specialising production lines and mills.
- ◾ To strengthen market position of the merchanting operations on the European market.

Priority products are coated paper on reels and in sheet format, and office paper. These are high added value products for which demand is estimated to show sustained strength. Expansion within these product areas is in line with the merchanting organisation's product portfolio.

Holmen and the environment

Holmen has carried out extensive environmental investments during the past years. These have helped to reduce the environmental impact of the business quite markedly.

Effects on the aqueous environment in the vicinity of Holmen's mills are now small. The Group's forests are harvested in such a way that the biodiversity in the forests is maintained.

It is, as yet, not quite certain that all the problems have definitely been solved. It is only nature itself that can answer such questions. But in "slow" ecosystems such as forests, it will take half a century, or even longer, before it can be said with certainty whether the measures have the intended effect.

On the other hand, when it comes to the aqueous environment in the vicinity of the mills, it is already possible to see distinct improvements, which have been confirmed by recent studies.

Holmen believes that it is important, with the aid of independent researchers, to continue to identify and analyse the effects of the business on the environment in order to establish the need for, and the value of, further environmental investments.

Capital expenditure and costs for environmental protection

Holmen divides the environmental capital expenditure in two categories: those which are *directly* related to environmental measures and those that are *integrated,* i.e. which are included in new equipment and the cost of which can therefore only be estimated.

DIRECT ENVIRONMENTAL CAPITAL EXPENDITURE consists of external measures, such as treatment plants. The entire amount represents an environmental capital expenditure.

INTEGRATED ENVIRONMENTAL CAPITAL EXPENDITURE is not primarily made for the sake of the environment but nevertheless has a positive impact on the environment, i.e. new process equipment with a superior environmental performance to the equipment it replaces. The cost of such environmental capital expenditure can only be determined by estimating its "environmental" share.

Environmental capital expenditure, SKr million	1999	1998
Direct	19	47
Integrated	120	37
Total	**139**	**84**

Environmental costs, SKr million	1999	1998
Operations	79	71
Capital	74	82
Environmental taxes and charges	40	36
Other	22	23
Total	**215**	**212**

Income from environmental protection

BENEFITS ON PROCESS ECONOMY. Environmental measures can provide benefits in the form of reductions in fibre and chemical losses. Recycled fibres, for example, can be used as a biofuel, which in turn helps to reduce energy costs.

LONG-TERM MARKET BENEFITS. Holmen's good environmental profile provides long-term market benefits, helps it to maintain its market share, and allows certain types of business to be transacted. A good environmental profile is also important for the image of the products, and for the image of the company as a long-term partner. Such advantages are, however, difficult to evaluate in financial terms.

INCREASED NATURAL VALUE. The environmental activities carried out by Holmen over the past thirty years have resulted in improvements to the quality of the water in the vicinity of the mills. By reducing emissions into air, Holmen has also helped to reduce the global impact of air pollution. Conditions have been created in the forests to ensure that species belonging to the natural ecosystem will continue to flourish.

Seen overall, natural values are improved markedly. This positive trend will continue since not all measures have yet had their full effect.

Holmen's view on income from environmental protection

A good environmental profile is as natural as good product quality, delivery reliability, good service and competitive prices.

A good environmental profile is an important instrument in maintaining close, long-term relationships with customers.

The aim is to make full use of those values that are inherent in the current good environmental profile.

Important environmental applications

HALLSTA. An application to increase production and bleaching was submitted at the end of 1998. Negotiations in the Environmental Court will take place during the first quarter of 2000.

BRAVIKEN. In October 1999, the Environmental Court granted a permit to incinerate waste chips and increase the quantity of filler in the paper produced. The decision is in line with the mill's application.

IGGESUNDS BRUK. In accordance with the wishes of the Environmental Court and other environmental authorities, supplementary information was appended at the end of 1998. The application means that the mill undertakes to implement certain measures to reduce emissions into water, and then to carry out a further investigation of the environmental impact of the emissions. Negotiations in the Environmental Court are expected to take place in 2000.

WORKINGTON. The British Environmental Agency issued a permit to raise production, and also to produce peroxide bleached products. The new equipment was commissioned in 1999.

Extensive investigations of the aqueous environment in the vicinity of the mill were carried out in co-operation with the Environmental Agency. The results have so far shown that the environmental situation is good.

Environmental management and certification

ISO 14001. Holmen Skog, Braviken, Wargön and the Iggesund Sawmill received certification in 1999. Hallsta, Iggesunds Bruk, Workington, Ströms Bruk, and the Domsjö sawmill shall receive certification in 2000.

CERTIFICATION OF FORESTRY. Holmen's forestry has been certificated since 1998 in accordance with the FSC forestry standard. This means that the forests are managed in accordance with the requirements of the Swedish FSC standard.

In 1999 Holmen Skog received further two FSC certifications:

FSC – CUSTODY CHAIN. Certification means that Holmen has a system to trace the origin of the wood.

FSC – GROUP CERTIFICATION. The certificate enables Holmen Skog to certificate its wood suppliers in accordance with the FSC forestry standard.

Waste

TAX ON WASTE. As of January 1, 2000 waste is taxed at a rate of SKr 250 per tonne of waste sent to landfill. In Holmen's case the proposed tax will amount to some SKr 20 million per year.

Responsibility for discontinued activities

STRÖMS BRUK. Waste containing mercury and arsenic from the now closed sulphur and chlorine plants has been deposited on the factory site.

DOMSJÖ. The site contains contamination from a chlorine factory that ceased production in 1990 in the form of mercury-containing sludge stored in a cement container on the site.

ROBERTSFORS. The ground of a closed wood impregnation plant contains arsenic. The contamination occurred before Holmen took over the site.

STOCKA. The ground at the closed sawmill will be further investigated to determine whether it has been contaminated with pentachlorophenol.

HÅSTAHOLMEN. The ground at the closed sawmill will be investigated to determine if it has been contaminated.

No decisions have been made on measures in any of these cases. It is, therefore, not possible to estimate what costs Holmen might incur in this connection.

Exceeded permits and complaints

HALLSTA. The permits for emissions of fibre residues (SS) were exceeded by 13 per cent in 1997. The County Administrative Board referred the matter to the public prosecutor for further investigation.

BRAVIKEN. Following investigation, the public prosecutor has decided to bring charges against the mill for having used bio-fuel ash from the bark boiler as landfill and topsoil on the mill site without a permit in 1997.

IGGESUNDS BRUK. Noise levels from the mill exceeded the permitted night-time level of 45 decibels. The County Administrative Board has referred the matter to the public prosecutor for further investigation.

HOLMEN SKOG has been accused by environmental organisations in Östergötland for incorrect harvesting and purchasing of wood. An internal investigation showed that in some cases Holmen Skog's procedures were inadequate. One case was due to poor communication between Holmen Skog and the authorities and among the authorities themselves. In the other cases Holmen Skog acted correctly.

Further environmental information:
Holmen Environmental Report 1999
The Holmen Environmental Report, which is distributed together with this annual report, provides a general account of the environmental activities within the Group. It is also available in Swedish and German and may be obtained from:
Holmen
Group Public Relations
P.O. Box 5407, SE-114 84 Stockholm, Sweden
Telephone: +46 8 666 21 00 · Fax +46 8 666 21 30
E-mail: info@holmen.com

Human Resources

Holmen's personnel policy is to provide all employees with increasingly stimulating tasks and, by different measures, developing their commitment to the Group. This creates the conditions needed to improve profitability as well as having positive effects on Holmen's long-term activities to recruit new employees.

The following is a selection of the various activities carried out within the Group on the basis of this policy.

Employee programme

As of 1998, 44 per cent of Holmen's personnel have acquired warrants or convertibles in the company. This employee programme will enable the employees eventually to become shareholders in Holmen and consequently share in its long-term development. A further aim is that this employee programme should strengthen commitment and motivation as a result of added interest in the Group and its stock market performance.

Closer ties with customers and suppliers

Detailed knowledge of customers and their product requirements is a key issue that all successful companies must nowadays

address. It is a question of creating an interactive relationship with customers, with the ultimate purpose of creating added value for both parties. Projects are therefore being run at various levels within the company with the object of developing understanding of customer needs and of strengthening customer relations. At *Holmen Paper*, attitude surveys have been carried out among personnel and customers to identify requirements and parameters that are important to the customer-supplier relationship.

They resulted in numerous activities that have helped to improve employees' ability to create value and efficiency in customer relationships.

At *Wargön* quality and delivery reliability goals have been established, which are conveyed to employees in the form of a "satisfied customer index".

At *Holmen Skog* a project was begun with the aim of improving wood purchasing efficiency. An essential aspect of the project is to strengthen relations between the company and its wood suppliers, i.e. some 20,000 private forest owners who supply most of the wood used by the Group's Swedish units. In 2000, training schemes and activities will be carried out for all employees who are involved in one way or another in contacts with the Group's wood suppliers.

Long-term recruitment

The activities that have been provided for many years for university students have continued. Holmen arranged numerous information days at various universities. The interest shown by students in the Group and the industry has steadily increased in the past few years. This can largely be ascribed to the activities for both university and upper secondary school students that the forestry products industry has carried out on a joint basis.

In the autumn of 1999, the sector project "Journey into the Future" began. The project consists of one-day programmes at schools throughout Sweden, where young employees in the Swedish forest products industry describe the stimulating and enriching jobs on offer in the industry. The project also includes a further training course for upper secondary school chemistry

teachers throughout the country. These activities were particularly well received. "Journey into the Future" will continue during 2000.

Induction

An in-depth induction programme was arranged for approximately 80 newly employed graduates from all parts of the Group. The purpose of the programme is to provide information about Holmen and also to give them a chance to create personal networks with colleagues from other parts of the Group. The induction programme comprises ten to twelve days during the course of one year.

Competence development

Competence is a key concept these days and it covers all areas of Holmen's business. A high level of competence helps to increase the growth in the value of the company. It is also a precondition for the increasingly autonomous, managerial positions that require employees with a high degree of competence in both their vocational and leadership roles. Competence requirements are expected to increase further in the coming years. The increasingly high-tech production equipment and the efficient, biologically adapted forestry methods will also increase the need for specialist expertise.

In the spring, *Holmen Paper* carried out an attitude survey among its Swedish employees. The results provided a valuable tool in the field of personnel development. For example, they generated a number of activities that helped to improve the company's human capital, i.e. the measure of the capability of the employees and the organisation to create value and efficiency.

In the new organisation that began to take shape at *Holmen Skog* in 1999, the number of graduate salaried employees at district level was increased. The central forestry department had four employees with doctorates at the end of the year. Since 1995, approximately 30 employees have studied at graduate level in fields such as forest biology and water protection.

At *Iggesund Timber*, the proportion of salaried employees with a university education rose to 26 per cent as a result of a specific recruitment policy.

At *Braviken*, a training scheme for supervisors and operators was begun with the aim of both increasing and broadening competence in this vocational field.

At the same mill, about a hundred employees took part in basic training courses in Swedish, mathematics, physics and chemistry.

At *Hallsta*, the distance learning programme for employees with irregular working hours continued with great success.

Extensive training schemes were carried out at *Iggesunds Bruk, the Iggesund Sawmill, Wargön* and *Workington* prior to the certification of their ISO 14001 environmental management systems, which have either been or are in the process of being introduced.

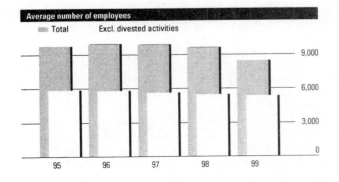

Average number of employees

Total | Excl. divested activities

95 · 96 · 97 · 98 · 99

9,000 / 6,000 / 3,000 / 0

Report of the Directors

The Board of Directors and the President of Holmen Aktiebolag (publ) co. reg. no. 556001-3301 herewith submit their report on the 1999 financial year for the parent company and the Group. The result of the year's operations and the financial position of the parent company and the Group are shown in the following profit and loss accounts and balance sheets together with the notes and supplementary information presented, along with the report of the auditors, on pages 27–51.

New name

An Extraordinary General Meeting held on February 10, 2000 decided to change the registered name of the parent company from Mo och Domsjö Aktiebolag to Holmen Aktiebolag. The Group name will be Holmen.

Strategic direction

Holmen's strategy is to focus on growth in the newsprint and magazine paper, and paperboard segments. Holmen's profitability in these segments is good and the company is highly competitive. The growth shall take place both organically and via acquisition. A strong financial position shall create the preconditions for this growth.

Structural changes

As of October 1, 1999, Holmen and SCA merged their operations in the areas of fine paper and merchanting into the new company, Modo Paper AB, in which Holmen owns 50 per cent. As of the fourth quarter, Holmen states its holding in Modo Paper under interests in earnings of associate companies.

The operating profit of the activities transferred from Holmen to Modo Paper for the first, second and third quarters respectively amounted to SKr 30 million, SKr 135 million and SKr 54 million. The interest in the fourth quarter earnings of Modo Paper, after interest costs of SKr 43 million, amounted to SKr 136 million.

The integration of the businesses is proceeding well, and the market development is good.

The pulp operations in Domsjö were divested with effect from December 31, 1999. The effect on the result was limited. Following the divestment, Holmen is no longer a net seller of pulp.

Distribution of shares in Modo Paper

In January, Holmen and SCA decided to initiate work with an exchange listing and broadening of ownership of Modo Paper AB, in which each holds a 50 per cent interest. The broadening of ownership is intended to be accomplished through Holmen distributing shares to its shareholders and SCA selling shares in a public offering.

Holmen's Board proposes that the ordinary Annual General Meeting resolves to distribute 35 per cent of the total number of shares in Modo Paper. It is SCA's intent in the public offering to sell shares corresponding to an equal number of shares. The Board's proposal to distribute shares in Modo Paper is conditional upon completion of SCA's planned sale and the subsequent listing of Modo Paper's shares on the OM Stockholm Exchange.

Assuming that the market conditions prevail for an exchange listing, the assessment is that Modo Paper will be listed on the OM Stockholm Exchange during the spring 2000.

■ Markets

Economic conditions in Sweden and Europe improved during the year. The North American economy remained strong, and there was a recovery in Asia. Demand for paper and paperboard improved gradually during the year and the market conditions for Holmen's main products were favourable at the end of the year.

Newsprint and magazine paper experienced strong demand in 1999 and capacity utilisation was high. Deliveries of newsprint to Western Europe rose by just over 2 per cent, of SC paper by some 5 per cent and of coated grades some 1 per cent. Prices in local currencies were stable after a slight reduction at the start of the year. Holmen Paper's capacity utilisation was high and total deliveries increased by 1 per cent to 1,413,000 tonnes.

Paperboard producers in Western Europe increased their deliveries by 5 per cent in 1999. Deliveries to Western Europe of virgin fibre-based paperboard increased by 1 per cent in total, of which solid bleached board increased by 6 per cent, while deliveries of folding boxboard remained unchanged. The strong demand meant that price increases were announced during the second half of the year. Iggesund Paperboard's deliveries rose by almost 3 per cent to 403,000 tonnes. Production disturbances in

connection with a major rebuild at the paperboard mill in Workington had an adverse effect on the year's delivery volume.

The *sawn timber* market was characterised by excess supply and depressed prices, despite firm demand. The market for whitewood products improved during the second half of the year and some price increases could be implemented, whilst the redwood market weakened. Iggesund Timber's deliveries increased by 5 per cent during the year.

Wood consumption within the Group (excluding divested activities) was slightly higher than in 1998. Supplies from the private forestry sector were more or less unchanged from last year. Holmen reduced its own harvesting slightly and increased imports. Pulpwood prices were reduced at the end of 1998 and the mills' cost per cubic metre of pulpwood was some 5 per cent lower in 1999 than in the previous year.

■ Production and deliveries

Holmen's production (excluding production from divested activities) of paper, paperboard and pulp for external delivery amounted to 1,839,000 tonnes (1,842,000). The fourth quarter production was 452,000 tonnes (third quarter: 477,000).

Deliveries (excluding deliveries from divested activities) of paper, paperboard and pulp rose by 2 per cent to 1,848,000 tonnes (1,814,000). Deliveries during the fourth quarter amounted to 489,000 tonnes (third quarter: 471,000).

■ Environment

HOLMEN is engaged in activities requiring a permit pursuant the Environmental Code. The Braviken paper mill, Hallsta paper mill, the Wargön mill, Iggesunds Bruk and the Iggesund Sawmill

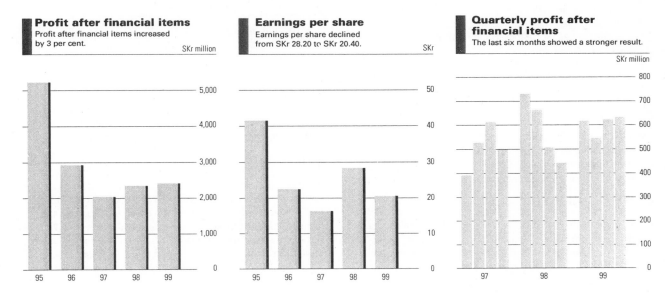

Profit after financial items
Profit after financial items increased by 3 per cent.
SKr million

Earnings per share
Earnings per share declined from SKr 28.20 to SKr 20.40.
SKr

Quarterly profit after financial items
The last six months showed a stronger result.
SKr million

71

have permits in accordance with the Environment Protection Act. The activities at the Domsjö Sawmill are regulated by the permits from the County Administrative Board. Ströms Bruk, which accounts for a small part of the Group's operations, has an insignificant impact on the environment. The County Administrative Board is deliberating whether the mill shall be deemed to require a permit, or only subject to a notification obligation under the terms of the environmental code. Workington has a permit from the British Environmental Agency. The capacity figures for these units are shown in the summary on page 54.

NEW ENVIRONMENTAL PERMITS. A comprehensive review will be made at Iggesunds Bruk and the Hallsta paper mill in 2000 in accordance with the Environment Protection Act. This review will take place in the Environmental Court.

ENVIRONMENTAL IMPACT. The Group's activities have an impact on the environment in the form of emissions into air and water, noise and deposits of waste on landfill sites. Braviken, Hallsta, Wargön, Iggesunds Bruk and Workington account for the greater part of the impact on the environment. The other units represent only a small proportion.

EXCEEDED PERMITS. Hallsta exceeded the permits for emissions of fibre residues (SS) by 13 per cent in 1997. The County Administrative Board submitted the case to the public prosecutor for further investigation.

After investigation, the prosecutor decided to prosecute Braviken for using bio-fuel ash from the bark boiler as filler and topsoil on the mill site in 1997 without a permit.

At Iggesunds Bruk, the level of noise from the mill exceeded the permitted night-time limit of 45 dBA. The County Administrative Board referred the case to the public prosecutor for further investigation.

These incidents have not affected operations at the units concerned.

More information on Holmen's environmental activities is provided on pages 23-24 and in the separate environmental report that is published together with this annual report.

Neither pages 23-24 of this annual report nor the separate environmental report are scrutinised by an external auditor.

Year 2000

Work to identify and resolve potential Y2K problems was completed as planned during the fourth quarter. The transition to the new millennium was problem-free, in terms of the Group's own business as well as effects from the company's external partners.

EU investigation

In the spring of 1995 the EU Commission began an investigation into the European newsprint market. The purpose was to establish whether there had been any form of co-operation in contravention of Article 85 of the Treaty of Rome. The investigation covered most newsprint producers in Europe, including Holmen

Paper. According to the Commission's preliminary conclusion, Holmen Paper has breached the EU's competition rules. The Commission is expected to make a decision on this case in 2000. No provisions have been made on account of the ongoing investigation.

Board and its procedures

Holmen's Board of Directors consists of seven members elected by the Annual General Meeting and three representatives of the employees and with the same number of deputy members. Among the members elected by the AGM are individuals having links with Holmen's major shareholders, as well as other individuals who are independent of these shareholders. The President is a member of the Board.

Members of the management of the company take part in meetings of the Board either to present business or in the role of secretary.

The Board held 14 meetings during the 1999 financial year. The Board devoted a great deal of time to strategic and structural issues.

The Board works in accordance with a plan intended to ensure that it obtains all necessary information. The company's auditors report personally to the Board their observations arising out of their audit and their assessment of the company's internal control systems, procedures and standards.

The Board has adopted a written set of procedures and issued written instructions pertaining to the division of responsibility between the Board and the President as well as to the information that shall be submitted regularly to the Board.

The members of the Board are listed on page 52.

New President and CEO

Per Ericson takes up his position as President and Chief Executive Officer on February 15. Per Ericson, previously President of AB Sandvik Steel, succeeds Bengt Pettersson who is retiring.

Reduction in restricted equity

In order to give the equity a more suitable structure, the Board proposes that the company's legal reserve be reduced by SKr 1,100 million by means of a transfer to non-restricted equity.

Dividend

The Board proposes that an ordinary dividend of SKr 11 (10) per share be paid. The proposed dividend will absorb SKr 977 million in total. Over and above this, the Board proposes that the Annual General Meeting resolve in favour of distributing 70 per cent of the shares in Modo Paper to Holmen's own shareholders. Such a distribution is subject to the conditions stated above.

See also "Proposed treatment of unappropriated earnings" on page 50.

Consolidated profit and loss account

SKr million		1999		1998
Net turnover	(Note 1)	20,508		22,676
Other operating income	(Note 2)	558		598
		21,066		23,274
Raw materials, goods for resale and consumables (Note 3)	−9,762		−10,879	
Change in inventory of finished products	−56		160	
Personnel costs	(Note 22) −3,344		−3,592	
Other external costs	−4,065	−17,227	−4,987	−19,298
Depreciation according to plan	(Note 4)	−1,387		−1,507
Interest in earnings of associate companies	(Note 6)	163		6
Operating profit		**2,615**		**2,475**
Net financial items	(Note 7)	−206		−137
Profit after financial items		**2,409**		**2,338**
Tax	(Note 8)	−595		166
Profit for the year		**1,814**		**2,504**
Earnings per share, SKr		**20.40**		**28.20**

By business area, SKr million	Net turnover		Operating profit/loss	
	1999	1998	1999	1998
Holmen Paper	7,327	7,432	1,494	1,511
Holmen Paper excl Holmen Kraft	*6,944*	*6,972*	*1,418*	*1,455*
Iggesund Paperboard	3,913	4,051	318	590
Iggesund Timber	767	727	−66	−59
Holmen Skog	4,397	4,713	521	548
Group adjustments and other	–	–	−178	−20
External currency hedging	–	–	158	−326
	16,404	16,923	2,247	2,244
Share in earnings Modo Paper	–	–	136	–
Divested activities*	8,345	10,905	232	231
Intra-group sales	−4,241	−5,152	–	–
Group	**20,508**	**22,676**	**2,615**	**2,475**

By product area, SKr million	Net turnover		Operating profit/loss	
	1999	1998	1999	1998
Newsprint and magazine paper	6,942	6,965	1,418	1,455
Paperboard	3,770	3,926	319	606
Pulp	230	214	−1	−16
Sawn timber	767	727	−66	−59
Wood	4,397	4,713	521	548
Power division	199	233	76	56
Group adjustments and other	–	–	−178	−20
External currency hedging	–	–	158	−326
	16,305	16,778	2,247	2,244
Share in earnings Modo Paper	–	–	136	–
Divested activities*	8,746	11,395	232	231
Intra-group sales	−4,543	−5,497	–	–
Group	**20,508**	**22,676**	**2,615**	**2,475**

* Relates to fine paper January–September as well as Domsjö sulphite mill, that was divested with effect from December 31.

73

Net turnover

Net turnover amounted to SKr 20,508 million (22,676). The decrease is mainly due to the fact that the fine paper operations, as of the fourth quarter, are part of the associate company Modo Paper. The year's total net turnover (excluding intra-group sales) for Holmen's current operations was SKr 14,565 million (15,000). The value of invoiced sales to customers outside Sweden corresponded to 70 per cent of turnover.

Operating profit

The operating profit amounted to SKr 2,615 million (2,475). The profit was favourably affected by higher delivery volumes and lower variable costs. Prices were lower and fixed costs slightly higher. The result of external currency hedging fully offset the negative effects of currency fluctuations. The 1998 result included the positive effect of the redemption of pension liabilities of SKr 130 million (Group adjustments and other).

Holmen Paper's profit amounted to SKr 1,494 million (1,511). This result was influenced by slightly lower prices expressed in Swedish kronor, which were largely offset by higher delivery volumes and cost reductions.

Iggesund Paperboard's profit decreased in relation to 1998, partly due to lower prices in Swedish kronor and sterling. Production disturbances due to the extensive rebuild of a paperboard machine in Workington, England, also had a negative effect of just over SKr 100 million on the fourth quarter result. The business area's result was also affected by certain non-recurring costs. Workington's competitive position was hit by the strength of sterling.

Iggesund Timber reported another poor result, mainly due to continued low selling prices and high saw log prices.

Holmen Skog's profit fell, largely on account of lower wood prices.

Profit after financial items

Net financial costs for 1999 amounted to SKr 206 million com-

pared with net costs of SKr 137 million for 1998. The change can largely be attributed to non-recurring items in 1998 having a favourable effect on financial items. The Group's profit after financial items was SKr 2,409 million (2,338).

Net profit and tax cost

The Group's tax charge amounted to SKr 595 million (refund 166). The previous year's tax figures were positive following the settlement of tax litigation in the company's favour and the re-entry of provisions that were no longer deemed necessary. The profit for the year after tax was SKr 1,814 million (2,504).

Key ratios

The operating margin was 12.0 per cent (10.9). The return on operating capital was 11.7 per cent (10.3).

The return on equity was 10.6 per cent (14.4). The decline is a reflection of the positive tax effects in 1998. Earnings per share amounted to SKr 20.40 (28.20).

Operating profit/loss, SKr million	1999	1998	1997	1996	1995
Holmen Paper	1,494	1,511	1,202	1,824	1,570
Holmen Paper excl					
Holmen Kraft	*1,418*	*1,455*	*1,149*	*1,858*	*1,566*
Iggesund Paperboard	318	590	639	591	896
Iggesund Timber	−66	−59	37	−53	17
Holmen Skog	521	548	578	357	391
Group adjustments and other	−178	−20	−246	−1,051	−94
External currency hedging	158	−326	−347	1,449	555
	2,247	2,244	1,863	3,117	3,335
Share in earnings					
Modo Paper	136	–	–	–	–
Divested activities	232	231	367	173	2,496
Group	2,615	2,475	2,230	3,290	5,831

Operating profit / Operating margin

Operating margin increased from 10.9 to 12.0 per cent

Operating profit ▪ Operating margin

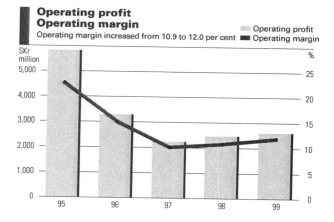

Change in profit after financial items
1999 compared with 1998

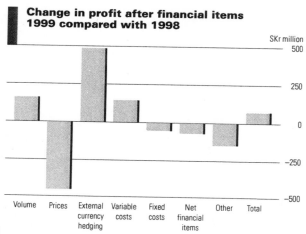

Consolidated balance sheet

at December 31, SKr million		1999	1998
ASSETS			
Fixed assets			
Intangible assets			
Goodwill, leases and similar rights	(Note 9)	16	32
		16	**32**
Tangible assets			
Forest land	(Note 10)	4,577	4,585
Buildings, other land and land installations	(Note 10)	1,805	2,565
Machinery and equipment	(Note 10)	8,190	13,216
Fixed plant under construction and advance payments		253	341
		14,825	**20,707**
Financial assets	(Note 11)		
Shares and participations			
Associate companies		4,345	89
Other shares and participations		47	59
Financial receivables		15	–
Other long-term receivables		20	44
		4,427	**192**
		19,268	**20,931**
Current assets			
Inventories etc.	(Note 12)	2,102	3,648
Current receivables			
Operating receivables	(Note 13)	2,966	4,614
Financial receivables	(Note 14)	3,380	–
Short-term placements		1,224	780
Cash and bank		232	461
		9,904	**9,503**
		29,172	**30,434**
EQUITY AND LIABILITIES			
Equity	(Note 15)		
Restricted equity			
Share capital		4,443	4,443
Restricted reserves		5,343	7,819
Non-restricted equity			
Non-restricted reserves		4,283	3,611
Profit for the year		1,814	2,504
		15,883	**18,377**
Minority interests		–	5
Provisions			
Interest-bearing			
Pension provisions	(Note 17)	60	135
Interest-free			
Tax provisions	(Note 8)	2,702	3,228
Other provisions	(Note 17)	221	240
		2,983	**3,603**
Liabilities			
Financial liabilities	(Note 18)	6,845	4,249
Operating liabilities	(Note 19)	3,461	4,200
		10,306	**8,449**
		29,172	**30,434**
Pledged assets	(Note 20)	**40**	**445**
Contingent liabilities	(Note 21)	**333**	**233**

Assets and operating capital

The Group's operating capital amounted to SKr 20,345 million (24,445). The decrease is largely due to the transfer of the fine paper operations to the associate company, Modo Paper, as of the fourth quarter. See the table below for operating capital by business area.

Capital expenditure amounted to SKr 1,988 million (1,642), of which investments relating to divested activities amounted to SKr 546 million. Main projects were the rebuild of a paperboard machine at Workington, England (SKr 381 million), increased evaporation capacity at Iggesunds Bruk (SKr 106 million), a soft calender at Hallsta (SKr 130 million), a soft calender and shoe press at Braviken (SKr 105 million) and the start of a project to raise drying capacity at the Iggesund Sawmill (SKr 25 million).

Equity

Equity decreased by SKr 2,494 million and amounted to SKr 15,883 million (18,377) on December 31, 1999. The reduction is largely the result of dividend payments of SKr 3,999 million, of which an extra dividend accounted for SKr 3,110 million.

Net financial liability

The Group's net financial liability fell during the year and amounted to SKr 2,054 million (3,143) at the close.

At the end of the year short-term placements and cash and bank amounted to SKr 1,456 million (1,241), and financial receivables to SKr 3,395 million (–), of which SKr 3,140 million relate to Modo Paper. Financial liabilities and interest-bearing provisions amounted to SKr 6,905 million (4,384).

Key ratios

The closing debt/equity ratio was 0.13 (0.17).

The equity ratio fell to 54.4 per cent from the opening level of 60.4 per cent.

Operating capital, SKr million	1999	1998	1997	1996	1995
Holmen Paper	7,296	7,250	6,184	5,912	5,465
Holmen Paper excl					
Holmen Kraft	*6,459*	*6,412*	*6,127*	*5,885*	*5,433*
Iggesund Paperboard	4,442	4,036	4,095	3,854	3,827
Iggesund Timber	415	442	418	394	394
Holmen Skog	4,935	4,960	4,896	5,015	5,202
Group adjustments	–1,000	–511	–355	–507	–325
	16,088	16,177	15,238	14,668	14,563
Divested activities	4,257	8,268	8,430	7,965	8,218
	20,345	24,445	23,668	22,633	22,781

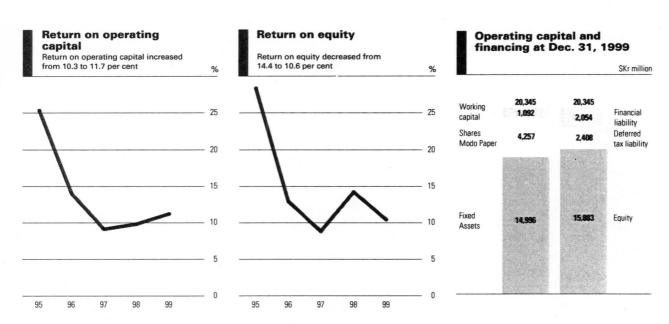

Return on operating capital
Return on operating capital increased from 10.3 to 11.7 per cent

Return on equity
Return on equity decreased from 14.4 to 10.6 per cent

Operating capital and financing at Dec. 31, 1999
SKr million

Consolidated cash flow statement

SKr million		1999	1998
Operating profit		2,615	2,475
Adjustments for items not included in cash flow*		1,551	1,388
Change in working capital		–3	169
Net financial items	(Note 7)	–206	–137
Paid tax		–122	253
Cash flow before capital expenditure		**3,835**	**4,148**
Capital expenditure		–1,988	–1,642
Acquisition		–	–915
Effects from divested activities**		3,258	–
Cash flow before dividend		**5,105**	**1,591**
Issue of warrants and convertible loan***		–	46
Dividend paid to shareholders			
Ordinary		–889	–800
Extra		–3,110	–
Cash flow net financial liability		**1,106**	**837**
Currency effects		–17	–111
Change in net financial liability		**1,089**	**726**
Financing			
Financial receivables			
Long-term receivables		15	–
Current receivables		3,380	–
Liquid funds			
Short-term placements		1,224	780
Cash and bank		232	461
Pension provisions		–60	–135
Financial liabilities			
Long-term liabilities	(Note 18)	–1,313	–2,180
Current liabilities	(Note 18)	–5,532	–2,069
Net financial liability		**–2,054**	**–3,143**
Cash flow net financial liability		1,106	837
Cash flow financial receivables, liabilities and provisions		–871	–1,300
Cash flow liquid funds		**235**	**–463**
Opening liquid funds		1,241	1,636
Cash flow liquid funds		235	–463
Currency effects		–20	68
Closing liquid funds		**1,456**	**1,241**

* The main adjustments made are depreciation according to plan, residual value according
to plan of retired fixed assets and re-entry of interest in earnings of associate companies.

** Of the effects from divested activities, SKr 2,029 million were allocated to fixed
assets, SKr 3,713 million to operating receivables, and SKr 2,484 million to operating
liabilities. A further effect was a reduction of liquid funds by SKr 346 million.

*** Refers to rights to convert attached to the convertible loan.

Cash flow

The Group's cash flow before capital expenditure amounted to SKr 3,835 million (4,148). Working capital remained more or less unchanged in relation to the start of the year (previous year: decrease by SKr 169 million).

Capital expenditure amounted to a total of SKr 1,988 million (1,642), of which SKr 546 million related to divested activities.

The effects of the divestments amounted to SKr 3,258 million and relate to capital released by the formation of Modo Paper and the sale of the Domsjö sulphite mill.

The cash flow before payment of dividend amounted to SKr 5,105 million. Dividends paid to shareholders amounted to SKr 3,999 million, of which the extra dividend paid accounted for SKr 3,110 million.

Financing

Net financial liability decreased during the year by SKr 1,089 million as a result of positive cash flow.

The year's financing was mainly arranged by the issue of commercial paper and the use of contracted long-term credit facilities. At the end of the year, financial liabilities and interest-bearing provisions amounted to SKr 6,905 million (4,384). Financial assets amounted to SKr 4,851 million, of which SKr 3,395 million were financial receivables. In addition, the Group had access to binding credit facilities of some SKr 6,280 million, of which SKr 1,535 million were drawn at the end of the year. The maturity profile for financial liabilities and credit facilities is provided on page 37.

Cash flow before capital expenditure, SKr million	1999	1998	1997	1996	1995
Holmen Paper	2,059	1,920	1,559	2,538	1,497
Holmen Paper excl Holmen Kraft	*1,969*	*1,852*	*1,526*	*2,561*	*1,460*
Iggesund Paperboard	690	982	755	836	1,168
Iggesund Timber	–3	–30	34	–2	89
Holmen Skog	567	564	737	595	309
Other	292	–566	–473	627	1,079
	3,605	2,870	2,612	4,594	4,142
Net financial items	–206	–137	–204	–371	–615
Paid tax	–122	253	–200	–409	–652
	3,277	2,986	2,208	3,814	2,875
Cash flow divested activities	558	1,162	856	1,270	3,299
	3,835	4,148	3,064	5,084	6,174

Capital expenditure, SKr million	1999	1998	1997	1996	1995
Holmen Paper	606	1,597*	618	1,183	1,170
Holmen Paper excl Holmen Kraft	*599*	*680*	*617*	*1,183*	*1,170*
Iggesund Paperboard	752	302	253	180	807
Iggesund Timber	39	54	19	55	15
Holmen Skog	38	82	42	50	35
Other	7	10	4	47	43
	1,442	2,045	936	1,515	2,070
Divested activities	546	512	920	900	584
	1,988	2,557	1,856	2,415	2,654

* Incl. repurchase of hydro-electric power stations SKr 915 million.

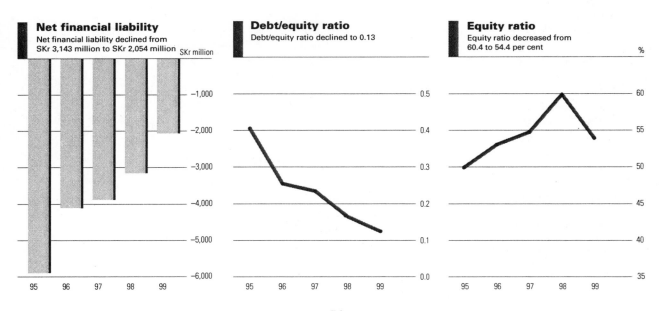

Net financial liability
Net financial liability declined from SKr 3,143 million to SKr 2,054 million. SKr million

Debt/equity ratio
Debt/equity ratio declined to 0.13

Equity ratio
Equity ratio decreased from 60.4 to 54.4 per cent %

Financial risks

The Group's financial activities and management of financial transactions are centralised to Group Finance. The aim is to minimise the Group's capital costs by using means of suitable financing and by effective risk control and management. The activities are carried out on the basis of the financial policy established by the Board and are characterised by a low level of risk.

CURRENCY RISK. The Group's commercial payment flows in foreign currency are estimated to amount to some SKr 7.7 billion net for 2000, of which EUR accounts for 73 per cent (see graph below). In order to reduce the effect of currency fluctuations on the result, Holmen hedges its currency flows for a certain period into the future. Hedging is normally made to cover the flows that are nearest in time, and is carried out by means of forwards and options. The degree of hedging is decided by the Board on the basis of the profitability of the products, competitive position and estimates of currency movements.

At the beginning of 1999, the Group had hedged just under five months of currency flows. During the year, between four or five months of currency flows were hedged. At the end of 1999, hedges covered currency flows for four months, which corresponds mainly to accounts receivable and contracted flows.

The result from currency hedging is included in the consolidated operating profit by translating sales hedged against currency fluctuations at the hedging rate. Currency fluctuations therefore have an effect on the Group's operating result when hedging contracts mature. The effect of the currency hedging on the result for 1999 amounted to SKr 158 million, of which SKr 102 million is accounted for centrally in the Group, and SKr 56 million

is stated in the result of the business area in question. (See also under Accounting Principles, page 40). The value of hedging contracts not yet recognised in income amounted to a deficit of SKr 1 million at December 31, 1999. As of 2000, the hedging result will be stated under each separate business area.

Holmen's operating capital in foreign currency amounted to SKr 1,731 million as of December 31, of which SKr 1,543 million is in sterling. Liabilities in foreign currency (loans and forwards) amounted to SKr 888 million at the turn of the year, and have been assumed as financing or hedging of foreign assets. During the year operating capital in foreign currency decreased by SKr 3,434 million, and financial liabilities in foreign currency by SKr 3,385 million, primarily as a consequence of the establishment of Modo Paper. The conversion of foreign currency loans and forwards had no effect on the result.

The financial result of foreign Group and associate companies is not hedged.

Holmen's competitive position is influenced by currency fluctuations in relation to producers whose production costs are incurred in other currencies. Such currencies include the US dollar, the Canadian dollar, and the euro. Holmen does not normally hedge such risks.

INTEREST RATE AND FUNDING RISK. Holmen's net financial liabilities at the year end amounted to SKr 2,054 million (3,143), divided into loan SKr 6,905 million (4,384), liquid funds SKr 1,456 million (1,241) and financial receivables SKr 3,395 million (–).

The duration of the debt is normally short, but it can be lengthened in order to limit the negative effects of an increase in

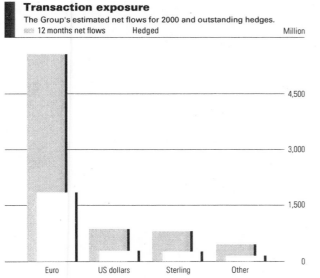

Transaction exposure
The Group's estimated net flows for 2000 and outstanding hedges.
12 months net flows   Hedged   Million

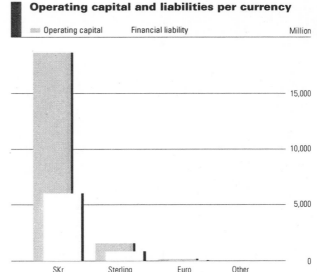

Operating capital and liabilities per currency
Operating capital   Financial liability   Million

interest rates. Changes in duration are decided by the Board. The duration has varied between three and five months during the year, and was three months at the end of 1999.

Contracted long-term credit facilities at fixed interest rate margins are used to reduce the risk that raising capital in the future will be difficult or expensive. At the end of the year the contracted credit facilities amounted to SKr 6,820 million, of which SKr 5,285 million were unutilised. The maturity profile of the financial liabilities and the existing credit facilities is shown in the graph below.

During 1999, the funding was primarily managed through Holmen's Swedish commercial paper programme and the utilisation of a contracted credit facility.

The limit of Holmen's Swedish commercial paper programme were raised from SKr 2,000 million to SKr 4,000 million during the year. In 1999 a Swedish Medium Term Note programme with a limit of SKr 4,000 million was set up. The programme, which has not yet been utilised, provides Holmen with the possibility to issue bonds in Swedish kronor or euro to primarily Swedish investors.

Holmen was assigned a BBB+ corporate rating from the Standard & Poor rating institution during the year. Holmen already holds a short-term K-1 rating.

CREDIT RISKS IN RELATION TO FINANCIAL COUNTERPARTIES. The Group's financial transactions give rise to credit risks in relation to financial counterparties. Limiting these is an important part of the financial management.

The Group's liquid funds are placed without currency risk

with banks or on the Swedish money market. Holmen only invests in securities with high liquidity and very low credit risk.

The risk of a counterparty not fulfilling its contractual obligations is limited by selecting creditworthy counterparties and by limiting the exposure to each of them. ISDA agreements regulate netting of outstanding exposure with individual counterparties which have been entered into with all counterparties to interest and currency derivative transactions which are not cleared via an exchange. The Group had outstanding derivative contracts with a nominal amount of SKr 13 billion and a market value of SKr 112 million as of December 31, 1999. Calculated in accordance with the regulations of the Swedish Financial Supervisory Authority for financial institutions, Holmen's total counterparty risks on its derivative instruments amount to SKr 226 million at December 31, 1999.

Insurance

Holmen insures its mills against property damage and sequential loss. The level of risk accepted within the Group varies from one mill to another, but is at most SKr 20 million for an individual damage. The Group's forests are not insured as they are widely dispersed throughout the country and the risk of simultaneous damage to large parts of the holdings is therefore small.

Maturities

Financial liabilities and interest-bearing provisions
Credit facilities   SKr million

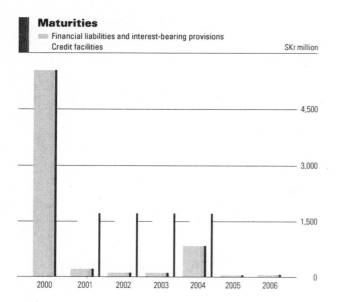

Quarterly figures

SKr million	1999					1998				
	Full year	IV	III	II	I	Full year	IV	III	II	I
NET TURNOVER										
Holmen Paper	7,327	1,971	1,808	1,710	1,838	7,432	2,064	1,833	1,782	1,753
Holmen Paper excl Holmen Kraft	*6,944*	*1,855*	*1,743*	*1,644*	*1,702*	*6,972*	*1,923*	*1,738*	*1,706*	*1,605*
Iggesund Paperboard	3,913	963	1,005	972	973	4,051	1,007	992	990	1,062
Iggesund Timber	767	198	168	200	201	727	186	171	175	195
Holmen Skog	4,397	1,128	965	1,119	1,185	4,713	1,168	1,046	1,183	1,316
	16,404	**4,260**	**3,946**	**4,001**	**4,197**	**16,923**	**4,425**	**4,042**	**4,130**	**4,326**
Divested activities *	8,345	276	2,530	2,739	2,800	10,905	2,640	2,567	2,727	2,971
	24,749	**4,536**	**6,476**	**6,740**	**6,997**	**27,828**	**7,065**	**6,609**	**6,857**	**7,297**
Intra-group sales	−4,241	−562	−1,073	−1,262	−1,344	−5,152	−1,313	−1,196	−1,229	−1,414
	20,508	**3,974**	**5,403**	**5,478**	**5,653**	**22,676**	**5,752**	**5,413**	**5,628**	**5,883**
PROFIT/LOSS										
Holmen Paper	1,494	348	404	353	389	1,511	428	473	323	287
Holmen Paper excl Holmen Kraft	*1,418*	*310*	*434*	*367*	*307*	*1,455*	*419*	*476*	*347*	*213*
Iggesund Paperboard	318	−14	138	106	88	590	104	139	141	206
Iggesund Timber	−66	−13	−17	−24	−12	−59	−25	−12	−17	−5
Holmen Skog	521	176	109	124	112	548	157	126	164	101
Group adjustments and other	−178	−23	−34	−52	−69	−20	84	−35	−51	−18
External currency hedging	158	1	20	8	129	−326	−126	−179	14	−35
	2,247	**475**	**620**	**515**	**637**	**2,244**	**622**	**512**	**574**	**536**
Share in earnings Modo Paper	136	136	−	−	−	−	−	−	−	−
Divested activities *	232	43	72	106	11	231	−150	3	142	236
Operating profit	**2,615**	**654**	**692**	**621**	**648**	**2,475**	**472**	**515**	**716**	**772**
Net financial items	−206	−23	−72	−78	−33	−137	−31	−9	−54	−43
Profit after financial items	**2,409**	**631**	**620**	**543**	**615**	**2,338**	**441**	**506**	**662**	**729**
Tax	−595	−22	−201	−175	−197	166	751	−154	−205	−226
Profit for the year	**1,814**	**609**	**419**	**368**	**418**	**2,504**	**1,192**	**352**	**457**	**503**

*Relates to fine paper January–September as well as Domsjö sulphite mill, that was divested with effect from December 31.

Parent company

Profit and loss account, SKr million

		1999	1998
Net turnover	(Note 1)	15,840	16,813
Other operating income	(Note 2)	466	445
		16,306	17,258
Raw materials and consumables		−7,019	−7,287
Change in inventory of finished products		−32	121
Personnel costs	(Note 22)	−2,416	−2,491
Other external costs		−4,499 −13,966	−5,115 −14,772
Depreciation according to plan	(Note 4)	−291	−362
Items affecting comparability	(Note 5)	−6	−82
Operating profit		**2,043**	**2,042**
Net financial items	(Note 7)	1,860	749
Profit after financial items		**3,903**	**2,791**
Appropriations			
Group contributions			
Income		336	98
Cost		−1,143	−1,200
Other appropriations	(Note 16)	1,778	−64
Profit before tax		**4,874**	**1,625**
Tax	(Note 8)	−199	120
Profit for the year		**4,675**	**1,745**

Cash flow statement, SKr million

	1999	1998
Operating profit	2,043	2,042
Adjustments for items not included in cash flow*	328	463
Change in working capital etc.	−3,410	−246
Net financial items	1,860	749
Paid tax	80	120
Cash flow before capital expenditure	**901**	**3,128**
Capital expenditure	−2,208	−1,048
Effects from divested activities**	3,159	–
Cash flow before dividend	**1,852**	**2,080**
Issue of warrants and convertible loan***	–	46
Dividend paid to shareholders	−3,999	−800
Cash flow net financial liability	**−2,147**	**1,326**
Financial receivables	466	–
Liquid funds	1,561	765
Pension provisions	−53	−73
Financial liabilities	−6,832	−3,403
Net financial liability	**−4,858**	**−2,711**
Cash flow net financial liability	−2,147	1,326
Cash flow financial receivables, liabilities and provisions	2,943	−1,465
Cash flow liquid funds	**796**	**−139**
Opening liquid funds	765	904
Cash flow	796	−139
Closing liquid funds	**1,561**	**765**

* The main adjustments made are depreciation according to plan and residual value according to plan of retired fixed assets.

** Of the effects from divested activities, SKr 776 million were allocated to fixed assets, SKr 3,217 million to operating receivables and SKr 834 million to operating liabilities.

*** Refers to rights to convert attached to the convertible loan.

Balance sheet at December 31, SKr million

		1999	1998
Assets			
Fixed assets			
Intangible assets			
Leases and similar rights	(Note 9)	9	9
		9	9
Tangible assets			
Forest land	(Note 10)	1,789	1,794
Buildings, other land and land installations	(Note 10)	39	437
Machinery and equipment	(Note 10)	77	2,840
Fixed plant under construction and advance payments		–	122
		1,905	5,193
Financial assets	(Note 11)		
Shares and participations			
Group companies		19,148	19,237
Associate companies		4,516	50
Other shares and participations		1	1
Financial receivables		15	–
Other long-term receivables		303	470
		23,983	19,758
		25,897	24,960
Current assets			
Inventories etc.	(Note 12)	1,762	2,461
Current receivables			
Operating receivables	(Note 13)	2,487	2,974
Financial receivables	(Note 14)	451	–
Short-term placements		1,216	695
Cash and bank		345	70
		6,261	6,200
		32,158	31,160
Equity and liabilities			
Equity	(Note 15)		
Restricted equity			
Share capital		4,443	4,443
Revaluation reserve		100	100
Statutory reserve		1,952	1,952
Share premium reserve		46	46
Non-restricted equity			
Profit brought forward		2,500	4,754
Profit for the year		4,675	1,745
		13,716	13,040
Untaxed reserves	(Note 16)	**1,072**	**2,856**
Provisions			
Interest-bearing			
Pension provisions	(Note 17)	53	73
Non-interest bearing			
Tax provisions	(Note 8)	15	11
Other provisions	(Note 17)	217	225
		285	309
Liabilities			
Financial liabilities	(Note 18)	14,205	11,786
Operating liabilities	(Note 19)	2,880	3,169
		17,085	14,955
		32,158	31,160
Pledged assets	(Note 20)	40	67
Contingent liabilities	(Note 21)	**514**	**227**

Accounting principles

General accounting principles. The Annual Accounts Act, which is harmonised with the EU, has been applied with effect from 1997. The company complies with the recommendations issued by the Swedish Accounting Standards Board.

Principles of valuation, etc. Assets and liabilities are valued at acquisition value except where otherwise stated below. Receivables are stated at the value that is expected to be received, after individual appraisal.

Commission companies. The Group's business is largely conducted through the following commission companies: Holmen Paper AB, Iggesund Paperboard AB, Iggesund Timber AB and Holmen Skog AB.

These companies are wholly-owned Group companies of Holmen AB. The parent company is liable for all the undertakings and commitments of these commission companies. All income, costs, assets and liabilities, which arise in the operations conducted by the commission companies are stated either in the accounts of Holmen AB, or in the accounts of Group companies other than the commission companies.

MoDo Paper AB and MoDo Merchants AB were included as companies operating on commission until September 30th 1999. Following the formation of Modo Paper, these companies are no longer commission companies within Holmen.

Principles of consolidation. The consolidated financial statements relate to the parent company and those companies in which the parent company directly or indirectly controls more than half the votes, or exercises control in some other way.

The consolidated financial statements are made up using the purchase method, where shares in Group companies are replaced in the consolidated financial statements by the assets and liabilities of the Group companies, valued at the Group's acquisition cost. Any differences between the acquisition cost and the assets and liabilities of the acquired company valued on a commercial basis is treated as positive or negative goodwill. Goodwill and excess values in respect of assets subject to decrease in value are depreciated according to plan in the consolidated profit and loss account. The consolidated equity includes – apart from the parent company's equity – only changes in the equity of Group companies that have arisen after acquisition.

The accounts of foreign Group companies are translated using the current method, whereby all assets, provisions, and other liabilities are translated at closing date rates and exchange rate differences arising are taken direct to the consolidated restricted and non-restricted reserves respectively. All items in profit and loss accounts are translated at average rates for the year.

Associate companies. Shareholdings in associate companies, in which the Group controls a minimum of 20 per cent and a maximum of 50 per cent of the votes, or otherwise exercises a significant influence over their operational and financial control, are stated in accordance with the capital interest method, except for associate companies having a negligible effect on the Group's results and financial position.

The capital interest method means that the book value of the shares in the associate company stated in the consolidated accounts corresponds to the Group's interest in the associate company's equity and any residual value of excess values and discounts arising upon consolidation. The Group's interest in associate companies' earnings after financial income and costs adjusted for any write-downs or reversals of acquired goodwill and negative goodwill respectively is stated in the consolidated profit and loss account as interest in earnings of associate companies. The Group's interest in the booked taxes of associate companies is included in the Group's tax costs and minority interests in the associate companies' result are included in minority interests in the consolidated accounts.

Interests in profits earned after the acquisition of associate companies which have not been realised in the form of a dividend, are transferred to capital interest reserve, which is included in the Group's restricted equity. If the associate company is stated at a lower value than the value according to the acquisition-value method, the difference is taken against consolidated non-restricted equity.

Net turnover. By net turnover is meant invoiced sales, excluding value added tax and after allowing for discounts, and similar reductions in income, but before allowing for the cost of delivery.

Other operating income. Revenue from secondary activities not forming part of the main business are stated as other operating income.

Items affecting comparability. The effect on the result of specific events and transactions of significance is stated within the respective income level.

Capital gains and losses on the divestment of fixed assets and lines of business, restructuring costs, etc, are normally stated within the operating result of the business area in question or as Group adjustment.

Depreciation principles for fixed assets. Depreciation according to plan is based on the acquisition value of the assets, and is provided on a straight-line basis during the economic life of the assets.

The following economic lives are used:

Administrative and warehouse buildings, residential property . . . . .20–33 years	Machinery for sawmills . . . . 12 years
Production buildings, land installations, and machinery for pulp, paper and paperboard production . . .20 years	Other machinery and equipment . . 4–10 years
	Forest roads . . . . .10 years
	Goodwill . . . . . . .3–20 years

Group contributions. Group contributions are stated via the parent company's profit and loss account together with the associated tax effect.

Taxes. *Estimated full tax.* The tax charge for the year is stated as tax to be paid on taxable profit, changes in deferred tax and tax on the Group's interest in earnings of associate companies. The tax charge is calculated using the tax rules applicable in each country.

Deferred tax liability. The following are stated under the heading deferred tax liability in the consolidated balance sheet:

Deferred tax liability included in untaxed reserves

Deferred tax liability and deferred tax receivable respectively in Group adjustments

Deferred tax attributable to other significant differences between taxable and stated results

Deferred tax relating to the difference between the book and taxable values of holdings of shares for which definite plans exist for sale in the near future.

Deferred tax receivables relating to loss allowances.

The tax rates applicable in each country are used for calculating deferred tax. Loss allowances are taken into account if it is considered likely that they can be utilised.

Receivables and liabilities in foreign currencies. Receivables and liabilities denominated in foreign currencies are translated at closing date rates or, if they have been hedged, at hedging rates. Exchange rate differences are included in the operating result, except for differences relating to short-term placements, cash and bank, financial liabilities, and interest-bearing provisions, which are stated within net financial items. For the hedging of future currency flows, exchange rate differences are taken into the result during the same period as the underlying flow. The result of the consolidated internal hedging is stated within the operating result for each business area.

Definitions of financial ratios

The offsetting item for internal hedging is stated within the operating result under Group adjustments and other.

The currency structure of financial liabilities has been altered by means of forward hedging contracts. These forward contracts are valued at closing date rates and the unrealised profit or loss is stated net as a liability. Any premiums/discounts are regarded as interest, periodised and stated within net interest cost.

Loans and forward contracts in foreign currencies can be used to reduce the currency effect of the translation of foreign net assets into Swedish kronor. Currency differences on these are eliminated – to the extent that they correspond to currency differences on foreign net assets, after tax effects are taken into account – from the profit and loss account, and taken direct to equity in the balance sheet. These hedging measures are based on the value at Group level of the net assets per currency.

Valuation of inventories. Inventories are valued at the lower of acquisition value or production cost after allowing for obsolescence at the standard rate of three per cent, or at actual value. The actual value of finished products is their sales value less estimated selling costs. The actual value of timber and pulp wood and other raw materials, inventory materials and the like is the lower of replacement value or acquisition value after allowing for actual obsolescence.

Convertible loan and warrants. The amount of the convertible loan has been calculated on the basis of the market yield. The difference between the loan amount arrived at in this way and proceeds is transferred to premium reserve as a premium on the price of the shares that will eventually be issued. The size of the stated loan liability is successively increased during the term of the loan by accruing interest so that upon maturity the stated amount of the loan will coincide with the nominal amount of the loan. The proceeds of the issue of warrants are taken direct to premium reserve.

Partnership financing. Under the terms of partnership financing agreements from 1983 and 1990, Holmen has sold hydro-electric power assets to two companies (Junkaravan AB and Iggesund Kraft AB) in which Holmen owns less than 50 per cent. Under separate supply agreements, Holmen purchases all the power generated at a cost which corresponds to production costs plus a financing cost that is based on a real return of four to five per cent plus actual inflation. Under the terms of option agreements Holmen is entitled, but not bound, to buy back the hydro-electric power assets on specified dates at prices which will give the financiers the agreed real return. The exercise prices are estimated at some SKr 2,237 million at the end of 1999.

Merger of fine paper and merchanting business areas. The merger between SCA's and Holmen's fine paper and merchanting units took the form of the acquisition of SCA's corresponding businesses by a wholly-owned subsidiary in return for shares in this company. As a merger is stated in Holmen's books as an exchange of assets, it had no effect on the result.

The holding in the new company, Modo Paper, is treated as an associate company and is stated using the capital interest method as of the fourth quarter 1999.

Operating capital. Balance sheet total less financial receivables, short-term placements, cash and bank, operating liabilities and interest-free provisions excluding deferred tax liability.

Average is defined as: $\dfrac{\text{opening balance} + \text{closing balance}}{2}$

(When operating capital is calculated in accordance with the recommendation of the Business Stock Exchange Committee (NBK), a reduction is also made for deferred tax liability.)

Equity. For the period between 1988 and 1994 convertible participating loan (KVB) is included.

Average is defined as: $\dfrac{\text{opening balance} + \text{closing balance}}{2}$

Debt/equity ratio. Net financial liabilities (financial liabilities and interest-bearing provisions less financial receivables, short-term placements and cash and bank) divided by the sum of equity and minority interests.

Equity ratio. Equity plus minority interests expressed as a percentage of the balance sheet total.

Interest coverage. Operating profit/loss divided by net financial items.

Return on operating capital. Operating profit/loss expressed as a percentage of the average operating capital.

Return on equity. Profit/loss for the year, expressed as a percentage of the average equity.

Operating margin. Operating profit/loss (excluding items affecting comparability, and interest in earnings of associate companies) expressed as a percentage of net turnover.

Net margin. Profit/loss for the year expressed as a percentage of net turnover.

Capital turnover rate. Net turnover divided by average operating capital (expressed as times per year).

Earnings per share. Profit/loss for the year divided by the weighted average number of shares (and up to 1993 also of KVBs) during the year.

Earnings per share after dilution. The profit for the year, adjusted for interest costs after tax attributable to outstanding convertibles, divided by the weighted average number of shares in issue during the year after adjustment for the number of shares issued in the event of conversion and premiums, if any, over the book value of outstanding warrants.

Notes (Amounts in million Swedish kronor, except where otherwise stated)

1 Net turnover

External net turnover by market	Group 1999	1998
Sweden	4,301	4,471
Great Britain	3,438	4,098
Germany	2,683	2,952
France	2,072	2,258
Holland	1,412	1,691
Italy	765	767
Other EU-countries	2,976	2,450
Rest of Europe	1,506	2,626
Rest of the world	1,355	1,363
	20,508	22,676

Of the parent company's net turnover of SKr 15,840 million (16,813) ,
9 per cent (12) were sales to Group companies. The parent company's purchases from Group companies are negligible.

2 Other operating income

Other operating income mainly comprises rental income and property leasing income, freight forwarding income, sales of by-products and capital gains/losses on sales of fixed assets.

3 Raw materials, goods for resale and consumables

As goods for resale account for a small proportion of the Group's turnover, this item is grouped together with raw materials and consumables.

4 Depreciation according to plan

	Group 1999	1998	Parent company 1999	1998
Goodwill and leases	5	56	–	–
Buildings, other land and land installations	159	168	35	45
Machinery and equipment	1,223	1,283	256	317
	1,387	1,507	291	362

5 Items affecting comparability

	Parent company 1999	1998
Capital gains/losses on divestments		
Group companies	10	–
Associate companies	8	–
Other	–12	–14
Write-down in value of shares		
Group companies	–3	–17
Associate companies	–8	–41
Write-down of receivables from associate companies	–	–10
	–5	–82

6 Interest in earnings of associate companies

	Group 1999	1998
Interest in earnings after financial items	163	6
Tax	–49	–2
Holmen's interest in earnings after tax	114	4

The associate companies concerned are Modo Paper AB, Les Bois de la Baltique SA, Svensk Etanolkemi AB and Sydved AB.

7 Net financial items

	Group 1999	1998	Parent company 1999	1998
Dividend income				
Associate companies	–	–	7	6
Group companies	–	–	1,755	1,419
Interest income from current assets ...				
External	86	122	57	110
Group companies	–	–	1	2
Interest costs				
External	–297	–262	–279	–220
Group companies	–	–	–164	–148
Other financial items				
Foreign exchange differences on other long-term loans	–	–	234	–274
Arrangement costs, loans	–3	–1	–3	–1
Other	8	4	252	–145
	–206	–137	1,860	749

8 Tax

	1999		1998
Booked tax		−469		−83
Estimated full tax in respect of			
Interest in earnings of associate			
companies	−49		−2	
Appropriations for the year	−143		−122	
Change in capitalised loss			
allowances, etc.	66	−126	373	249
		−595		166

The parent company's tax cost amounted to SKr 199 million.

The parent company has transferred this business to Modo Paper AB by means of a "transfer of business". This transfer satisfies the conditions for exemption from immediate taxation, which means that the reversal of certain untaxed reserves will not be subject to tax.

Tax liabilities	Group 1999	Group 1998	Parent company 1999	Parent company 1998
Tax provisions				
Deferred tax liabilities	2,408	2,920	−	−
Other provisions	294	308	15	11
Total tax provisions	2,702	3,228	15	11
Net of short-term tax liability				
and tax receivable	778	427	539	264
	3,480	3,655	554	275

A sum of SKr 320 million has been reserved in the Group's accounts for deferred tax liabilities in respect of the proportion of Holmen's interest in Modo Paper's share capital that is to be distributed as dividend. A corresponding reservation has not been made by the parent company.

Unsettled tax disputes

Holmen is currently engaged in a number of tax disputes relating to the parent company and to certain Swedish Group companies. The disputes originate from the audit of the tax returns submitted by the parent company and certain Group companies for the financial years 1992–1997, as a result of which the companies' taxed income was increased.

During the year, several court rulings were made in Holmen's favour. Holmen had, for instance, acquired interests in aircraft through associate companies abroad. The Swedish Tax Authorities questioned at which point in time the company was entitled to make deductions for the deficits arising. The case, which reached the County Administrative Court, has been settled in Holmen's favour.

Provisions have been made, in certain cases and for reasons of prudence, for tax supplements in those cases where a decision has been made, but where the cases have not yet been finally settled. Holmen will, in those cases in which it has not yet done so, appeal against the decision of the tax authority.

9 Intangible fixed assets

Goodwill, leases and similar rights	Group	Parent company
Accumulated acquisition values		
Opening value	174	9
Divested activities, Modo Paper	−156	−
	18	9
Accumulated depreciation according to plan		
Opening value	142	−
Depreciation for the year	5	−
Divested activities, Modo Paper	−145	−
	2	−
Closing residual value according to plan	16	9

10 Tangible fixed assets

Group	Forest land	Buildings, other land and land installations	Machinery and equipment
Accumulated acquisition values			
Opening balance	310	5,065	26,921
Acquisitions	1	190	1,786
Divested activities, Modo Paper	–	–1,659	–10,772
Divestments and retirements	–2	–210	–1,192
Translation differences arising for the year	–	–45	–357
	309	3,341	16,386
Accumulated depreciation according to plan			
Opening balance	–	2,608	12,961
Depreciation for the year	–	159	1,223
Divested activities, Modo Paper	–	–912	–4,785
Divestments and retirements	–	–194	–1,018
Translation differences arising for the year	–	–21	–185
	–	1,640	8,196
Accumulated revaluations			
Opening balance	4,275	108	–
Divested activities, Modo Paper	–	–4	–
Divestments and retirements	–7	–	–
	4,268	104	–
Accumulated write-downs			
Opening balance	–	–	744
Divested activities, Modo Paper	–	–	–686
Translation differences arising for the year	–	–	–58
	–	–	–
Closing residual value according to plan	4,577	1,805	8,190

Parent company	Forest land	Buildings, other land and land installations	Machinery and equipment
Accumulated acquisition values			
Opening balance	43	1,340	6,188
Acquisitions	–	19	481
Divested activities, Modo Paper	–	–997	–5,440
Divestments and retirements	–	–185	–914
	43	177	315
Accumulated depreciation according to plan			
Opening balance	–	904	3,348
Depreciation for the year	–	35	256
Divested activities, Modo Paper	–	–624	–2,563
Divestments and retirements	–	–176	–803
	–	139	238
Accumulated revaluations			
Opening balance	1,751	1	–
Divestments and retirements	–5	–	–
	1,746	1	–
Closing residual value according to plan	1,789	39	77

In January, an agreement was reached with AssiDomän to exchange some 80,000 hectares of forest land in northern Sweden. The Swedish Board of Agriculture gave its consent to the exchange in April. The transactions have been taken into Holmen's accounts with no effect on the result.

Assessed tax values

Assessed tax values relate to assets in Sweden.

	Group		Parent company	
	1999	1998	**1999**	1998
Forest and agricultural property	6,699	6,050	3,421	3,105
Buildings, other land and land installations	2,701	4,012	63	1,059
	9,400	10,062	3,484	4,164

11 Financial fixed assets

SHARES AND PARTICIPATIONS Group	Associate companies	Other shares and parti- cipations
Accumulated acquisition values		
Opening balance	161	59
Shares in Modo Paper	4,166	–
Capital contribution	8	–
Divestments	–7	–8
Translation differences arising for the year	–2	–4
	4,326	47
Accumulated interest in earnings		
Opening balance	37	–
Interest in earnings/dividends for the year	114	–
Divestments	–15	–
	136	–
Accumulated write-downs		
Opening balance	109	–
Write-downs for the year	8	–
	117	–
Closing book value	4,345	47

Parent company	Group companies	Associate companies	Other shares and parti- cipations
Accumulated acquisition values			
Opening balance	18,587	159	1
Purchases	1,813	–	–
Shares in Modo Paper	–	4,473	–
Capital contribution	–	8	–
Divested activities, Modo Paper	–1,987	–	–
Divestments	–	–7	–
	18,413	4,633	1
Accumulated revaluations			
Opening balance	2,299	–	–
	2,299	–	–
Accumulated write-downs			
Opening balance	1,649	109	–
Write-downs for the year	3	8	–
Divested activities, Modo Paper	–88	–	–
	1,564	117	–
Closing book value	19,148	4,516	1

List of shareholdings, see pages 48–49.

	Group		Parent company	
LONG-TERM RECEIVABLES	**1999**	1998	**1999**	1998
Receivables from Group companies . .	–	–	286	435
Receivables from associate companies	–	11	–	11
Other long-term receivables	20	33	17	24
	20	44	303	470

87

12 Inventories etc.

	Group		Parent company	
	1999	1998	**1999**	1998
Raw materials and consumables	689	1,065	563	722
Timber and pulpwood	182	296	125	206
Finished products, goods for resale and work in progress	886	1,926	731	1,188
Felling rights	335	336	334	335
Advance payments to suppliers	10	25	9	10
	2,102	3,648	1,762	2,461

13 Operating receivables

	Group		Parent company	
	1999	1998	**1999**	1998
Accounts receivable	2,051	3,586	1,761	2,066
Receivables from Group companies ..	–	–	159	280
Receivables from associate companies	272	45	265	45
Prepaid costs and accrued income	130	323	86	240
Tax receivable	6	44	–	–
Other receivables	507	616	216	343
	2,966	4,614	2,487	2,974

14 Financial receivables

Of the Group's financial receivables of SKr 3,380 million, SKr 3,140 million relate to associate companies. Of the parent company's receivables of SKr 451 million, SKr 212 million relate to associate companies.

15 Equity

	Restricted equity		Non-restricted equity		
Group	Share capital	Restricted reserves	Non-restricted reserves	Profit for the year	Total
Opening balance, January 1, 1999	4,443	7,819	3,611	2,504	18,377
Transfer of profit for the year 1998	–	–	2,504	–2,504	–
Dividend paid					
Ordinary	–	–	–889	–	–889
Extra	–	–	–3,110	–	–3,110
Restatements between restricted and non-restricted equity and exchange rate differences of foreign Group and associate companies	–	–2,476	2,167	–	–309
Profit for the year	–	–	–	1,814	1,814
Closing balance, Dec. 31, 1999 .	4,443	5,343	4,283	1,814	15,883

Accumulated currency differences from and including January 1st 1999, amount to a deficit of SKr 309 million, after a reduction of SKr 141 million as a result of currency hedging during the period.

Parent company	December 31, 1999		December 31, 1998	
	Number	SKr million	Number	SKr million
Share capital				
Series "A"	22,623,234	1,131.2	22,623,234	1,131.2
Series "B"	66,235,044	3,311.7	66,235,044	3,311.7
	88,858,278	4,442.9	88,858,278	4,442.9

Further information concerning Holmen shares is provided on pages 6–7.

	Restricted equity			Non-restricted equity		
	Share capital	Revaluation reserve	Other restricted equity	Profit brought forward	Profit for the year	Total
Opening balance January 1, 1999	4,443	100	1,998	4,754	1,745	13,040
Transfer of profit for the year 1998	–	–	–	1,745	–1,745	–
Dividend paid						
Ordinary	–	–	–	–889	–	–889
Extra	–	–	–	–3,110	–	–3,110
Profit for the year	–	–	–	–	4,675	4,675
Closing balance, December 31, 1999 .	4,443	100	1,998*	2,500	4,675	13,716

* Other restricted equity consists of statutory reserve SKr 1,952 million and share premium reserve SKr 46 million.

16 Untaxed reserves parent company

	Total January 1, 1999	Change during the year	Total Dec. 31, 1999
Accumulated depreciation in excess of plan	2,059	–2,018	41
Profit equalisation reserve	797	234	1,031
	2,856	–1,784	1,072

The year's allocations of SKr 1,778 million include a change of SKr 1,784 million in untaxed reserves. Of the untaxed reserves, deferred tax accounted for SKr 300 million. The deferred tax is not included in the parent company balance sheet, but is stated in the consolidated balance sheet.

17 Provisions

The pension liabilities correspond to the present value of the pension commitments arrived at on actuarial grounds.

Other provisions mainly consist of reserves to cover future forestry levies and personnel reductions.

18 Financial liabilities

	Group 1999	Group 1998	Parent company 1999	Parent company 1998
Long-term				
Bond loans	–	16	–	–
Subordinated loans	376	374	376	374
Liabilities to Group companies	–	–	7,373	8,383
Other long-term liabilities				
Liabilities to credit institutions	924	1,776	874	1,312
Other liabilities	13	14	8	8
	1,313	2,180	8,631	10,077
Current				
Liabilities to credit institutions	1,569	80	1,799	205
Commercial paper	3,167	–	3,167	–
Current proportion of long-term liabilities				
Bond loans	16	13	–	–
Liabilities to credit institutions	634	590	462	153
Other liabilities	–	3	–	2
Other current liabilities	146	1,383	146	1,349
	5,532	2,069	5,574	1,709
	6,845	4,249	14,205	11,786

Financial liabilities are in all essentials interest-bearing. The parent company's liabilities to Group companies include a significant volume of interest-free liabilities between wholly-owned Swedish Group companies.

In 1998 an SKr 361 million convertible loan was issued to employees, of which SKr 332 million (326) are stated under loan stock. The loan may be converted into Holmen Series "B" shares between February 1, 2004 and March 31, 2004 at a conversion price of SKr 148.10. Under certain circumstances, such as the payment of large dividends, the conversion price may be adjusted.

Long-term financial liabilities maturing later than five years from the closing date are specified below.

	Group 1999	Parent company 1999
Subordinated loans	44	44
Liabilities to credit institutions	3	–
	47	44

Information concerning the breakdown of liabilities by currency and maturity is provided in the section entitled Financial risks, page 36–37.

19 Operating liabilities

	Group 1999	Group 1998	Parent company 1999	Parent company 1998
Advance payments from customers	1	2	–	–
Liabilities to suppliers	1,475	2,001	1,190	1,312
Bills payable	3	145	–	–
Liabilities to Group companies	–	–	254	531
Liabilities to associate companies	83	92	141	152
Accrued costs and deferred income	527	909	485	580
Tax liability	784	471	539	264
Other current liabilities	588	580	271	330
	3,461	4,200	2,880	3,169

Operating liabilities relate entirely to items falling due for payment no later than one year after the closing date.

Accrued costs and deferred income consist largely of personnel costs, discounts and complaints.

20 Pledged assets

	Value of pledged assets — Property mortgages	Value of pledged assets — Other pledged assets	Total pledged assets 1999	Total pledged assets 1998
Group				
Own liabilities				
Liabilities to credit institutions	–	–	–	373
Other liabilities	10	–	10	30
Other commitments	–	30	30	42
	10	30	40	445
Parent company				
Own liabilities				
Other liabilities	10	–	10	25
Other commitments	–	30	30	42
	10	30	40	67

21 Contingent liabilities

	Group 1999	Group 1998	Parent company 1999	Parent company 1998
Guarantees on behalf of Group companies	–	–	255	66
Other guarantees and contingent liabilities	333	233	259	161
	333	233	514	227

The parent company has provided guarantees for certain undertakings which may become incumbent on Group companies.

22 Personnel, wages and salaries

	1999 No. of employees	1999 Of whom men	1998 No. of employees	1998 Of whom men
Average No. of employees				
Parent company				
Sweden	5,960	4,935	6,490	5,394
Group companies				
Sweden	216	165	264	198
Australia	2	1	2	1
Belgium	20	12	27	14
Belarus	22	11	32	20
Denmark	6	3	8	4
Estonia	50	35	58	39
France	720	609	982	822
Germany	52	31	69	34
Great Britain	910	760	1,008	833
Holland	225	173	234	192
Italy	6	1	8	2
Latvia	60	37	64	42
Lithuania	51	39	58	42
Norway	30	20	40	27
Russia	54	34	167	133
Singapore	6	5	5	4
Spain	31	22	44	33
Switzerland	8	6	20	14
Ukraine	–	–	4	3
USA	4	3	2	1
Total Group companies	2,473	1,967	3,096	2,458
Total Group	8,433	6,902	9,586	7,852

Wages, salaries, other remunerations and social security charges	1999				1998			
	Wages, salaries and remune-rations	Of which Board of Directors and President	Social security charges	Of which pension costs	Wages, salaries and remune-rations	Of which Board of Directors and President	Social security charges	Of which pension costs
Parent company								
Sweden	1,690	14[1]	726	192[2]	1,806	15[1]	685	31[2]
Group companies								
Sweden	60	2	27	5	73	3	32	5
Other Nordic countries	14	2	2	1	17	2	3	1
France	205	8	91	2	278	7	122	6
Germany	27	3	7	2	32	5	7	2
Great Britain	294	9	51	24	315	10	52	24
Holland	69	5	17	3	68	5	12	2
Eastern Europe	17	1	5	0	24	3	8	0
Rest of Europe	29	11	8	1	41	11	11	2
Other countries	5	2	0	0	5	2	1	0
Total Group companies	720	43[4]	208	38	853	48[4]	248	42
Total Group	2,410	57	934	230[3][5]	2,659	63	933	73[3]

1) Of this amount, SKr 5.8 million (5.8) relate to the category Board and President of parent company, and SKr 8.2 million (9.2) relate to the category presidents of commission companies.

2) Of the pension costs, SKr 3.3 million (2.3) relate to the category Board and President of parent company, and SKr 1.9 million (3.1) to the category presidents of commission companies. Outstanding pension commitments, stated under Pension provisions, amount in total to SKr 0 (9.4 million) for these categories.

3) Of the Group's pension costs, SKr 11.3 million (9.9) relate to the category Boards and Presidents of parent company and Group companies. The Group's outstanding pension commitments, stated under Pension provisions, amount to SKr 0.8 million (33.0) for these categories.

4) Bonuses totalling SKr 0.8 million (0.9) were paid to Boards and Presidents of Group companies.

5) SPP has reported that Holmen's share of SPP's surplus funds is SKr 184 million. As the procedures for repayment of these funds have not yet been decided on, the amount has not been taken into the company's accounts.

Information provided in compliance with the Business Stock Exchange Committee's recommendation concerning the conditions of employment of senior executives.

Chairman of the Board
Fee: SKr 300,000

President
Salaries and other perquisites: SKr 5,028,774

Pension
The pension agreement provides for retirement at the age of 65, but with either party being entitled to request retirement from 61 years of age. Pension will be paid between 61 and 65 at 60 per cent of the salary, and corresponds thereafter to the ITP plan, complemented with certain old-age and family pension benefits for that part of the salary which exceeds 20 base amounts.

Period of notice and severance pay
The period of notice is twelve months on the part of the company and six months on the part of the President. In the event of the company giving notice, severance pay of two-years' salary will be paid.

Business area Presidents and Senior Vice Presidents
Pension
Pension agreements provide for retirement at the age of 65, but with either party being entitled to request retirement on pension after 60. Pension will be paid between 60 and 65 at 65 per cent of the salary providing entitlement to pension. The normal pension follows the ITP plan or equivalent. Over and above this, it will be complemented with certain pension benefits for the part of the annual salary which exceeds 20 base amounts.

Period of notice and severance pay
The period of notice is twelve months on the part of the company and six months on the part of the employee. In the event of the company giving notice, severance pay corresponding to between one year's and 2.5 years' salary will be paid, depending on age.

Auditors' fees

The audit fees were SKr 6.6 million for the Group and SKr 3.5 million for the parent company. Consulting and other such fees amounted to SKr 8.9 million for the Group and SKr 7.4 million for the parent company.

List of shareholdings

	Reg. no.	Registered office	No. of parti-cipations	1999 Parti-cipations [1] %	1999 Book value SKr 1,000	1998 Parti-cipations [1] %	1998 Book value SKr 1,000
Holmen Paper AB	556005-6383	Norrköping	100	100	100	100	100
Iggesund Paperboard AB	556088-5294	Hudiksvall	1,000	100	100	100	100
Iggesund Timber AB	556099-0672	Hudiksvall	1,000	100	100	100	100
Holmen Skog AB (former MoDo Skog AB)	556220-0658	Örnsköldsvik	1,000	100	83	100	83
MoDo Paper AB	556082-1570	Örnsköldsvik	–	–	–	100	95
MoDo Merchants AB	556018-2338	Stockholm	–	–	–	100	120
AB Ankarsrums Skogar	556002-5495	Örnsköldsvik	1,000	100	41,609	100	41,609
Domsjö Klor AB	556227-5361	Örnsköldsvik	1,000	100	1,079	100	1,079
Fiskeby AB	556000-9218	Norrköping	2,000,000	100	646,160	100	646,160
Haradsskogarna AB	556000-6909	Örnsköldsvik	100,640	100	129,450	100	129,450
Harrsele Linjeaktiebolag	556003-6344	Örnsköldsvik	48,000	100	16,985	100	16,985
Holmens Bruk AB	556002-0264	Norrköping	49,514,201	100	4,061,703	100	4,061,703
Holmen Kraft AB	556340-9191	Norrköping	1,194,600	100	346,242	100	346,242
Husum Copy AB	556114-7058	Örnsköldsvik	100	100	100	100	100
AB Iggesunds Bruk	556000-8053	Hudiksvall	6,002,500	100	3,933,735	100	3,933,735
Lammbi AB	556037-1196	Örnsköldsvik	–	–	–	100	66
Lägernskog AB	556003-2806	Örnsköldsvik	1,480	100	1,385	100	1,385
MoDo-Iggesund CTMP AB	556245-2556	Örnsköldsvik	400,000	100	40,000	100	40,000
MoDo Paper East AB	556126-2279	Örnsköldsvik	–	–	–	90,1	0
MoDo Forest Management AB	556031-9047	Stockholm	100	100	16,200	100	16,200
AB PM 8 i Husum	556255-4070	Örnsköldsvik	–	–	–	100	50
Skärnäs Terminal AB	556008-3171	Hudiksvall	4,800	100	1,913	100	1,913
Ströms Trävaru AB	556000-7857	Örnsköldsvik	400	100	166,200	100	166,200
Svenskt Papper AB	556076-2022	Stockholm	–	–	–	95	86,400
Basberg Papir AS, Norway		Oslo	–	–	–	100	–
AB Överums Skogar	556156-0557	Norrköping	1,000	100	53,005	100	53,005
Örnsköldsviks Stuveri AB	556008-1530	Örnsköldsvik	–	–	–	100	5,185
Other Swedish Group companies					7,023		7,022
MoDo Ltd, Great Britain		Westerham	1,197,100	100	996,779	100	996,779
Iggesund Paperboard (Workington) Ltd		Workington	–	100	–	100	–
MoDo Holdings Ltd		Westerham	–	–	–	100	–
MoDo Merchants Ltd		West Byfleet	–	–	–	100	–
MoDo France Finances SAS, France		Paris	2,200,007	100	856,824	100	856,824
MoDo France Holding SAS, France		Paris	17,800,007	100	6,931,308	100	6,931,308
MoDo France SA*		Paris	–	100	–	100	–
MoDo Paper Alizay-Alicel SA		Paris	–	–	–	100	–
MoDo Paper Alizay-Alipap SA		Paris	–	–	–	100	–
MoDo Paper PSM SA		Paris	–	–	–	100	–
MoDo International Finance, Ireland		Dublin	823,565,413	100	823,565	100	823,565
MoDo Merchants Benelux BV, Holland		Amsterdam	–	–	–	100	9,592
MoDo Van Gelder NV		Amsterdam	–	–	–	100	–
Partaros BV, Holland		Amsterdam	800	100	25,421	100	25,421
Noord-Europese Houtimport BV		Amsterdam	–	100	–	100	–
Comercial Papelera Aldi SA, Spain		Madrid	–	–	–	100	–
Iggesund Paperboard Asia Pte Ltd, Singapore		Singapore	800,000	100	4,273	100	4,273
Other foreign Group companies					46,703		34,148
					19,148,045		**19,236,997**

1) Percentage of shares and percentage of votes are the same except where otherwise stated.

* MoDo France SA is 89 % owned by MoDo France Holding SAS and 11 % by MoDo France Finances SAS.

Parent company and Group holdings of shares and participations in associate companies

	Reg.no.	Registered office	No. of parti-cipations	Parti-cipations[1] %	1999 Book value at parent company SKr 1,000	1999 Value of parti-cipation in consoli-dated accounts SKr 1,000	Parti-cipations[1] %	1998 Book value at parent company SKr 1,000	1998 Value of parti-cipations in consoli-dated accounts SKr 1,000
Iggesund Kraft AB	556422-0902	Örnsköldsvik	58,000	50.0	5,800	5,800	50.0	5,800	5,800
Industriskog AB	556193-9470	Falun	25,000	33.3	2,503	2,503	33.3	2,503	2,503
Junkaravan AB	556227-3630	Örnsköldsvik	343,000	22.3	12,200	12,200	22.3	12,200	12,200
Lumosi AB	556528-1051	Stockholm	–	–	–	–	26.5	0	0
Modo Paper AB	556552-6158	Stockholm	5,000,000	50.0	4,473,398	4,257,480	–	–	–
Svensk Etanolkemi AB	556263-4088	Örnsköldsvik	10,000	50.0	10,000	43,538	50.0	10,000	36,676
Sydved AB	556171-0814	Jönköping	–	–	–	–	33.3	7,060	7,060
Les Bois de la Baltique SA, France		Rouen	75,000	33.3	7,591	17,144	33.3	7,591	18,570
Miscellanous shares									
Parent company					4,703	4,703		4,652	4,652
Other Group companies					–	1,179		–	1,302
					4,516,195	4,344,547		49,806	88,763

1) Percentage of shares and percentage of votes are the same except where otherwise stated.

The capital interest reserve amounts to SKr 43 million (see Accounting Principles on page 40).

Parent company and Group holdings of shares and participations in other companies

	Reg.no.	Registered office	No. of parti-cipations	Parti-cipations[1] %	1999 Book value SKr 1,000	Parti-cipations[1] %	1998 Book value SKr 1,000
Parent company							
Miscellanous shares					656		656
Subtotal parent company					656		656
Group							
Brännälvens Kraft AB	556017-6678	Arbrå	5,556	13.9	36,400	13.9	36,400
MoBaSa-MoDo Battistella Reflorestamento SA, Brazil		Curitiba	234,951	1.9	8,910	1.9	12,491
Ukhta Ltd, Isle of Man		Douglas	–	–	–	99*	7,992
Miscellaneous shares					690		918
Subtotal Group					46,000		57,801
Total					46,656		58,457

1) Percentage of shares and percentage of votes are the same except where otherwise stated.

* Share of votes 9 per cent.

Proposed treatment of unappropriated earnings

The following unappropriated earnings in the accounts of the
parent company are at the disposal of the Annual General Meeting: Kronor

Net profit for the 1999 financial year	4,675,000,000
Retained earnings from previous year	2,500,219,584
	7,175,219,584

The Board of Directors and the President propose

that a dividend of SKr 11 per share (88,858,278 shares) be paid	977,441,058
and, subject to the conditions stipulated in the report of the directors, that a total of 70 per cent of the company's shares in Modo Paper AB, the total value of which in the parent company's accounts is SKr 4,473,398,314, also be distributed by way of dividend	3,131,378,820
and that the remaining amount be carried forward	3,066,399,706
	7,175,219,584

It is proposed that of the consolidated non-restricted equity of SKr 6,097 million,
no transfer be made to consolidated restricted equity.

Stockholm February 14, 2000

Fredrik Lundberg

Steewe Björklundh	**Matts Jutterström**	**Carl Kempe**
Hans Larsson	**Arne Mårtensson**	**Thomas Nilsson**
Per Welin	**Christer Zetterberg**	**Bengt Pettersson**
		President

Our audit report was submitted on February 21, 2000

KPMG Bohlins AB
Thomas Thiel
Authorised Public Accountant

Audit Report

To the general meeting of the shareholders of Holmen Aktiebolag (publ)
Co. reg. No. 556001-3301

We have audited the annual accounts, the consolidated accounts, the accounting records and the administration of the Board of Directors and the President of Holmen Aktiebolag for the year 1999. These accounts and the administration of the company are the responsibility of the Board of Directors and the President. Our responsibility is to express an opinion on the annual accounts, the consolidated accounts and the administration based on our audit.

We conducted our audit in accordance with generally accepted auditing standards in Sweden. Those standards require that we plan and perform the audit to obtain reasonable assurance that the annual accounts and the consolidated accounts are free of material misstatement. An audit includes examining, on a test basis, evidence supporting the amounts and disclosures in the accounts. An audit also includes assessing the accounting principles used and their application by the Board of Directors and the President, as well as evaluating the overall presentation of information in the annual accounts and the consolidated accounts. As a basis for our opinion concerning discharge from liability, we examined significant decisions, actions taken and circumstances of the company in order to be able to determine the liability, if any, to the company of any Board member or the President. We also examined whether any Board member or the President has, in any other way, acted in contravention of the Companies Act, the Annual Accounts Act or the Articles of Association. We believe that our audit provides a reasonable basis for our opinion set out below.

The annual accounts and the consolidated accounts have been prepared in accordance with the Annual Accounts Act and, thereby, give a true and fair view of the company's and the Group's financial position and results of operations in accordance with generally accepted accounting principles in Sweden.

We recommend to the general meeting of shareholders that the income statements and balance sheets of the parent company and the Group be adopted, that the profit for the parent company be dealt with in accordance with the proposal in the Report of the Directors and that the members of the Board of Directors and the President be discharged from liability for the financial year.

Stockholm, February 21, 2000

KPMG Bohlins AB

Thomas Thiel
Authorised Public Accountant

Board of Directors

CARL KEMPE

FREDRIK LUNDBERG

ARNE MARTENSSON

CHRISTER ZETTERBERG

PER WELIN

BENGT PETTERSSON

STEEWE BJÖRKLUNDH

TORGNY HAMMAR

ANDERS LIDÉN

THOMAS NILSSON

HANS LARSSON

MATTS JUTTERSTRÖM

KARIN NORIN

Fredrik Lundberg, Djursholm. Born 1951. Chairman of the Board. Member since 1988. President and CEO of L E Lundbergföretagen AB. Other significant appointments: Chairman of the Board; Cardo AB and Hufvudstaden AB. Member of the Board; L E Lundbergföretagen AB, Modo Paper AB, and NCC AB.
Shareholding in Holmen, direct and via private company: 584,724 shares.

Carl Kempe, Örnsköldsvik. Born 1939. Deputy Chairman. Member since 1983. Other significant appointments: Chairman of the Kempe Foundations.
Shareholding in Holmen: 300,218 shares

Steewe Björklundh, Hudiksvall. Born 1958. Member since 1998. Representative of the employees, LO. Chairman of the Forest and Wood Union at the Iggesund Sawmill.
Shareholding in Holmen: 800 convertibles.

Matts Jutterström, Forsa. Born 1961. Member since 1999. Representative of the employees, LO. Chairman of Paper-branch 15, Iggesund.
Shareholding in Holmen: 900 convertibles.

Hans Larsson, Stockholm. Born 1942. Member since 1990. Other significant appointments: Chairman of the Board: NCC AB, Althin Medical AB, Biolight International AB, and Nobia AB. Member of the Board: Handelsbanken and Bilia AB.
Shareholding in Holmen: 1,000 shares.

Arne Mårtensson, Djursholm. Born 1951. Member since 1991. CEO of Handelsbanken. Other significant appointments: Deputy Chairman of the Board: Swedish Bankers' Association and KSSS. Member of the Board: Handelsbanken, Sandvik AB, the Swedish Association for Share Promotion, OM Group AB, Svenska ICC, Teleoptimering i Sverige AB and V & S Vin & Sprit AB.
Shareholding in Holmen: 0.

Thomas Nilsson, Åby. Born 1945. Member since 1992. Representative of the employees, PTK. Chairman of SIF branch Holmen, Norrköping and of SIF's industrial delegation for the forest industry.
Shareholding in Holmen: 1,000 convertibles.

Bengt Pettersson, Stockholm. Born 1938. President and CEO until Feb 14, 2000. Member since 1994. Other significant appointments: Member of the Board: Cardo AB, L E Lundbergföretagen AB, Federation of Swedish Industries and Swedish Forest Industries' Association.
Shareholding in Holmen: 3,000 shares, 10,000 call options and 1,000 warrants.

Per Welin, Stockholm. Born 1936. Member since 1991. Chairman of the Board: L E Lundbergföretagen AB. Other significant appointments: Member of the Board: Allgon, Autoliv, NCC AB and Östgöta Enskilda Bank.
Shareholding in Holmen: 3,200 shares.

Christer Zetterberg, Trosa. Born 1941. Member since 1994. Other significant appointments: Chairman of the Board: IDI, Segerström & Svensson, Ekman & Co, Turn IT, and Micronic Laser Systems. Member of the Board (among others): Caenfil AB and L E Lundbergföretagen AB.
Shareholding in Holmen: 1,000 shares.

Deputy members

Torgny Hammar, Hallstavik. Born 1943. Deputy member since 1993. Representative of the employees, PTK. Chairman: Leaders Hallstavik and member of the Board of Central Leaders. Shareholding in Holmen: 900 convertibles.

Anders Lidén, Herräng. Born 1969. Deputy member since 1999. Representative of the employees LO, Hallstavik. Shareholding in Holmen: 300 warrants.

Karin Norin, Forsa. Born 1950. Deputy member since 1999. Representative of the employees PTK. Chairman of SIF's-club Holmen-Iggesund. Member of SIFs industrial delegation for the forest industry. Shareholding in Holmen: 0.

Auditors

KPMG Bohlins AB
Principal auditor: **Thomas Thiel.** Authorized public accountant.

Senior Management

President and CEO

Bengt Pettersson
Up to February 14, 2000.

Per Ericson
As of February 15, 2000. Born 1946.
Joined Holmen 2000.
Shareholding in Holmen: 10,000 call options

Group staffs

Johan Flodström
Senior Vice President. Group Legal Affairs.
Company Secretary. Born 1945. Joined Holmen 1976.
Shareholding in Holmen: 500 shares, 900 warrants,
10,000 call options.

Ingalill Landfors
Senior Vice President. Group Human Resources.
Born 1939. Joined Holmen 1964. Shareholding
in Holmen: 900 warrants, 10,000 call options.

Christer Lewell
Senior Vice President. Group Public Relations.
Born 1948. Joined Holmen 1987. Shareholding
in Holmen: 10,000 call options.

Lennart Svensson
Senior Vice President. Group Finance.
Born 1945. Joined Holmen 1977. Shareholding
in Holmen: 900 warrants, 10,000 call options.

Olle Svensson
Senior Vice President. Group Technology.
Born 1936. Joined Holmen 1965. Shareholding in Holmen: 400 shares, 900 convertibles, 4,000 call options.

PER ERICSON

OLLE SVENSSON

LENNART SVENSSON

BENGT PETTERSSON

INGALILL LANDFORS

JOHAN FLODSTRÖM

CHRISTER LEWELL

Business areas

Göran Lundin
President Holmen Paper
Born 1940. Joined Holmen 1964. Shareholding
in Holmen: 900 warrants, 10,000 call options.

Erik Sjölund
President Iggesund Paperboard
Born 1941. Joined Holmen 1969. Shareholding
in Holmen: 1,000 warrants, 10,000 call options.

Per Erik Frick
President Iggesund Timber
Born 1938. Joined Holmen 1966. Shareholding in
Holmen: 2,282 shares, 900 warrants, 5,000 call options.

Björn Andrén
President Holmen Skog
Born 1946. Joined Holmen 1971. Shareholding in
Holmen: 1,000 convertibles, 10,000 call options.

BJÖRN ANDRÉN

PER ERIK FRICK

GÖRAN LUNDIN

ERIK SJÖLUND

Call options are issued by L E Lundbergföretagen AB.

Production units

Holmen Paper

BRAVIKEN
Raw material: Spruce wood, recovered paper.
Process: Production of TMP and DIP pulp, and paper.
Product: Newsprint, coloured newsprint and telephone directory paper.
Production capacity: 700,000 tonnes/year.
Average No. of employees: 741.
Brand names: Holmen News, Holmen Coloured News, Holmen Guide.

HALLSTA
Raw material: Spruce wood, recovered paper.
Process: Production of TMP, groundwood and DIP pulp, and paper.
Product: Newsprint, MF Magazine (improved newsprint), SC paper and book paper.
Production capacity: 670,000 tonnes/year.
Average No. of employees: 1,053.
Brand names: Holmen News (Super News, Super Print, Super Bright, Ultra Bright, Ultra Bright Plus), SCANMAG, ECO.

WARGÖN
Raw material: Spruce wood.
Process: Production of sulphite and groundwood pulp, and paper.
Product: Coated printing paper, MWC, on reels and in sheets.
Production capacity: 130,000 tonnes/year.
Average No. of employees: 385.
Brand names: SCANGLOSS, SCANMATT, SCANPLUS.

HOLMEN KRAFT
Responsible for the supply of electric power to Holmen's Swedish mills. Company-owned and partnerfinanced hydro-electric power stations in the rivers Umeälven, Faxälven, Gideälven, Ljusnan, Iggesundsån and Motala Ström.
Production/purchases of electric power 1999.
Company owned and associate hydro-electric power stations: 1,135 GWh.
Back pressure power at mills: 338 GWh.
Purchased electric power: 2,464 GWh.
Total: 3,937 GWh.
Average No. of employees: 18.

Iggesund Paperboard

IGGESUNDS BRUK
Raw material: Softwood and hardwood.
Process: Production of sulphate pulp and paperboard.
Product: Solid bleached board for packaging and graphic purposes.
Production capacity: Paperboard: 300,000 tonnes. Market pulp: 20,000 tonnes /year.
Average No. of employees: 942.
Brand names: Invercote, Invercote Albato, Invercote Creato, etc.

WORKINGTON
Raw material: Spruce wood and purchased sulphate pulp.
Process: Production of RMP pulp and paperboard.
Product: Folding boxboard for packaging and graphic purposes.
Production capacity: 235,000 tonnes/year.
Average No. of employees: 611.
Brand names: Graphique-Silkia, Carton-Silkia, Tabac-Silkia, Carton-Cote, Carton-Excel.

STRÖMS BRUK
Raw material: Paperboard from Iggesunds Bruk and Workington, purchased plastic granules, foil etc.
Process: Plastic coating of paperboard.
Product: Plastic-coated and laminated paperboard.
Production capacity: 40,000 tonnes/year.
Average No. of employees: 141.
Brand names: Invercote, Carton-Cote, Carton-Excel.

Iggesund Timber

IGGESUND SAWMILL
Raw material: Spruce and pine wood.
Process: Sawmill.
Product: Sawn timber.
Production capacity: 300,000 m³/year.
Average No. om employees: 171.
Brand names: MONOLIT, DUOLIT, QUATROLIT.

DOMSJÖ SAWMILL
Raw material: Pine wood.
Process: Sawmill.
Product: Sawn timber.
Production capacity: 90,000 m³/year.
Average No. of employees: 75.
Brand name: MONOLIT.

Holmen Skog

Forest regions: Lycksele, Örnsköldsvik, Iggesund and Norrköping. Wholly-owned purchasing company in Estonia.

Land holdings	1,303,000 hectares	**Wood procurement 1999**
Productive forest land	1,029,000 hectares	excl. procurement for divested mills 4.27 million m³
Share of Sweden's forest land	4.5 per cent	**Average No. of employees:** 556
Wood stock	106 m³ per hectare	
Total wood stock	109 million m³	

Glossary

Chemical pulp
Sulphate and sulphite pulp. The cellulose fibres have been separated by chemical means.

Coated paper
Paper coated with clay, for instance, to get a smooth surface which increases the printing quality.

DIP
(De-inked pulp). Recycled fibre pulp which has been de-inked.

FBB
Folding Boxboard – a board which comprises several layers produced from mechanical and chemical pulp.

FSC
Forest Stewardship Council. A world-wide organisation with its head office in Mexico. The FSC has formulated ten basic principles, which take into account the environmental, economic and social aspects of forestry in all parts of the world. The Swedish FSC standard is adapted to the specific conditions in Sweden. Behind the Swedish FSC standard are forest companies, environmental organisations, customers, the Sami community, the Swedish Church and trade unions. Holmen Skog received certification in accordance with FSC during 1998.

Grammage
The weight of one square metre of paper. Measured in grammes.

Hardwood
Mainly birchwood.

ISO 14001
An international environmental management system. Indicates how the environmental activities are to be organised and conducted in order to achieve continuous improvements.

Mechanical pulp
Pulp where the fibres have been liberated entirely by mechanical means.

MF Journal
Improved newsprint with high brightness for newspaper supplements and advertising prints.

MF Special
MF Journal (improved newsprint), telephone directory paper and coloured newsprint.

MWC paper
Medium Weight Coated. Coated paper in grammages between 80 and 110 g/m^2.

Newsprint
Paper for daily newspapers, often made of TMP pulp, mechanical pulp and DIP.

Productive forest land
Forest land where the trees within one hectare grow on aggregate by more than one cubic metre of wood per year.

Pulpwood
Wood used for production of pulp. Often small dimensions; wood from thinnings or from the top of the stems.

Recycled fibre
Wood fibre recovered from collected used paper.

Saw logs
The thick parts of the stem that are used by the sawmills for sawn timber.

SBB
Solid Bleached Board – a single layered board of bleached chemical pulp.

SC Paper
Super calendered paper. Uncoated glossed magazine paper in grammages between 50 and 65 g/m^2.

Softwood
Pine wood and spruce wood.

Sulphate pulp
See Chemical pulp.

TMP pulp
Thermomechanical pulp. A high yield pulp (94–96 per cent yield from the wood) which is obtained by heating spruce chips and then grinding them in refiners.

Virgin fibre
Fibre from fresh wood direct from the tree.

Addresses

Head office

Holmen AB
(Strandvägen 1)
P.O. Box 5407
SE-114 84 STOCKHOLM
Telephone: +46 8 666 21 00
Fax: +46 8 666 21 35
E-mail: info@holmen.com
www.holmen.com

Holmen Paper

Holmen Paper AB
(Vattengränden 2)
SE-601 88 NORRKÖPING
Telephone: +46 11 23 50 00
Fax: +46 11 23 63 04
E-mail:
info@holmenpaper.com
www.holmenpaper.com

Holmen Paper AB
Braviken Paper Mill
SE-601 88 NORRKÖPING
Telephone: +46 11 23 50 00
Fax: +46 11 23 66 30
E-mail:
braviken@holmenpaper.com

Holmen Paper AB
Hallsta Paper Mill
SE-763 81 HALLSTAVIK
Telephone: +46 175 260 00
Fax: +46 175 264 01
E-mail:
hallsta@holmenpaper.com

Holmen Paper AB
Wargön Mill
SE-468 81 VARGÖN
Telephone: +46 521 27 75 00
Fax: +46 521 22 38 45
E-mail:
wargon@holmenpaper.com

Iggesund Paperboard

Iggesund Paperboard AB
SE-825 80 IGGESUND
Telephone: +46 650 280 00
Fax: +46 650 288 00
E-mail:
info@iggesundpaperboard.com
www.iggesundpaperboard.com

Iggesund Paperboard AB
Iggesunds Bruk
SE-825 80 IGGESUND
Telephone: +46 650 280 00
Fax: +46 650 285 32
E-mail: info.ib@
iggesundpaperboard.com

Iggesund Paperboard AB
Ströms Bruk
P.O. Box 67
SE-820 72 STRÖMSBRUK
Telephone: +46 650 289 00
Fax: +46 650 289 30
E-mail: info.sb@
iggesundpaperboard.com

Iggesund Paperboard
(Workington) Ltd
WORKINGTON Cumbria
CA14 1JX
Great Britain
Telephone: +44 1900 601000
Fax: +44 1900 605000
E-mail: info.wo@
iggesundpaperboard.com

Iggesund Timber

Iggesund Timber AB
P.O. Box 45
SE-825 21 IGGESUND
Telephone: +46 650 280 00
Fax: +46 650 280 57
E-mail:
info@iggesundtimber.com
www.iggesundtimber.com

Iggesund Timber AB
Iggesund Sawmill
P.O. Box 45
SE-825 21 IGGESUND
Telephone: +46 650 280 00
Fax: +46 650 178 65
E-mail:
info@iggesundtimber.com

Iggesund Timber AB
Domsjö Sawmill
(Domsjövägen 82)
P.O. Box 44
SE-892 21 DOMSJÖ
Telephone: +46 660 754 00
Telex: 6040
Fax: +46 660 759 88
E-mail:
info@iggesundtimber.com

Holmen Skog

Holmen Skog AB
(Hörneborgsvägen 6)
SE-891 80 ÖRNSKÖLDSVIK
Telephone: +46 660 754 00
Fax: +46 660 759 85
E-mail:
info@holmenskog.com
www.holmenskog.com

The complete list of addresses
may be obtained from
Holmen AB
Group Public Relations
P. O. Box 5407
SE-114 84 Stockholm
Telephone: +46 8 666 21 00
Fax: +46 8 666 21 30
E-mail: info@holmen.com

The Holmen annual report is printed on paperboard and paper produced by Holmen and Modo Paper.
Cover: Invercote® Creato 260 g. Inside Pages: Silverblade® matt 130 g.
Graphic design: Energi Reklambyrå and Nova Print AB, Linköping, Sweden.
Photo: Anders Engman, Malcolm Hanes, Bo-Göran Backström and others.
Translation: Ian M Beck AB.

Pfizer Inc.
Annual Report 1999

Financial Review

Proposed Merger with Warner-Lambert Company

On February 7, 2000, we announced an agreement to merge with Warner-Lambert Company (Warner-Lambert). Under terms of the merger agreement, which has been approved by the Board of Directors of both Pfizer and Warner-Lambert, we will exchange 2.75 shares of Pfizer voting common stock for each outstanding share of Warner-Lambert voting common stock in a tax-free transaction valued at $98.31 per Warner-Lambert share, or an equity value of $90 billion based on the closing price of our stock on February 4, 2000 of $35.75 per share. Customary and usual provisions will be made for outstanding options and warrants.

The combined company, which will be called Pfizer Inc, is expected to have (excluding any impact of anticipated restructuring charges and transaction fees of $1.7 billion to $2.2 billion):

- compounded annual revenue growth of 13% and earnings growth of 25% through 2002
- $4.7 billion in annual research and development expenses in 2000
- anticipated annual cost savings and efficiencies of $1.6 billion by 2002 ($200 million of these savings are expected to be achieved in 2000, $1 billion in 2001 and $1.6 billion in 2002)
- diluted earnings per share of $.98 on a pro forma basis in 2000, $1.27 for 2001 and $1.56 for 2002 (these numbers include the $1.6 billion of cost savings phased in over this time period, but do not include any increased sales from collaborative activities and the $1.8 billion termination fee paid by Warner-Lambert to American Home Products Corporation)

This transaction is subject to customary conditions, including the use of pooling-of-interests accounting, qualifying as a tax-free reorganization, shareholder approval at both companies and usual regulatory approvals. The transaction is expected to close in mid-2000.

The following financial review reflects the results of operations and financial condition of Pfizer and does not consider the impact of the proposed merger with Warner-Lambert.

Overview of Consolidated Operating Results

In 1999, total revenues grew 20% to $16,204 million, reflecting the strong worldwide demand for our in-line products, as well as our alliance products. Our operating results in 1999 were impacted by the recording of a charge to write off certain Trovan inventories. Our 1998 operating results reflect:

- the sale of our Medical Technology Group (MTG)
- the recording of certain significant charges associated with adjustments to asset values, the exiting of certain product lines, plant rationalizations, severance payments, co-promotion payments to Searle, a contribution to The Pfizer Foundation and other miscellaneous charges

Analysis of the Consolidated Statement of Income

(millions of dollars)	1999	1998	1997	% Change 99/98	98/97
Net sales	$14,133	$12,677	$10,739	11	18
Alliance revenue	2,071	867	316	139	175
Total revenues	16,204	13,544	11,055	20	23
Cost of sales	2,528	2,094	1,776	21	18
Selling, informational and administrative expenses	6,351	5,568	4,401	14	27
% of total revenues	39.2%	41.1%	39.8%		
R&D expenses	2,776	2,279	1,805	22	26
% of total revenues	17.1%	16.8%	16.3%		
Other deductions—net	101	1,009	206	(90)	391
Income from continuing operations before taxes	$ 4,448	$ 2,594	$ 2,867	71	(10)
% of total revenues	27.5%	19.2%	25.9%		
Taxes on income	$ 1,244	$ 642	$ 775	94	(17)
Effective tax rate	28.0%	24.8%	27.0%		
Income from continuing operations	$ 3,199	$ 1,950	$ 2,082	64	(6)
% of total revenues	19.7%	14.4%	18.8%		
Discontinued operations—net of tax	(20)	1,401	131	—	972
Net income	$ 3,179	$ 3,351	$ 2,213	(5)	51
% of total revenues	19.6%	24.7%	20.0%		

Percentages may reflect rounding adjustments.

Total Revenues

Total revenues increased 20% or $2,660 million in 1999 and 23% or $2,489 million in 1998. Revenue increases in both years were primarily due to sales volume growth of our in-line products and revenue generated from product alliances (alliance revenue).

Revenue growth in 1999 was not significantly impacted by foreign exchange. Total revenues grew by 26% in 1998 excluding the impact of foreign exchange.

Elements of Total Revenue Growth

Volume has been the major contributor to total revenue growth in each of the last three years.

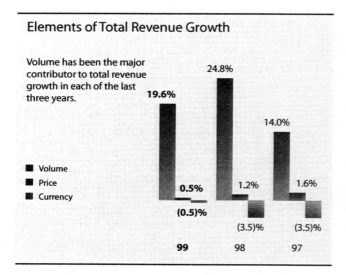

- ■ Volume
- ■ Price
- ■ Currency

Percentage Change in Total Revenues

	Total % Change	Analysis of % Change		
		Volume	Price	Currency
Pharmaceutical				
1999 vs. 1998	**21.5**	**21.1**	**0.5**	**(0.1)**
1998 vs. 1997	25.8	28.1	1.0	(3.3)
Animal Health				
1999 vs. 1998	**2.4**	**4.9**	**1.2**	**(3.7)**
1998 vs. 1997	(1.1)	0.6	2.4	(4.1)
Total				
1999 vs. 1998	**19.6**	**19.6**	**0.5**	**(0.5)**
1998 vs. 1997	22.5	24.8	1.2	(3.5)

Total Revenues by Business Segment

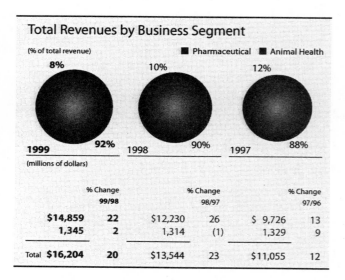

Pharmaceutical revenues increased 22% to $14,859 million in 1999 and 26% to $12,230 million in 1998. In the U.S. market, revenue growth was 21% in 1999 and 38% in 1998, while international growth was 22% in 1999 and 10% in 1998. The introduction of Viagra accounts for 12 percentage points of the 1998 U.S. growth. Pharmaceutical revenue growth in 1999 was not significantly impacted by foreign exchange. In 1998, pharmaceutical revenue grew 29% excluding the impact of foreign exchange. The currency impact on the 1998 revenue growth reflects the strengthening of the dollar relative to the Japanese yen, as well as several European and other Asian currencies.

In 1999, we had seven products, including alliance products, with sales to third parties in excess of $1 billion each. The five Pfizer-discovered products in this group—Norvasc, Zoloft, Zithromax, Viagra and Diflucan—grew at a combined annual rate of 18% in 1999 and are patent-protected well into this decade, or beyond.

Net Sales—Major Pharmaceutical Products

				% Increase	
(millions of dollars)	**1999**	1998	1997	**99/98**	98/97
Cardiovascular Diseases:	**$4,635**	$4,186	$3,806	**11**	10
Norvasc	**3,030**	2,575	2,217	**18**	16
Cardura	**794**	688	626	**15**	10
Infectious Diseases:	**3,145**	2,822	2,475	**11**	14
Zithromax	**1,333**	1,041	821	**28**	27
Diflucan	**1,002**	916	881	**9**	4
Central Nervous System Disorders:	**2,156**	1,924	1,553	**12**	24
Zoloft	**2,034**	1,836	1,507	**11**	22
Viagra	**1,033**	788	—	**31**	—
Allergy:	**557**	422	273	**32**	55
Zyrtec/Reactine	**552**	416	265	**33**	57

Certain prior year data have been reclassified to conform to the current year presentation.

In June 1999, the European Union's Committee for Proprietary Medicinal Products suspended the European Union (EU) licenses of the oral and intravenous formulations of our antibiotic Trovan for 12 months. In the rest of the world, including the U.S., the use of Trovan is limited to serious infections in institutionalized patients. As a result of these limitations, Trovan net sales declined to $86 million in 1999 from $160 million in 1998. See "Cost of sales" for a discussion of a charge recorded in 1999 to write off certain Trovan inventories.

Alliance revenue was $2,071 million in 1999, reflecting revenue associated with the co-promotion of Lipitor, Aricept and our new alliance product, Celebrex.

In February 1999, we launched Celebrex with G.D. Searle & Co. (Searle), the pharmaceutical division of Monsanto Company, which discovered and developed the drug. Celebrex is used for the relief of symptoms of adult rheumatoid arthritis and osteoarthritis. During 1999, Celebrex achieved total global sales of approximately $1.5 billion.

Together with our alliance partner, the Parke-Davis Division of Warner-Lambert, the company that discovered and developed Lipitor, we co-promote this product in most major world markets. During 1999, Lipitor achieved third-party sales of approximately $3.7 billion.

These alliances allow us to co-promote or license these products for sale in certain countries. Under the co-promotion agreements, these products are marketed and promoted with our alliance partners. We provide cash, staff and other resources to sell, market, promote and further develop these products. Revenue from co-promotion agreements is reported in the Statement of Income as *Alliance revenue*.

Certain alliance agreements include additional provisions that enable our product alliance partners the right to negotiate to co-promote certain specified Pfizer-discovered products.

Rebates under Medicaid and related state programs reduced revenues by $146 million in 1999, $150 million in 1998 and $99 million in 1997. The 1998 increase in rebates reflects growth of in-line products and the introduction in 1998 of two products—Trovan and Viagra. We also provided to the federal government legislatively mandated discounts of $95 million in 1999, $105 million in 1998 and $88 million in 1997. Performance-based contracts also provide rebates to several customers as a result of the increasing influence of managed care groups on the pricing of our products.

In the fourth quarter of 1999, we sold the Bain de Soleil sun care product line for $26 million in cash to Schering-Plough HealthCare Products, Inc. Proceeds from the sale approximated the total of the carrying value of net assets associated with this product line and selling costs. The sale of Bain de Soleil will not have a material impact on our future results of operations.

Animal Health net sales increased 2% to $1,345 million in 1999 and decreased 1% to $1,314 million in 1998. Excluding the impact of foreign exchange, net sales increased 6% in 1999 and 3% in 1998. The increase in net sales in 1999 was due to:
- the performance of the companion animal business partially offset by
- the continuing weakness in the livestock market in the U.S. and Europe
- the decision of the European Commission to ban certain antibiotic feed additives, including Stafac (virginiamycin) in the EU after June 30, 1999

We do not expect the ban on sales of virginiamycin to have a material effect on our future results of operations.

Sales of companion animal products increased by 30% in 1999 primarily due to the launch of Revolution and the growth of Rimadyl. Revolution was approved in the U.S. in July 1999 as the first and only topically applied medication for dogs and cats that is effective against heartworm, fleas and many other parasites. Rimadyl is a treatment for the relief of pain and inflammation associated with osteoarthritis in dogs.

Net sales decreased 1% in 1998 due to a weak livestock market in the U.S. and poor Asian economies.

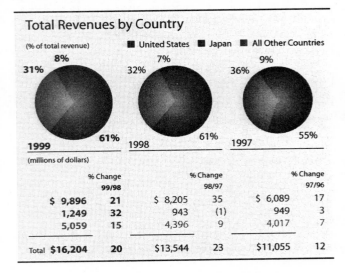

Total Revenues by Country

(% of total revenue)	United States	Japan	All Other Countries
1999	8% / 31% / 61%		
1998	7% / 32% / 61%		
1997	9% / 36% / 55%		

(millions of dollars)

	1999	% Change 99/98	1998	% Change 98/97	1997	% Change 97/96
	$ 9,896	21	$ 8,205	35	$ 6,089	17
	1,249	32	943	(1)	949	3
	5,059	15	4,396	9	4,017	7
Total	$16,204	20	$13,544	23	$11,055	12

Revenues were in excess of $100 million in each of 12 countries outside the U.S. in 1999. The U.S. was the only country to contribute more than 10% to total revenues.

Percentage Change in Geographic Total Revenues by Business Segment

	% Change in Total Revenues			
	U.S.		International	
	99/98	98/97	99/98	98/97
Pharmaceutical	21	38	22	10
Animal Health	14	3	(7)	(4)
Total	21	35	18	8

Product Developments

We continue to invest in R&D to provide future sources of revenue through the development of new products, as well as through additional uses for existing in-line and alliance products. Certain significant regulatory actions by, and filings pending with, the U.S. Food and Drug Administration (FDA) follow:

U.S. FDA Approvals

Product	Indication	Date Approved
Zoloft	Posttraumatic stress disorder (PTSD)	December 1999
Zoloft	Oral liquid dosage form	December 1999
Celebrex	Familial adenomatous polyposis (a rare and devastating hereditary disease that, left untreated, almost always leads to colorectal cancer)	December 1999
Tikosyn	Atrial fibrillation	October 1999

Zoloft is the first and only medicine to receive FDA approval for the treatment of PTSD.

We have developed a comprehensive program to educate institutions and health care professionals on the required in-hospital initiation and dosing regimen for Tikosyn. We expect to launch Tikosyn in the U.S. in the first quarter of 2000, and it will be available to those prescribers and hospitals that have participated in this educational program.

Pending U.S. New Drug Applications

Product	Indication	Date Filed
Relpax	Migraine headaches	October 1998
Zeldox	Psychotic disorders— intramuscular dosage form	December 1997
Zeldox	Psychotic disorders— oral dosage form	March 1997

In October 1999, we received an approvable letter from the FDA for Relpax for the treatment of migraines. Regulatory review is continuing in Europe.

We received a non-approvable letter from the FDA for Zeldox in 1998. Analysis and interpretation of the results of a recently completed study on the effects of Zeldox will be included in an amended New Drug Application, which we expect to file by midyear 2000.

Ongoing or planned clinical trials for additional uses and dosage forms for our currently marketed products include:

Product	Indication
Norvasc	Pediatric hypertension
Zithromax	Decrease cardiovascular risk in patients with atherosclerosis (a process in which fatty substances are deposited within blood vessels) caused by certain infections Treatment of mycobacterium avium complex Accelerated dosing regimen (three-day treatment)
Viagra	Female sexual arousal disorder
Zoloft	Pediatric depression Social phobia
Zyrtec	Decongestant formulation Pediatric
Lipitor	Broad cardiovascular-care clinical program
Aricept	Oral liquid dosage form
Celebrex	Sporadic adenomatous polyposis Pain

Together with Warner-Lambert, we are jointly exploring potential Lipitor line extensions and product combinations and other areas of mutual interest. This includes a program to develop a combination product that contains the cholesterol-lowering and antihypertensive medications in Lipitor and Norvasc—two of the world's most widely prescribed medicines.

Ongoing or planned clinical trials for new product development programs include:

Product	Indication
lasofoxifene	Prevention and treatment of osteoporosis Prevention of breast cancer Reduction of risk of coronary heart disease
Vfend (voriconazole)	Serious systemic fungal infections
darifenacin	Overactive bladder
inhaled insulin	Diabetes
valdecoxib (under co-development with Searle)	Osteoarthritis Rheumatoid arthritis Pain

Additional product development programs are in various stages of discovery.

In 1998, we entered into worldwide agreements with Aventis Pharma to manufacture insulin and co-develop and co-promote inhaled insulin. Under the agreements, Aventis Pharma and Pfizer will contribute expertise in the development and production of insulin products, as well as selling and marketing resources. We bring to the alliance our development of inhaled insulin from our collaboration with Inhale Therapeutic Systems, Inc. Together with Aventis Pharma we are building a new insulin manufacturing plant in Frankfurt, Germany, to support the product currently in development.

We have decided not to pursue further development of ezlopitant for the treatment of chemotherapy-induced nausea and vomiting in cancer patients, as well as Alond for the treatment of diabetic neuropathy.

Costs and Expenses

In 1999, we substantially completed the actions under the restructuring plans announced in 1998.

In 1998, we recorded charges for the restructuring in addition to charges for certain asset impairments. These pre-tax charges were recorded in the 1998 Statement of Income as follows:

(millions of dollars)	Total	COS*	SI&A*	R&D	OD*
Restructuring charges	$177	$68	$17	$1	$ 91
Asset impairments	213	18	—	—	195

*COS—Cost of sales; SI&A—Selling, informational and administrative expenses; OD— Other deductions—net.

The components of the 1998 restructuring charges follow:

(millions of dollars)	Charges in 1998	Utilization		
		1998	1999	Beyond
Property, plant and equipment	$ 49	$ 49	$ —	$ —
Write-down of intangibles	44	44	—	—
Employee termination costs	40	12	28	—
Other	44	11	17	16
Total	$177	$116	$45	$16

As a result of the restructuring, our workforce was reduced by approximately 500 manufacturing, sales and corporate personnel. In 1998, restructuring charges of $90 million are reflected in the pharmaceutical segment and $87 million are in the animal health segment.

In 1998, we recorded an impairment charge of $110 million in the pharmaceutical segment to adjust intangible asset values, primarily goodwill and trademarks, related to consumer health care product lines. These charges resulted from significant changes in the marketplace and a revision of our strategies.

As noted in our discussion of revenues, our animal health antibiotic feed additive Stafac was banned throughout the EU, resulting in 1998 asset impairment charges of $103 million ($85 million to adjust intangible asset values, primarily goodwill and trademarks, and $18 million to adjust the carrying value of machinery and equipment in the pharmaceutical segment).

In 1999, revenues declined approximately $41 million as a result of exiting certain product lines. In 1999, as a result of the restructuring activities and the asset impairments, we realized cost savings of approximately $39 million and a reduction in amortization and depreciation expense of approximately $12 million.

Cost of sales increased 21% in 1999 and 18% in 1998. Based on our evaluation of the actions noted in our discussion of revenues, we determined that it was unlikely that certain Trovan inventories of finished goods, bulk, work-in-process and raw materials will be used. Accordingly, in the third quarter of 1999, we recorded a charge of $310 million in *Cost of sales* to write off Trovan inventories in excess of the amount required to support expected sales. Also included in *Cost of sales* for 1999 is a benefit of $6.6 million related to the change in accounting for the cost of inventories from the "Last-in, first-out" method to the "First-in, first-out" method. Excluding the Trovan inventory charge and the benefit related to the accounting change for inventories in 1999 and the asset impairments and restructuring charges in 1998, cost of sales increased 11%, comparable to the increase in 1999 net sales.

Excluding the 1998 asset impairments and restructuring charges, cost of sales increased 13% in 1998 as compared to an increase in net sales of 18%.

SI&A increased 14% in 1999 and 27% in 1998. These increases reflect support for previously introduced products and new products. Such support included substantial global investments, begun in 1998, in our pharmaceutical sales force, including the creation of a new U.S. primary-care sales force and a new U.S. specialty sales force dedicated to rheumatology. In addition, personnel increases in other specialty sales forces in the U.S. and the expansion of international sales forces contributed to the increase in SI&A. Our past investments in SI&A are enabling us to maximize the financial return realized from our products.

R&D increased 22% in 1999 and 26% in 1998. These expenditures were necessary to support the advancement of potential drug candidates in all stages of development (from initial discovery through final regulatory approval). In 2000, we expect total R&D spending to be about $3.2 billion. See "Proposed Merger with Warner-Lambert Company" for the expected R&D spending in 2000 of a combined Pfizer/Warner-Lambert entity.

Other deductions—net decreased 90% in 1999 due to the absence of certain significant charges recorded in 1998 of $883 million.

Other deductions—net increased substantially in 1998 primarily due to:

- asset impairments—$195 million
- restructuring charges—$91 million
- co-promotion payments to Searle for rights to Celebrex—$240 million
- a contribution to The Pfizer Foundation—$300 million
- legal settlements involving the brand-name prescription drug antitrust litigation—$57 million

partially offset by

- an increase in interest income on the investment of cash generated from operations and the divestiture of MTG
- foreign exchange effects

Our overall **effective tax rate** was 28.1% in 1999 and 35.4% in 1998. This decrease was due mainly to the 1998 gain on the disposal of MTG being recognized in jurisdictions with higher tax rates.

The effective tax rate for continuing operations was 28.0% in 1999 and 24.8% in 1998. Significant charges in both 1999 and 1998 were recorded in jurisdictions with higher tax rates. However, the level of these charges was greater in 1998 than in 1999. Excluding these charges in 1999 and 1998, the effective tax rate was 28.4% in 1999 and 28.0% in 1998. This increase in 1999 was primarily due to the mix of income by country.

We have received and are protesting assessments from the Belgian tax authorities. For additional details, see note 9, "Taxes on Income," beginning on page 49.

Discontinued Operations

In 1999, we agreed to pay a fine of $20 million to settle antitrust charges involving our former Food Science Group. This charge is reflected in *Discontinued operations — net of tax.* For additional details, see note 18, "Litigation," beginning on page 54.

During 1998, we exited the medical devices business with the sale of our remaining MTG businesses:

- Howmedica to Stryker Corporation in December for $1.65 billion in cash
- Schneider to Boston Scientific Corporation in September for $2.1 billion in cash
- American Medical Systems to E.M. Warburg, Pincus & Co., LLC, in September for $130 million in cash
- Valleylab to U.S. Surgical Corporation in January for $425 million in cash

The net proceeds from these divestitures were used for general corporate purposes, including the repayment of commercial paper borrowings. Net income of these businesses up to the date of their divestiture and divestiture gains are included in *Discontinued operations — net of tax.*

Net Income

Net income for 1999 decreased 5% from 1998. Diluted earnings per share were $.82 and decreased by 4% from 1998. Excluding the impact of the 1999 Trovan inventory charge and certain significant charges and discontinued operations in 1998, net income increased by 29% in 1999 over 1998. On that same basis, diluted earnings per share were $.87 in 1999 and increased by 30% over 1998. The 1998 pre-tax significant charges related to:

- asset impairments — $213 million
- restructuring charges — $177 million
- co-promotion payments to Searle — $240 million
- contribution to The Pfizer Foundation — $300 million
- other, which is primarily related to legal settlements — $126 million

Financial Condition, Liquidity and Capital Resources

Our net financial asset position as of December 31 was as follows:

(millions of dollars)	1999	1998	1997
Financial assets*	$6,436	$5,835	$3,034
Short- and long-term debt	5,526	3,256	2,976
Net financial assets	$ 910	$2,579	$ 58

Consists of cash and cash equivalents, short-term loans and investments, and long-term loans and investments.

Selected Measures of Liquidity and Capital Resources

	1999	1998	1997
Cash and cash equivalents and short-term loans and investments (millions of dollars)*	$4,715	$4,079	$1,704
Working capital (millions of dollars)	2,006	2,739	2,448
Current ratio	1.22:1	1.38:1	1.49:1
Shareholders' equity per common share**	$ 2.36	$ 2.33	$ 2.10

Cash is managed jurisdictionally and is not always available to be used in every location throughout the world. When necessary, we utilize short-term borrowings for various corporate purposes.

**Represents shareholders' equity divided by the actual number of common shares outstanding (which excludes treasury shares and those held by the employee benefit trusts).*

The decrease in working capital from 1998 to 1999 was primarily due to the following:

- Decrease in *Inventories* — due to the writeoff of Trovan inventory
- Increase in *Short-term borrowings* — primarily to fund common stock purchases of $2.5 billion

offset by

- Net increase in *Cash and cash equivalents* and *Short-term investments* — mainly from profits earned overseas
- Increase in *Accounts receivable* — resulting from growth in sales volume and higher alliance revenue receivables due to sales growth of alliance products and the launch of Celebrex in February 1999
- Decrease in *Income taxes payable*

The increase in working capital from 1997 to 1998 was primarily due to the following:

- Increase in *Cash and cash equivalents* and *Short-term investments*—due to the receipt of cash from the MTG divestiture
- Increase in *Accounts receivable*—due to the alliance revenue receivables and growth in sales volume
- Increase in *Inventories*—due to higher pharmaceutical inventory levels as a result of new products

offset by

- Decrease in *Net assets of discontinued operations*—due to the sale of the MTG businesses
- Increase in *Short-term borrowings*—due to an increase in funding for common stock purchases at a higher average price net of repayments made with cash received from the MTG divestiture
- Increase in *Dividends payable*—related to the first-quarter 1999 dividend declared in December 1998
- Increase in *Income taxes payable*—primarily due to changes in operations and the divestiture of the MTG businesses
- Increase in *Other current liabilities*—primarily due to accrued charges associated with the divestiture of the MTG businesses and our plan to exit certain product lines

The decline in the current ratio from 1998 to 1999 was primarily due to higher short-term borrowings due to an increase in funding for common stock purchases. The increase in shareholders' equity per common share in 1998 was primarily due to growth in net income.

Summary of Cash Flows

(millions of dollars)	1999	1998	1997
Cash provided by/(used in):			
Operating activities	$ 3,076	$ 3,282	$ 1,580
Investing activities	(2,768)	(335)	(963)
Financing activities	(1,127)	(2,277)	(981)
Discontinued operations	(20)	4	118
Effect of exchange-rate changes on cash and cash equivalents	26	1	(27)
Net (decrease)/increase in cash and cash equivalents	$ (813)	$ 675	$ (273)

Net cash provided by operating activities decreased in 1999 primarily due to:

- higher receivable levels related to increased sales and alliance revenue
- higher taxes paid

reduced by

- higher income from continuing operations

Net cash provided by operating activities increased in 1998 primarily due to:

- higher taxes payable associated with sales growth of existing and new products as well as the MTG

divestitures, partially offset by tax benefits associated with charges for asset impairment, restructuring, co-promotion payments to Searle and the contribution to The Pfizer Foundation
- higher compensation related accruals

reduced by

- higher receivable and inventory levels related to new products

Net cash used in investing activities in 1999 changed primarily due to:

- the absence of proceeds from the sale of MTG which occurred in 1998
- increased purchases of property, plant and equipment in 1999

Net cash used in investing activities decreased in 1998 primarily due to:

- proceeds from the sale of the MTG businesses, some of which accounts for our increase in short-term investments

reduced by

- increased long-term investments
- increased purchases of property, plant and equipment

Net cash used in financing activities decreased in 1999 primarily due to:

- increased short-term borrowings for common stock purchases

reduced by

- higher dividend payments to our shareholders

Net cash used in financing activities increased in 1998 primarily due to:

- the increase in common stock purchases at a higher average price
- higher dividend payments to our shareholders

reduced by

- more cash received from employee stock option exercises

Under the current share-purchase program begun in September 1998, we are authorized to purchase up to $5 billion of our common stock. In 1999, we purchased approximately 65.6 million shares of our common stock in the open market for approximately $2.5 billion. Since the beginning of this program, we have purchased 80.4 million shares of our common stock for approximately $3 billion. In September 1998, we completed a program under which we purchased 79.2 million shares of our common stock at a total cost of $2 billion. Purchased shares are available for general corporate purposes.

We have available lines of credit and revolving-credit agreements with a select group of banks and other financial intermediaries. Major unused lines of credit totaled approximately $1.5 billion at December 31, 1999.

Our short-term debt has been rated P1 by Moody's Investors Services (Moody's) and A-1+ by Standard and Poor's (S&P). Also, our long-term debt has been rated Aaa by Moody's and AAA by S&P for the past 14 years. Moody's and S&P are the major corporate debt-rating organizations and these are their highest ratings.

Cash Dividends Paid Per Common Share

The 1999 cash dividends paid represented the 32nd consecutive year of dividend increases.

(dollars)

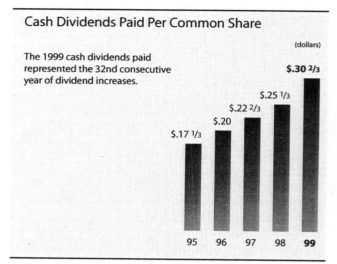

$.17 1/3	$.20	$.22 2/3	$.25 1/3	$.30 2/3
95	96	97	98	99

Dividends on Common Stock

Our dividend payout ratio, which represents cash dividends paid per common share divided by diluted earnings per common share, was approximately 37% in 1999, 30% in 1998 and 40% in 1997. In 1999, excluding the effect on net income of the Trovan inventory charge, the dividend payout ratio was approximately 35%. In 1998, excluding the effects on net income of discontinued operations and charges for asset impairment, restructuring, co-promotion payments to Searle and the contribution to The Pfizer Foundation, the dividend payout ratio was 38%. In December 1999, the Board of Directors declared a first-quarter 2000 dividend of $.09. The first-quarter 2000 cash dividend will mark the 33rd consecutive year of quarterly dividend increases.

Banking Operation

Our international banking operation, Pfizer International Bank Europe (PIBE), operates under a full banking license from the Central Bank of Ireland. The results of its operations are included in *Other deductions — net.*

PIBE extends credit to financially strong borrowers, largely through U.S. dollar loans made primarily for short and medium terms, with floating interest rates. Generally, loans are made on an unsecured basis. When deemed appropriate, guarantees and certain covenants may be obtained as a condition to the extension of credit.

To reduce credit risk, PIBE has established credit approval guidelines, borrowing limits and monitoring procedures. Credit risk is further reduced through an active policy of diversification with respect to borrower, industry and

geographic location. PIBE continues to have S&P's highest short-term rating of A-1+.

The net income of PIBE is affected by changes in market interest rates because of repricing and maturity mismatches between its interest-sensitive assets and liabilities. PIBE is currently asset sensitive (more assets than liabilities repricing in a given period) and, therefore, we expect that in an environment of increasing interest rates, net income would increase. PIBE's asset and liability management reflects its liquidity, interest-rate outlook and general market conditions.

For additional details regarding our banking operation, see note 3, "Financial Subsidiaries," beginning on page 44.

Forward-Looking Information and Factors That May Affect Future Results

The Securities and Exchange Commission encourages companies to disclose forward-looking information so that investors can better understand a company's future prospects and make informed investment decisions. This annual report and other written and oral statements that we make from time to time contain such forward-looking statements that set out anticipated results based on management's plans and assumptions. We have tried, wherever possible, to identify such statements by using words such as "anticipate," "estimate," "expects," "projects," "intends," "plans," "believes" and words and terms of similar substance in connection with any discussion of future operating or financial performance.

We cannot guarantee that any forward-looking statement will be realized, although we believe we have been prudent in our plans and assumptions. Achievement of future results is subject to risks, uncertainties and inaccurate assumptions. Should known or unknown risks or uncertainties materialize, or should underlying assumptions prove inaccurate, actual results could vary materially from those anticipated, estimated or projected. Investors should bear this in mind as they consider forward-looking statements.

We undertake no obligation to publicly update forward-looking statements, whether as a result of new information, future events or otherwise.

Certain risks, uncertainties and assumptions are discussed here and under the heading entitled "Cautionary Factors That May Affect Future Results" in Item 1 of our annual report on Form 10-K for the year ended December 31, 1999, which will be filed at the end of March 2000.

Prior to the filing of Form 10-K, you should refer to the discussion under the same heading in our quarterly report on Form 10-Q for the quarter ended October 3, 1999, and to the extent incorporated by reference therein, in our Form 10-K filing for 1998. This discussion of potential risks and uncertainties is by no means complete but is designed to highlight important factors that may impact our outlook.

Competition and the Health Care Environment

In the U.S., many pharmaceutical products are subject to increasing pricing pressures, which could be significantly impacted by the current national debate over Medicare reform.

If the Medicare program provided outpatient pharmaceutical coverage for its beneficiaries, the federal government, through its enormous purchasing power under the program, could demand discounts from pharmaceutical companies that may implicitly create price controls on prescription drugs. On the other hand, a Medicare drug reimbursement provision may increase the volume of pharmaceutical drug purchases, offsetting at least in part these potential price discounts. In addition, managed care organizations, institutions and other government agencies continue to seek price discounts. Government efforts to reduce Medicare and Medicaid expenses are expected to increase the use of managed care organizations. This may result in managed care influencing prescription decisions for a larger segment of the population. International operations are also subject to price and market regulations. As a result, it is expected that pressures on pricing and operating results will continue.

Financial Risk Management

The overall objective of our financial risk management program is to seek a reduction in the potential negative earnings effects from changes in foreign exchange and interest rates arising in our business activities. We manage these financial exposures through operational means and by using various financial instruments. These practices may change as economic conditions change.

Foreign Exchange Risk

A significant portion of our revenues and earnings are exposed to changes in foreign exchange rates. Where practical, we seek to relate expected local currency revenues with local currency costs and local currency assets with local currency liabilities. Generally, we do not use financial instruments for trading activities.

Foreign exchange risk is also managed through the use of foreign currency forward-exchange contracts. These contracts are used to offset the potential earnings effects from short-term foreign currency assets and liabilities that arise during operations. For additional details on foreign exchange exposures, see note 4-D, "Derivative Financial Instruments— Instruments Outstanding," on page 47.

In addition, foreign currency put options are purchased to reduce a portion of the potential negative effects on earnings related to certain of our significant anticipated intercompany inventory purchases for up to one year. These purchased options hedge Japanese yen versus the U.S. dollar.

Also, under certain market conditions, we protect against possible declines in the reported net assets of our subsidiaries in Japan and in countries that are a member of the European Monetary Union. We do this through currency swaps and borrowing in Japanese yen and borrowing in euros.

Our financial instrument holdings at year-end were analyzed to determine their sensitivity to foreign exchange rate changes. The fair values of these instruments were determined as follows:

- forward-exchange contracts and currency swaps—net present values
- purchased foreign currency options—foreign exchange option pricing model

- foreign receivables, payables, debt and loans—changes in exchange rates

In our sensitivity analysis, we assumed that the change in one currency's rate relative to the U.S. dollar would not have an effect on other currencies' rates relative to the U.S. dollar. All other factors were held constant.

If there were an adverse change in foreign exchange rates of 10%, the expected effect on net income related to our financial instruments would be immaterial. For additional details, see note 4-D, "Derivative Financial Instruments— Accounting Policies," on page 46.

Interest Rate Risk

Our U.S. dollar interest-bearing investments, loans and borrowings are subject to interest rate risk. We invest and borrow primarily on a short-term or variable-rate basis. We are also subject to interest rate risk on Japanese yen and on euro short-term borrowings. Under certain market conditions, interest rate swap contracts are used to adjust interest-sensitive assets and liabilities.

Our financial instrument holdings at year-end were analyzed to determine their sensitivity to interest rate changes. The fair values of these instruments were determined by net present values.

In our sensitivity analysis, we used the same change in interest rate for all maturities. All other factors were held constant. If interest rates increased by 10%, the expected effect on net income related to our financial instruments would be immaterial.

International Markets

Thirty-nine percent of our 1999 revenues arise from international operations and we expect revenue and net income growth in 2000 to be impacted by changes in foreign exchange rates.

Revenues from Asia comprised approximately 11% of total revenues in 1999, including 8% from Japan.

European Currency

A new European currency (euro) was introduced in January 1999 to replace the separate currencies of 11 individual countries. The major changes during its first year of existence have occurred in the banking and financial sectors. The impact at the commercial and retail level has been limited but is expected to increase during the next two years through December 31, 2001, when the separate currencies will cease to exist. We are modifying systems and commercial arrangements to deal with the new currency, including the availability of dual currency processes to permit transactions to be denominated in the separate currencies, as well as the euro. The cost of this effort is not expected to have a material effect on our businesses or results of operations. We continue to evaluate the economic and operational impact of the euro, including its impact on competition, pricing and foreign currency exchange risks. There is no guarantee, however, that all problems have been foreseen and corrected, or that no material disruption will occur in our businesses.

Tax Legislation

Pursuant to the Small Jobs Protection Act of 1996 (the Act), Section 936 of the Internal Revenue Code (the U.S. possessions corporation income tax credit) was repealed for tax years beginning after December 31, 1995. The Act allows us to continue using the credit against the tax arising from manufacturing income earned in a U.S. possession for an additional 10-year period. The amount of manufacturing income eligible for the credit during this additional period is subject to a cap based on income earned prior to 1996 in the U.S. possession. This 10-year extension period does not apply to investment income earned in a U.S. possession, the credit on which expired as of July 1, 1996. The Act does not affect the amendments made to Section 936 by the 1993 Omnibus Budget Reconciliation Act, which provided for a five-year phase-down of the U.S. possession tax credit from 100% to 40%. In addition, the Act permitted the extension of the R&D tax credit through June 30, 1998. In 1998, this credit was again extended to June 30, 1999, and in 1999, it was further extended to June 30, 2004.

Recently Issued Accounting Standards

In June 1999, the Financial Accounting Standards Board issued Statement of Financial Accounting Standards (SFAS) No. 137, *Accounting for Derivative Instruments and Hedging Activities—Deferral of the Effective Date of FASB Statement No. 133.* This pronouncement requires us to adopt SFAS No. 133, *Accounting for Derivative Instruments and Hedging Activities,* on January 1, 2001. SFAS No. 133 requires a company to recognize all derivative instruments as assets or liabilities in its balance sheet and measure them at fair value. We do not expect the adoption of SFAS No. 133 to have a material impact on our financial position, results of operations or cash flows.

Year 2000

We have not experienced any operational problems as a result of Year 2000 issues, and Year 2000 had no material effect on our revenues. Although the transition from 1999 to 2000 did not adversely impact our company, there can be no assurances that we will not experience any negative effects or disruptions in our businesses in the future as a result of Year 2000 issues.

The total cost of our Year 2000 Program was $130 million, of which we incurred $94 million in 1999, $31 million in 1998 and $5 million in 1997. These costs were expensed as incurred, except for capitalizable hardware of approximately $8 million in 1999, $4 million in 1998 and $1 million in 1997 and were funded through operating cash flows. Such costs did not include normal system upgrades and replacements. Immaterial costs may be incurred in 2000 to address remaining non-critical Year 2000 issues.

Litigation, Tax and Environmental Matters

Claims have been brought against us and our subsidiaries for various legal and tax matters. In addition, our operations are subject to international, federal, state and local environmental laws and regulations. It is possible that our cash flows and results of operations could be affected by the one-time impact of the resolution of these contingencies. We believe that the ultimate disposition of these matters to the extent not previously provided for will not have a material impact on our financial condition, results of operations or cash flows, except where specifically commented on in note 18, "Litigation," beginning on page 54 and note 9, "Taxes on Income," beginning on page 49.

Management's Report

We prepared and are responsible for the financial statements that appear on pages 39 to 61. These financial statements are in conformity with generally accepted accounting principles and, therefore, include amounts based on informed judgments and estimates. We also accept responsibility for the preparation of other financial information that is included in this document.

We have designed a system of internal control to:
- safeguard the Company's assets,
- ensure that transactions are properly authorized, and
- provide reasonable assurance, at reasonable cost, of the integrity, objectivity and reliability of the financial information.

An effective internal control system has inherent limitations no matter how well designed and, therefore, can provide only reasonable assurance with respect to financial statement preparation. The system is built on a business ethics policy that requires all employees to maintain the highest ethical standards in conducting Company affairs. Our system of internal control includes:
- careful selection, training and development of financial managers,
- an organizational structure that segregates responsibilities,
- a communications program which ensures that the Company's policies and procedures are well understood throughout the organization, and
- an extensive program of internal audits, with prompt follow-up, including reviews of separate operations and functions around the world.

112

Our independent certified public accountants, KPMG LLP, have audited the annual financial statements in accordance with generally accepted auditing standards. The independent auditors' report expresses an informed judgment as to the fair presentation of the Company's reported operating results, financial position and cash flows. Their judgment is based on the results of auditing procedures performed and such other tests that they deemed necessary, including their consideration of our internal control structure.

We consider and take appropriate action on recommendations made by KPMG LLP and our internal auditors. We believe that our system of internal control is effective and adequate to accomplish the objectives discussed above.

W. C. Steere, Jr., *Principal Executive Officer*

D. L. Shedlarz, *Principal Financial Officer*

L. V. Cangialosi, *Principal Accounting Officer*
February 14, 2000

Audit Committee's Report

The Audit Committee reviews the Company's financial reporting process on behalf of the Board of Directors. Management has the primary responsibility for the financial statements and the reporting process, including the system of internal controls. In this context, the Committee has met and held discussions with management and the independent auditors. Management represented to the Committee that the Company's consolidated financial statements were prepared in accordance with generally accepted accounting principles, and the Committee has reviewed and discussed the consolidated financial statements with management and the independent auditors. The Committee discussed with the independent auditors matters required to be discussed by Statement of Auditing Standards No. 61 (Communication With Audit Committees). In addition, the Committee has discussed with the independent auditors, the auditors' independence from the Company and its management, including the matters in the written disclosures required by the Independence Standards Board Standard No. 1 (Independence Discussions with Audit Committees). The Committee discussed with the Company's internal and independent auditors the overall scope and plans for their respective audits. The Committee meets with the internal and independent auditors, with and without

management present, to discuss the results of their examinations, the evaluations of the Company's internal controls, and the overall quality of the Company's financial reporting. In reliance on the reviews and discussions referred to above, the Committee recommended to the Board of Directors, and the Board has approved, that the audited financial statements be included in the Company's Annual Report on Form 10-K for the year ended December 31, 1999, for filing with the Securities and Exchange Commission. The Committee and the Board also have recommended, subject to shareholder approval, the selection of the Company's independent auditors.

G. B. Harvey, *Chair, Audit Committee*
February 14, 2000

Independent Auditors' Report

To the Shareholders and Board of Directors of Pfizer Inc:

We have audited the accompanying consolidated balance sheets of Pfizer Inc and subsidiary companies as of December 31, 1999, 1998 and 1997 and the related consolidated statements of income, shareholders' equity and cash flows for each of the years then ended. These consolidated financial statements are the responsibility of the Company's management. Our responsibility is to express an opinion on these consolidated financial statements based on our audits.

We conducted our audits in accordance with generally accepted auditing standards. Those standards require that we plan and perform the audit to obtain reasonable assurance about whether the consolidated financial statements are free of material misstatement. An audit includes examining, on a test basis, evidence supporting the amounts and disclosures in the consolidated financial statements. An audit also includes assessing the accounting principles used and significant estimates made by management, as well as evaluating the overall consolidated financial statement presentation. We believe that our audits provide a reasonable basis for our opinion.

In our opinion, the consolidated financial statements referred to above present fairly, in all material respects, the financial position of Pfizer Inc and subsidiary companies at December 31, 1999, 1998 and 1997, and the results of their operations and their cash flows for each of the years then ended, in conformity with generally accepted accounting principles.

New York, NY
February 14, 2000

Consolidated Statement of Income

(millions, except per share data)	Year ended December 31		
	1999	1998	1997
Net sales	$14,133	$12,677	$10,739
Alliance revenue	2,071	867	316
Total revenues	16,204	13,544	11,055
Costs and expenses:			
Cost of sales	2,528	2,094	1,776
Selling, informational and administrative expenses	6,351	5,568	4,401
Research and development expenses	2,776	2,279	1,805
Other deductions—net	101	1,009	206
Income from continuing operations before provision for taxes on income and minority interests	4,448	2,594	2,867
Provision for taxes on income	1,244	642	775
Minority interests	5	2	10
Income from continuing operations	3,199	1,950	2,082
Discontinued operations—net of tax	(20)	1,401	131
Net income	$ 3,179	$ 3,351	$ 2,213
Earnings per common share—basic			
Income from continuing operations	$ .85	$ .51	$ .55
Discontinued operations—net of tax	(.01)	.37	.04
Net income	$ .84	$ .88	$ .59
Earnings per common share—diluted			
Income from continuing operations	$ .82	$ .49	$ .53
Discontinued operations—net of tax	—	.36	.04
Net income	$ .82	$ .85	$ .57
Weighted average shares — basic	3,775	3,789	3,771
Weighted average shares — diluted	3,884	3,945	3,909

See Notes to Consolidated Financial Statements which are an integral part of these statements.

Consolidated Balance Sheet

(millions, except per share data)	December 31		
	1999	1998	1997
Assets			
Current Assets			
Cash and cash equivalents	$ 739	$ 1,552	$ 877
Short-term investments	3,703	2,377	712
Accounts receivable, less allowance for doubtful accounts:			
1999—$68; 1998—$67; 1997—$35	3,864	2,914	2,220
Short-term loans	273	150	115
Inventories			
Finished goods	650	697	442
Work in process	711	890	808
Raw materials and supplies	293	241	211
Total inventories	1,654	1,828	1,461
Prepaid expenses and taxes	958	1,110	637
Net assets of discontinued operations	—	—	1,420
Total current assets	11,191	9,931	7,442
Long-term loans and investments	1,721	1,756	1,330
Property, plant and equipment, less accumulated depreciation	5,343	4,415	3,793
Goodwill, less accumulated amortization:			
1999—$129; 1998—$109; 1997—$90	763	813	989
Other assets, deferred taxes and deferred charges	1,556	1,387	1,437
Total assets	$20,574	$18,302	$14,991
Liabilities and Shareholders' Equity			
Current Liabilities			
Short-term borrowings, including current portion of long-term debt	$ 5,001	$ 2,729	$ 2,251
Accounts payable	951	971	660
Dividends payable	349	285	—
Income taxes payable	869	1,162	729
Accrued compensation and related items	669	614	456
Other current liabilities	1,346	1,431	898
Total current liabilities	9,185	7,192	4,994
Long-term debt	525	527	725
Postretirement benefit obligation other than pension plans	346	359	394
Deferred taxes on income	301	197	127
Other noncurrent liabilities	1,330	1,217	818
Total liabilities	11,687	9,492	7,058
Shareholders' Equity			
Preferred stock, without par value; 12 shares authorized, none issued	—	—	—
Common stock, $.05 par value; 9,000 shares authorized;			
issued: 1999—4,260; 1998—4,222; 1997—4,165	213	210	207
Additional paid-in capital	5,416	5,506	3,101
Retained earnings	13,396	11,439	9,349
Accumulated other comprehensive expense	(399)	(234)	(85)
Employee benefit trusts	(2,888)	(4,200)	(2,646)
Treasury stock, at cost:			
1999—413; 1998—339; 1997—283	(6,851)	(3,911)	(1,993)
Total shareholders' equity	8,887	8,810	7,933
Total liabilities and shareholders' equity	$20,574	$18,302	$14,991

See Notes to Consolidated Financial Statements which are an integral part of these statements.

Consolidated Statement of Shareholders' Equity

(millions)	Common Stock Shares	Common Stock Par Value	Additional Paid-In Capital	Employee Benefit Trusts Shares	Employee Benefit Trusts Fair Value	Treasury Stock Shares	Treasury Stock Cost	Retained Earnings	Accum. Other Comprehensive Inc./(Exp.)	Total
Balance January 1, 1997	1,378	$ 69	$1,693	(36)	$(1,488)	(87)	$(1,482)	$ 8,017	$ 145	$6,954
Restatement for the 1999 stock split	2,756	138	(138)	(72)	—	(175)	—	—	—	—
Balance January 1, 1997, as restated	4,134	207	1,555	(108)	(1,488)	(262)	(1,482)	8,017	145	6,954
Comprehensive income:										
Net income								2,213		2,213
Other comprehensive expense— net of tax:										
Currency translation adjustment									(253)	(253)
Net unrealized gain on available-for-sale securities									20	20
Minimum pension liability									3	3
Total other comprehensive expense									(230)	(230)
Total comprehensive income										1,983
Cash dividends declared								(881)		(881)
Stock option transactions	29	—	343			13	68			411
Purchases of common stock						(34)	(586)			(586)
Employee benefit trusts transactions—net			1,177	1	(1,158)	—	7			26
Other	2	—	26							26
Balance December 31, 1997	4,165	207	3,101	(107)	(2,646)	(283)	(1,993)	9,349	(85)	7,933
Comprehensive income:										
Net income								3,351		3,351
Other comprehensive expense— net of tax:										
Currency translation adjustment									(74)	(74)
Net unrealized loss on available-for-sale securities									(2)	(2)
Minimum pension liability									(73)	(73)
Total other comprehensive expense									(149)	(149)
Total comprehensive income										3,202
Cash dividends declared								(1,261)		(1,261)
Stock option transactions	55	3	745			—	(18)			730
Purchases of common stock						(58)	(1,912)			(1,912)
Employee benefit trusts transactions—net			1,633	5	(1,554)	2	12			91
Other	2	—	27							27
Balance December 31, 1998	4,222	210	5,506	(102)	(4,200)	(339)	(3,911)	11,439	(234)	8,810
Comprehensive income:										
Net income								3,179		3,179
Other comprehensive expense— net of tax:										
Currency translation adjustment									(222)	(222)
Net unrealized gain on available-for-sale securities									81	81
Minimum pension liability									(24)	(24)
Total other comprehensive expense									(165)	(165)
Total comprehensive income										3,014
Cash dividends declared								(1,222)		(1,222)
Stock option transactions	35	3	526			—	(16)			513
Purchases of common stock						(66)	(2,500)			(2,500)
Employee benefit trusts transactions—net			(735)	13	1,312	(8)	(424)			153
Other	3	—	119							119
Balance December 31, 1999	4,260	$213	$5,416	(89)	$(2,888)	(413)	$(6,851)	$13,396	$(399)	$8,887

See Notes to Consolidated Financial Statements which are an integral part of these statements.

Consolidated Statement of Cash Flows

(millions of dollars)	Year ended December 31		
	1999	1998	1997
Operating Activities			
Income from continuing operations	$ 3,199	$ 1,950	$2,082
Adjustments to reconcile income from continuing operations to net cash provided by operating activities:			
Depreciation and amortization	542	489	428
Trovan inventory write-off	310	—	—
Asset impairments and restructuring charges	—	323	—
Deferred taxes and other	286	22	83
Changes in assets and liabilities, net of effect of businesses divested:			
Accounts receivable	(978)	(765)	(477)
Inventories	(240)	(439)	(350)
Prepaid and other assets	68	(350)	(128)
Accounts payable and accrued liabilities	61	628	(63)
Income taxes payable	(179)	951	(54)
Other deferred items	7	473	59
Net cash provided by operating activities	3,076	3,282	1,580
Investing Activities			
Purchases of property, plant and equipment	(1,561)	(1,198)	(878)
Proceeds from disposals of property, plant and equipment	71	79	47
Purchases net of maturities of short-term investments	(8,633)	(5,845)	(221)
Proceeds from redemptions of short-term investments	7,309	4,209	28
Proceeds from sales of businesses—net	26	3,059	21
Purchases of long-term investments	(322)	(752)	(74)
Other investing activities	342	113	114
Net cash used in investing activities	(2,768)	(335)	(963)
Financing Activities			
Repayments of long-term debt	(4)	(202)	(269)
Increase in short-term debt—net	2,083	402	325
Proceeds from stock issuances	62	—	—
Purchases of common stock	(2,500)	(1,912)	(586)
Cash dividends paid	(1,148)	(976)	(881)
Stock option transactions and other	380	411	430
Net cash used in financing activities	(1,127)	(2,277)	(981)
Net cash (used in)/provided by discontinued operations	(20)	4	118
Effect of exchange-rate changes on cash and cash equivalents	26	1	(27)
Net (decrease)/increase in cash and cash equivalents	(813)	675	(273)
Cash and cash equivalents at beginning of year	1,552	877	1,150
Cash and cash equivalents at end of year	$ 739	$ 1,552	$ 877
Supplemental Cash Flow Information			
Cash paid during the period for:			
Income taxes	$ 1,293	$ 1,073	$ 809
Interest	238	155	149

See Notes to Consolidated Financial Statements which are an integral part of these statements.

Notes to Consolidated Financial Statements

1 Significant Accounting Policies

A—Consolidation and Basis of Presentation

The consolidated financial statements include the parent company and all significant subsidiaries, including those operating outside the U.S. Balance sheet amounts for the international operations are as of November 30 of each year and income statement amounts are for the full-year periods ending on the same date. Substantially all unremitted earnings of international subsidiaries are free of legal and contractual restrictions. All significant transactions among our businesses have been eliminated. We made certain reclassifications to the 1998 and 1997 financial statements to conform to the 1999 presentation.

In preparing the financial statements, we must use some estimates and assumptions that may affect reported amounts and disclosures. Estimates are used when accounting for depreciation, amortization, employee benefits and asset valuation allowances. We are also subject to risks and uncertainties that may cause actual results to differ from estimated results, such as changes in the health care environment, competition, foreign exchange and legislation. "Forward-Looking Information and Factors That May Affect Future Results," beginning on page 35, discusses these and other uncertainties.

B—Cash Equivalents

Cash equivalents include items almost as liquid as cash, such as certificates of deposit and time deposits with maturity periods of three months or less when purchased. If items meeting this definition are part of a larger investment pool, we classify them as *Short-term investments.*

C—Inventories

We value inventories at cost or fair value, if lower. Cost is determined as follows:

- finished goods and work-in-process at average actual cost
- raw materials and supplies at average or latest actual cost

In 1999, we changed the method of determining the cost of all of our remaining inventories previously on the "Last-in, first-out" (LIFO) method to the "First-in, first-out" (FIFO) method. Those inventories consisted of U.S. sourced pharmaceuticals and part of the animal health inventories. We believe that the change in accounting for inventories from LIFO to FIFO is preferable because inventory costs are stable and substantially unaffected by inflation. The change in the method of inventory costing resulted in a pre-tax benefit of $6.6 million included in *Cost of sales* for 1999.

D—Long-Lived Assets

Long-lived assets include:

- property, plant and equipment—These assets are recorded at original cost and increased by the cost of any significant improvements after purchase. We depreciate the cost evenly over the assets' estimated useful lives. For tax purposes, accelerated depreciation methods are used as allowed by tax laws.
- goodwill—Goodwill represents the difference between the purchase price of acquired businesses and the fair value of their net assets when accounted for by the purchase method. We amortize goodwill evenly over periods not exceeding 40 years. The average amortization period is 37 years.
- other intangible assets—Other intangible assets are included in *Other assets, deferred taxes and deferred charges.* We amortize these assets evenly over their estimated useful lives.

We review long-lived assets to assess recoverability from future operations using undiscounted cash flows. When necessary, we record charges for impairments of long-lived assets for the amount by which the present value of future cash flows exceeds the carrying value of these assets.

E—Foreign Currency Translation

For most international operations, local currencies are considered their functional currencies. We translate assets and liabilities to their U.S. dollar equivalents at rates in effect at the balance sheet date and record translation adjustments in *Shareholders' Equity.* We translate Statement of Income accounts at average rates for the period. Transaction adjustments are recorded in *Other deductions—net.*

For operations in highly inflationary economies, we translate the balance sheet items as follows:

- monetary items (that is, assets and liabilities that will be settled for cash) at rates in effect at the balance sheet date, with translation adjustments recorded in *Other deductions—net*
- non-monetary items at historical rates (that is, those rates in effect when the items were first recorded)

F—Product Alliances

We have agreements to promote pharmaceutical products developed by other companies. *Alliance revenue* represents revenue recorded under these co-promotion agreements and is derived from the sale of products. The revenue is earned when our co-promotion partners ship the related goods and the sale is consummated with a third party. Such revenue is based in most cases upon a percentage of our co-promotion partners' net sales. *Selling, informational and administrative expenses* in most cases includes other expenses for selling and marketing these products.

We have license agreements in certain foreign countries for these products. When products are sold under license agreements, we record *Net sales* instead of *Alliance revenue* and record related costs and expenses in the appropriate caption in the Statement of Income.

G—Stock-Based Compensation

In accordance with Statement of Financial Accounting Standards No. 123, *Accounting for Stock-Based Compensation,* we elected to account for our stock-based compensation under Accounting Principles Board Opinion No. 25, *Accounting for Stock Issued to Employees.*

The exercise price of stock options granted equals the market price on the date of grant. In general, there is no recorded expense related to stock options.

H—Advertising Expense

We record advertising expense as follows:

- production costs as incurred
- costs of radio time, television time and space in publications are deferred until the advertising first occurs

Advertising expense totaled $1,310 million in 1999, $1,139 million in 1998, and $898 million in 1997.

2 Discontinued Operations

In 1999, we agreed to pay a fine of $20 million to settle antitrust charges involving our former Food Science Group, divested in 1996. For additional details, see note 18, "Litigation."

In 1998, we completed the sale of the Medical Technology Group (MTG) segment. Accordingly, the consolidated financial statements and related notes reflect the results of operations and net assets of the MTG businesses—Valleylab, Schneider, American Medical Systems (AMS), Howmedica and Strato/Infusaid—as discontinued operations. We completed the sales of:

- Howmedica to Stryker Corporation in December for $1.65 billion in cash
- Schneider to Boston Scientific Corporation in September for $2.1 billion in cash
- AMS to E.M. Warburg, Pincus & Co., LLC in September for $130 million in cash
- Valleylab to U.S. Surgical Corporation in January for $425 million in cash

In 1997, we sold Strato/Infusaid to Horizon Medical Products and Arrow International for $21 million in cash.

The contractual net assets identified as part of the disposition of Valleylab, Schneider, AMS and Howmedica are recorded as *Net assets of discontinued operations* at December 31, 1997. The net cash flows of our discontinued operations are reported as *Net cash (used in)/provided by discontinued operations.*

Net assets of discontinued operations consisted of the following:

(millions of dollars)	1997
Net current assets	$ 397
Property, plant and equipment—net	383
Other net noncurrent assets and liabilities	640
Net assets of discontinued operations	$1,420

Discontinued operations—net of tax were as follows:

(millions of dollars)	1999	1998	1997
Net sales	$ —	$1,160	$1,449
Pre-tax income/(loss)	$(20)	$ 92	$ 232
Provision for taxes on income	—	57	93
Income/(loss) from operations of discontinued businesses—net of tax	(20)	35	139
Pre-tax gain/(loss) on disposal of discontinued businesses	—	2,504	(11)
Provision/(benefit) for taxes on gain/(loss)	—	1,138	(3)
Gain/(loss) on disposal of discontinued businesses—net of tax	—	1,366	(8)
Discontinued operations—net of tax	$(20)	$1,401	$ 131

3 Financial Subsidiaries

Our financial subsidiaries include Pfizer International Bank Europe (PIBE) and a small captive insurance company. PIBE periodically adjusts its loan portfolio to meet its business needs. Information about these subsidiaries follows:

Condensed Balance Sheet

(millions of dollars)	1999	1998	1997
Cash and interest-bearing deposits	$114	$103	$115
Loans—net	380	433	408
Other assets	13	15	8
Total assets	$507	$551	$531
Certificates of deposit and other liabilities	$ 24	$ 97	$ 73
Shareholders' equity	483	454	458
Total liabilities and shareholders' equity	$507	$551	$531

Condensed Statement of Income

(millions of dollars)	1999	1998	1997
Interest income	$27	$30	$29
Interest expense	(2)	(2)	(2)
Other income—net	8	1	13
Net income	$33	$29	$40

4 Financial Instruments

Most of our financial instruments are recorded in the Balance Sheet. Several "derivative" financial instruments are "off-balance-sheet" items.

A—Investments in Debt and Equity Securities

Information about our investments follows:

(millions of dollars)	1999	1998	1997
Trading securities	$ 113	$ 99	$ —
Amortized cost and fair value of held-to-maturity debt securities:*			
Corporate debt	3,624	2,306	626
Certificates of deposit	445	670	655
Municipals	—	—	56
Other	19	21	104
Total held-to-maturity debt securities	4,088	2,997	1,441
Cost and fair value of available-for-sale debt securities*	686	686	686
Cost of available-for-sale equity securities	60	54	81
Gross unrealized gains	230	106	106
Gross unrealized losses	—	(8)	(4)
Fair value of available-for-sale equity securities	290	152	183
Total investments	$5,177	$3,934	$2,310

*Gross unrealized gains and losses are not significant.

These investments are in the following captions in the Balance Sheet:

(millions of dollars)	1999	1998	1997
Cash and cash equivalents	$ 443	$ 660	$ 636
Short-term investments	3,703	2,377	712
Long-term loans and investments	1,031	897	962
Total investments	$5,177	$3,934	$2,310

The contractual maturities of the held-to-maturity and available-for-sale debt securities as of December 31, 1999, were as follows:

(millions of dollars)	Years				
	Within 1	Over 1 to 5	Over 5 to 10	Over 10	Total
Held-to-maturity debt securities:					
Corporate debt	$3,590	$ 34	$ —	$—	$3,624
Certificates of deposit	443	2	—	—	445
Other	—	2	8	9	19
Available-for-sale debt securities:					
Certificates of deposit	—	370	75	—	445
Corporate debt	—	91	150	—	241
Total debt securities	$4,033	$499	$233	$ 9	$4,774
Available-for-sale equity securities					290
Trading securities					113
Total investments					$5,177

B—Short-Term Borrowings

The weighted average effective interest rate on short-term borrowings outstanding at December 31 was 4.3% in 1999, 3.7% in 1998 and 2.9% in 1997. We had approximately $1.5 billion available to borrow under lines of credit at December 31, 1999.

C—Long-Term Debt

(millions of dollars)	1999	1998	1997
Floating-rate unsecured notes	$491	$491	$686
Other borrowings and mortgages	34	36	39
Total long-term debt	$525	$527	$725
Current portion not included above	$ 2	$ 4	$ 4

The floating-rate unsecured notes mature on various dates from 2001 to 2005 and bear interest at a defined variable rate based on the commercial paper borrowing rate. The weighted average interest rate was 6.1% at December 31, 1999. These notes minimize credit risk on certain available-for-sale debt securities that may be used to satisfy the notes at maturity. In September 1998, we repaid $195 million of the outstanding floating-rate unsecured notes prior to their scheduled maturity by using the proceeds from the issuance of short-term commercial paper.

Long-term debt outstanding at December 31, 1999, matures as follows:

(millions of dollars)	2001	2002	2003	2004	After 2004
Maturities	$131	$161	$—	$—	$233

D—Derivative Financial Instruments

Purpose

"Forward-exchange contracts," "currency swaps" and "purchased currency options" are used to reduce exposure to foreign exchange risks. Also, "interest rate swap" contracts are used to adjust interest rate exposures.

Accounting Policies

We consider derivative financial instruments to be "hedges" (that is, an offset of foreign exchange and interest rate risks) when certain criteria are met. Under hedge accounting for a purchased currency option, its impact on earnings is deferred until the recognition of the underlying hedged item (inventory) in earnings. We recognize the earnings impact of the other instruments during the terms of the contracts, along with the earnings impact of the items they offset.

Purchased currency options are recorded at cost and amortized evenly to operations through the expected inventory delivery date. Gains at the transaction date are included in the cost of the related inventory purchased.

As interest rates change, we accrue the difference between the debt interest rates recognized in the Statement of Income and the amounts payable to or receivable from counterparties under interest rate swap contracts. Likewise, amounts arising from currency swap contracts are accrued as exchange rates change.

The financial statements include the following items related to derivative and other financial instruments serving as hedges or offsets:

Prepaid expenses and taxes includes:
- purchased currency options

Other current liabilities includes:
- fair value of forward-exchange contracts
- net amounts payable related to interest rate swap contracts

Other noncurrent liabilities includes:
- net amounts payable related to currency swap contracts

Accumulated other comprehensive expense includes changes in the:
- foreign exchange translation of currency swaps and foreign debt
- fair value of forward-exchange contracts for net investment hedges

Other deductions—net includes:
- changes in the fair value of foreign exchange contracts and changes in foreign currency assets and liabilities
- payments under swap contracts to offset, primarily, interest expense or, to a lesser extent, net foreign exchange losses
- amortization of discounts or premiums on currencies sold under forward-exchange contracts

Our criteria to qualify for hedge accounting are:
Foreign currency instruments must:
- relate to a foreign currency asset, liability or an anticipated transaction that is probable and whose characteristics and terms have been identified
- involve the same currency as the hedged item
- reduce the risk of foreign currency exchange movements on our operations

Interest rate instruments must:
- relate to an asset or a liability
- change the character of the interest rate by converting a variable rate to a fixed rate or vice versa

The following table summarizes the exposures hedged or offset by the various instruments we use:

Instrument	Exposure	Maximum Maturity in Years		
		1999	1998	1997
Forward-exchange contracts	Foreign currency assets and liabilities	.5	.5	.5
Currency swaps	Net investments	4	5	—
	Loans	.3	1	2
Purchased currency options	Inventory purchases and sales	.9	1	1
Interest rate swaps	Debt interest	4	5	1

Instruments Outstanding

The notional amounts of derivative financial instruments, except for currency swaps, do not represent actual amounts exchanged by the parties, but instead represent the amount of the item on which the contracts are based.

The notional amounts of our foreign currency and interest rate contracts follow:

(millions of dollars)	1999	1998	1997
Foreign currency contracts:			
Commitments to sell foreign currencies, primarily in exchange for U.S. dollars:			
Euro*	$1,050	$ —	$ —
U.K. pounds	781	482	548
Japanese yen	412	298	224
Irish punt*	91	61	107
Australian dollars	76	98	59
German marks*	39	50	158
Netherlands guilders*	—	316	4
French francs*	—	216	134
Other currencies	192	201	240
Commitments to purchase foreign currencies, primarily in exchange for U.S. dollars:			
Euro*	339	—	—
U.K. pounds	101	53	60
Irish punt*	50	532	92
German marks*	47	67	73
Netherlands guilders*	—	156	4
Swiss francs	—	8	187
Other currencies	196	144	136
Total forward-exchange contracts	$3,374	$2,682	$2,026
Currency swaps:			
Japanese yen	$ 829	$ 754	$ —
U.K. pounds	40	40	40
Total currency swaps	$ 869	$ 794	$ 40
Purchased currency options, primarily for U.S. dollars:			
Japanese yen	$ 393	$ 364	$ 198
German marks	—	—	130
French francs	—	—	46
Belgian francs	—	—	29
Other currencies	30	25	61
Total purchased currency options	$ 423	$ 389	$ 464
Interest rate swap contracts:			
Japanese yen	$ 353	$ 321	$ 814
Swiss francs	—	—	405
Total interest rate swaps	$ 353	$ 321	$1,219

*On January 1, 1999, members of the European Monetary Union were permitted to use the new currency, the euro, or their old currency.

The Japanese yen for U.S. dollar currency swaps require that we make interim payments of a fixed rate of 1.1% on the Japanese yen payable and have interim receipts of a variable rate based on a commercial paper rate on the U.S. dollar receivable. These currency swaps replaced $625 million of Japanese yen debt, which previously served as a hedge of our net investments in Japan, as well as related interest rate swaps.

The Japanese yen and Swiss franc interest rate swaps effectively fixed the interest rate on floating rate debt as follows:

- the Japanese yen debt at 1.4% in 1999, 1998 and 1997
- the Swiss franc debt at 2.1% in 1997

The floating interest rates were based on "LIBOR" rates related to the contract currencies. In connection with the sale of the Schneider Swiss subsidiary in 1998, we terminated the Swiss franc interest rate swap contracts and ceased borrowing Swiss francs.

E — Fair Value

The following methods and assumptions were used to estimate the fair value of derivative and other financial instruments at the balance sheet date:

- short-term financial instruments (cash equivalents, accounts receivable and payable, forward-exchange contracts, short-term investments and borrowings)— cost approximates fair value because of the short maturity period
- loans—cost approximates fair value because of the short interest reset period
- long-term investments, long-term debt, forward-exchange contracts and purchased currency options—fair value is based on market or dealer quotes
- interest rate and currency swap agreements—fair value is based on estimated cost to terminate the agreements (taking into account broker quotes, current interest rates and the counterparties' creditworthiness)

The differences between fair and carrying values of our derivative and other financial instruments were not material at December 31, 1999, 1998 and 1997, except for a difference of $230 million at December 31, 1999 for available-for-sale equity securities.

F — Credit Risk

We periodically review the creditworthiness of counterparties to foreign exchange and interest rate agreements and do not expect to incur a loss from failure of any counterparties to perform under the agreements. In general, there is no requirement for collateral from customers. There are no significant concentrations of credit risk related to our financial instruments. No individual counterparty credit exposure exceeded 10% of our consolidated *Shareholders' Equity* at December 31, 1999.

5 Comprehensive Income

Changes in accumulated other comprehensive income/(expense) follow:

(millions of dollars)	Currency Translation Adjustment	Net Unrealized Gain/(Loss) on Available-For-Sale Securities	Minimum Pension Liability	Accumulated Other Comprehensive Income/(Expense)*
Balance January 1, 1997	$ 174	$ 40	$ (69)	$ 145
Period change	(253)	20	3	(230)
Balance December 31, 1997	(79)	60	(66)	(85)
Period change	(74)	(2)	(73)	(149)
Balance December 31, 1998	(153)	58	(139)	(234)
Period change	(222)	81	(24)	(165)
Balance December 31, 1999	**$(375)**	**$139**	**$(163)**	**$(399)**

Income tax benefit for other comprehensive expense was $76 million in 1997, $116 million in 1998 and $33 million in 1999.

6 Inventories

In June 1999, the European Union's Committee for Proprietary Medicinal Products suspended the European Union licenses of the oral and intravenous formulations of Trovan for 12 months. Based on our evaluation of these events and related matters, we determined that it was unlikely that certain Trovan inventories of finished goods, bulk, work-in-process, and raw materials will be used. Accordingly, in the third quarter of 1999, we recorded a charge of $310 million ($205 million after-tax, or $.05 after-tax per diluted share) in *Cost of sales* to write off Trovan inventories in excess of the amount required to support expected sales.

7 Property, Plant and Equipment

The major categories of property, plant and equipment follow:

(millions of dollars)	Useful Lives (years)	1999	1998	1997
Land	—	$ 174	$ 151	$ 126
Buildings	33⅓	2,008	1,669	1,534
Machinery and equipment	8–20	3,040	2,685	2,459
Furniture, fixtures and other	3–12½	1,618	1,383	1,232
Construction in progress	—	1,197	956	516
		8,037	6,844	5,867
Less: accumulated depreciation		2,694	2,429	2,074
Total property, plant and equipment		$5,343	$4,415	$3,793

8 Other Deductions—Net

The components of other deductions—net follow:

(millions of dollars)	1999	1998	1997
Interest income	$(301)	$ (185)	$(156)
Interest expense	236	143	149
Interest expense capitalized	(13)	(7)	(2)
Net interest income	(78)	(49)	(9)
Co-promotion payments to Searle	—	240	—
Contribution to The Pfizer Foundation	—	300	—
Legal settlements involving the brand-name prescription drug antitrust litigation	2	57	—
Amortization of goodwill and other intangibles	43	45	48
Net exchange (gains)/losses	(20)	(16)	26
Other, net	154	432	141
Other deductions—net	$ 101	$1,009	$ 206

In 1999, we substantially completed the actions under the restructuring plans announced in 1998.

In 1998, we recorded charges for the restructuring in addition to charges for certain asset impairments. The components of these pre-tax charges follow:

(millions of dollars)	Total	COS*	SI&A*	R&D	OD*
Restructuring charges	$177	$68	$17	$ 1	$ 91
Asset impairments	213	18	—	—	195

COS—Cost of sales; SI&A—Selling, informational and administrative expenses; OD—Other deductions-net.

The components of the 1998 restructuring charges follow:

(millions of dollars)	Charges in 1998	Utilization		
		1998	1999	Beyond
Property, plant and equipment	$ 49	$ 49	$ —	$ —
Write-down of intangibles	44	44	—	—
Employee termination costs	40	12	28	—
Other	44	11	17	16
Total	$177	$116	$45	$16

These charges resulted from a review of our global operations to increase efficiencies and return on assets, thereby resulting in plant and product line rationalizations. In addition to the disposition of our MTG businesses, we exited certain product lines including certain lines associated with our animal health business and certain of our fermentation operations.

We wrote off assets related to the product lines we exited, including inventory, intangible assets—primarily goodwill—as well as certain buildings, machinery and equipment which we do not plan to use or sell.

As a result of the restructuring, our work force was reduced by approximately 500 manufacturing, sales and corporate personnel. Employee termination costs represent payments for severance, outplacement counseling fees, medical and other benefits and a $5 million noncash charge for the acceleration of nonvested employee stock options.

Other restructuring charges consist of charges for inventory for product lines we have exited—$12 million, contract termination payments—$9 million, facility closure costs—$7 million and environmental remediation costs associated with the disposal of certain facilities—$16 million.

In 1998, we recorded an impairment charge of $110 million in the pharmaceutical segment to adjust intangible asset values, primarily goodwill and trademarks, related to consumer health care product lines. These charges resulted from significant changes in the marketplace and a revision of our strategies, including:

- the decision to redeploy resources from personal care and minor brands to over-the-counter switches of prescription products
- the withdrawal of one of our major over-the-counter products in Italy
- an acquired product line which experienced declines in market share

In 1998, our animal health antibiotic feed additive, Stafac, was banned, effective in mid-1999, throughout the European Union, resulting in asset impairment charges of $103 million ($85 million was to adjust intangible asset values, primarily goodwill and trademarks, and $18 million was to adjust the carrying value of machinery and equipment in the pharmaceutical segment).

9 Taxes on Income

Income from continuing operations before taxes consisted of the following:

(millions of dollars)	1999	1998	1997
United States	$2,557	$1,184	$1,215
International	1,891	1,410	1,652
Total income from continuing operations before taxes	$4,448	$2,594	$2,867

The provision for taxes on income from continuing operations consisted of the following:

(millions of dollars)	1999	1998	1997
United States:			
Taxes currently payable:			
Federal	$ 621	$ 344	$344
State and local	38	24	9
Deferred income taxes	(72)	(162)	(23)
Total U.S. tax provision	587	206	330
International:			
Taxes currently payable	606	550	462
Deferred income taxes	51	(114)	(17)
Total international tax provision	657	436	445
Total provision for taxes on income	$1,244	$ 642	$775

Amounts are reflected in the preceding tables based on the location of the taxing authorities. As of December 31, 1999, we have not made a U.S. tax provision of approximately $1.9 billion for approximately $8.2 billion of unremitted earnings of our international subsidiaries. These earnings are expected, for the most part, to be reinvested overseas.

We operate a manufacturing subsidiary in Puerto Rico that benefits from a Puerto Rican incentive grant in effect through the end of 2002. Under this grant, we are partially exempt from income, property and municipal taxes. For further information on U.S. taxation of Puerto Rican operations, see "Tax Legislation" on page 37.

Reconciliation of the U.S. statutory income tax rate to our effective tax rate for continuing operations follows:

(percentages)	1999	1998	1997
U.S. statutory income tax rate	35.0	35.0	35.0
Effect of partially tax-exempt operations in Puerto Rico	(1.5)	(2.2)	(1.8)
Effect of international operations	(4.8)	(5.5)	(5.0)
All other—net	(0.7)	(2.5)	(1.2)
Effective tax rate for continuing operations	28.0	24.8	27.0

Deferred taxes arise because of different treatment between financial statement accounting and tax accounting, known as "temporary differences." We record the tax effect of these temporary differences as "deferred tax assets" (generally items that can be used as a tax deduction or credit in future periods) and "deferred tax liabilities" (generally items that we received a tax deduction for, but have not yet been recorded in the Statement of Income).

The tax effects of the major items recorded as deferred tax assets and liabilities are:

(millions of dollars)	1999 Deferred Tax Assets	1999 Deferred Tax Liabs.	1998 Deferred Tax Assets	1998 Deferred Tax Liabs.	1997 Deferred Tax Assets	1997 Deferred Tax Liabs.
Prepaid/deferred items	$ 361	$ 197	$ 411	$ 169	$ 252	$189
Inventories	471	109	322	72	218	60
Property, plant and equipment	22	514	39	433	30	350
Employee benefits	544	131	391	97	297	113
Restructurings and special charge*	244	—	301	—	133	—
Foreign tax credit carryforwards	181	—	117	—	159	—
Other carryforwards	165	—	97	—	135	—
Unremitted earnings	—	335	—	335	—	—
All other	121	170	169	73	119	76
Subtotal	2,109	1,456	1,847	1,179	1,343	788
Valuation allowance	(27)	—	(30)	—	(27)	—
Total deferred taxes	$2,082	$1,456	$1,817	$1,179	$1,316	$788
Net deferred tax asset	$ 626		$ 638		$ 528	

*Includes tax effect of the 1991 charge for potential future Shiley C/C heart valve fracture claims.

These amounts, netted by taxing location, are in the following captions in the Balance Sheet:

(millions of dollars)	1999	1998	1997
Prepaid expenses and taxes	$ 744	$ 809	$ 425
Other assets, deferred taxes and deferred charges	183	26	230
Deferred taxes on income	(301)	(197)	(127)
Net deferred tax asset	$ 626	$ 638	$ 528

A valuation allowance is recorded because some items recorded as foreign deferred tax assets may not be deductible or creditable. The "foreign tax credit carryforwards" were generated from dividends paid or deemed to be paid by subsidiaries to the parent company between 1997 and 1999. We can carry these credits forward for five years from the year of actual payment and apply them to certain U.S. tax liabilities.

The Internal Revenue Service (IRS) has completed and closed its audits of our tax returns through 1992. The IRS completed its audits in January 2000 of our tax returns for 1993 through 1995. We are awaiting the agent's final report for those years. We do not expect any material adjustments to be proposed.

In November 1994, Belgian tax authorities notified Pfizer Research and Development Company N.V./S.A. (PRDCO), an indirect, wholly owned subsidiary of our company, of a proposed adjustment to the taxable income of PRDCO for fiscal year 1992. The proposed adjustment arises from an assertion by the Belgian tax authorities of jurisdiction with respect to income resulting primarily from certain transfers of property by our non-Belgian subsidiaries to the Irish branch of PRDCO. In January 1995, PRDCO received an assessment from the tax authorities for additional taxes and interest of approximately $432 million and $97 million, respectively, relating to these matters. In January 1996, PRDCO received an assessment from the tax authorities, for fiscal year 1993, for additional taxes and interest of approximately $86 million and $18 million, respectively. The additional assessment arises from the same assertion by the Belgian tax authorities of jurisdiction with respect to all income of the Irish branch of PRDCO. Based upon the relevant facts regarding the Irish branch of PRDCO and the provisions of the Belgian tax laws and the written opinions of outside counsel, we believe that the assessments are without merit.

We believe that our accrued tax liabilities are adequate for all years.

10 Benefit Plans

Our pension plans cover most employees worldwide. Our postretirement plans provide medical and life insurance benefits to retirees and their eligible dependents.

Information regarding our pension and postretirement benefit obligation follows:

(percentages)	Pension 1999	Pension 1998	Pension 1997	Postretirement 1999	Postretirement 1998	Postretirement 1997
Weighted-average assumptions:						
Discount rate:						
U.S. plans	7.5	6.8	7.0	7.5	6.8	7.0
International plans	5.1	5.3	5.9			
Rate of compensation increase:						
U.S. plans	4.5	4.5	4.5			
International plans	3.7	3.4	3.9			

The following tables present reconciliations of the benefit obligation of the plans; the plan assets of the pension plans and the funded status of the plans:

(millions of dollars)	Pension			Postretirement		
	1999	1998	1997	**1999**	1998	1997
Change in benefit obligation						
Benefit obligation at beginning of year	**$3,177**	$2,674	$2,130	**$ 286**	$ 287	$ 285
Service cost	**169**	151	105	**7**	10	7
Interest cost	**192**	181	145	**18**	20	19
Employee contributions	**9**	6	6			
Plan amendments	**13**	15	274	**2**	—	—
Plan net (gains)/losses	**87**	354	240	**(30)**	(3)	(7)
Foreign exchange impact	**28**	36	(103)			
Acquisitions	**—**	—	3	**—**	—	—
Divestitures	**(42)**	(26)	—	**—**	—	—
Curtailments	**—**	(26)	(1)	**—**	(10)	—
Settlements	**(1)**	(10)	(1)	**—**	—	—
Benefits paid	**(221)**	(178)	(124)	**(20)**	(18)	(17)
Benefit obligation at end of year	**$3,411**	$3,177	$2,674	**$ 263**	$ 286	$ 287
Change in plan assets						
Fair value of plan assets at beginning of year	**$3,194**	$2,793	$2,410			
Actual return on plan assets	**464**	530	491			
Company contributions	**76**	63	50			
Employee contributions	**9**	6	6			
Foreign exchange impact	**26**	3	(57)			
Acquisitions	**—**	—	1			
Divestitures	**(34)**	(23)	—			
Settlements	**(1)**	(13)	(1)			
Benefits paid	**(206)**	(165)	(107)			
Fair value of plan assets at end of year	**$3,528**	$3,194	$2,793			
Funded status:						
Plan assets in excess of/(less than) benefit obligation	**$ 117**	$ 17	$ 119	**$(263)**	$(286)	$(287)
Unrecognized:						
Net transition asset	**(4)**	(4)	(10)	**—**	—	—
Net (gains)/ losses	**(75)**	1	(86)	**(56)**	(26)	(24)
Prior service costs/(gains)	**240**	248	310	**(27)**	(47)	(83)
Net amount recognized	**$ 278**	$ 262	$ 333	**$(346)**	$(359)	$(394)

The components in the balance sheet consist of:

(millions of dollars)	Pension			Postretirement		
	1999	1998	1997	**1999**	1998	1997
Prepaid benefit cost	**$ 537**	$ 504	$ 499	**$ —**	$ —	$ —
Accrued benefit liability	**(655)**	(562)	(362)	**(346)**	(359)	(394)
Intangible asset	**79**	71	53	**—**	—	—
Accumulated other comprehensive income	**317**	249	143	**—**	—	—
Net amount recognized	**$ 278**	$ 262	$ 333	**$(346)**	$(359)	$(394)

Information related primarily to International plans:

(millions of dollars)	Pension		
	1999	1998	1997
Pension plans with an accumulated benefit obligation in excess of plan assets:			
Fair value of plan assets	**$400**	$323	$294
Accumulated benefit obligation	**752**	693	553
Pension plans with a benefit obligation in excess of plan assets:			
Fair value of plan assets	**$496**	$435	$422
Benefit obligation	**949**	901	774

At December 31, 1999, the major U.S. pension plan held approximately 6.8 million shares of our common stock with a fair value of approximately $220 million. The Plan received approximately $2 million in dividends on these shares in 1999.

The assumptions used and the annual cost related to these plans follow:

(percentages)	Pension			Postretirement		
	1999	1998	1997	**1999**	1998	1997
Weighted average assumptions:						
Expected return on plan assets:						
U.S. plans	**10.0**	10.0	10.0			
International plans	**7.3**	8.1	7.5			

(millions of dollars)						
Service cost	**$169**	$ 151	$ 105	**$ 7**	$ 10	$ 7
Interest cost	**192**	181	145	**18**	20	19
Expected return on plan assets	**(275)**	(249)	(208)			
Amortization of:						
Prior service costs/ (gains)	**19**	24	34	**(18)**	(24)	(24)
Net transition asset	**(5)**	(6)	(5)	**—**	—	—
Net losses/(gains)	**12**	10	2	**—**	(1)	(1)
Curtailments and settlements—net*	**—**	28	—	**—**	(22)	—
Net periodic benefit cost/(gain)	**$112**	$ 139	$ 73	**$ 7**	$(17)	$ 1

*Includes approximately $12 million of special termination pension benefits for certain MTG employees in 1998.

An average increase of 6.9% in the cost of health care benefits was assumed for 2000 and is projected to decrease over the next five years to 5.2% and to then remain at that level.

A 1% change in the medical trend rate assumed for postretirement benefits would have the following effects at December 31, 1999:

(millions of dollars)	1% Increase	1% Decrease
Total of service and interest cost components	$ 1	$ (1)
Postretirement benefit obligation	13	(12)

We have savings and investment plans for most employees in the U.S., Puerto Rico, the U.K. and Ireland. Employees may contribute a portion of their salaries to the plans and we match a portion of the employee contributions. Our contributions were $50 million in 1999, $48 million in 1998 and $43 million in 1997.

11 Lease Commitments

We lease properties for use in our operations. In addition to rent, the leases require us to pay directly for taxes, insurance, maintenance and other operating expenses, or to pay higher rent when operating expenses increase. Rental expense, net of sublease income, was $158 million in 1999, $131 million in 1998 and $127 million in 1997. This table shows future minimum rental commitments under noncancellable leases at December 31, 1999:

(millions of dollars)	2000	2001	2002	2003	2004	After 2004
Lease commitments	$54	$45	$40	$29	$27	$286

12 Common Stock

We effected a three-for-one stock split of our common stock in the form of a 200% stock dividend in 1999 and a two-for-one split of our common stock in the form of a 100% stock dividend in 1997. All share and per share information in this report reflects both splits. Per share data may reflect rounding adjustments as a result of the three-for-one split.

Under the current share-purchase program begun in September 1998, we are authorized to purchase up to $5 billion of our common stock. In 1999, we purchased approximately 65.6 million shares of our common stock in the open market at an average price of $38 per share. Since the beginning of this program, we have purchased 80.4 million shares of our common stock for approximately $3 billion. In September 1998, we completed a program under which we purchased 79.2 million shares of our common stock at a total cost of $2 billion. In 1998, we purchased approximately 57.8 million shares of our common stock at an average price of $33 per share under these share-purchase programs. Of the 57.8 million shares repurchased in 1998, 14.8 million shares were repurchased under the share-purchase program which started in September 1998, for a total cost of $525 million.

13 Preferred Stock Purchase Rights

Preferred Stock Purchase Rights have a scheduled term through October 2007, although the term may be extended or the Rights may be redeemed prior to expiration. One right was issued for each share of common stock issued by our company. These rights are not exercisable unless certain change-in-control events transpire, such as a person acquiring or obtaining the right to acquire beneficial ownership of 15% or more of our outstanding common stock or an announcement of a tender offer for at least 30% of our stock. The rights are evidenced by corresponding common stock certificates and automatically trade with the common stock unless an event transpires that makes them exercisable. If the rights become exercisable, separate certificates evidencing the rights will be distributed and each right will entitle the holder to purchase a new series of preferred stock at a defined price from our company. The preferred stock, in addition to preferred dividend and liquidation rights, will entitle the holder to vote with the company's common stock.

The rights are redeemable by us at a fixed price until 10 days, or longer as determined by the Board, after certain defined events, or at any time prior to the expiration of the rights.

We have reserved 3.0 million preferred shares to be issued pursuant to these rights. No such shares have yet been issued. At the present time, the rights have no dilutive effect on the earnings per common share calculation.

14 Employee Benefit Trusts

In 1993, we sold 120 million shares of treasury stock to the Pfizer Inc. Grantor Trust in exchange for a $600 million note. The Trust was established primarily to fund our employee benefit plans. In February 1999, the Trust transferred 10 million shares to us to satisfy the balance due on its note and contributed its remaining 90 million shares to the newly established Pfizer Inc. Employee Benefit Trust (EBT). The Grantor Trust was then dissolved and the shares of the EBT will now be used to fund employee benefit plans. The Balance Sheet reflects the fair value of the shares owned by the EBT as a reduction of *Shareholders' Equity.*

15 Earnings Per Share

The weighted average common shares used in the computations of basic earnings per common share and earnings per common share assuming dilution were as follows:

(millions, except per share data)	1999	1998	1997
Earnings:			
Income from continuing operations	**$3,199**	$1,950	$2,082
Discontinued operations—net of tax	**(20)**	1,401	131
Net income	**$3,179**	$3,351	$2,213
Basic:			
Weighted average number of common shares outstanding	**3,775**	3,789	3,771
Earnings per common share			
Income from continuing operations	**$ .85**	$ .51	$ .55
Discontinued operations—net of tax	**(.01)**	.37	.04
Net income	**$ .84**	$ .88	$ .59
Diluted:			
Weighted average number of common shares outstanding	**3,775**	3,789	3,771
Common share equivalents— stock options and stock issuable under employee compensation plans	**109**	156	138
Weighted average number of common shares and common share equivalents	**3,884**	3,945	3,909
Earnings per common share			
Income from continuing operations	**$ .82**	$ .49	$ .53
Discontinued operations—net of tax	**—**	.36	.04
Net income	**$ .82**	$ .85	$ .57

Options to purchase 115 million shares were outstanding during 1999 but were not included in the computation of diluted earnings per share because the options' exercise prices were greater than the average market price of the common shares.

16 Stock Option and Performance Awards

We may grant stock options to any employee, including officers, under our Stock and Incentive Plan. Options are exercisable after five years or less, subject to continuous employment and certain other conditions and expire 10 years after the grant date. Once exercisable, the employee can purchase shares of our common stock at the market price on the date we granted the option.

The Plan also allows for stock appreciation rights, stock awards and performance awards. In 1999, shareholders approved amendments to increase the shares available in the Plan and to extend its term through 2008.

The following table summarizes information concerning options outstanding under the Plan at December 31, 1999:

(thousands of shares)	Options Outstanding			Options Exercisable	
Range of Exercise Prices	Number Outstanding at 12/31/99	Weighted Average Remaining Contractual Term (years)	Weighted Average Exercise Price	Number Exercisable at 12/31/99	Weighted Average Exercise Price
$ 0 – $10	85,308	4.0	$ 6.40	84,401	$ 6.38
10 – 15	36,677	6.6	12.42	34,439	12.42
15 – 20	35,486	7.7	18.34	21,145	18.35
20 – 40	48,730	8.7	35.18	14,114	35.18
over 40	66,904	9.2	42.07	—	—

The following table summarizes the activity for the Plan:

(thousands of shares)	Shares Available for Grant	Under Option	
		Shares	Weighted Average Exercise Price Per Share
Balance January 1, 1997	105,042	259,284	$ 7.21
Granted	(42,612)	42,612	18.35
Exercised	—	(46,983)	5.38
Cancelled	1,959	(2,016)	12.89
Balance December 31, 1997	64,389	252,897	9.39
Granted	(52,860)	52,860	35.21
Exercised	—	(54,888)	7.04
Cancelled	1,212	(1,257)	19.91
Balance December 31, 1998	12,741	249,612	15.32
Authorized	165,000	—	—
Granted	(67,963)	67,963	42.07
Exercised	—	(41,524)	9.57
Cancelled	2,928	(2,946)	35.41
Balance December 31, 1999	**112,706**	**273,105**	**22.63**

Options granted in 1999 include options for 450 shares granted to every eligible employee worldwide in celebration of our 150th Anniversary.

The tax benefits related to certain stock option transactions were $228 million in 1999, $274 million in 1998 and $88 million in 1997.

The weighted-average fair value per stock option granted was $13.57 for 1999 options, $11.31 for 1998 options and $5.59 for the 1997 options. We estimated the fair values using the Black-Scholes option pricing model, modified for dividends and using the following assumptions:

	1999	1998	1997
Expected dividend yield	**1.02%**	1.02%	1.76%
Risk-free interest rate	**5.26%**	5.23%	6.23%
Expected stock price volatility	**25.98%**	26.29%	25.56%
Expected term until exercise (years)	**5.75**	5.75	5.50

The following table summarizes results as if we had recorded compensation expense for the 1999, 1998 and 1997 option grants:

(millions of dollars, except per share data)	**1999**	1998	1997
Net income:			
As reported	**$3,179**	$3,351	$2,213
Pro forma	**2,750**	3,149	2,087
Basic earnings per share:			
As reported	**$ .84**	$ .88	$ .59
Pro forma	**.73**	.83	.55
Diluted earnings per share:			
As reported	**$ .82**	$ .85	$ .57
Pro forma	**.71**	.80	.53

The Performance-Contingent Share Award Program was established effective in 1993 to provide executives and other key employees the right to earn common stock awards. We determine the award payouts after the performance period ends, based on specific performance criteria. Under the Program, up to 120 million shares may be awarded. We awarded approximately 2,276,000 shares in 1999, approximately 1,959,000 shares in 1998 and approximately 1,347,000 shares in 1997. At December 31, 1999, program participants had the right to earn up to 12.3 million additional shares. Compensation expense related to the Program was $64 million in 1999, $202 million in 1998 and $74 million in 1997.

We entered into two forward-purchase contracts in 1998 and on maturity they were extended. These contracts offset the potential impact on net income of our liability under the Program. At settlement date we will, at the option of the counterparty to the contract, either receive our own stock or settle the contracts for cash. Other contract terms are as follows:

		Maximum Maturity in Years	
Number of Shares (thousands)	Per Share	**1999**	1998
3,000	$33.73	—	.9
3,017	33.75	**.9**	—

The financial statements include the following items related to these contracts:

Prepaid expenses and taxes includes:
- fair value of these contracts

Other deductions—net includes:
- changes in the fair value of these contracts

17 Insurance

We maintain insurance coverage adequate for our needs. Under our insurance contracts, we usually accept self-insured retentions appropriate for our specific business risks.

18 Litigation

The Company is involved in a number of claims and litigations, including product liability claims and litigations considered normal in the nature of its businesses. These include suits involving various pharmaceutical and hospital products that allege either reaction to or injury from use of the product. In addition, from time to time the Company is involved in, or is the subject of, various governmental or agency inquiries or investigations relating to its businesses.

In 1999, the Company pleaded guilty to one count of price fixing of sodium erythorbate from July 1992 until December 1994, and one count of market allocation of maltol from December 1989 until December 1995, and paid a total fine of $20 million. The activities at issue involved the Company's former Food Science Group, a division that manufactured food additives and that the Company divested in 1996. The Department of Justice has stated that no further antitrust charges will be brought against the Company relating to the former Food Science Group, that no antitrust charges will be brought against any current director, officer or employee of the Company for conduct related to the products of the former Food Science Group, and that none of the Company's current directors, officers or employees was aware of any aspect of the activity that gave rise to the violations. Five purported class action suits involving these products have been filed against the Company; two in California State Court, and three in New York Federal Court. The Company does not believe that this plea and settlement, or civil litigation involving these products, will have a material effect on its business or results of operations.

On June 9, 1997, the Company received notice of the filing of an Abbreviated New Drug Application (ANDA) by Mylan Pharmaceuticals for a sustained-release nifedipine product asserted to be bioequivalent to Procardia XL. Mylan's notice asserted that the proposed formulation does not infringe relevant licensed Alza and Bayer patents and thus that approval of their ANDA should be granted before patent expiration. On July 18, 1997, the Company, together with Bayer AG and Bayer Corporation, filed a patent-infringement suit against Mylan Pharmaceuticals Inc. and Mylan Laboratories Inc. in the United States District Court for the Western District of Pennsylvania with respect to Mylan's ANDA. Suit was filed under Bayer AG's U.S. Patent No. 5,264,446, licensed to the Company, relating to nifedipine of a specified particle size range. Mylan has filed its answer denying infringement and a scheduling order has been entered. On December 17, 1999, Mylan received final approval from the FDA for its 30 mg. extended-release nifedipine tablet. On March 16, 1999, the United States District Court granted Mylan's motion to file an amended answer and antitrust counterclaims. All discovery on the antitrust counterclaims is stayed pending resolution of the patent misuse claims. On March 29, 1999, Mylan filed a motion for summary judgment based on an adverse decision against Bayer in Bayer's litigation against Elan Pharmaceutical Research Corp. which involved the same nifedipine particle size patent. Discovery has been essentially completed and the parties dispositive motions were filed by an extended deadline of July 19, 1999, including Pfizer and Bayer's summary judgment motion seeking to dismiss Mylan's patent misuse defenses and counterclaims. On December 13, 1999, Mylan filed its opposition to plaintiffs' motion for summary judgment dismissing Mylan's patent misuse defense and counterclaim, and Bayer and the Company filed their opposition to Mylan's motion for summary judgment of non-infringement. The parties reply memoranda in support of their motions were filed on December 28, 1999.

On or about February 23, 1998, Bayer AG received notice that Biovail Laboratories Incorporated had filed an ANDA for a sustained-release nifedipine product asserted to be bioequivalent to one dosage strength (60 mg.) of Procardia XL. The notice was subsequently received by the Company as well. The notice asserts that the Biovail product does not infringe Bayer's U.S. Patent No. 5,264,446. On March 26, 1998, the Company received notice of the filing of an ANDA by Biovail Laboratories of a 30 mg. dosage formulation of nifedipine alleged to be bioequivalent to Procardia XL. On April 2, 1998, Bayer and Pfizer filed a patent-infringement action against Biovail, relating to their 60 mg. nifedipine product, in the United States District Court for the District of Puerto Rico. On May 6, 1998, Bayer and Pfizer filed a second patent infringement action in Puerto Rico against Biovail under the same patent with respect to Biovail's 30 mg. nifedipine product. These actions have been consolidated for discovery and trial. On April 24, 1998, Biovail Laboratories Inc. brought suit in the United States District Court for the Western District of Pennsylvania against the Company and Bayer seeking a declaratory judgment of invalidity of and/or non-infringement of the 5,264,446 nifedipine patent as well as a finding of violation of the antitrust laws. Biovail has also moved to transfer the patent infringement actions from Puerto Rico to the Western District of Pennsylvania. Pfizer has opposed this motion to transfer and on June 19, 1998, moved to dismiss Biovail's declaratory judgment action and antitrust action in the Western District of Pennsylvania, or in the alternative, to stay the action pending the outcome of the infringement actions in Puerto Rico. On January 4, 1999, the District Court in Pennsylvania granted Pfizer's motion for a stay of the antitrust action pending the outcome of the infringement actions in Puerto Rico. On January 29, 1999, the District Court in Puerto Rico denied Biovail's motion to transfer the patent infringement actions from Puerto Rico to the Western District of Pennsylvania. On April 12, 1999, Biovail filed a motion for summary judgment also based in part on the summary judgment motion granted to Elan in the Bayer v. Elan litigation in the Northern District of Georgia. Pfizer and Bayer's response was filed on April 26, 1999. On September 20, 1999, the United States District Court in Puerto Rico denied Biovail's motion for summary judgment without prejudice to their refiling after completion of discovery in the Procardia XL patent-infringement litigation. The court set an expedited discovery schedule with a deadline of December 30, 1999, to complete discovery of parties and fact witnesses and February 29, 2000, to complete discovery of expert witnesses. On December 20, 1999, the court extended the date to complete fact discovery to January 28, 2000, and that of expert discovery to March 15, 2000. A status conference with the court is scheduled for March 17, 2000.

On April 2, 1998, the Company received notice from Lek U.S.A. Inc. of its filing of an ANDA for a 60 mg. formulation of nifedipine alleged to be bioequivalent to Procardia XL. On May 14, 1998, Bayer and Pfizer commenced suit against Lek for infringement of Bayer's U.S. Patent No. 5,264,446, as well as for infringement of a second Bayer patent, No. 4,412,986 relating to combinations of nifedipine with certain polymeric materials. On September 14, 1998, Lek was served with the summons and complaint. Plaintiffs amended the complaint on November 10, 1998, limiting the action to infringement of U.S. Patent 4,412,986. On January 19, 1999, Lek filed a motion to dismiss the complaint alleging infringement of U.S. Patent 4,412,986. Pfizer responded to this motion and oral argument has been held in abeyance pending a settlement conference. In September 1999, a settlement agreement was entered into among the parties staying this litigation until the expiration of U.S. Patent No. 4,412,986 on November 2, 2000.

On February 10, 1999, the Company received a notice from Lek U.S.A. of its filing of an ANDA for a 90 mg. formulation of nifedipine alleged to be bioequivalent to Procardia XL. On March 25, 1999, Bayer and Pfizer commenced suit against Lek for infringement of the same two Bayer patents originally asserted against Lek's 60 mg. formulation. This case was also the subject of a settlement conference. In September, 1999, a settlement agreement was entered into among the parties staying this litigation until the expiration of U.S. patent No. 4,412,986 on November 2, 2000.

On November 9, 1998, Pfizer received an ANDA notice letter from Martec Pharmaceutical, Inc. for generic versions (30 mg., 60 mg., 90 mg.) of Procardia XL. On or about December 18, 1998, Pfizer received a new ANDA certification letter stating that the ANDA had actually been filed in the name of Martec Scientific, Inc. On December 23, 1998, Pfizer brought an action against Martec Pharmaceutical, Inc. and Martec Scientific, Inc. in the Western District of Missouri for infringement of Bayer's patent relating to nifedipine of a specific particle size. On January 26, 1999, a second complaint was filed against Martec Scientific in the Western District of Missouri based on Martec's new ANDA certification letter. Martec filed its response to this complaint on February 26, 1999. A hearing to determine claim scope is scheduled for June 1, 2000.

Pfizer filed suit on July 8, 1997, against the FDA in the United States District Court for the District of Columbia, seeking a declaratory judgment and injunctive relief enjoining the FDA from processing Mylan's ANDA or any other ANDA submission referencing Procardia XL that uses a different extended-release mechanism. Pfizer's suit alleges that extended-release mechanisms that are not identical to the osmotic pump mechanism of Procardia XL constitute different dosage forms requiring the filing and approval of suitability petitions under the Food Drug and Cosmetics Act before the FDA can accept an ANDA for filing. Mylan intervened in Pfizer's suit. On March 31, 1998, the U.S. District Judge granted the government's motion for summary judgment against the Company. On July 16, 1999, the D.C. Court of Appeals dismissed the appeal on the ground that since the FDA had not approved any ANDA referencing Procardia XL that uses a different extended-release mechanism than the osmotic pump mechanism of Procardia XL, it was premature to maintain this action, stating that Pfizer has the right to bring such an action if, and when, the FDA approves such an ANDA. Subsequent to FDA's final approval of Mylan's ANDA, on December 18, 1999 Pfizer filed suit against FDA in the United States District Court for the District of Delaware. The suit alleges that FDA unlawfully approved Mylan's 30 mg. extended release product because FDA had not granted an ANDA suitability petition reflecting a difference in dosage form from Procardia XL.

On March 31, 1999, the Company received notice from TorPharm of its filing, through its U.S. agent Apotex Corp., of an ANDA for 1 mg., 2 mg., 4 mg. and 8 mg. tablets alleged to be bioequivalent to Cardura (doxazosin mesylate). The notice letter alleges that Pfizer's patent on doxazosin is invalid in view of certain prior art references. Following a review of these allegations, suit was filed in the United States District Court for the Northern District of Illinois against TorPharm and Apotex Corp. on May 14, 1999. The defendants requested a 90-day period in which to file their answer. The request was granted and TorPharm/Apotex's answer was filed by August 19, 1999. Discovery is in progress. On June 2, 1999, FDA was notified that given the patent litigation and pursuant to provisions of the Federal Food Drug and Cosmetic Act, the FDA may not approve the TorPharm application for thirty months from filing or resolution of the litigation.

On May 5, 1999, the Company filed an action against Sibia Neurosciences, Inc. in the United States District Court for the District of Delaware seeking a declaratory judgment that two Sibia patents claiming reporter gene drug screening assays are invalid, not infringed by the Company, and unenforceable due to Sibia's misuse of its patent rights in seeking certain license terms. On May 27, 1999, Sibia Neurosciences, Inc. filed an answer to the Company's declaratory judgment action in which Sibia denies that a prior case or controversy existed, but admits that a case or controversy does now exist regarding at least one patent in suit, denies the invalidity, unenforceability and non-infringement of the patents in suit, and asserts various jurisdictional and equitable defenses, affirmative defenses, and lack of standing by the Company to assert patent misuse. Sibia Neurosciences also filed a counterclaim alleging willful infringement by the Company of one of the patents in suit. A reply to that counterclaim denying Sibia's allegation has been filed. The parties submitted a joint status report to the court on December 14, 1999, in which the parties agreed to complete fact discovery by August 21, 2000, and commence trial on January 8, 2001.

On May 19, 1999, Abbott Laboratories filed an action against the Company in the United States District Court of the Northern District of Illinois alleging that the Company's use, sale or manufacture of trovafloxacin infringes Abbott's United States Patent No. 4,616,019 claiming naphthyridine antibiotics and seeking a permanent injunction and damages. An answer denying these allegations was filed on June 9, 1999. Discovery is in progress.

On December 17, 1999, the Company received notice of the filing of an ANDA by Zenith Goldline Pharmaceuticals for 50 mg. and 100 mg. tablets of sertraline hydrochloride alleged to be bioequivalent to Zoloft. Zenith has certified to the FDA that it will not engage in the manufacture, use or sale of sertraline hydrochloride until the expiration of Pfizer's U.S. Patent 4,536,518, which covers sertraline per se and expires December 30, 2005. Zenith has also alleged in its certification to the FDA that the manufacture, use and sale of Zenith's product will not infringe Pfizer's U.S. Patent 4,962,128, which covers methods of treating an anxiety-related disorder or Pfizer's U.S. Patent 5,248,699, which covers a crystalline polymorph of sertraline hydrochloride. These patents expire in November 2009 and August 2012, respectively. On January 28, 2000, the Company filed a patent infringement action against Zenith Goldline and its parent Ivax Corporation in the United States District Court for the District of New Jersey for infringement of the '128 and '699 patents.

On February 1, 2000, the Company received notice of the filing of an ANDA by Novopharm Limited for 50 mg, 100 mg, 150 mg and 200 mg tablets of fluconazole alleged to be bioequivalent to DIFLUCAN. Novopharm has certified to the FDA its position that the Company's U.S. Patent 4,404,216, which covers fluconazole, is invalid. This patent expires in January 2004. The Company is evaluating Novopharm's notice.

In pre-existing litigation between Pioneer Hi-Bred International, Inc. and DeKalb Genetics Corporation in the United States District Court for the Southern District of Iowa, the court granted on October 8, 1999 Pioneer's motion to add additional parties, including Pfizer Inc. and Monsanto Co. (the present owner of DeKalb Genetics Corporation), as codefendant parties. The amended complaint, which claims violations of the federal Lanham Act and Iowa state law stemming from the codefendants' alleged use of Pioneer's corn seed germplasm in the development of competitive corn seed products, was served on the Company on October 19. The Company filed its answer on December 15, 1999.

On September 22, 1999, the jury in a trademark-infringement litigation brought against the Company by Trovan Ltd. and Electronic Identification Devices, Ltd. relating to use of the TROVAN mark for trovafloxacin issued a verdict in favor of the plaintiffs with respect to liability, holding that the Company had infringed Trovan Ltd.'s mark and had acted in bad faith. Following a further damage trial, on October 12, 1999, the jury awarded Trovan Ltd. a total of $143 million in damages, comprised of $5 million actual damages, $3 million as a reasonable royalty and $135 million in punitive damages. The court held a hearing on December 27, 1999, on whether to award the plaintiffs profits based on the Company's sales of Trovan and, if so, the amount of same. The Company's motion for mistrial remains outstanding.

As previously disclosed, a number of lawsuits and claims have been brought against the Company and Shiley Incorporated, a wholly owned subsidiary, alleging either personal injury from fracture of 60° or 70° Shiley Convexo Concave ("C/C") heart valves, or anxiety that properly functioning implanted valves might fracture in the future, or personal injury from a prophylactic replacement of a functioning valve.

In an attempt to resolve all claims alleging anxiety that properly functioning valves might fracture in the future, the Company entered into a settlement agreement in January 1992 in Bowling v. Shiley, et al., a case brought in the United States District Court for the Southern District of Ohio, that established a worldwide settlement class of people with C/C heart valves and their spouses, except those who elected to exclude themselves. The settlement provided for a Consultation Fund of $90 million, which was fixed by the number of claims filed, from which valve recipients received payments that are intended to cover their cost of consultation with cardiologists or other health care providers with respect to their valves. The settlement agreement established a second fund of at least $75 million to support C/C valve-related research, including the development of techniques to identify valve recipients who may have significant risk of fracture, and to cover the unreimbursed medical expenses that valve recipients may incur for certain procedures related to the valves. The Company's obligation as to coverage of these unreimbursed medical expenses is not subject to any dollar limitation. Following a hearing on the fairness of the settlement, it was approved by the court on August 19, 1992, and all appeals have been exhausted.

Generally, the plaintiffs in all of the pending heart valve litigations seek money damages. Based on the experience of the Company in defending these claims to date, including insurance proceeds and reserves, the Company is of the opinion that these actions should not have a material adverse effect on the financial position or the results of operations of the Company. Litigation involving insurance coverage for the Company's heart valve liabilities has been resolved.

The Company's operations are subject to federal, state, local and foreign environmental laws and regulations. Under the Comprehensive Environmental Response Compensation and Liability Act of 1980, as amended ("CERCLA" or "Superfund"), the Company has been designated as a potentially responsible party by the United States Environmental Protection Agency with respect to certain waste sites with which the Company may have had direct or indirect involvement. Similar designations have been made by some state environmental agencies under applicable state Superfund laws. Such designations are made regardless of the extent of the Company's involvement. There are also claims that the Company may be a

responsible party or participant with respect to several waste site matters in foreign jurisdictions. Such claims have been made by the filing of a complaint, the issuance of an administrative directive or order, or the issuance of a notice or demand letter. These claims are in various stages of administrative or judicial proceedings. They include demands for recovery of past governmental costs and for future investigative or remedial actions. In many cases, the dollar amount of the claim is not specified. In most cases, claims have been asserted against a number of other entities for the same recovery or other relief as was asserted against the Company. The Company is currently participating in remedial action at a number of sites under federal, state, local and foreign laws.

To the extent possible with the limited amount of information available at this time, the Company has evaluated its responsibility for costs and related liability with respect to the above sites and is of the opinion that the Company's liability with respect to these sites should not have a material adverse effect on the financial position or the results of operations of the Company. In arriving at this conclusion, the Company has considered, among other things, the payments that have been made with respect to the sites in the past; the factors, such as volume and relative toxicity, ordinarily applied to allocate defense and remedial costs at such sites; the probable costs to be paid by the other potentially responsible parties; total projected remedial costs for a site, if known; existing technology; and the currently enacted laws and regulations. The Company anticipates that a portion of these costs and related liability will be covered by available insurance.

Through the early 1970s, Pfizer Inc. (Minerals Division) and Quigley Company, Inc. ("Quigley"), a wholly owned subsidiary, sold a minimal amount of one construction product and several refractory products containing some asbestos. These sales were discontinued thereafter. Although these sales represented a minor market share, the Company has been named as one of a number of defendants in numerous lawsuits. These actions, and actions related to the Company's sale of talc products in the past, claim personal injury resulting from exposure to asbestos-containing products, and nearly all seek general and punitive damages. In these actions, the Company or Quigley is typically one of a number of defendants, and both are members of the Center for Claims Resolution (the "CCR"), a joint defense organization of sixteen defendants that is defending these claims. The Company and Quigley are responsible for varying percentages of defense and liability payments for all members of the CCR. A number of cases alleging property damage from asbestos-containing products installed in buildings have also been brought against the Company, but most have been resolved.

As of January 29, 2000, there were 57,328 personal injury claims pending against Quigley and 26,890 such claims against the Company (excluding those that are inactive or have been settled in principle), and 68 talc cases against the Company.

The Company believes that its costs incurred in defending and ultimately disposing of the asbestos personal injury claims, as well as the property damage and talc claims, will be largely covered by insurance policies issued by several primary insurance carriers and a number of excess carriers that have agreed to provide coverage, subject to deductibles, exclusions, retentions and policy limits. Litigation against excess insurance carriers seeking damages and/or declaratory relief to secure their coverage obligations has now been largely resolved, although claims against several of such insureds do remain pending. Based on the Company's experience in defending the claims to date and the amount of insurance coverage available, the Company is of the opinion that the actions should not ultimately have a material adverse effect on the financial position or the results of operations of the Company.

In 1993, the Company was named, together with numerous other manufacturers of brand-name prescription drugs and certain companies that distribute brand-name prescription drugs, in suits in federal and state courts brought by various groups of retail pharmacy companies, alleging that the manufacturers violated the Sherman Act by agreeing not to give retailers certain discounts and that the failure to give such discounts violated the Robinson Patman Act. A class action was brought on the Sherman Act claim, as well as additional actions by approximately 3,500 individual retail pharmacies and a group of chain and supermarket pharmacies (the "individual actions") on both the Sherman Act and Robinson Patman Act claims. A retailer class was certified in 1994 (the "Federal Class Action"). In 1996, fifteen manufacturer defendants, including the Company, settled the Federal Class Action. The Company's share was $31.25 million, payable in four annual installments without interest. Trial began in September 1998 for the class case against the non-settlers, and the District Court also permitted the opt-out plaintiffs to add the wholesalers as named defendants in their cases. The District Court dismissed the case at the close of the plaintiffs' evidence. The plaintiffs appealed and, on July 13, 1999, the Court of Appeals upheld most of the dismissal but remanded on one issue, while expressing doubts that the plaintiffs could prove any damages.

Retail pharmacy cases also have been filed in state courts in five states, and consumer class actions were filed in state courts in fourteen states and the District of Columbia alleging injury to consumers from the failure to give discounts to retail pharmacy companies.

In addition to its settlement of the retailer Federal Class Action (see above), the Company has also settled several major opt-out retail cases, and along with other manufacturers: (1) has entered into an agreement to settle all outstanding consumer class actions (except Alabama, California and North Dakota), which settlement is going through the approval process in the various courts in which the actions are pending; and (2) has entered into an agreement to settle the California consumer case, which has been approved by the Court there.

The Company believes that these brand-name prescription drug antitrust cases, which generally seek damages and certain injunctive relief, are without merit.

The Federal Trade Commission opened an investigation focusing on the pricing practices at issue in the above pharmacy antitrust litigation. In July 1996, the Commission issued a subpoena for documents to the Company, among others, to which the Company responded. A second subpoena was issued to the Company for documents in May 1997 and the Company again responded. We are not aware of any further activity.

FDA administrative proceedings relating to Plax are pending, principally an industry-wide call for data on all anti-plaque products by the FDA. The call-for-data notice specified that products that have been marketed for a material time and to a material extent may remain on the market pending FDA review of the data, provided the manufacturer has a good faith belief that the product is generally recognized as safe and effective and is not misbranded. The Company believes that Plax satisfied these requirements and prepared a response to the FDA's request, which was filed on June 17, 1991. This filing, as well as the filings of other manufacturers, is still under review and is currently being considered by an FDA Advisory Committee. The Committee has issued a draft report recommending that plaque removal claims should not be permitted in the absence of data establishing efficacy against gingivitis. The process of incorporating the Advisory Committee recommendations into a final monograph is expected to take several years. If the draft recommendation is ultimately accepted in the final monograph, although it would have a negative impact on sales of Plax, it will not have a material adverse effect on the sales, financial position or operations of the Company.

On January 15, 1997, an action was filed in Circuit Court, Chambers County, Alabama, purportedly on behalf of a class of consumers, variously defined by the laws or types of laws governing their rights and encompassing residents of up to 47 states. The complaint alleges that the Company's claims for Plax were untrue, entitling them to a refund of their purchase price for purchases since 1988. A hearing on Plaintiffs' motion to certify the class was held on June 2, 1998. We are awaiting the Court's decision. The Company believes the complaint is without merit.

Since December 1998, four actions have been filed, in state courts in Houston, San Francisco, Chicago and New Orleans, purportedly on behalf of statewide (California) or nationwide (Houston, Chicago and New Orleans) classes of consumers who allege that the Company's and other manufacturers' advertising and promotional claims for Rid and other pediculicides were untrue, entitling them to refunds, other damages and/or injunctive relief. The Houston case has been voluntarily dismissed and proceedings in the San Francisco, Chicago and New Orleans cases are still in early stages of the proceedings. The Company believes the complaints are without merit.

In December, 1999 and January, 2000, two suits were filed in California state courts against the Company and other manufacturers of zinc oxide-containing powders. The first suit was filed by the Center for Environmental Health and the second was filed by an individual plaintiff on behalf of a purported class of purchasers of baby powder products. The suits generally allege that the label of Desitin powder violates California's "Proposition 65" by failing to warn of the presence of lead, which is alleged to be a carcinogen. In January, 2000, the Company received a notice from a California environmental group alleging that the labeling of Desitin ointment and powder violates Proposition 65 by failing to warn of the presence of cadmium, which is alleged to be a carcinogen. Several other manufacturers of zinc oxide-containing topical baby products have received similar notices. The Company believes that the labeling for Desitin complies with applicable legal requirements.

In April 1996, the Company received a Warning Letter from the FDA relating to the timeliness and completeness of required post-marketing reports for pharmaceutical products. The letter did not raise any safety issue about Pfizer drugs. The Company has been implementing remedial actions designed to remedy the issues raised in the letter. During 1997, the Company met with the FDA to apprise them of the scope and status of these activities. A review of the Company's new procedures was undertaken by FDA in 1999. The Company and Agency met to review the findings of this review and agreed that commitments and remedial measures undertaken by the Company related to the Warning Letter have been accomplished. The Company agreed to keep the Agency informed of its activities as it continues to modify its processes and procedures.

During May and June, 1999, the FDA and the European Union's Committee for Proprietary Medicinal Products (CPMP) reconsidered the approvals to market Trovan, a broad-spectrum antibiotic, following post-market reports of severe adverse liver reactions to the drug. On June 9, the Company announced that, regarding the marketing of Trovan in the United States, it had agreed to restrict the indications, limit product distribution, make certain other labeling changes and to communicate revised warnings to health care professionals in the United States. On July 1, Pfizer received the opinion of the CPMP recommending a one-year suspension of the licenses to market Trovan in the European Union. The CPMP opinion has been finalized in a Final Decision by the European Commission. Since June, 1999, three suits and several claims have been received by the Company alleging liver injuries due to the ingestion of Trovan. The majority of these claims have been resolved without litigation. In June and July, 1999, two of the lawsuits were filed in the Circuit Court, Hampton County, South Carolina on behalf of a purported class of all persons who received Trovan, seeking compensatory and punitive damages and injunctive relief. One of the suits, seeking injunctive relief, has been dismissed. No substantitive proceedings have yet occurred in the other suit and the Company believes that it is not properly maintainable as a class action, and will defend against it accordingly.

In October 1999 the Company was sued in an action seeking unspecified damages, costs and attorney's fees on behalf

of a purported class of people whose dogs had suffered injury or death after ingesting Rimadyl, an antiarthritic medication for older dogs. The suit, which was filed in state court in South Carolina, is in the early pretrial stages. The Company believes it is without merit.

During 1998, the Company completed the sale of all of the businesses and companies that were part of the Medical Technology Group. As part of the sale provisions, the Company has retained responsibility for certain items, including matters related to the sale of MTG products sold by the Company before the sale of the MTG businesses. A number of cases have been brought against Howmedica Inc. (some of which also name the Company) alleging that P.C.A. one-piece acetabular hip prostheses sold from 1983 through 1990 were defectively designed and manufactured and pose undisclosed risks to implantees. These cases have now been resolved. Between 1994 and 1996, seven class actions alleging various injuries arising from implantable penile prostheses manufactured by American Medical Systems were filed and ultimately dismissed or discontinued. Thereafter, between late 1996 and early 1998, approximately 700 former members of one or more of the purported classes, represented by some of the same lawyers who filed the class actions, filed individual suits in Circuit Court in Minneapolis alleging damages from their use of implantable penile prostheses. Most of these claims, along with a number of filed and unfiled claims from other jurisdictions, have now been resolved. The Company believes that most if not all of these cases are without merit.

In June 1993, the Ministry of Justice of the State of Sao Paulo, Brazil, commenced a civil public action against the Company's Brazilian subsidiary, Laboratorios Pfizer Ltda. ("Pfizer Brazil") asserting that during a period in 1991 Pfizer Brazil withheld sale of the pharmaceutical product Diabinese in violation of antitrust and consumer protection laws. The action sought the award of moral, economic and personal damages to individuals and the payment to a public reserve fund. In February 1996, the trial court issued a decision holding Pfizer Brazil liable. The trial court's opinion also established the amount of moral damages for individuals who might make claims later in the proceeding and set out a formula for calculating the payment into the public reserve fund which could have resulted in a sum of approximately $88 million. Pfizer Brazil appealed this decision. In September 1999, the appeals court issued a ruling upholding the trial court's decision as to liability. However, the appeals court decision overturned the trial court's decision concerning damages, ruling that criteria to apply in the calculation of damages, both as to individuals and as to payment of any amounts to the reserve fund, should be established only in a later stage of the proceeding. The Company believes that this action should not have a material adverse effect on the financial position or the results of operations of the Company.

19 Segment Information and Geographic Data

We operate in the following two business segments:
- pharmaceutical—including treatments for heart diseases, infectious diseases, central nervous system disorders, diabetes, arthritis, erectile dysfunction and allergies, as well as self-medications
- animal health—products for food animals and companion animals, including antibiotics, vaccines and other veterinary items

Each separately managed segment offers different products requiring different marketing and distribution strategies.

We sell our products primarily to customers in the wholesale sector. In 1999, sales to our two largest wholesalers accounted for 14% and 12% of total revenues. These sales were concentrated in the pharmaceutical segment.

Revenues were in excess of $100 million in each of 12 countries outside the U.S. in 1999. The U.S. was the only country to contribute more than 10% to total revenues. The following tables present segment and geographic information:

Segment Information

(millions of dollars)		Pharmaceutical	Animal Health	Corporate/ Other	Consolidated
Total revenues	1999	$14,859	$1,345	$ —	$16,204
	1998	12,230	1,314	—	13,544
	1997	9,726	1,329	—	11,055
Segment profit	1999	4,898[1]	67	(517)[2]	4,448[3]
	1998	3,574	(77)	(903)[2]	2,594[3]
	1997	3,129	112	(374)[2]	2,867[3]
Identifiable assets[4]	1999	9,723	2,144	8,707	20,574
	1998	7,987	2,109	8,206	18,302
	1997	6,464	2,197	6,330[5]	14,991
Property, plant and equipment additions[4]	1999	1,387	90	84	1,561
	1998	991	97	110	1,198
	1997	687	69	122	878
Depreciation and amortization[4]	1999	438	74	30	542
	1998	386	82	21	489
	1997	337	75	16	428

Geographic Data

(millions of dollars)		United States[6]	Japan	All Other Countries	Consolidated
Total revenues	1999	$9,896	$1,249	$5,059	$16,204
	1998	8,205	943	4,396	13,544
	1997	6,089	949	4,017	11,055
Long-lived assets	1999	3,430	487	2,750	6,667
	1998	2,905	369	2,499	5,773
	1997	2,910	283	2,155	5,348

[1] Includes $310 million charge to write off Trovan inventories.

[2] Includes interest income/(expense) and corporate expenses. Corporate also includes other income/(expense) of the financial subsidiaries (see note 3, "Financial Subsidiaries") and certain performance-based compensation expenses not allocated to the operating segments.

[3] Consolidated total equals income from continuing operations before provision for taxes on income and minority interests.

[4] Certain production facilities are shared by various segments. Property, plant and equipment, as well as capital additions and depreciation, are allocated based on physical production. Corporate assets are primarily cash, short-term investments and long-term loans and investments.

[5] Includes net assets of discontinued operations.

[6] Includes operations in Puerto Rico.

20 Subsequent Event

On February 7, 2000, we announced an agreement to merge with Warner-Lambert Company (Warner-Lambert). Under terms of the merger agreement, which has been approved by the Board of Directors of both Pfizer and Warner-Lambert, we will exchange 2.75 shares of Pfizer voting common stock for each outstanding share of Warner-Lambert voting common stock in a tax-free transaction valued at $98.31 per Warner-Lambert share, or an equity value of $90 billion based on the closing price of our stock on February 4, 2000 of $35.75 per share. Customary and usual provisions will be made for outstanding options and warrants.

This transaction is subject to customary conditions, including the use of pooling-of-interests accounting, qualifying as a tax-free reorganization, shareholder approval at both companies and usual regulatory approvals. The transaction is expected to close in mid-2000.

Quarterly Consolidated Financial Data (Unaudited)

(millions of dollars, except per share data)	Quarter			
	First	Second	Third	Fourth
1999				
Net sales	$3,524	$3,298	$3,423	$3,887
Alliance revenue	403	481	569	619
Total revenues	3,927	3,779	3,992	4,506
Costs and expenses	2,778	2,751	3,025	3,202
Income from continuing operations before provision for taxes on income and minority interests	1,149	1,028	967	1,304
Provision for taxes on income	333	298	265	348
Minority interests	1	1	1	2
Income from continuing operations	815	729	701	954
Discontinued operations—net of tax	—	(20)	—	—
Net income	$ 815	$ 709	$ 701	$ 954
Earnings per common share—basic				
Income from continuing operations	$ .22	$ .19	$ .19	$ .25
Discontinued operations—net of tax	—	(.01)	—	—
Net income	$ .22	$ .18	$ .19	$ .25
Earnings per common share—diluted				
Income from continuing operations	$ .21	$ .18	$ .18	$ .25
Discontinued operations—net of tax	—	—	—	—
Net income	$ .21	$ .18	$ .18	$ .25
Cash dividends paid per common share	$ .07 1/3	$ .07 1/3	$ .08	$ .08
Stock prices				
High	$ 48 1/64	$ 50 3/64	$ 40 1/16	$ 42 1/8
Low	$ 36 3/64	$ 31 3/64	$ 32	$ 32 3/16
1998				
Net sales	$ 2,886	$ 3,114	$ 3,110	$ 3,567
Alliance revenue	150	198	220	299
Total revenues	3,036	3,312	3,330	3,866
Costs and expenses	2,294	2,468	2,628	3,560
Income from continuing operations before provision for taxes on income and minority interests	742	844	702	306
Provision for taxes on income	206	249	186	1
Minority interests	1	1	1	(1)
Income from continuing operations	535	594	515	306
Discontinued operations—net of tax	157	34	882	328
Net income	$ 692	$ 628	$ 1,397	$ 634
Earnings per common share—basic				
Income from continuing operations	$ .14	$ .16	$ .13	$ .08
Discontinued operations—net of tax	.04	.01	.24	.08
Net income	$ .18	$ .17	$ .37	$ .16
Earnings per common share—diluted				
Income from continuing operations	$ .14	$ .15	$ .13	$ .07
Discontinued operations—net of tax	.04	—	.23	.09
Net income	$ .18	$ .15	$ .36	$ .16
Cash dividends paid per common share	$ .06 1/3	$ .06 1/3	$ .06 1/3	$ .06 1/3
Stock prices				
High	$ 32 1/2	$ 40 37/64	$ 40 13/64	$ 42 63/64
Low	$ 23 11/16	$ 32 1/8	$ 30 4/64	$ 28 4/64

All data reflects the 1999 three-for-one stock split.

As of January 31, 2000, there were 149,747 record holders of our common stock (symbol PFE).

Financial Summary

(millions, except per share data)	1999	1998	1997	1996	1995	1994	1993	1992	1991	1990	1989
						Year Ended December 31					
Net sales	$14,133	12,677	10,739	9,864	8,684	6,825	6,080	5,816	5,352	4,757	4,220
Alliance revenue	2,071	867	316	—	—	—	—	—	—	—	—
Total revenues	16,204	13,544	11,055	9,864	8,684	6,825	6,080	5,816	5,352	4,757	4,220
Research and development	2,776	2,279	1,805	1,567	1,340	1,036	880	776	654	545	449
Other costs and expenses	8,980	8,671	6,383	5,769	5,327	4,212	3,822	3,829	3,675	3,288	3,045
Divestitures, restructuring and unusual items — net[1]	—	—	—	—	—	—	741	(141)	300	—	—
Income from continuing operations before taxes and minority interests	$ 4,448	2,594	2,867	2,528	2,017	1,577	637	1,352	723	924	726
Provision for taxes on income	$ 1,244	642	775	758	609	445	106	368	141	235	171
Income from continuing operations before cumulative effect of accounting changes	$ 3,199	1,950	2,082	1,764	1,401	1,127	529	981	579	684	551
Discontinued operations — net of tax	(20)	1,401	131	165	172	171	129	113	143	117	130
Cumulative effect of accounting changes	—	—	—	—	—	—	—	(283)[2]	—	—	—
Net income	$ 3,179	3,351	2,213	1,929	1,573	1,298	658	811	722	801	681
Effective tax rate — continuing operations	28.0%	24.8%	27.0%	30.0%	30.2%	28.2%	16.6%	27.2%	19.5%	25.4%	23.6%
Depreciation	$ 473	420	363	309	277	236	206	209	183	167	160
Property, plant and equipment additions	1,561	1,198	878	690	635	620	575	592	505	466	388
Cash dividends paid	1,148	976	881	771	659	594	536	487	437	397	364
As of December 31											
Working capital[3]	$ 2,006	2,739	2,448	1,914	1,787	1,582	1,875	2,749	1,978	1,920	2,026
Property, plant and equipment — net	5,343	4,415	3,793	3,456	3,113	2,747	2,320	1,994	2,061	1,808	1,565
Total assets[3]	20,574	18,302	14,991	14,251	12,339	10,797	8,986	9,346	9,387	8,782	8,099
Long-term debt	525	527	725	681	828	604	571	571	393	189	181
Long-term capital[4]	9,738	9,551	8,819	7,907	6,518	5,150	4,643	5,453	5,725	5,643	5,034
Shareholders' equity	8,887	8,810	7,933	6,954	5,506	4,324	3,866	4,719	5,026	5,092	4,536
Per common share data:											
Basic:											
Income from continuing operations before effect of accounting changes	$ .85	.51	.55	.47	.38	.31	.14	.25	.15	.17	.14
Discontinued operations — net of tax	(.01)	.37	.04	.05	.05	.04	.03	(.04)[2]	.03	.03	.03
Net income	$ .84	.88	.59	.52	.43	.35	.17	.21	.18	.20	.17
Diluted:											
Income from continuing operations before effect of accounting changes	$ .82	.49	.53	.46	.37	.30	.14	.24	.14	.17	.14
Discontinued operations — net of tax	—	.36	.04	.04	.05	.05	.03	(.04)[2]	.04	.03	.03
Net income	$ .82	.85	.57	.50	.42	.35	.17	.20	.18	.20	.17
Market value per share (December 31)	$ 32.44	41.67	24.85	13.83	10.50	6.44	5.75	6.04	7.00	3.37	2.90
Return on shareholders' equity	35.9%	40.0%	29.7%	31.0%	32.0%	31.7%	15.3%	16.6%	14.3%	16.6%	15.4%
Cash dividends paid per share	$ .30⅔	.25⅓	.22⅔	.20	.17⅓	.15⅔	.14	.12⅓	.11	.10	.09⅓
Shareholders' equity per share	$ 2.36	2.33	2.10	1.85	1.48	1.18	1.04	1.21	1.27	1.29	1.14
Current ratio	1.22:1	1.38:1	1.49:1	1.36:1	1.37:1	1.35:1	1.60:1	1.92:1	1.62:1	1.67:1	1.75:1
Weighted average shares used to calculate:											
Basic earnings per share amounts	3,775	3,789	3,771	3,743	3,687	3,670	3,785	3,948	3,963	3,966	3,972
Diluted earnings per share amounts	3,884	3,945	3,909	3,864	3,777	3,729	3,845	4,038	4,072	4,046	4,073
Employees of continuing operations (thousands)	51	46	41	39	37	34	33	33	35	33	33
Total revenues per employee (thousands)	$ 318	292	269	256	238	202	184	177	154	145	129

All financial information reflects the divestitures of our MTG and food science businesses as discontinued operations.

We have restated all common share and per share data for the 1999, 1997, 1995 and 1991 stock splits.

[1] Divestitures, restructuring and unusual items — net includes the following:

    1993 — Pre-tax charges of approximately $745 million and $56 million to cover worldwide restructuring programs, as well as unusual items and a gain of approximately $60 million realized on the sale of our remaining interest in Minerals Technologies Inc.

    1992 — Pre-tax gain of $259 million on the sale of a business, offset by pre-tax charges of $175 million for restructuring, consolidating and streamlining. In addition, it includes pre-tax curtailment gains of $57 million associated with postretirement benefits other than pensions of divested operations.

    1991 — A pre-tax charge of $300 million for potential future Shiley C/C heart valve fracture claims.

[2] Accounting changes adopted January 1, 1992: SFAS No. 106 — charge of $313 million or $.08 per share; SFAS No. 109 — credit of $30 million or $.01 per share. Per share amounts of accounting changes are included in per share amounts presented for discontinued operations.

[3] Includes net assets of discontinued operations of our MTG businesses through 1997.

[4] Defined as long-term debt, deferred taxes on income, minority interests and shareholders' equity.

Roche
Annual Report 2000

Finance

In 2000 Roche achieved a record net income of CHF 8.6 billion, an increase of 50% over 1999. As in the previous year the operating result was enhanced through placing Genentech shares in the market which contributed CHF 3.9 billion to Group operating profit and CHF 2.5 billion to Group net income. In addition, finance and treasury operations contributed a strong net financial income of CHF 2.3 billion including gains from the sale of LabCorp shares. On an adjusted basis, excluding the effects from these items, changes in accounting policies and the Fragrances and Flavours business spun off in June 2000, Group net income increased 14% over 1999. As a result of the strong cash flow Roche has – three years after the Corange acquisition – become a net creditor again with a net liquidity position of CHF 3.2 billion. The ratio of equity and minority interests to total assets improved from 43% to 46%.

Financial Review

Highlights <small>in millions of CHF</small>

	Figures reported in the financial statements			Figures reported on an adjusted basis		
	2000	1999	% change	2000	1999	% change
Sales	28,672	27,567	+4	27,543	25,496	+8
EBITDA	11,126	8,874	+25	7,068	6,647	+6
Operating profit	7,131	6,421	+11	4,301	4,094	+5
Net income	8,647	5,764	+50	5,014	4,401	+14

Record results

In 2000 the Roche Group achieved record results. Consolidated sales reached 28.7 billion Swiss francs, an increase of 4% over the previous year, EBITDA increased by 25% to 11.1 billion Swiss francs, operating profit reached 7.1 billion Swiss francs, a rise of 11% compared to 1999, and net income rose by 50% to 8.6 billion Swiss francs. These results were driven by higher operating and financial income and substantial gains on the sale of Genentech and LabCorp shares.

On an adjusted basis, the results of the Roche Group also reflect a strong performance. Group sales rose by 8% to 27.5 billion Swiss francs, EBITDA increased by 6% to 7.1 billion Swiss francs, operating profit by 5% to 4.3 billion Swiss francs and net income by 14% to 5.0 billion Swiss francs. The adjusted figures are presented to improve the comparability of current and future results and are given for both 2000 and 1999. They are shown on a continuing basis, without the Fragrances and Flavours business, and adjust for the accounting effects of various special items and changes in International Accounting Standards. A description of the adjustments is given on page 50.

In 2000 Roche again recorded record profits, as net income rose 50% over the previous year to 8.6 billion Swiss francs.

Henri B. Meier, Chief Financial Officer until 31 December 2000

Double-digit sales growth in Diagnostics; sales growth in Pharmaceuticals reduced due to patent expiry and generic competition

The reported Group sales growth of 4% was influenced by the spin-off of Givaudan in June 2000. On an adjusted basis, i.e. excluding the sales of Fragrances and Flavours, the Roche Group achieved a growth rate of 8% in Swiss francs or 2% in local currencies. Furthermore, the sale of the Medicinal Feed Additives (MFA) products in May 2000 influenced the top-line results. Excluding MFA and Fragrances and Flavours, the Group posted a sales growth of 9% in Swiss francs and 3% in local currencies.

With growth rates of 18% in Swiss francs and 12% in local currencies, sales of the Diagnostics Division once again outpaced the market. Sales in Patient Care, Molecular Systems and Molecular Biochemicals all grew at double-digit rates in local currencies. Pharma sales rose 7% in Swiss francs and 1% in local currencies. The good performance of certain established and new products such as Mabthera/Rituxan, Herceptin, NeoRecormon, Cellcept and Roaccutan/Accutane was partially offset by generic competition for Versed and Ticlid in the United States after patents had expired. After a strong start sales of Xenical levelled off in 2000. Sales by the Vitamins and Fine Chemicals Division increased by 2% in Swiss francs, but declined by 4% in local currencies, excluding the MFA products. Sales volumes continued to grow strongly while price levels after a 7-year decline on average have now stabilised.

Further increase of EBITDA and operating profit

Group EBITDA increased by 25% to 11.1 billion Swiss francs and the operating profit increased by 11% to 7.1 billion Swiss francs. The main drivers for this strong result are a 4% increase in gross profit, another substantial gain on the sale of Genentech shares and the absence of further unprovided expenses for settling the vitamin case. The gross profit margin remained stable. Marketing and distribution costs grew faster than sales to exploit the market potential of established and new products. Net other operating income reflected gains from the continuing realignment of the product portfolio. On an adjusted basis, i.e. excluding special items, changes in accounting policies and the Fragrances and Flavours business, EBITDA rose by 6% to 7.1 billion Swiss francs and operating profit by 5% to 4.3 billion Swiss francs.

Roche has by far the highest amortisation charge of the large pharmaceutical companies as a result of its acquisitions (instead of mergers) and the use of International Accounting Standards. In 2000, the amortisation charge was 1.5 billion Swiss francs or 5% of sales compared to 0–2% of sales for our main competitors.

The EBITDA margins for Diagnostics and Pharmaceuticals remained practically unchanged, while the Vitamins EBITDA margin declined slightly as a result of lower average prices.

Givaudan spin-off completed

On 8 June 2000 the Fragrances and Flavours Division was listed on the Swiss Exchange as an independent company under the name Givaudan. The shares in Givaudan were distributed as a special dividend to all holders of Roche shares and non-voting equity securities on a one-for-one basis. The annual impact of the spin-off on the results of the Roche Group, as shown in the adjusted figures, is a reduction of sales by 8%, operating profit by 6% and net income by 3%.

Acquisition of Kytril to strengthen Roche's oncology portfolio

In December 2000 Roche acquired the global rights to Kytril for 1.1 billion US dollars from SmithKline Beecham in connection with its merger with Glaxo Wellcome. In 1999 Kytril achieved net sales of 550 million Swiss francs. Roche also sold to SmithKline Beecham the exclusive rights to Coreg in the United States and Canada for 400 million US dollars.

Substantial gain on sale of Genentech shares

On 29 March 2000 the Group sold 17.3 million shares of Genentech through a public offering yielding proceeds of 2.8 billion US dollars. The resulting pre-tax gain after incidental costs was 3.9 billion Swiss francs. Roche now holds 58% of Genentech, which corresponds approximately to the majority holding acquired in 1990.

Major steps in settling vitamin case in the United States

During 2000 Roche completed two major steps for settling the vitamin case in the United States. On 28 March 2000 a US federal judge approved the overall settlement agreement to a class action suit brought by the US buyers of bulk vitamins. Several customers in the class action have decided to opt out of the overall settlement and pursue claims against the Group individually. On 10 October 2000 an overall agreement with indirect customers and end-consumers in the United States was announced. Outside the United States, the European Commission issued a Statement of Objections in July 2000 against 13 producers of bulk vitamins, including Roche. The global provisions recorded in 1999 remain the current best estimate of the total liability.

Another strong financial result

Total financial income reached 2.3 billion Swiss francs in 2000. This strong positive result is primarily driven by net gains on sales of marketable securities including shares of LabCorp. In June 2000 LabCorp called for redemption its entire convertible preferred stock, part of which was held by Roche as a portfolio investment. During the conversion process Roche realised a pre-tax gain of 296 million Swiss francs. In October 2000 Roche reduced its holding in LabCorp to 33%, realising a pre-tax gain of 660 million Swiss francs. The gain on the October sale is excluded from the adjusted results.

With our capacity to generate a high cash flow and our very solid financing we are highly flexible and well equipped for the future.

Anton Affentranger, Chief Financial Officer since 1 January 2001

Financial condition strengthened further

In 2000, the Group achieved an impressive cash flow. The gross cash flow of the Group (EBITDA) increased by 25% to 11.1 billion Swiss francs reflecting the improvements in the operating result including the gain from the sale of Genentech shares. Furthermore, the improvement of the working capital turnover and the financial income contributed substantially. Net liquidity was strengthened by 6.1 billion Swiss francs in total during the year. At 31 December 2000 the net liquidity amounted to 3.2 billion Swiss francs (compared to net debt of 2.9 billion Swiss francs at 31 December 1999). The ratio of equity and minority interests to total assets increased from 43% at year-end 1999 to 46% at the end of 2000.

Offsetting impacts of new and revised International Accounting Standards

Several new and revised standards issued by the International Accounting Standards Committee became effective from 1 January 2000. The effects of the changes in accounting policies regarding business combinations and intangible assets amount to 1.4 billion Swiss francs, which was largely offset by the impact from the new standard on impairment of assets of 1.2 billion Swiss francs. The accounting effects of all major acquisitions since 1990 are now reported in a consistent manner.

Consolidated income statements _in millions of CHF_

	Figures reported in the financial statements			Figures reported on an adjusted basis		
	2000	1999	% change	2000	1999	% change
Sales	28,672	27,567	+4	27,543	25,496	+8
Cost of sales	(9,163)	(8,874)	+3	(8,445)	(7,813)	+8
Gross profit	19,509	18,693	+4	19,098	17,683	+8
Marketing and distribution	(8,746)	(7,813)	+12	(8,507)	(7,377)	+15
Research and development	(3,950)	(3,782)	+4	(3,919)	(3,732)	+5
Administration	(1,242)	(1,174)	+6	(1,201)	(1,103)	+9
Amortisation of intangible assets	(1,474)	(1,207)	+22	(1,439)	(1,371)	+5
Impairment of long-term assets	(1,147)	–	–	14	–	–
Other operating income (expense), net	232	14	+1,557	255	(6)	–
Gain from sales of Genentech shares	3,949	4,461	–11	–	–	–
Vitamin case	–	(2,426)	–100	–	–	–
Genentech legal settlements	–	(345)	–100	–	–	–
Operating profit	7,131	6,421	+11	4,301	4,094	+5
Financial income (expense), net	2,337	1,134	+106	1,723	1,242	+39
Profit before taxes	9,468	7,555	+25	6,024	5,336	+13
Income taxes	(2,272)	(1,902)	+19	(1,026)	(992)	+3
Profit after taxes	7,196	5,653	+27	4,998	4,344	+15
Changes in accounting policies	1,395	27	+5,067	–	–	–
Income applicable to minority interests	33	88	–63	(7)	61	–
Share of result of associated companies	23	(4)	–	23	(4)	–
Net income	8,647	5,764	+50	5,014	4,401	+14
Diluted earnings per share and non-voting equity security (CHF)	1,024	668		596	510	

Adjusted results: The consolidated results for 2000 and 1999 are significantly influenced by various special items and also by changes in International Accounting Standards. To improve the comparability of current and future consolidated results adjusted figures are calculated for both years. They are used in the internal management of the business and are helpful when reviewing the trends in the Group's results.

- The adjusted results are shown on a continuing basis. The results of the Fragrances and Flavours Division are excluded as if the Givaudan spin-off had already taken place on 1 January 1999. Sales by the Vitamins and Fine Chemicals Division to the Fragrances and Flavours Division are reclassified as sales to third parties.
- The adjusted results also exclude the gains on the sales of Genentech shares, the gain on the sale of LabCorp shares in October 2000, the costs of the vitamin case and Genentech legal settlements.
- The 1999 adjusted results show the recurring accounting effects of the new and revised International Accounting Standards that became effective on 1 January 2000, and of the acquisition of the remaining outstanding shares in Genentech in 2000 as if they had already taken place at the beginning of 1999.
- The adjusted figures exclude the charges recorded in the second half of 1999 and in 2000 relating to the fair-value adjustments of inventories associated with the Genentech acquisition.
- The above adjustments have also led to corresponding modifications to income taxes and to income applicable to minority interests. The minority interest figure for 1999 is calculated as if the participation in Genentech as at 31 December 1999 had applied throughout the whole of 1999.

An analysis of the adjustments is given on page 95, and explanations of the adjusting items are given in Notes 1, 3, 5, 6 and 7 to the Consolidated Financial Statements.

Sales on an adjusted basis ^{in millions of CHF}

By division	2000	1999	% change (CHF)	% change (local currencies)
Pharmaceuticals	17,686	16,487	+7	+1
Diagnostics	6,252	5,282	+18	+12
Vitamins and Fine Chemicals	3,605	3,727	−3	−9
Total sales	27,543	25,496	+8	+2

Gross profit

In 2000 gross profit increased by 816 million Swiss francs to 19.5 billion Swiss francs. The gross profit margin remained at 68%. On an adjusted basis, i.e. excluding primarily Fragrances and Flavours, gross profit reached 19.1 billion Swiss francs, an increase of 1.4 billion Swiss francs. On this basis, the gross profit margin also remained stable at 69%. The gross profit margin was improved by a favourable change in the division mix with a higher share of high-margin businesses and further productivity improvements in all divisions. However, this was offset by continued pressure on prices, in particular for Vitamins and Fine Chemicals, and a new generation of products in Diagnostics with increased production and service costs.

Marketing and distribution

Marketing and distribution expenses increased by 933 million Swiss francs or 12% to 8.7 billion Swiss francs. On an adjusted basis, i.e. excluding Fragrances and Flavours, marketing and distribution expenses rose by 1.1 billion Swiss francs or 15% to 8.5 billion Swiss francs. The major factors involved were the increased efforts in Pharmaceuticals to build the market for Xenical and Tamiflu, the increased support for the new oncology products and pre-marketing expenses for upcoming product launches. Other factors were the increased marketing spend by Diagnostics to foster its leading position in the industry and to build new markets.

Research and development

The 4% rise in research and development costs was almost exclusively attributable to Genentech's in-license and collaboration agreements and increased spending on later-stage clinical trials. Excluding Genentech, research and development costs remained at the level of 1999. Research and development costs as a percentage of sales on Group level were stable at 14%. For Pharmaceuticals, which account for more than 80% of the Group's research and development expenses, they remained at 18%.

Administration

Administration costs grew by 6%, and by 9% on an adjusted basis, i.e. excluding Fragrances and Flavours. This increase was slightly greater than the growth in sales mainly as a result of increased legal costs due to competitive conditions and governmental inquiries more than offsetting savings from improved processes.

Amortisation of intangible assets

The significant increase of amortisation expenses was primarily driven by a half-year amortisation of intangible assets and goodwill resulting from the acquisition of the remaining outstanding Genentech shares in June 1999. On an adjusted basis, the increase in amortisation of intangible assets was primarily due to foreign currency effects.

Impairment of long-term assets

The adoption of new International Accounting Standards resulted in impairment charges of 1.2 billion Swiss francs relating to intangible assets acquired prior to 2000. Further impairment entries during 2000 resulted in a net impairment credit of 14 million Swiss francs as shown in the adjusted results.

Other operating income (expense), net

Other operating income (expense), net increased by more than 0.2 billion Swiss francs mainly due to higher gains from ongoing realignments of the product portfolio and higher royalty income despite increased royalty and restructuring expenses.

Operating profit

Operating profit rose by 11% to 7.1 billion Swiss francs primarily driven by a 4% increase in gross profit, the 3.9 billion Swiss francs gain on the sale of Genentech shares and no further unprovided expenses for the vitamin case. Operating profit on an adjusted basis increased from 4.1 to 4.3 billion Swiss francs in 2000. The margin on sales on an adjusted basis declined from 16.1% in 1999 to 15.6%.

Divisional results on an adjusted basis in millions of CHF

	Pharma-ceuticals	Diagnostics	Vitamins and Fine Chemicals	Other	Group
Year ended 31 December 2000					
Divisional sales to third parties	17,686	6,252	3,605	–	27,543
EBITDA	4,970	1,639	719	(260)	7,068
– as % of sales	28	26	20	–	26
Operating profit	3,249	822	494	(264)	4,301
– as % of sales	18	13	14	–	16
Year ended 31 December 1999					
Divisional sales to third parties	16,487	5,282	3,727	–	25,496
EBITDA	4,656	1,380	799	(188)	6,647
– as % of sales	28	26	21	–	26
Operating profit	3,069	633	584	(192)	4,094
– as % of sales	19	12	16	–	16

EBITDA (Earnings before interest and other financial income, tax, depreciation and amortisation including impairment) measures the gross cash generation of the divisions. The divisional operating profit margins furthermore reflect the different fixed asset intensities of the businesses and the acquisition history.

The EBITDA margin of the Pharmaceuticals Division remained at 28%. The higher marketing costs for Xenical, Tamiflu and the new oncology products and the pre-marketing expenses for upcoming product launches were offset by higher sales with an improved gross profit margin and by gains from the continuing realignment of the product portfolio.

The Diagnostics Division maintained its EBITDA margin at 26%. The higher marketing efforts led to correspondingly higher sales. The operating profit margin increased by 1 percentage point.

The strong long-term competitive pressure in the Vitamins and Fine Chemicals business continued. However, the division was able to offset the sales price decline to some extent by further productivity improvements and volume increases. EBITDA decreased by one percentage point to 20%.

The result of 'Other' consists of the costs of Corporate Headquarters. In 2000 they increased substantially due to restructuring costs relating to the Basel Institute for Immunology and the voluntary solidarity contribution to the Holocaust Victim Assets Litigation (Swiss Banks Litigation).

Financial income (expense), net

Total financial income (expense), net showed a substantial increase of over 100% to 2.3 billion Swiss francs. Key factors were profits achieved on the marketable securities portfolio, despite weak stock markets, together with the gain on the sale of LabCorp shares, which reduced the Group's participation to 33%, and the gain on the portfolio investment in LabCorp convertibles. With higher net liquidity available than in 1999, interest income increased substantially. This increase largely compensated the rise in interest expenses resulting from additional debt and from increases in the discounted value of provisions. The net result on foreign exchange transactions also improved compared to the previous year. Even after exclusion of the gain on the October sale of LabCorp shares, total financial income (expense), net rose by 39%.

An analysis of its components is given in Note 10 to the Consolidated Financial Statements.

Net income

Net income rose by 50% to 8.6 billion Swiss francs in 2000. This represents a return on sales of 30%. On an adjusted basis, the increase amounted to 14%.

Balance sheet in millions of CHF

	2000	1999	% change
Long-term assets	34,798	35,800	−3
Current assets	34,737	34,631	=
Total assets	69,535	70,431	−1
Equity	27,608	26,954	+2
Minority interests	4,428	3,047	+45
Non-current liabilities	23,642	25,574	−8
Current liabilities	13,857	14,856	−7
Total equity, minority interests and liabilities	69,535	70,431	−1

One of the most notable factors in the development of the Group's balance sheet during the year was the spin-off of Givaudan, excluding assets of 3.9 billion Swiss francs and liabilities of 1.2 billion Swiss francs from the Roche Group's balance sheet. A further significant development was the acquisition of the global rights to Kytril for 1.1 billion US dollars, which added to intangible assets. There was also a change in accounting policy under which the Group reclassified as a reduction from equity 4.2 billion Swiss francs of own equity instruments, which in previous years were reported as marketable securities.

The record earnings, fed by the Genentech and LabCorp share sales and the strong results of on-going activities, were largely responsible for turning the net debt position of 2.9 billion Swiss francs at the start of the year into a net liquidity position of 3.2 billion Swiss francs by its end. They also helped raise the Group's ratio of equity and minority interests to total assets from 43% to 46% over the same period.

The 'Knock Out' bonds were repaid at maturity, and some of the 'Helveticus' convertible bonds were also exercised. The consequent reduction in the Group's borrowings was nevertheless more than offset by the issue of the 'Sumo' and 'LYONs' bonds.

The implementation of new and revised International Accounting Standards on intangible assets and business combinations at 1 January 2000 resulted in an increase of 1.4 billion Swiss francs in intangible assets. However, a reduction in intangible assets of a similar magnitude arose following the implementation of the new Standard on impairment of assets at the same date, so that the net effect on the balance sheet was minor. The changes are purely of an accounting nature and have no impact on the Group's cash flows.

Cash flows in millions of CHF

	2000	1999
Operating activities before income taxes	6,204	2,557
Income taxes paid (all activities)	(2,288)	(830)
Operating activities	3,916	1,727
Financing activities	(2,538)	(895)
Investing activities	(832)	(867)
Net effect of currency translation on cash	(36)	103
Increase (decrease) in cash	510	68

Cash flows from operating activities (before income taxes) increased by 3.6 billion Swiss francs due to the improved operating result, better working capital performance and reduced outflows in respect of the vitamin case and restructuring. Income taxes paid in 2000 were considerably higher, mainly due to the Genentech and LabCorp share sales. Financing activities cash flows benefited from the 4.1 billion Swiss francs proceeds from the issue of the 'Sumo' and 'LYONs IV' bonds which exceeded the outflows on the 'Knock Out' and 'Helveticus' bonds. Meanwhile, the 5.7 billion Swiss francs proceeds from the Genentech and LabCorp transactions were partly used in the Kytril acquisition (1.9 billion Swiss francs) and in additions to property, plant and equipment (2.2 billion Swiss francs). The remainder was reinvested in net purchases of marketable securities, to give a net cash outflow from investing activities of 0.8 billion Swiss francs.

Foreign exchange rates

Exchange rates against the Swiss franc were:

	31 December 2000	Average 2000	31 December 1999	Average 1999	31 December 1998
1 USD	1.64	1.69	1.60	1.50	1.37
1 EUR	1.52	1.56	1.61	1.60	1.60
1 GBP	2.45	2.56	2.58	2.43	2.29
100 JPY	1.43	1.57	1.57	1.33	1.18

Compared to 1999 the US dollar was on average 13% stronger against the Swiss franc, while the euro was around 3% weaker. The net effect of these differing exchange rate patterns on the Group's sales was a positive 6 percentage points.

The US dollar's 3% strengthening against the Swiss franc on a year-end basis contrasted with the weakening of the euro (–6%) and the Japanese yen (–9%). The divergence in trends tended to mitigate effects on the Group's balance sheet.

CHF/USD exchange rate

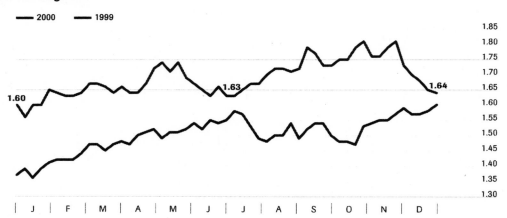

Introduction of the euro

The introduction of the euro has presented various opportunities to streamline the conduct of the business. With regard to systems, the business processes and IT systems of European Group companies have been adapted to handle euro-denominated transactions. The companies concerned are able to deal with dual-currency transactions in the transition period to 2002, and those located in EMU countries will be converting to the euro for accounting purposes during the course of 2001.

Consolidated Financial Statements

Reference numbers indicate corresponding Notes to the Consolidated Financial Statements

Consolidated income statement in millions of CHF

	Year ended 31 December 2000	1999
Sales[4]	28,672	27,567
Cost of sales	(9,163)	(8,874)
Gross profit	19,509	18,693
Marketing and distribution	(8,746)	(7,813)
Research and development[4]	(3,950)	(3,782)
Administration	(1,242)	(1,174)
Amortisation of intangible assets[13]	(1,474)	(1,207)
Impairment of long-term assets[1, 13]	(1,147)	–
Other operating income (expense), net[9]	232	14
Gain from sales of Genentech shares[3]	3,949	4,461
Vitamin case[5]	–	(2,426)
Genentech legal settlements[6]	–	(345)
Operating profit	7,131	6,421
Financial income (expense), net[10]	2,337	1,134
Profit before taxes	9,468	7,555
Income taxes[11]	(2,272)	(1,902)
Profit after taxes	7,196	5,653
Changes in accounting policies[1]	1,395	27
Income applicable to minority interests[23]	33	88
Share of result of associated companies[14]	23	(4)
Net income	8,647	5,764
Basic earnings per share and non-voting equity security (CHF)[22]	1,036	668
Diluted earnings per share and non-voting equity security (CHF)[22]	1,024	668

Consolidated balance sheet in millions of CHF

	31 December 2000	1999
Long-term assets		
Property, plant and equipment[12]	13,785	14,240
Intangible assets[13]	15,870	15,672
Investments in associated companies[14]	652	535
Other investments	1,558	1,736
Deferred income tax assets[11]	460	1,170
Other long-term assets[15]	2,473	2,447
Total long-term assets	34,798	35,800
Current assets		
Inventories[16]	5,754	6,546
Accounts receivable – trade[17]	5,519	6,178
Current income tax assets[11]	435	408
Other current assets[18]	2,381	2,633
Marketable securities[19]	18,086	16,814
Cash[19]	2,562	2,052
Total current assets	34,737	34,631
Total assets	69,535	70,431
Equity		
Share capital[21]	160	160
Non-voting equity securities *(Genussscheine)*[21]	p.m.	p.m.
Own equity instruments[21]	(4,166)	
Retained earnings	31,839	26,669
Other reserves	(225)	125
Total equity	27,608	26,954
Minority interests[23]	4,428	3,047
Non-current liabilities		
Long-term debt[24]	16,167	15,962
Deferred income tax liabilities[11]	2,535	3,895
Liabilities for post-employment benefits[8]	2,502	2,764
Provisions[26]	2,036	1,694
Other non-current liabilities	402	1,259
Total non-current liabilities	23,642	25,574
Current liabilities		
Short-term debt[24]	5,451	5,702
Current income tax liabilities[11]	882	728
Provisions[26]	1,959	2,660
Accounts payable – trade and other	2,215	2,378
Accrued and other current liabilities[20]	3,350	3,388
Total current liabilities	13,857	14,856
Total equity, minority interests and liabilities	69,535	70,431

p.m. = pro memoria. Non-voting equity securities have no nominal value (see Note 21).

Consolidated statement of changes in equity in millions of CHF

	Year ended 31 December	
	2000	1999
Share capital[21]		
Balance at 1 January and at 31 December	160	160
Non-voting equity securities *(Genussscheine)*[21]		
Balance at 1 January and at 31 December	p.m.	p.m.
Own equity instruments[21]		
Balance at 1 January as previously reported	–	
Adjustment from change in accounting policies	(3,291)	
Balance at 1 January as restated	(3,291)	
Movements during the year	(875)	
Balance at 31 December	(4,166)	
Retained earnings		
Balance at 1 January	26,669	21,655
Net income	8,647	5,764
Dividends paid[21]	(835)	(750)
Givaudan spin-off – special dividend and transfer of net assets[7, 21]	(2,642)	–
Balance at 31 December	31,839	26,669
Other reserves		
– Equity conversion options		
Conversion option embedded in 'Sumo' bonds[24]	24	–
– Currency translation differences		
Balance at 1 January	125	(149)
Gains (losses) recognised during the year	(374)	274
Balance at 31 December	(249)	125
Balance other reserves at 31 December	(225)	125
Total equity at 31 December	27,608	26,954

p.m. = pro memoria. Non-voting equity securities have no nominal value (see Note 21).

Consolidated cash flow statement in millions of CHF

	Year ended 31 December	
	2000	1999
Cash flows from operating activities		
Net income	8,647	5,764
Non-operating income and expenses*	(1,516)	657
Operating profit	7,131	6,421
Depreciation of property, plant and equipment[12]	1,374	1,246
Amortisation of intangible assets[13]	1,474	1,207
Impairment of long-term assets[1, 13]	1,147	–
Effects of Genentech transactions, vitamin case and Genentech legal settlements[28]	(3,791)	(1,550)
Other adjustments for non-cash operating income and expense[28]	(90)	619
(Increase) decrease in working capital	367	(2,618)
Costs of vitamin case paid[5]	41	(1,282)
Costs of Genentech legal settlements paid[6]	(337)	(75)
Restructuring costs paid[26]	(338)	(910)
Payments made for defined benefit post-employment plans[8]	(309)	(290)
Other operating cash flows	(465)	(211)
Cash flows from operating activities, before income taxes paid	6,204	2,557
Income taxes paid	(2,288)	(830)
Total cash flows from operating activities	3,916	1,727
Cash flows from financing activities		
Proceeds from issue of long-term debt[28]	4,143	4,175
Repayment of long-term debt[28]	(3,062)	(3,689)
Transactions in own equity instruments[21]	(875)	
Increase (decrease) in short-term borrowings	(747)	70
Interest and dividends paid[28]	(1,737)	(1,436)
Givaudan spin-off – special dividend and Givaudan cash balances[7, 21]	(465)	–
Other	205	(15)
Total cash flows from (used in) financing activities	(2,538)	(895)
Cash provided by operating and financing activities	1,378	832
Cash flows from investing activities		
Purchase of property, plant and equipment, and intangible assets[12, 13]	(2,402)	(2,413)
Disposal of property, plant and equipment, and intangible assets[12, 13]	200	376
Acquisition of subsidiaries, associated companies and products[28]	(2,686)	(6,222)
Divestments of subsidiaries, associated companies and products[28]	6,809	7,353
Interest and dividends received[28]	743	459
Purchases of marketable securities, net of sales, and other	(3,496)	(420)
Total cash flows from (used in) investing activities	(832)	(867)
Net effect of currency translation on cash	(36)	103
Increase (decrease) in cash	510	68
Cash at beginning of year	2,052	1,984
Cash at end of year[19]	2,562	2,052

*Non-operating income and expenses consist of the following income statement items: financial income (expense), net, income taxes, changes in accounting policies, income applicable to minority interests, and share of result of associated companies.

Notes to the Consolidated Financial Statements

Reference numbers indicate corresponding Notes to the Consolidated Financial Statements

1. Summary of significant accounting policies

Basis of preparation of the consolidated financial statements

The consolidated financial statements of the Roche Group have been prepared in accordance with International Accounting Standards, using the historical cost convention. They were authorised for issue by the Board of Directors on 26 February 2001.

The preparation of the consolidated financial statements requires management to make estimates and assumptions that affect the reported amounts of revenues, expenses, assets and liabilities, disclosure of contingent liabilities at the date of the financial statements. If in the future such estimates and assumptions, which are based on management's best judgement at the date of the financial statements, deviate from the actual circumstances, the original estimates and assumptions will be modified as appropriate in the year in which the circumstances change.

Consolidation policy

These financial statements are the consolidated financial statements of Roche Holding Ltd, a company registered in Switzerland, and its subsidiaries (hereafter 'the Group').

The subsidiaries are those companies controlled, directly or indirectly, by Roche Holding Ltd, where control is defined as the power to govern the financial and operating policies of an enterprise so as to obtain benefits from its activities. This control is normally evidenced when Roche Holding Ltd owns, either directly or indirectly, more than 50% of the voting rights of a company's share capital. Companies acquired during the year are consolidated from the date on which operating control is transferred to the Group, and subsidiaries to be divested are included up to the date of divestment. Companies acquired to be resold are not consolidated but are classified as assets held for sale and carried at cost. Assets identified for divestment in the following year are reclassified as assets held for sale within other current assets. These assets normally consist mainly of inventories, property, plant and equipment, and other long-term assets.

Investments in associated companies are accounted for by the equity method. These are companies over which the Group exercises significant influence, but which it does not control. This is normally evidenced when the Group owns 20% or more of the voting rights of the company. Interests in joint ventures are reported using the line-by-line proportionate consolidation method. Other investments are carried at cost after deducting appropriate provisions for permanent impairment and are included in long-term assets.

Foreign currency valuation

Assets and liabilities of Group companies reporting in currencies other than Swiss francs (foreign entities) are translated into Swiss francs using year-end rates of exchange. Sales, costs, expenses, net income and cash flows are translated at the average rates of exchange for the year. Translation differences due to the changes in exchange rates between the beginning and the end of the year and the difference between net income translated at the average and year-end exchange rates are taken directly to equity. Exchange gains and losses on hedges of non-Swiss franc net investments and on intercompany balances of a long-term investment nature are also taken to equity. On the divestment of a foreign entity, the cumulative currency translation differences relating to that foreign entity are recognised in income as part of the gain or loss on divestment.

Gains and losses on exchange arising in Group companies from the translation into their local reporting currency of their financial assets and liabilities denominated in foreign currencies and from the settlement of foreign currency transactions are included in income.

Certain Group companies maintain financial information for Group reporting purposes in US dollars, Swiss francs or euros where these are the functional currencies of the companies concerned. The effect of exchange rate differences between the local currency and the US dollar, Swiss franc or euro in respect of financial assets and liabilities is included in income.

Sales and cost of sales

Sales represent amounts received and receivable for goods supplied and services rendered to customers after deducting volume discounts and sales taxes. Cost of sales includes the corresponding direct production costs and related production overhead of goods manufactured and services rendered.

Research and development

Research costs are charged against income as incurred, with the exception of buildings and major items of equipment, which are capitalised and depreciated. Development costs are also charged against income as incurred since the criteria for their recognition as an asset are not met.

Employee benefits

Wages, salaries, social security contributions, paid annual leave and sick leave, bonuses, options and non-monetary benefits are accrued in the year in which the associated services are rendered by employees of the Group. Where the Group provides long-term employee benefits, the cost is accrued to match the rendering of the services by the employees concerned.

The Group operates a number of defined benefit and defined contribution plans throughout the world. The cost for the year for defined benefit plans is determined using the projected unit credit method. This reflects service rendered by employees to the dates of valuation and incorporates actuarial assumptions primarily regarding discount rates used in determining the present value of benefits, projected rates of remuneration growth, and long-term expected rates of return for plan assets. Discount rates are based on the market yields of high-quality corporate bonds in the country concerned. Differences between assumptions and actual experiences, and effects of changes in actuarial assumptions are allocated over the estimated average remaining working lives of employees, where these differences exceed a defined corridor. Past service costs are allocated over the average period until the benefits become vested. Pension assets and liabilities in different defined benefit schemes are not offset unless the Group has a legally enforceable right to use the surplus in one plan to settle obligations in the other plan.

The Group's contributions to the defined contribution plans are charged to the income statement in the year to which they relate.

Taxation

Income taxes include all taxes based upon the taxable profits of the Group, including withholding taxes payable on the distribution of retained earnings within the Group. Other taxes not based on income, such as property and capital taxes, are included within operating expenses or financial expenses according to their nature.

Provision for income taxes, mainly withholding taxes, which could arise on the remittance of retained earnings, principally relating to subsidiaries, is only made where there is a current intention to remit such earnings.

Deferred income taxes are provided using the liability method, under which deferred tax consequences are recognised for temporary differences between the tax bases of assets and liabilities and their carrying values for financial reporting purposes. Deferred income tax assets relating to the carry-forward of unused tax losses are recognised to the extent that it is probable that future taxable profit will be available against which the unused tax losses can be utilised.

Current and deferred income tax assets and liabilities are offset when the income taxes are levied by the same taxation authority and when there is a legally enforceable right to offset them.

Property, plant and equipment

Property, plant and equipment are initially recorded at cost of purchase or construction and are depreciated on a straight-line basis, except for land, which is not depreciated. Estimated useful lives of major classes of depreciable assets are as follows:

Buildings and land improvements	40 years
Machinery and equipment	5–15 years
Office equipment	3 years
Motor vehicles	5 years

Investment grants or similar assistance for projects are initially recorded as deferred income (in other non-current liabilities) and are subsequently recognised as income over the useful lives of the related assets. Repairs and maintenance costs are recognised as expenses as incurred. Borrowing costs are not capitalised. Assets acquired under finance leases are depreciated over their estimated useful lives. Payments made under operating leases are charged against income on a straight-line basis over the period of the lease.

Inventories

Inventories are stated at the lower of cost or net realisable value. Cost is determined by the first-in first-out method.

Cash and marketable securities

Cash comprises cash on hand and time, call and current balances with banks and similar institutions. This definition is also used for the cash flow statement. Marketable securities are shown at the lower of cost or market value.

Debt instruments

The proceeds, net of expenses, of bonds issued with warrants are allocated between the bonds and the warrants in proportion to their respective fair market values at the time of issue. Any discount arising from the low coupon rate and represented by the difference between the principal amount and the net proceeds is charged to interest expense over the life of the bonds. Obligations arising from warrants issued with debt instruments are accrued over the period the warrants are outstanding, to meet the maximum cash obligation at the date when the warrants are exercisable.

Provisions

Provisions are recognised where a legal or constructive obligation has been incurred which will probably lead to an outflow of resources that can be reasonably estimated.

Financial instruments

Gains and losses from forward exchange contracts, options and currency swaps used to hedge potential exchange rate exposures are deferred and then offset against losses and gains on the specific transactions being hedged. The fee agreed in establishing each contract is amortised over the duration of the contract. Interest differentials under swap arrangements, forward rate agreements and interest rate caps used to manage interest rate exposures are recognised by adjustments to interest expense. When such derivative financial instruments are used for trading purposes any gains and losses from changes in their market value are taken to income as they arise. Certain covered call option contracts entered into by the Group require that underlying securities be lodged with the financial institutions involved in the arrangement.

The fair values at the balance sheet date are approximately in line with their reported carrying values unless specifically mentioned in the Notes to the Consolidated Financial Statements.

International Accounting Standards

Several revised or new standards issued by the International Accounting Standards Committee and interpretations of the Standing Interpretations Committee became effective from 1 January 2000. These are listed below and their effects, if any, are described.

In total, recurring operating costs in 2000 are 33 million Swiss francs higher than under the previous methods of accounting. In recording the effects of changes in accounting policy the Group follows the allowed alternative of retaining the previous year's figures as reported and of displaying the effect in the current year's income statement.

'Property, plant and equipment', 'Provisions, contingent liabilities and contingent assets' and 'Events after the balance sheet date'. No adjustments were necessary as a result of these implementations, as the Group's accounting policies previously reflected the measurement principles in these new or revised standards.

'Share capital – reacquired own equity instruments'. The Group's holdings in its own equity instruments are recorded as a deduction from equity. The original cost of acquisition, consideration received for subsequent resale of these equity instruments and other movements are reported as changes in equity. Previously these instruments were recorded in marketable securities. Had they been treated as own equity instruments in 1999, reported earnings per share would have been approximately 3% higher. These instruments have been acquired primarily to meet the obligations that may arise in respect of certain of the Group's debt instruments.

'Impairment of assets'. When the recoverable amount of an asset, being the higher of its net selling price and its value in use, is less than its carrying amount, then the carrying amount is reduced to its recoverable value. This reduction is reported in the income statement as an impairment loss. Value in use is calculated using estimated cash flows, generally over a five-year period, with extrapolating projections for subsequent years. These are discounted using an appropriate long-term interest rate. Previously the value in use was calculated using cash flow projections on an undiscounted basis. The new standard is required to be adopted on a prospective basis.

As a result, effective 1 January 2000, the Group recognised impairment charges of 1,161 million Swiss francs relating to acquired intangible assets. A reduction in deferred tax liabilities of 348 million Swiss francs was also recorded, giving a net charge of 813 million Swiss francs in the consolidated results. Under the Group's previous accounting treatment, no impairment would have arisen. As a result of the impairment, the net book value of intangible assets was reduced by the amount of the impairment charge, and consequently amortisation in 2000 was 130 million Swiss francs lower than it would have been under the previous policy.

Further impairment entries that arose during the year are disclosed in Note 13.

'Intangible assets' and 'Business combinations'. Goodwill is recorded as an intangible asset and is the surplus of the cost of acquisition over the fair value of identifiable assets acquired. Any goodwill and fair value adjustments are treated as assets and liabilities of the acquired company and are recorded in the local currency of that company.

Patents, licences, trademarks and other intangible assets are initially recorded at fair value. Where these assets have been acquired through a business combination, this will be the fair value allocated in the acquisition accounting. Where these have been acquired other than through a business combination, the initial fair value will be cost.

All intangible assets are amortised over their useful lives on a straight-line basis. Estimated useful lives of major classes of intangible assets are as follows:

Goodwill	5–20 years
Patents, licences, trademarks and other intangible assets	Lower of legal duration and economic useful life, up to a maximum of 20 years

As required for the implementation of these new and revised standards the Group has reviewed the accounting for its previous acquisitions. This process included the acquisitions of Genentech, Nicholas, Syntex, Tastemaker and Corange. The Group has recalculated the goodwill and other assets and liabilities arising from significant acquisitions since 1995 and has adjusted the carrying values accordingly, as is required by the new and revised standards. Furthermore, in connection with acquisitions made prior to 1995, the Group now reports as intangible assets the goodwill which had previously been written-off to equity, and has recalculated this goodwill and other assets and liabilities arising from these acquisitions. Thus the accounting effects of the Group's acquisitions are reported in a consistent manner. In addition, non-acquisition-related intangible assets have been reviewed to ensure that they meet the recognition and measurement criteria of the new standard.

As a result, as of 1 January 2000, the Group recorded certain reclassifications and adjustments of the original purchase accounting allocations to reflect the revised balances, the approximate amount of amortisation up to 1 January 2000 and effects on taxation balances and minority interests. These are as follows:

In millions of CHF	Goodwill	Other intangible assets	Deferred income taxes	Minority interests	Total
Items not previously recognised	12,901	1,727	–	–	14,628
Provisions now charged to expense	(711)	–	–	–	(711)
Transfers	1,079	(1,079)	–	–	–
Prior changes in Group organisation	(628)	–	–	–	(628)
Amortisation, net	(10,283)	(1,505)	–	–	(11,788)
Deferred income tax effects, net	–	–	49	–	49
Minority interests	–	–	–	(155)	(155)
Net credit to income	2,358	(857)	49	(155)	1,395

As a result of this change in accounting policy, the carrying value of intangible assets increased as of 1 January 2000. Consequently the Group's amortisation charge in 2000 was 104 million Swiss francs higher than it would have been under the previous policy. Most of this increase was in the Diagnostics Division.

If the new and revised standards on 'Intangible assets' and 'Business combinations' had been applied in 1999 then the Group's net assets at 31 December 1999 would have been higher by 1,395 million Swiss francs, and the recurring operating costs would have been 187 million Swiss francs higher than reported.

New standards for 2001. For the Consolidated Financial Statements for 2001, a new International Accounting Standard 'Financial instruments: recognition and measurement' will come into effect. The standard requires that all financial assets and financial liabilities are recognised on the balance sheet, including all derivatives. The financial statements will be affected by the introduction of fair value accounting for certain marketable securities, investments and derivatives. For certain marketable securities and investments designated as available for sale, the Group intends to recognise the changes in fair value in equity until the asset is sold.

The assessment of the impact of the standard on the Group's financial position as of 1 January 2001 will be reported in the 2001 consolidated financial statements as an adjustment to retained earnings at 1 January 2001, with no restatement of previously reported amounts for the year ended 31 December 2000. As a result retained earnings will increase by approximately one billion Swiss francs. The most significant part of this relates to other investments, the fair value of which is approximately one billion Swiss francs higher than the carrying value as at 31 December 2000.

The new International Accounting Standard on 'Investment property', effective from 1 January 2001, is not expected to have a significant impact on the Group's financial statements.

International Accounting Standards will continue to be developed and revised in the future. This will lead to further adaptations of the Group's accounting policies in the coming years.

2. Financial risk management

Financial risk management within the Group is governed by policies approved by senior management. These policies cover foreign exchange risk, interest rate risk, market risk, credit risk and liquidity risk. Group policies also cover areas such as cash management, investment of excess funds and the raising of short- and long-term debt.

When deemed appropriate, certain of the above risks are altered through the use of financial instruments. Group management believes that, in order to create the optimum value for the Group, it is not desirable to eliminate or mitigate all possible market fluctuations. Financial instruments are selectively used to create and optimise value. Group companies report details of the financial instruments outstanding and financial liquidity position to Group Treasury on at least a monthly basis.

Foreign exchange risk

The Group operates across the world and is exposed to movements in foreign currencies affecting its net income and financial position, as expressed in Swiss francs.

Transaction exposure arises because the amount of local currency paid or received for transactions denominated in foreign currencies may vary due to changes in exchange rates. For many Group companies income will be primarily in the local currency. A significant amount of expenditure, especially for purchase of goods for resale and interest on and repayment of loans will be in foreign currencies. Similarly, transaction exposure arises on net balances of monetary assets held in foreign currencies. Group companies manage this exposure at a local level, if necessary by means of financial instruments such as options and forward contracts. In addition, Group Treasury monitors total worldwide exposure with the help of comprehensive data received on a monthly basis.

Translation exposure arises from the consolidation of the foreign currency denominated financial statements of the Group's foreign subsidiaries. The effect on the Group's consolidated equity is shown as a currency translation movement. The Group hedges significant net investments in foreign currencies by taking foreign currency loans or issuing foreign currency denominated debt instruments. Major translation exposures are monitored on a regular basis.

A significant part of the Group's cash outflows for research, development, production and administration is denominated in Swiss francs, while a much smaller proportion of the Group's cash inflows are Swiss franc denominated. As a result, an increase in the value of the Swiss franc relative to other currencies has an adverse impact on consolidated net income. Similarly, a relative fall in the value of the Swiss franc has a favourable effect on results published in Swiss francs.

Interest rate risk

Interest rate risk arises from movements in interest rates which could have adverse effects on the Group's net income or financial position. Changes in interest rates cause variations in interest income and expenses on interest-bearing assets and liabilities. In addition, they can affect the market value of certain financial assets, liabilities and instruments as described in the following section on market risk.

The interest rates on the Group's major debt instruments are fixed, as described in Note 24, which reduces the Group's exposure to changes in interest rates. Group companies manage their short-term interest rate risk at a local level, if necessary using financial instruments such as interest rate forward contracts, swaps and options.

Market risk

Changes in the market value of certain financial assets, liabilities and instruments can affect the net income or financial position of the Group. The Group's long-term investments are held for strategic purposes, and changes in market value do not affect the carrying value, unless a permanent loss in value is indicated. The Group's marketable securities are held for fund management purposes. The risk of loss in value is reduced by a very careful review prior to investing, concentration of investments and continuous monitoring of the performance of investments and changes in their risk configuration.

Credit risk

Credit risk arises from the possibility that the counter-party to a transaction may be unable or unwilling to meet their obligations causing a financial loss to the Group.

Trade receivables are subject to a policy of active risk management focussing on the assessment of country risk, credit availability, ongoing credit evaluation and account monitoring procedures. There are no significant concentrations within trade receivables of counter-party credit risk, due to the Group's large number of customers and their wide geographical spread. Country risk limits and exposures are continuously monitored.

The exposure of other financial assets and liabilities to credit risk is controlled by setting a policy for limiting credit exposure to high-quality counter-parties, continuously reviewing credit ratings, and limiting individual aggregate credit exposure accordingly.

Liquidity risk

Group companies need to have sufficient availability of cash to meet their obligations. Individual companies are responsible for their own cash management, including the short-term investment of cash surpluses and the raising of loans to cover cash deficits, subject to guidance by the Group and, in certain cases, to approval at Group level.

The Group maintains sufficient reserves of cash and readily realisable marketable securities to meet its liquidity requirements at all times. In addition, the strong international creditworthiness of the Group allows it to make efficient use of international capital markets for financing purposes.

3. Group organisation

An overview of the operating subsidiaries and associated companies is included on pages 110 to 111. In addition to the operating companies, the Group has holding and finance companies.

Genentech

On 13 June 1999 the Group exercised its option to acquire the remaining outstanding Special Common Stock of Genentech, Inc. on 30 June 1999. As a result, Genentech became a wholly owned subsidiary of the Group. The total consideration of 4,007 million US dollars (6,222 million Swiss francs) included the contribution by the Group to Genentech of the funds required by Genentech to purchase the outstanding Genentech Special Common Stock and the cost to Genentech of settling outstanding obligations under its employee stock option plan. The consideration paid was allocated to the assets and liabilities of Genentech, and consequently the total carrying value of Genentech increased by 6,222 million Swiss francs. As part of this the Group recorded a write-up of inventory of 298 million Swiss francs. During 2000 158 million Swiss francs of this was recognised as cost of sales through the sale of inventory (1999: 140 million Swiss francs).

On 23 July 1999 and 21 October 1999 the Group sold a total of 34% of the Common Stock of Genentech through public offerings yielding total proceeds of 4.9 billion US dollars (7.4 billion Swiss francs). The total resulting pre-tax gain of 4.5 billion Swiss francs is calculated as the difference between the proceeds of the sales, net of incidental costs, and the proportion of net assets.

On 29 March 2000 the Group sold 17.3 million shares of Genentech through a public offering yielding proceeds of 2,771 million US dollars (4,599 million Swiss francs). The resulting pre-tax gain after incidental costs was 3,949 million Swiss francs. Roche's ownership interest in Genentech at 31 December 2000 was 58%.

Other acquisitions and divestments

On 22 December 2000 the Group acquired the global rights to Kytril (granisetron) from SmithKline Beecham for a cash consideration of 1,114 million US dollars (1,871 million Swiss francs).

On 22 December 2000 the Group also sold its exclusive rights to Coreg (carvedilol) in the United States and Canada to SmithKline Beecham for 400 million US dollars (660 million Swiss francs). The Group will remain the supplier of carvedilol in all markets outside the United States and Canada.

As a result of the acquisition of Kytril, the acquisition of the medical instruments division of AVL and certain other smaller acquisitions, additional intangible assets of 2,267 million Swiss francs were recorded. Total cash outflow from other acquisitions was 2,351 million Swiss francs and the inflow from other divestments was 1,087 million Swiss francs.

4. Segment information in millions of CHF

Divisional information

2000	Pharma-ceuticals	Diagnostics	Vitamins and Fine Chemicals	Others	Continuing operations	Fragrances and Flavours	Group
Segment revenues							
Segment revenue/ divisional sales	17,831	6,252	3,696	–	27,779	1,193	28,972
Less inter-divisional sales[a]	(145)	–	(125)	–	(270)	(30)	(300)
Divisional sales to third parties	17,686	6,252	3,571	–	27,509	1,163	28,672
Segment results/ operating profit	5,879	822	494	(264)	6,931	200	7,131
Segment assets and liabilities							
Divisional assets[b]	24,657	11,962	4,406	60	41,085	–	41,085
Other segment assets[c]	530	41	82	–	653	–	653
Segment assets	25,187	12,003	4,488	60	41,738	–	41,738
Non-segment assets[d]							27,797
Total assets							69,535
Divisional liabilities[b]	(501)	(280)	(158)	(1)	(940)	–	(940)
Other segment liabilities[c]	(2,007)	(1,496)	(1,196)	–	(4,699)	–	(4,699)
Segment liabilities	(2,508)	(1,776)	(1,354)	(1)	(5,639)	–	(5,639)
Non-segment liabilities[d]							(31,860)
Total liabilities							(37,499)
Other segment information							
Capital expenditure[e]	3,209	1,023	385	8	4,625	68	4,693
Depreciation	742	387	209	4	1,342	32	1,374
Amortisation	993	430	16	–	1,439	35	1,474
Impairment of long-term assets	1,147	–	–	–	1,147	–	1,147
Research and development costs	3,201	558	122	38	3,919	31	3,950
Share of result of associated companies	–	34	(11)	–	23	–	23
Investments in associated companies	101	432	31	88	652	–	652
Number of employees	41, 409	15,631	7,257	461	64,758	–	64,758

a) Transfer prices for inter-divisional sales are set on an arm's length basis.

b) Divisional assets consist primarily of property, plant and equipment, intangible assets, receivables and inventories. Divisional liabilities consist of trade accounts payable.

c) Other segment assets and liabilities consist of assets and liabilities which can be reasonably attributed to the reported business segments. These include pension assets and liabilities and some provisions.

d) Non-segment assets and liabilities mainly include current and deferred income tax balances, and financial assets and liabilities, principally cash, marketable securities, investments in associated companies, other investments and debt.

e) Capital expenditure comprises additions to intangible assets (including goodwill) and additions to property, plant and equipment, including those arising from acquisitions.

1999	Pharma-ceuticals	Diagnostics	Vitamins and Fine Chemicals	Others	Continuing operations	Fragrances and Flavours	Group
Segment revenues							
Segment revenue/ divisional sales	16,684	5,283	3,832	–	25,799	2,231	28,030
Less inter-divisional sales[a]	(197)	(1)	(183)	–	(381)	(82)	(463)
Divisional sales to third parties	16,487	5,282	3,649	–	25,418	2,149	27,567
Segment results/ operating profit	7,287	771	(1,842)	(192)	6,024	397	6,421
Segment assets and liabilities							
Divisional assets[b]	25,138	10,142	4,440	56	39,776	2,977	42,753
Other segment assets[c]	534	35	100	–	669	17	686
Segment assets	25,672	10,177	4,540	56	40,445	2,994	43,439
Non-segment assets[d]							26,992
Total assets							70,431
Divisional liabilities[b]	(674)	(346)	(149)	(1)	(1,170)	(72)	(1,242)
Other segment liabilities[c]	(2,033)	(1,660)	(1,384)	–	(5,077)	(141)	(5,218)
Segment liabilities	(2,707)	(2,006)	(1,533)	(1)	(6,247)	(213)	(6,460)
Non-segment liabilities[d]							(33,970)
Total liabilities							(40,430)
Other segment information							
Capital expenditure[e]	6,507	633	477	6	7,623	131	7,754
Depreciation	672	336	169	4	1,181	65	1,246
Amortisation	776	323	46	–	1,145	62	1,207
Research and development costs	3,048	516	130	38	3,732	50	3,782
Share of result of associated companies	–	(4)	–	–	(4)	–	(4)
Investments in associated companies	–	515	2	18	535	–	535
Number of employees	40,299	14,456	7,551	482	62,788	4,907	67,695

a) Transfer prices for inter-divisional sales are set on an arm's length basis.

b) Divisional assets consist primarily of property, plant and equipment, intangible assets, receivables and inventories. Divisional liabilities consist of trade accounts payable.

c) Other segment assets and liabilities consist of assets and liabilities which can be reasonably attributed to the reported business segments. These include pension assets and liabilities and some provisions.

d) Non-segment assets and liabilities mainly include current and deferred income tax balances, and financial assets and liabilities, principally cash, marketable securities, investments in associated companies, other investments and debt.

e) Capital expenditure comprises additions to intangible assets (including goodwill) and additions to property, plant and equipment, including those arising from acquisitions.

Geographical information

2000	Sales to third parties (by destination)	Segment assets[a]	Capital expenditure[b]
Switzerland	509	4,083	1,313
European Union	9,012	15,157	867
Rest of Europe	1,266	435	43
Europe	10,787	19,675	2,223
North America	10,636	17,296	1,992
Latin America	2,928	2,143	253
Asia	3,394	2,214	175
Africa, Australia and Oceania	927	410	50
Segment total	28,672	41,738	4,693
Non-segment assets[c]	–	27,797	–
Consolidated total	28,672	69,535	4,693

1999			
Switzerland	455	4,168	515
European Union	9,326	14,107	842
Rest of Europe	1,090	395	30
Europe	10,871	18,670	1,387
North America	10,130	18,922	6,076
Latin America	2,577	2,372	133
Asia	3,109	2,923	124
Africa, Australia and Oceania	880	552	34
Segment total	27,567	43,439	7,754
Non-segment assets[c]	–	26,992	–
Consolidated total	27,567	70,431	7,754

a) Segment assets consist primarily of property, plant and equipment, intangibles, receivables and inventories. Segment liabilities are not included.

b) Capital expenditure comprises additions to intangible assets (including goodwill) and additions to property, plant and equipment, including those arising from acquisitions.

c) Non-segment assets mainly include current and deferred income tax assets, and financial assets, principally cash, marketable securities, investments in associated companies and other investments.

5. Vitamin case

Following the settlement agreement with the US Department of Justice on 20 May 1999 regarding pricing practices in the vitamin market, the Group recorded pre-tax expenses of 2,426 million Swiss francs in respect of the vitamin case in 1999. Cash outflows in 1999 were 1,282 million Swiss francs.

On 28 March 2000 a US federal judge approved the overall settlement agreement to a class action suit brought by the US buyers of bulk vitamins. Several customers in the class action have decided to opt out of the proposed settlement and pursue claims against the Group individually. As these individual suits are still in process it is not possible to determine the timing and amount of the ultimate settlement of these claims.

On 10 October 2000 settlement agreements were executed with Attorneys General and private class counsels representing US indirect purchasers and consumers in 22 states and with Attorneys General in respect of governmental entities in 43 states. The class action settlements remain subject to court approval. If approved, Roche will pay up to 171 million US dollars, plus interest and legal fees. Certain suits in other states are still in process and it is not possible to determine the outcome of these claims.

On 6 July 2000 the European Commission issued a Statement of Objections against 13 producers of bulk vitamins, including Roche. This is the beginning of the Commission's formal investigation into the vitamin case and it is not yet possible to determine the ultimate outcome of this investigation.

The provisions that were recorded in respect of the vitamin case at 31 December 1999, less the amounts utilised during 2000, remain the Group's best current estimate of the total liability that may arise. Therefore no additional expenses have been charged in 2000. Net cash inflows in 2000 were 41 million Swiss francs. Following the opt-out of some of the US buyers of bulk vitamins from settlement agreement, the Group received a repayment of part of the amounts paid into a trust fund in 1999.

6. Genentech legal settlements

On 19 November 1999 the Group's subsidiary Genentech reached a settlement agreement with the University of California regarding alleged patent infringement involving Genentech's human growth hormone products. Furthermore, Genentech made a payment to settle an investigation by the United States federal authorities relating to past clinical, sales and marketing activities associated with a human growth hormone. The total pre-tax expense recorded in 1999 was 345 million Swiss francs. All payments in respect of these matters have been made.

7. Givaudan spin-off in millions of CHF

On 8 June 2000 the Group's Fragrances and Flavours Division was spun off as an independent company under the name of Givaudan. The shares in Givaudan were distributed on this date as a special dividend to the holders of Roche shares and non-voting equity securities. As a result of the spin-off, assets totalling 3.9 billion Swiss francs and liabilities totalling 1.2 billion Swiss francs were transferred to Givaudan.

The results and cash flows of the Fragrances and Flavours Division up until the spin-off in June 2000 are included in the consolidated figures. However, the consolidated balance sheet is shown after the spin-off and does not include this Division's assets and liabilities.

The sales, results, assets, liabilities and net cash flows of the Fragrances and Flavours Division as part of the Roche Group are shown as discontinuing operations in the following table.

Statement of income	Continuing operations 2000	1999	Discontinuing operations 2000	1999	Group 2000	Group 1999
Sales	27,779	25,799	1,193	2,231	28,972	28,030
Less inter-divisional sales*	(270)	(381)	(30)	(82)	(300)	(463)
Sales to third parties	27,509	25,418	1,163	2,149	28,672	27,567
Operating profit	6,931	6,024	200	397	7,131	6,421
Financial income (expense), net	2,383	1,242	(46)	(108)	2,337	1,134
Result before taxes	9,314	7,266	154	289	9,468	7,555
Income taxes	(2,226)	(1,797)	(46)	(105)	(2,272)	(1,902)
Result after taxes	7,088	5,469	108	184	7,196	5,653
Changes in accounting policies	1,395	29	–	(2)	1,395	27
Minority interests	33	88	–	–	33	88
Share of result of associated companies	23	(4)	–	–	23	(4)
Net income	8,539	5,582	108	182	8,647	5,764

Balance sheet at 31 December

	Continuing operations 2000	1999	Discontinuing operations 2000	1999	Group 2000	Group 1999
Property, plant and equipment	13,785	13,304	–	936	13,785	14,240
Intangible assets	15,870	14,492	–	1,180	15,870	15,672
Other long-term assets	5,143	5,577	–	311	5,143	5,888
Current assets	34,737	33,329	–	1,302	34,737	34,631
Total assets	69,535	66,702	–	3,729	69,535	70,431
Long-term debt	16,167	15,948	–	14	16,167	15,962
Other non-current liabilities	7,475	7,730	–	1,882	7,475	9,612
Current liabilities	13,857	13,754	–	1,102	13,857	14,856
Total liabilities	37,499	37,432	–	2,998	37,499	40,430
Net assets	32,036	29,270	–	731	32,036	30,001

Statement of cash flows

	Continuing operations 2000	1999	Discontinuing operations 2000	1999	Group 2000	Group 1999
Operating activities	3,726	1,436	190	291	3,916	1,727
Financing activities	(2,727)	(749)	189	(146)	(2,538)	(895)
Investing activities	(743)	(743)	(89)	(124)	(832)	(867)
Net effect of currency translation on cash	(51)	94	15	9	(36)	103
Increase (decrease) in cash	205	38	305	30	510	68

*Transfer prices for inter-divisional sales are set on an arm's length basis.

Amounts recognised in arriving at operating profit are as follows:

	2000	1999
Wages and salaries	6,156	5,613
Social security costs	746	719
Post-employment benefits: defined benefit plans	298	322
Post-employment benefits: defined contribution plans	58	41
Other employee benefits	325	236
Total employees' remuneration	7,583	6,931

The number of employees at the year-end was 64,758 (1999: 67,695).

Post-employment benefits

Most employees are covered by retirement benefit plans sponsored by Group companies. The nature of such plans varies according to legal regulations, fiscal requirements and economic conditions of the countries in which the employees are employed. Other post-employment benefits consist mostly of post-retirement healthcare and life insurance schemes, principally in the USA. Plans are usually funded by payments from the Group and by employees to trusts independent of the Group's finances. Where a plan is unfunded, a liability for the whole obligation is recorded in the Group's balance sheet.

The amounts recognised in arriving at operating profit for post-employment defined benefit plans are as follows:

	2000	1999
Current service cost	333	311
Interest cost	675	677
Expected return on plan assets	(714)	(645)
Net actuarial (gains) losses recognised	2	–
Past service cost	3	7
(Gains) losses on curtailment	(1)	(28)
Total included in employees' remuneration	298	322

The actual return on plan assets was 1,175 million Swiss francs (1999: 932 million Swiss francs).

The movements in the net asset (liability) recognised in the balance sheet for post-employment defined benefit plans are as follows:

	2000	1999
At the beginning of the year		
– as previously reported	(2,078)	(2,107)
– effect of implementing the revised International Accounting Standard for Employee Benefits in 1999	–	39
– as restated	(2,078)	(2,068)
Changes in Group organisation and Givaudan spin-off[3, 7]	84	(4)
Total expenses included in employees' remuneration (as above)	(298)	(322)
Contributions paid	174	165
Benefits paid (unfunded plans)	135	125
Currency translation effects and other	134	26
At end of year (as below)	(1,849)	(2,078)

Amounts recognised in the balance sheet for post-employment defined benefit plans are as follows:

	2000	1999
Unfunded plans		
Recognised asset (liability) for actuarial present value of unfunded obligations due to past and present employees	(2,423)	(2,648)
Funded plans		
Actuarial present value of funded obligations due to past and present employees	(9,034)	(9,028)
Plan assets held in trusts at fair value	10,448	10,046
Plan assets in excess of actuarial present value of funded obligations	1,414	1,018
Less		
– unrecognised actuarial (gains) losses	(862)	(467)
– unrecognised past service costs	22	19
Recognised asset (liability) for funded obligations due to past and present employees	574	570
Asset (liability) recognised		
Deficit recognised as part of liabilities for post-employment benefits	(2,502)	(2,764)
Surplus recognised as part of other long-term assets[15]	653	686
Total net asset (liability) recognised	(1,849)	(2,078)

The above amounts include non-pension post-employment benefit schemes, principally medical plans, with an actuarial present value of obligations of 690 million Swiss francs (1999: 703 million Swiss francs) and plan assets of 649 million Swiss francs (1999: 576 million Swiss francs). The related net liability recognised is 147 million Swiss francs (1999: 190 million Swiss francs). Actuarial gains of 106 million Swiss francs (1999: 63 million Swiss francs) were unrecognised.

Amounts recognised in the balance sheet for post-employment defined benefit plans are predominantly non-current and are reported as long-term assets and non-current liabilities.

Included within the fair value of the assets of the funded plans are 30 (1999: 1,700) of the Group's non-voting equity securities with a fair value of 0.5 million Swiss francs (1999: 32 million Swiss francs).

The Group operates defined benefit schemes in many countries and the actuarial assumptions vary based upon local economic and social conditions. The range of assumptions used in the actuarial valuations of the most significant defined benefit plans, which are in countries with stable currencies and interest rates, is as follows:

Discount rates	3 to 8%	(1999: 3 to 8%)
Projected rates of remuneration growth	2 to 9%	(1999: 2.5 to 9%)
Expected rates of return on plan assets	3 to 10%	(1999: 3.5 to 10%)
Healthcare cost trend rate	4 to 10%	(1999: 4 to 9%)

9. Other operating income (expense), net in millions of CHF

	2000	1999
Royalty income	626	504
Other operating income	1,132	826
Total other operating income	1,758	1,330
Royalty expense	(740)	(561)
Restructuring expense	(46)	(4)
Other operating expense	(740)	(751)
Total other operating expense	(1,526)	(1,316)
Total other operating income (expense), net	232	14

10. Financial income (expense), net in millions of CHF

	2000	1999
Gains from sale of marketable securities and other	3,522	2,529
Losses from sale of marketable securities and other	(761)	(621)
Net gain from sale of marketable securities and other	2,761	1,908
Interest and dividend income	738	532
Interest expense	(1,487)	(1,237)
Exchange gains (losses), net	325	(69)
Total financial income (expense), net	2,337	1,134

11. Income taxes in millions of CHF

Income tax expenses
The amounts charged in the income statement are as follows:

	2000	1999
Current income taxes	2,913	1,103
Deferred income taxes	(641)	799
Total charge for income taxes	2,272	1,902

The Group's parent company, Roche Holding Ltd, and several of the Group's operating companies are domiciled in Switzerland. The maximum effective rate of all income taxes on companies domiciled in Basel, Switzerland, is 8% for holding companies and 25% for operating companies (1999: 8% and 25%).

Since the Group operates across the world, it is subject to income taxes in many different tax jurisdictions. The Group calculates its average expected tax rate as a weighted average of the tax rates in the tax jurisdictions in which the Group operates.

The Group's effective tax rate differs from the Group's expected tax rate as follows:

	2000	1999
Group's average expected tax rate	20%	20%
Tax effect of		
– Income not taxable	(3%)	(2%)
– Expenses not deductible for tax purposes	3%	3%
– Benefit of prior year tax losses not previously recognised	–	–
– Other differences	(3%)	(3%)
– Gain from sales of Genentech shares	8%	2%
– Gain from sales of LabCorp shares	2%	–
– Impairment of long-term assets	(3%)	–
– Vitamin case	–	6%
– Genentech legal settlements	–	(1%)
Group's effective tax rate	24%	25%

Income tax assets and liabilities

Amounts recognised in the balance sheet for income taxes are as follows:

	2000	1999
Current income taxes		
Current income tax assets	435	408
Current income tax liabilities	(882)	(728)
Net current income tax asset (liability) in the balance sheet	(447)	(320)
Deferred income taxes		
Deferred income tax assets	460	1,170
Deferred income tax liabilities	(2,535)	(3,895)
Net deferred income tax asset (liability) in the balance sheet	(2,075)	(2,725)

Amounts recognised in the balance sheet for deferred taxes are reported as long-term assets and non-current liabilities, of which approximately 50% and 15% respectively is current.

Deferred income tax assets are recognised for tax loss carry forwards only to the extent that realisation of the related tax benefit is probable. The Group has no significant unrecognised tax losses. Deferred income tax liabilities have not been established for the withholding tax and other taxes that would be payable on the unremitted earnings of certain foreign subsidiaries, as such amounts are currently regarded as permanently reinvested. These unremitted earnings totalled 24.8 billion Swiss francs at 31 December 2000 (1999: 19.2 billion Swiss francs).

The deferred income tax assets and liabilities and the deferred income tax charges (credits) are attributable to the following items:

2000	Property, plant and equipment, and intangible assets	Restructuring provisions	Other temporary differences	Total
Net deferred income tax asset (liability) at beginning of year	(3,128)	302	101	(2,725)
Adjustment from changes in accounting policies[1]	49	–	–	49
On issue of debt instruments[24]	–	–	(128)	(128)
(Charged) credited to the income statement	312	(144)	473	641
Changes in Group organisation and Givaudan spin-off[3, 7]	(54)	(8)	(55)	(117)
Currency translation effects and other	(521)	(4)	730	205
Net deferred income tax asset (liability) at end of year	(3,342)	146	1,121	(2,075)

172

1999	Property, plant and equipment, and intangible assets	Restructuring provisions	Other temporary differences	Total
Net deferred income tax asset (liability) at beginning of year	(2,030)	637	237	(1,156)
Adjustment from change in accounting policies	–	–	(12)	(12)
(Charged) credited to the income statement	(358)	(363)	(78)	(799)
Changes in Group organisation	(646)	–	(89)	(735)
Currency translation effects and other	(94)	28	43	(23)
Net deferred income tax asset (liability) at end of year	(3,128)	302	101	(2,725)

12. Property, plant and equipment in millions of CHF

	Land	Buildings and land improve- ments	Machinery and equipment	Construction in progress	2000 Total	1999 Total
Net book value						
At beginning of year	739	5,634	6,159	1,708	14,240	12,704
Currency translation effects	(8)	2	(77)	(118)	(201)	1,121
Changes in Group organisation, including Givaudan spin-off[3,7]	(59)	(443)	(384)	(57)	(943)	25
Additions	36	128	951	1,068	2,183	2,150
Disposals	(32)	(18)	(33)	(37)	(120)	(514)
Transfers	–	337	849	(1,186)	–	–
Depreciation charge	–	(212)	(1,162)	–	(1,374)	(1,246)
At end of year	676	5,428	6,303	1,378	13,785	14,240
At 31 December						
Cost	676	8,319	13,498	1,378	23,871	24,199
Accumulated depreciation	–	(2,891)	(7,195)	–	(10,086)	(9,959)
Net book value	676	5,428	6,303	1,378	13,785	14,240

At 31 December 2000 the capitalised cost of machinery and equipment under finance leases amounts to 356 million Swiss francs (1999: 317 million Swiss francs) and the net book value of these assets amounts to 250 million Swiss francs (1999: 231 million Swiss francs).

Operating lease commitments

At 31 December the future minimum payments under non-cancellable operating leases were as follows:

	2000	1999
Within one year	191	184
Between one and five years	437	352
Thereafter	39	104
Total minimum payments	667	640

Total rental expense in 2000 for all operating leases was 322 million Swiss francs (1999: 305 million Swiss francs).

The Group has no significant capital commitments for the purchase or construction of property, plant and equipment.

13. Intangible assets in millions of CHF

	Goodwill	Patents, licences, trademarks and other	2000 Total	1999 Total
Net book value				
At beginning of year	5,389	10,283	15,672	10,757
Changes in accounting policies[1]	2,358	(857)	1,501	–
Currency translation effects	172	(104)	68	724
Changes in Group organisation, including Givaudan spin-off [3, 7]	(805)	1,859	1,054	5,316
Additions	–	219	219	263
Disposals	(2)	(21)	(23)	(181)
Amortisation charge	(562)	(912)	(1,474)	(1,207)
Impairment charge	–	(1,147)	(1,147)	–
At end of year	6,550	9,320	15,870	15,672
At 31 December				
Cost	17,762	16,849	34,611	20,207
Accumulated depreciation	(11,212)	(7,529)	(18,741)	(4,535)
At end of year	6,550	9,320	15,870	15,672

On 1 January 2000 the Group recognised an impairment charge of 1,161 million Swiss francs when implementing a change in accounting policy (see Note 1). In 2000 a credit of 14 million Swiss francs is recognised, based on changes in the recoverable amounts of impaired assets during the year.

14. Investments in associated companies in millions of CHF

The Group has investments in associated companies as listed below. Equity investments in associated companies have been accounted for using the equity method.

	Share of net income 2000	1999	Balance sheet value 2000	1999
Laboratory Corporation of America Holdings (USA)	34	(4)	429	17
Other investments accounted for using the equity method	(11)	–	223	20
Total investments accounted for using the equity method	23	(4)	652	37
Laboratory Corporation of America Holdings (USA) – non-voting convertible mandatorily redeemable 8.5% preferred stock (at cost)			–	498
Total investments in associated companies			652	535

Laboratory Corporation of America Holdings

The Group has a non-controlling 32.6% interest (1999: 47.6%) in Laboratory Corporation of America Holdings (LabCorp), which operates clinical laboratories in the United States. LabCorp was created in 1995 from the merger of Roche Biomedical Laboratories, Inc. with and into National Health Laboratories Holdings, Inc., with Roche owning 49.9% of the new company. In 1997 the Group purchased non-voting convertible preferred stock of LabCorp which was held at cost as a portfolio investment.

On 6 June 2000 LabCorp announced that it had called for the redemption on 7 July 2000 all of its outstanding convertible preferred stock. During this redemption period, the Group sold sufficient of its holding in LabCorp's ordinary stock such that the Group's non-controlling interest in LabCorp would be at a similar level after the redemption date as it was before. The Group realised a pre-tax gain of 296 million Swiss francs during this process. On 17 October 2000 the Group sold 4,000,000 shares of LabCorp, resulting in a pre-tax gain after incidental costs of 660 million Swiss francs. The above transactions resulted in a total cash inflow of 1,123 million Swiss francs.

Basilea Pharmaceutica

On 17 October 2000 the Group contributed cash of 206 million Swiss francs to establish a newly formed Swiss company, Basilea Pharmaceutica Ltd (Basilea). The Group also transferred certain know-how and intellectual property in antibiotics, antifungals and dermatology, and property, plant and equipment to Basilea for a consideration of 6 million Swiss francs. On 31 October 2000 the Group sold 51% of the shares of Basilea. The Group retains a non-controlling interest in Basilea.

15. Other long-term assets in millions of CHF

	2000	1999
Recognised surplus on funded pension plans[8]	653	686
Loans receivable	491	596
Prepaid employee benefits	420	375
Other	909	790
Total other long-term assets	2,473	2,447

Loans receivable comprise all loans to third parties with a term of over one year. Other long-term assets consist of various assets not otherwise shown separately from which the Group expects to derive economic benefits in over one year.

16. Inventories in millions of CHF

	2000	1999
Raw materials and supplies	963	1,298
Work in process	545	575
Finished goods	4,525	4,942
Less: provision for slow moving and obsolete inventory	(279)	(269)
Total inventories	5,754	6,546

Inventories held at net realisable value have a carrying value of 26 million Swiss francs (1999: 25 million Swiss francs).

17. Accounts receivable – trade in millions of CHF

	2000	1999
Accounts receivable	5,759	6,309
Notes receivable	109	123
Less: provision for doubtful accounts	(349)	(254)
Total accounts receivable – trade	5,519	6,178

At 31 December 2000, accounts receivable – trade include amounts denominated in US dollars equivalent to 2.0 billion Swiss francs (1999: 1.9 billion Swiss francs) and amounts denominated in euros and EMU national currencies equivalent to 1.9 billion Swiss francs (1999: 1.8 billion Swiss francs).

18. Other current assets in millions of CHF

	2000	1999
Accrued interest income	122	127
Prepaid expenses	1,346	1,122
Assets held for sale	–	367
Other receivables	913	1,017
Total other current assets	2,381	2,633

Assets held for sale include inventories, property, plant and equipment, and other long-term assets of products identified for divestment in the following year.

19. Cash and marketable securities in millions of CHF

	2000	1999
Equity securities	11,347	12,593
Bonds and debentures	4,669	2,700
Money market instruments	2,070	1,521
Total marketable securities	18,086	16,814
Total cash	2,562	2,052
Total cash and marketable securities	20,648	18,866

Equity securities: These consist primarily of readily saleable securities.

Bonds and debentures:

Contracted maturity	Amount	Range of interest rates
2000		
Within one year	1,054	3.0–9.8%
Between one and five years	1,163	1.0–11.8%
Over five years	2,452	2.0–7.6%
1999		
Within one year	378	4.0–6.9%
Between one and five years	1,285	1.5–7.8%
Over five years	1,037	2.8–8.2%

The weighted average interest rate is approximately 4.7% for the bonds and debentures (1999: 5.9%).

Money market instruments: These generally have fixed interest rates ranging from 3.1% to 4.8% (1999: 1.3% to 6.3%) depending upon the currency in which they are denominated. They are contracted to mature within one year of 31 December 2000.

As of 31 December 2000 the fair value of marketable securities is approximately 18.2 billion Swiss francs (1999: approximately 17.4 billion Swiss francs).

20. Accrued and other current liabilities in millions of CHF

	2000	1999
Deferred income	161	142
Accrued payroll and related items	768	668
Interest payable	298	302
Other accrued liabilities	2,123	2,276
Total accrued and other current liabilities	3,350	3,388

21. Equity

Share capital

At 31 December 2000 and 1999, the authorised and called-up share capital was 1,600,000 shares with a nominal value of CHF 100 each.

Based on information supplied to Roche by a shareholders' group with pooled voting rights, comprising the Hoffmann and Oeri-Hoffmann families, that group holds 800,200 shares as in the preceding year. (This figure does not include any shares without pooled voting rights that are held outside this group by individual members of the group.) There were no transactions with these individuals other than those in the ordinary course of business.

Non-voting equity securities *(Genussscheine)*

As of 31 December 2000 and 1999, 7,025,627 non-voting equity securities had been issued. Under Swiss company law these non-voting equity securities have no nominal value, are not part of the share capital and cannot be issued against a contribution which would be shown as an asset in the balance sheet of Roche Holding Ltd. Each non-voting equity security confers the same rights as any of the shares to participate in the net profit and any remaining proceeds from liquidation following repayment of the nominal value of the shares and, if any, participation certificates.
In accordance with the law and the Articles of Incorporation of Roche Holding Ltd, the company is entitled at all times to exchange all or some of the non-voting equity securities into shares or participation certificates.

Own equity instruments

As at 31 December 2000 the Group held 284,566 (1999: 251,589) of its own non-voting equity securities and financial instruments to acquire these securities. These have been acquired primarily to meet the obligations that may arise in respect of certain of the Group's debt instruments. For 2000 the Group's holdings in its own equity instruments are recorded as a deduction from equity.

Dividends

On 9 May 2000 the shareholders approved the distribution of a dividend of CHF 100 per share and non-voting equity security (1999: CHF 87) in respect of the 1999 business year. The distribution to holders of outstanding shares and non-voting equity securities totalled 835 million Swiss francs and has been charged to retained earnings in 2000. The shareholders also approved the special dividend in respect of the Givaudan spin-off. The accounting effect of this distribution, which primarily includes the carrying value in the Group's financial statements of the assets and liabilities of Givaudan, totalled 2,642 million Swiss francs and has been included with the special dividend as a movement in retained earnings in 2000.

22. Earnings per share and non-voting equity security

Basic earnings per share and non-voting equity security

	2000	1999
Net income (millions of CHF)	8,647	5,764
Number of shares (thousands)[21]	1,600	1,600
Number of non-voting equity securities (thousands)[21]	7,026	7,026
Weighted average number of own non-voting equity securities held (thousands)[21]	(277)	
Total (thousands)	8,349	8,626
Basic earnings per share and non-voting equity security (CHF)	1,036	668

177

Diluted earnings per share and non-voting equity security

For the calculation of diluted earnings per share and non-voting equity security in 2000, the weighted average number of shares and non-voting equity securities outstanding is adjusted to assume conversion of all dilutive potential shares or non-voting equity securities.

	2000
Net income (millions of CHF)	8,647
Elimination of interest expense, net of tax, of convertible debt instruments, where dilutive (millions of CHF)	114
Net income used to calculate diluted earnings per share (millions of CHF)	8,761
Weighted average number of shares and non-voting equity securities in issue (thousands)	8,349
Adjustment for assumed conversion of convertible debt instruments, where dilutive (thousands)	203
Weighted average number of shares and non-voting equity securities in issue used to calculate dilutive earnings per share (thousands)	8,552
Diluted earnings per share and non-voting equity security (CHF)	1,024

23. Minority interests in millions of CHF

	2000	1999
At beginning of year	3,047	1,149
Change in accounting policies[1]	155	–
Givaudan spin-off[7]	(2)	–
Acquisition of Genentech Special Common Stock	–	(1,298)
Sales of Genentech shares[3]	649	2,892
Conversion option embedded in the 'LYONs IV' notes issued in 2000[24]	172	–
Minority share of Group net income, net of tax	(33)	(88)
Exercise of Genentech stock options	381	240
Currency translation effects and other	59	152
At end of year	4,428	3,047
Of which:		
Genentech	4,377	2,993
Other	51	54
Total minority interests	4,428	3,047

Genentech

As of 31 December 2000 the minority interest of 42% in Genentech is publicly held by third parties. The Group's transactions in Genentech shares are described in Note 3.

At 31 December 2000 Genentech had options outstanding under its employee stock option plans which entitled the holders on exercise of the options to purchase 40.9 million shares at prices ranging from USD 12.53 to USD 95.66. Of these options outstanding 13.4 million were exercisable at that date.

24. Debt in millions of CHF

	2000	1999
Amounts due to banks and other financial institutions	4,427	5,157
Debt instruments	13,510	12,553
Capitalised lease obligations	206	213
Other borrowings	13	25
Total debt	18,156	17,948
Less: current portion of long-term debt (amounts due within one year)	(1,989)	(1,986)
Total long-term debt	16,167	15,962

Short-term debt totalling 5,451 million Swiss francs (1999: 5,702 million Swiss francs) consists of the current portion of long-term debt, as shown in the above table, together with short-term bank loans and overdrafts and other short-term debt amounting to 3,462 million Swiss francs (1999: 3,716 million Swiss francs).

Repayment terms of long-term debt

	2000	1999
Within one year	1,989	1,986
Between one and two years	2,519	3,180
Between two and three years	3,507	1,359
Between three and four years	3,470	4,625
Between four and five years	1,520	2,718
Thereafter	5,151	4,080
Total long-term debt	18,156	17,948

The 'LYONs' zero coupon US dollar exchangeable notes (see below) are reflected as due the first year that the holders of the notes can request the Group to purchase the notes.

The fair value of long-term debt is 20.8 billion Swiss francs (1999: 19.5 billion Swiss francs). This is calculated based upon the present value of the future cash flows on the instrument, discounted at a market rate of interest for instruments with similar credit status and cash flows.

Amounts due to banks and other financial institutions

Interest rates on these amounts, which are primarily denominated in US dollars, euros and EMU national currencies, average approximately 5% (1999: 5%). Repayment dates vary between 1 and 15 years.

Debt instruments

The carrying value of the Group's debt instruments is given in the table below. Supplementary information about the Group's debt instruments, including redemption and conversion terms, if any, is given on pages 99 to 101.

179

	Economic interest rate if held to maturity	2000	1999
Swiss franc bonds			
'Bullet' 2% due 2003, principal 1.25 billion Swiss francs	1.78%	1,245	1,242
'Rodeo' 1.75% due 2008, principal 1 billion Swiss francs	2.66%	923	912
US dollar bonds			
'Knock Out' 2.75% due 2000, principal 1 billion US dollars	6.20%	–	1,586
'Bull Spread' 3.5% due 2001, principal 1 billion US dollars	8.60%	1,610	1,506
'Chameleon' 6.75% due 2009, principal 1 billion US dollars	6.75%	1,622	1,584
Japanese yen bonds			
'Samurai' 1% due 2002, principal 100 billion Japanese yen	5.19%	1,051	1,011
Swiss franc convertible bonds			
'Helveticus' dividend-linked convertible bonds, due 2003, principal 1 billion Swiss francs	–	215	990
Zero coupon US dollar exchangeable notes			
'LYONs II' due 2010, principal 2.15 billion US dollars	7.00%	1,785	1,618
'LYONs III' due 2012, principal 3 billion US dollars	6.375%	2,301	2,098
'LYONs IV' due 2015, principal 1.506 billion US dollars	2.75%	1,363	–
Japanese yen exchangeable bonds			
'Sumo' 0.25% due 2005, principal 104.6 billion Japanese yen	1.00%	1,388	–
Limited conversion preferred stock	–	7	6
Total debt instruments		13,510	12,553

The economic interest rate if held to maturity is the market rate of interest at the date of issuance for a similar debt instrument, but with no conversion rights or discount upon issuance.

Issue of 'LYONs IV' US dollar notes exchangeable into Genentech shares

On 19 January 2000 the Group issued zero coupon US dollar exchangeable notes due 19 January 2015 with a principal amount of 1,506 million US dollars. The notes are exchangeable into shares of the Group's subsidiary, Genentech, at any time prior to maturity. If all of the notes were exchanged into Genentech shares, the Group's percentage of ownership of Genentech would decrease by 2.5%.

Net proceeds from the issue were 980 million US dollars (1,562 million Swiss francs). These were initially allocated as 2,369 million Swiss francs of debt, 1,094 million Swiss francs of unamortised discount, 172 million Swiss francs of minority interest (in respect of the conversion option embedded in the notes) and 115 million Swiss francs of deferred tax liability.

Issue of 'Sumo' Japanese yen bonds exchangeable into non-voting equity securities

On 26 April 2000 the Group issued 0.25% Japanese yen exchangeable bonds due 25 March 2005 with a principal amount of 104.6 billion Japanese yen. The bonds are exchangeable into non-voting equity securities until 17 March 2005.

Net proceeds from the issue were 98.76 billion Japanese yen (1,599 million Swiss francs). These were initially allocated as 1,694 million Swiss francs of debt, 132 million Swiss francs of unamortised discount, 24 million Swiss francs of equity (in respect of the conversion option embedded in the bonds) and 13 million Swiss francs of deferred tax liability.

Repayment of 'Knock Out' US dollar bonds

On the due date of 14 April 2000 the Group repaid the principal amount of 1 billion US dollars of the 2.75% US dollar bonds originally issued in 1993. The resulting cash outflow was 1,648 million Swiss francs.

Exercise of 'Helveticus' Swiss franc convertible bonds

During May 2000 'Helveticus' dividend-linked Swiss franc convertible bonds due 2003 with a principal amount of 698 million Swiss francs were exercised. The resulting cash outflow was 659 million Swiss francs. Other smaller amounts were exercised during the year.

Swiss franc convertible bonds

An annual payment distribution amount is paid on 31 July for each bond of CHF 9,530 par value in the place of a fixed rate of interest. This annual payment distribution amount equals two times the ordinary and/or extraordinary dividend declared on one non-voting equity security of Roche Holding Ltd for the business year ended on 31 December which was nineteen months prior to 31 July for the relevant year.

Unamortised discount

Included within the carrying value of debt instruments are the following unamortised discounts:

	2000	1999
Swiss franc bonds	82	96
US dollar bonds	41	124
Japanese yen bonds	55	95
Swiss franc convertible bonds	1	9
Zero coupon US dollar exchangeable notes	5,443	4,524
Japanese yen exchangeable bonds	103	–
Total unamortised discount	5,725	4,848

25. Financial instruments in millions of CHF

In appropriate circumstances the Group uses financial instruments as part of its risk management and trading strategies. This is discussed in Note 2. The majority of the derivative financial instruments outstanding at the year-end consist of forward contracts entered into by foreign affiliates for the purchase of currencies for settling intra-Group liabilities.

The notional principal values, fair values and carrying values of derivative financial instruments held by the Group are shown in the table on page 87. The notional amounts do not represent the amounts actually exchanged by the parties, and therefore are not a measure of the Group's exposure. Fair value is determined by reference to quoted market prices and the use of established estimation techniques. The carrying values are those included in the consolidated balance sheet as either other current assets or accrued liabilities.

2000	Notional principal amount	Fair value	Carrying value
Foreign currency derivatives			
– forward exchange contracts and swaps	8,223	156	84
– options	1,391	18	17
Interest rate derivatives			
– swaps	4,289	(34)	5
– other	114	–	1
Other derivatives	1,512	97	99
Total derivative financial instruments	15,529	237	206

1999	Notional principal amount	Fair value	Carrying value
Foreign currency derivatives			
– forward exchange contracts and swaps	7,933	(5)	(49)
– options	6,088	4	101
Interest rate derivatives			
– swaps	4,482	(48)	1
– other	633	(6)	–
Other derivatives	1,807	210	189
Total derivative financial instruments	20,943	155	242

The net unrecognised gains on open contracts which hedge future anticipated foreign currency sales amounted to 75 million Swiss francs (1999: 44 million Swiss francs). These gains will be recognised in the income statement when these open contracts mature at various dates up to one year from the balance sheet date.

26. Provisions in millions of CHF

	Restructuring provisions	Other provisions	2000 Total	1999 Total
At beginning of year	748	3,606	4,354	3,352
Changes in Group organisation and Givaudan spin-off [3, 7]	16	(10)	6	(54)
Additional provisions created	75	368	443	2,673
Unused amounts reversed	(69)	(96)	(165)	(62)
Utilised during the year	(338)	(632)	(970)	(1,903)
Increase in discounted amount due to passage of time or change in discounting rate	–	77	77	–
Currency translation effects and other	(4)	254	250	348
At end of year	428	3,567	3,995	4,354
Of which:				
Current portion of provisions	216	1,743	1,959	2,660
Non-current portions of provisions	212	1,824	2,036	1,694
Total provisions	428	3,567	3,995	4,354

Restructuring provisions arise from planned programmes that materially change the scope of business undertaken by the Group or the manner in which business is conducted. Such provisions include only the costs necessarily entailed by the restructuring which are not associated with the ongoing activities of the Group. The creation of such provisions is recorded as a charge against other operating income, except where they arise from the restructuring of newly acquired companies, in which case they are included in the acquisition accounting and hence form part of the goodwill.

Other provisions consist mainly of legal, environmental and similar matters. Other provisions include provisions in respect of the vitamin case (see Note 5).

27. Contingent liabilities

The operations and earnings of the Group continue, from time to time and in varying degrees, to be affected by political, legislative, fiscal and regulatory developments, including those relating to environmental protection, in the countries in which it operates. The industries in which the Group is engaged are also subject to physical risks of various kinds. The nature and frequency of these developments and events, not all of which are covered by insurance, as well as their effect on future operations and earnings are not predictable.

Provisions have been recorded in respect of the vitamin case, as disclosed in Note 5. These provisions are the Group's best current estimate of the total liability that may arise. As the various investigations outside the United States of America and private civil suits are still in progress it is possible that the ultimate liability may be different from this.

28. Cash flow statement in millions of CHF

Cash flows from operating activities

Cash flows from operating activities are those derived from the Group's primary activities, as described in the divisional review. This is calculated by the indirect method, by adjusting the Group's operating profit for any operating income and expenses that are not cash flows (for example depreciation and amortisation), and for movements in the Group's working capital. Operating cash flows also include income taxes paid on all activities, including, for example, the taxes paid on the Genentech and LabCorp share sales.

Effects of Genentech transactions, vitamin case and Genentech legal settlements	2000	1999
Gain on sale of Genentech shares[3]	(3,949)	(4,461)
Charge for vitamin case[5]	–	2,426
Charge for Genentech legal settlements[6]	–	345
Genentech inventory write-up charged[3]	158	140
Total	(3,791)	(1,550)

Other adjustments for non-cash operating income and expense		
Expense for defined benefit post-employment plans[8]	298	322
Other adjustments	(388)	297
Total	(90)	619

Cash flows from financing activities

Cash flows from financing activities are primarily the proceeds from issue and repayments of the Group's equity and debt instruments. They also include interest payments and dividend payments on these instruments. Cash flows from short-term financing, including finance leases, are also included. These cash flows indicate the Group's transactions with the providers of its equity and debt financing.

Cash flows from short-term borrowings are shown as a net movement, as these consist of a large number of transactions with short maturity.

Proceeds from issue of long-term debt	2000	1999
'LYONs IV' zero coupon exchangeable US dollar notes due 2015[24]	1,562	–
'Sumo' 0.25% exchangeable Japanese yen bonds due 2005[24]	1,599	–
'Chameleon' 6.75% US dollar bonds due 2009[24]	–	1,537
Long-term bank loans and other borrowings[24]	982	2,638
Total	4,143	4,175

Repayment of long-term debt		
Repayment of 'Knock Out' 2.75% US dollar bonds[24]	(1,648)	–
Exercise of 'Helveticus' dividend-linked Swiss francs convertible bonds[24]	(659)	(1)
Long-term bank loans and other borrowings[24]	(755)	(3,688)
Total	(3,062)	(3,689)

Interest and dividends paid		
Interest paid	(902)	(686)
Dividends paid	(835)	(750)
Total	(1,737)	(1,436)

Cash flows from investing activities

Cash flows from investing activities are principally those arising from the Group's investments in property, plant and equipment and intangible assets, and from the acquisition and divestment of subsidiaries, associated companies and businesses. Cash flows connected with the Group's portfolio of marketable securities and other investments are also included as are any interest and dividend payments received in respect of these securities and investments. These cash flows indicate the Group's net reinvestment in its operating assets and the cash flow effects of the changes in Group organisation, as well as the cash generated by the Group's other investments.

Cash flows from marketable securities, including income and capital gains and losses, are shown as a net movement on the Group's portfolio, as these consist of a large number of positions which are not held on a long-term basis.

Acquisitions of subsidiaries, associated companies and products	2000	1999
Cash contribution to Basilea[14]	(206)	–
Acquisition of Genentech Special Common Stock[3]	–	(6,222)
Other acquisitions[3, 14]	(2,480)	–
Total	(2,686)	(6,222)

Divestments of subsidiaries, associated companies and products		
Proceeds on sales of Genentech shares[3]	4,599	7,353
Proceeds on sales of LabCorp shares[14]	1,123	–
Other divestments[3]	1,087	–
Total	6,809	7,353

Interest and dividends received		
Interest received	542	303
Dividends received	201	156
Total	743	459

29. Subsequent events

At the Annual General Meeting on 3 April 2001, the shareholders will be asked to approve a 100 for 1 stock split of the shares and non-voting equity securities of Roche Holding Ltd. If approved the split will take place after changes in the relevant Swiss company law will have entered into force.

Report of the Group Auditors

As auditors of the Group, we have audited the Consolidated Financial Statements of the Roche Group on pages 56 to 90 for the year ended 31 December 2000.

These Consolidated Financial Statements are the responsibility of the Board of Directors of Roche Holding Ltd. Our responsibility is to express an opinion on these Consolidated Financial Statements based on our audit. We confirm that we meet the Swiss legal requirements concerning professional qualification and independence.

Our audit was conducted in accordance with auditing standards promulgated by the Swiss profession and with the International Standards on Auditing issued by the International Federation of Accountants, which require that an audit be planned and performed to obtain reasonable assurance about whether the Consolidated Financial Statements are free from material misstatement. We have examined on a test basis evidence supporting the amounts and disclosures in the Consolidated Financial Statements. We have also assessed the accounting principles used, significant estimates made and the overall consolidated financial statement presentation. We believe that our audit provides a reasonable basis for our opinion.

In our opinion, the Consolidated Financial Statements of the Roche Group present fairly, in all material respects, the financial position at 31 December 2000, and the results of operations and the cash flows for the year then ended in accordance with International Accounting Standards, and comply with relevant Swiss law.

We recommend that the Consolidated Financial Statements submitted to you be approved.

PricewaterhouseCoopers AG

William D. Kirst

Ralph R. Reinertsen

Basel, 26 February 2001

Multi-Year Overview

Statistics, as reported	1991	1992
Statement of income in millions of CHF		
Sales	11,451	12,953
EBITDA	2,208	2,893
Operating profit	1,386	2,013
Net income	1,482	1,916
Research and development	1,727	1,998
Balance sheet in millions of CHF		
Long-term assets	8,478	9,293
Current assets	16,567	18,290
Total assets	25,045	27,583
Equity	14,429	16,046
Minority interests	511	581
Non-current liabilities	7,029	6,809
Current liabilities	3,076	4,147
Additions to property, plant and equipment	1,139	1,293
Personnel		
Number of employees at end of year	55,134	56,335
Key Ratios		
Net income as % of sales	13	15
Net income as % of equity	10	12
Research and development as % of sales	15	15
Current ratio %	539	441
Equity and minority interests as % of total assets	60	60
Sales per employee in thousands of CHF	208	230
Data on shares and non-voting equity securities		
Number of shares	1,600,000	1,600,000
Number of non-voting equity securities *(Genussscheine)*	7,025,627	7,025,627
Total shares and non-voting equity securities	8,625,627	8,625,627
Total dividend in millions of CHF	236	312
Earnings per share and non-voting equity security (diluted) in CHF	172	222
Dividend per share and non-voting equity security in CHF	28	37
Cash and warrants in addition to dividend (adjusted) in CHF	13	–
Cash and warrants in addition to dividend (unadjusted) in CHF	25	–

a) If 1991 warrants held to final exercise date.

b) In addition to the normal dividend, the shareholders approved for each share and each non-voting equity security a special
RO 100 centenary warrant worth CHF 36 on date of issue or, at the holder's option, a cash equivalent of CHF 36.

c) 1997 net income and related key ratios are shown after special charges of 6,308 million Swiss francs, net of tax, incurred following
the Corange acquisition and include Corange only in respect of balance sheet data.

	1993	1994	1995	1996	1997 e)	1998	1999	2000
	14,315	14,748	14,722	15,966	18,767	24,662	27,567	28,672
	3,278	3,635	4,176	4,629	5,076	6,423	8,874	11,126
	2,348	2,656	3,057	3,420	3,590	4,350	6,421	7,131
	2,478	2,860	3,372	3,899	(2,031)	4,392	5,764	8,647
	2,269	2,332	2,290	2,446	2,903	3,408	3,782	3,950
	9,522	13,549	12,632	15,487	32,453	27,952	35,800	34,798
	21,404	22,684	22,932	24,289	22,323	27,927	34,631	34,737
	30,926	36,233	35,564	39,776	54,776	55,879	70,431	69,535
	17,914	16,422	17,554	20,780	18,250	21,666	26,954	27,608
	625	861	799	835	1,187	1,149	3,047	4,428
	7,921	10,034	11,554	12,727	21,181	21,416	25,574	23,642
	4,466	8,916	5,657	5,434	14,158	11,648	14,856	13,857
	1,407	1,355	1,490	1,624	1,802	1,883	2,150	2,183
	56,082	61,381	50,497	48,972	51,643	66,707	67,695	64,758
	17	19	23	24	−11	18	21	30
	14	17	19	19	−11	20	21	31
	16	16	16	15	15	14	14	14
	479	254	405	447	158	240	233	251
	60	48	51	54	36	41	43	46
	255	240	292	326	363	370	407	443
	1,600,000	1,600,000	1,600,000	1,600,000	1,600,000	1,600,000	1,600,000	1,600,000
	7,025,627	7,025,627	7,025,627	7,025,627	7,025,627	7,025,627	7,025,627	7,025,627
	8,625,627	8,625,627	8,625,627	8,625,627	8,625,627	8,625,627	8,625,627	8,625,627
	404	474	552	647	716	750	863 e)	992 f)
	287	332	391	452	(235)	509	668	1,024
	48	55	64 b)	75	83	87	100 e)	115 f)
	–	77 a)	–	36	–	190 d)	–	–
	–	153 a)	–	36	–	190 d)	–	–

d) If 1996 warrants held to final exercise date.

e) Dividend 1999 does not include the special dividend relating to the spin-off of the Fragrances and Flavours Division.

f) Dividend 2000 as proposed by the Board of Directors.

Sales by division in millions of CHF

	1996	1997	1998	1999	2000
Pharmaceuticals	10,460	12,070	14,376	16,487	17,686
Diagnostics	757	966	4,616	5,282	6,252
Vitamins and Fine Chemicals	3,329	3,803	3,630	3,649	3,571
Fragrances and Flavours	1,414	1,928	2,040	2,149	1,163
Others	6	–	–	–	–
Total	15,966	18,767	24,662	27,567	28,672

Sales by geographical area in millions of CHF

	1996	1997	1998	1999	2000
Switzerland	291	320	445	455	509
European Union	4,923	5,588	8,799	9,326	9,012
Rest of Europe	635	841	1,017	1,090	1,266
Europe	5,849	6,749	10,261	10,871	10,787
North America	5,946	6,974	8,698	10,130	10,636
Latin America	1,568	1,991	2,455	2,577	2,928
Asia	2,003	2,333	2,453	3,109	3,394
Africa, Australia and Oceania	600	720	795	880	927
Total	15,966	18,767	24,662	27,567	28,672

Additions to property, plant and equipment by division in millions of CHF

	1996	1997	1998	1999	2000
Pharmaceuticals	1,156	1,204	858	963	1,132
Diagnostics	72	128	439	568	603
Vitamins and Fine Chemicals	282	394	442	450	372
Fragrances and Flavours	84	71	144	165	68
Others	30	5	–	4	8
Total	1,624	1,802	1,883	2,150	2,183

Additions to property, plant and equipment by geographical area in millions of CHF

	1996	1997	1998	1999	2000
Switzerland	366	307	295	335	361
European Union	420	457	703	826	731
Rest of Europe	6	13	28	30	31
Europe	792	777	1,026	1,191	1,123
North America	650	793	591	668	610
Latin America	40	74	98	133	229
Asia	129	138	141	124	173
Africa, Australia and Oceania	13	20	27	34	48
Total	1,624	1,802	1,883	2,150	2,183

Consolidated Income Statement on an Adjusted Basis

Reconciliation of reported figures to adjusted basis in millions of CHF

2000	Sales to third parties	EBITDA	Operating profit	Net income
As reported in the financial statements	28,672	11,126	7,131	8,647
Discontinuing operations	(1,163)	(267)	(200)	(108)
Reclassification of sales to Givaudan as sales to third parties	34	–	–	–
Impact of fair value adjustment to Genentech inventories	–	158	158	158
Impairment of long-term assets	–	–	1,161	1,161
Gain on sale of Genentech shares	–	(3,949)	(3,949)	(3,949)
Gain on sale of LabCorp shares	–	–	–	(660)
Income taxes	–	–	–	1,200
Change in accounting policies	–	–	–	(1,395)
Income applicable to minority interests	–	–	–	(40)
Adjusted	27,543	7,068	4,301	5,014
1999				
As reported in the financial statements	27,567	8,874	6,421	5,764
Discontinuing operations	(2,149)	(524)	(397)	(182)
Reclassification of sales to Givaudan as sales to third parties	78	–	–	–
Impact of fair value adjustment to Genentech inventories	–	140	140	140
Impact of new/revised IAS	–	(153)	(187)	(187)
Additional amortisation on Genentech acquisition as if effective 1 January 1999	–	–	(193)	(193)
Gain on sale of Genentech shares	–	(4,461)	(4,461)	(4,461)
Vitamin case	–	2,426	2,426	2,426
Genentech legal settlements	–	345	345	345
Income taxes	–	–	–	805
Change in accounting policies	–	–	–	(29)
Income applicable to minority interests	–	–	–	(27)
Adjusted	25,496	6,647	4,094	4,401

Sears
Annual Report 1999

millions, except per share data	1999	1998	1997
Revenues	$ 41,071	$ 41,575	$ 41,574
Income before extraordinary loss	1,453	1,072	1,188
Net income	1,453	1,048	1,188
Per common share			
Income before extraordinary loss	3.81	2.74	2.99
Net income	3.81	2.68	2.99
Excluding impact of noncomparable items			
Income excluding noncomparable items	1,482	1,300	1,303
Per common share	3.89	3.32	3.27
Total assets	36,954	37,675	38,700
Debt	18,038	19,669	20,840
Shareholders' equity	6,839	6,066	5,862

This annual report, including the chairman's comments, contains forward-looking statements which should be read in the context of the cautionary language found in the financial statements section of this report.

ARTHUR C. MARTINEZ
Chairman and
Chief Executive Officer

(Letter to Our Shareholders)

Dear Fellow Shareholder:

In 1999,Sears demonstrated what can happen when its two powerful profit engines—retail and credit—begin firing simultaneously. The strong finish to the year resulted in record earnings for the fourth quarter and for the year. We saw earnings per share grow from $2.68 in 1998 to $3.81 in 1999,an increase of 42 percent. Excluding noncomparable items,earnings per share increased 17 percent,from $3.32 to $3.89 in 1999. Our return on equity increased to 23 percent in 1999,up from 18 percent in 1998. What's more, we are confident that the changes we are making throughout our organization will further strengthen our competitiveness.

Retail,Credit Drive Record Earnings

Sears recorded revenues in 1999 of $41.1 billion,up 2.7 percent from 1998, excluding the impact of divested businesses. We expanded our margins by 20 basis points while investing in our online capabilities and our technology platform. In the end, we produced record earnings for the fourth quarter and a record $2.41 billion in operating earnings for the year.

On the retail side, we generated strong sales growth in both appliances and home electronics. While the apparel businesses showed more modest growth, our important private brands such as TKS Basics for kids, Crossroads and Fieldmaster showed genuine strength. Sears Canada also turned in another strong performance, and we look for continued growth from Canada's only Full-line department store chain.

In our credit business, we worked tirelessly to strengthen our portfolio quality, reduce our losses and improve our collection processes.Our success drove earnings from the receivables portfolio up 18 percent to $1.35 billion in operating income. Our active accounts reached 38.9 million in 1999 and we added 4.4 million new accounts during the year. All 63 million customers in our portfolio were converted to the new TSYS system,which will give Sears greater flexibility in customer offerings. In addition, we converted 11 million of our accounts to the new Sears Premier Card.

Following a challenging 1998, our management team spent several intense months reevaluating the entire Sears enterprise—inside and out. Most important, we doubled our focus on our customers. We hear them loud and clear. And the actions we took helped us set these impressive performance marks in 1999.

Listening and Learning

By closely examining our customers' opinions, we wanted to confirm precisely where we have equity with them,and what it will take to draw them to other areas of our business. Our research provided some powerful insights:

> Customers are drawn to Sears largely because of our powerful brands—especially our private brands.

> Our guarantees create confidence in Sears and our products and strongly motivate purchase decisions.

> Our customers want us to more clearly define what we offer and create a more focused,simpler, trend-right store.

> Today's customers seek a dynamic shopping experience, which includes an easy-to-navigate and an easy-to-check-out shopping environment.

> Customers often view Sears in a limited or singular dimension instead of seeing the whole-house appeal we offer.

> Customers often do not recognize that we meet or beat our competitors for price and overall value on a consistent basis.

Turning Feedback into Action

We concentrated on translating our customers' suggestions into in-store initiatives that will capture their imaginations and transform their Sears shopping experience.

First, we created the most strategically developed marketing program our company has ever launched—one that communicates a much stronger whole-house value and event message. Our new ad campaign, built around our core value proposition, **"The good life at a great price. Guaranteed,"** strikes a chord with consumers. We punctuated the launch with our sponsorship of the Backstreet Boys' successful Millennium Tour and the rollout of a Pulse Card, which creates a membership loyalty program for younger shoppers. The new advertising produced an immediate improvement in sales. In fact, the day after Thanksgiving we recorded the single biggest day in our history for sales volume.

Next, we took several important steps to ensure that we consistently deliver what our value proposition promises. We developed a strategy to orient our stores more clearly around the home and the good life our customers strive to create there. In 2000, we will introduce in select Sears stores a new format that concentrates on five key focal areas that support today's lifestyles and our strengths: Appliances, Home Fashions, Tools, Kids and Electronics. Other areas such as Women's and Men's Apparel, Shoes, Sporting Goods and Home Office will assume more of a support role.

Our private brands remain critical to our success. In the appliance sector, we strengthened our dominant Kenmore brand when we introduced the highly successful Kenmore Elite series. In the hardware business, we successfully piloted our new Tool Territory format, which provides an unparalleled selection of Craftsman and other tools in a bright, spacious, hands-on environment. To showcase our private apparel brands, we built a new in-store shop program built around private brands like Crossroads and Fieldmaster. This format will reach 450 stores in 2000. At the same time, we're integrating new national brands into our apparel assortment, including distinctive products from Nike and others.

We took seriously our customers' call for a more focused shopping experience and began to review the breadth and depth of our merchandise. We started with our kids selections through our TKS Exceptional Value lines. Our customers clearly liked what they saw, and sales increased substantially. Next, we will continue the editing of our men's and women's offerings which will be reduced a further 20 percent in 2000. As a result, customers will see a deeper selection and inventory of sizes and colors in the merchandise we carry.

Our customers told us they would like wider aisles, clearer signage and shopping carts, and we're responding with a new, less cluttered store design. We tested carts in a number of stores in the fourth quarter, and customers responded enthusiastically. We plan to have them in all locations by year-end.

As our customers are faced with more credit alternatives than ever before, we need to provide them with good reasons to use their Sears Card. We're enhancing our credit product to make it more attractive to more customers. We introduced the new Sears Premier Card, which rewards our best customers with additional savings opportunities.

Winning through Innovation

Sears has a long history of providing innovative products and services to our customers. That tradition continued in 1999 as our customers responded very well to the innovations we presented them. To give them greater access to our products and services, Sears launched the sale of appliances, parts and the Tool Territory over the sears.com Web site. Our online customers appreciate the "bricks behind the clicks" and the convenience of our nationwide delivery system. The results have been exciting. Online sales in the fourth quarter exceeded expectations. But this is just the beginning. We see some extraordinary innovations for the home coming from our online businesses in 2000 with some exciting strategic alliances. We'll significantly boost our investment in our online business in 2000.

We also continue to delight customers with exciting new products and The Great Indoors format. We took valuable lessons in innovation from our successful Denver store and applied them to our new Scottsdale store to an overwhelming response from customers. Sales in Scottsdale started out strong and Denver sales grew 20 percent in 1999. We look forward to the opening of our Dallas store this year and have made plans for additional stores. On the product side, our new Kenmore Elite line–the ultimate in innovative styling and technology– has quickly become a favorite for Sears customers.

A New Framework for Success

As we digested the insights gained from examining our organization and listening to our customers, we took two necessary steps to create the infrastructure and cost structure we need to succeed in our highly competitive environment.

We restructured the organization to focus on the whole of Sears so we could more effectively leverage our individual businesses for the greater good of the company.

We also looked hard at our entire cost structure. We engaged our associates to help us examine every aspect of our operations. Our charge was to identify savings opportunities without compromising direct customer service. We also focused on headcount in our headquarters and eliminated approximately 1,000 positions.

This strategy, of course, placed added pressure on our associates, and they responded valiantly. With their hard work and commitment, we are saving an estimated $5 to $10 million each month—funds we can deploy to strengthen our customer value proposition. We will realize the full effect of these cost-cutting actions in 2000.

To support our effort to streamline processes and create whole-house focus, we formed an office of the chief executive to assist me in our decision making. Alan Lacy is responsible for all services, which includes both the Services and Credit business segments. Julian Day assumed the role of chief operating officer and manages all operations, logistics, information technology and finance. By working together, we've discovered many more opportunities to exploit synergies between various businesses.

Reaching Out to Communities
Each year we invest our time and resources to support the communities that support our stores. In 1999, active and retired Sears associates, along with their families, gave more than 275,000 hours of volunteer service through the America's Promise campaign. They also made significant contributions to various disaster relief efforts and pledged more than $5.4 million to nonprofit organizations through the You Can Make a Difference workplace giving campaign. Sears and its associates, along with The Sears Roebuck Foundation, gave nearly $30 million in funding and merchandise to a variety of family-focused arts and human services agencies.

Commitment to Sears
I would like to take special note of another significant 1999 event at Sears, when in October, Jack Rogers retired from Sears Board of Directors after nearly 20 years of distinguished service. Jack's tenure spanned a period of great change in our company. His commitment to Sears inspired us when prospects were unclear. And his wise counsel made him an extraordinary contributor. We miss him, and I sincerely thank him for his service.

Opportunities for 2000
Our success in 1999 was clearly no accident. We made deliberate moves to get our business back on track, and our customers responded. We expect to generate even greater success from many of the programs initiated in 1999. At the same time, we will find new ways to engineer success in other businesses. Here are some of our priorities and opportunities:

> Revitalize our Full-line Stores. Specifically, we will roll out the new Tool Territory format, which tested very well in 1999. Further, we will continue to build apparel brands and expand our in-store brand shops. We also will build our dominance in appliances through additional innovation. And we will test the new store designs—which include everything from wider aisles to edited merchandise to shopping carts—to make our stores more inviting to shop.

> Build on our tradition of innovation in retailing. For example, we will roll out The Great Indoors format at a faster pace, opening 15 stores in the next one to two years. We will also open new Dealer Stores—the only ones of their kind in retailing—with formats customized for small town and urban locations. In 2000, our Sears Hardware format will continue to evolve as we combine the best of our existing Sears Hardware and Orchard Supply formats.

> Aggressively grow sears.com to offer the best of Sears Online. We will develop new business designs around home maintenance, home remodeling and home decorating, all delivered through strategic alliances.

> Strengthen key brands. We will build on the success of Kenmore Elite by expanding the product line. Craftsman will see a new professional line of tools. The recently introduced DieHard Security Battery demonstrates our commitment to a higher standard for innovation.

> Enhance Credit performance. We will make the Sears Card more relevant, launch Sears co-branded MasterCard and forge tighter links with our retail organization.

> Focus relentlessly on costs and asset productivity.

As I said earlier, we spent a great deal of 1999 listening to our customers. We found the experience both informative and inspiring. They are refreshingly open and honest and tell us exactly what they expect from Sears. They are also very loyal to us, even as they tell us we must meet their needs to keep their business. And, most important, we confirmed something we already knew—that our customers are truly amazing people who invite us into their busy lives every day.

This year's annual report focuses on our customers. We asked them to help us define, in their own words, how Sears delivers **"The good life at a great price. Guaranteed."** It wasn't hard to find customers who were glad to help. They're the reason we enhance our Web site and open our doors every day. We're honored to be such an integral part of their lives. We hope you enjoy meeting them.

ARTHUR C MARTINEZ
Chairman and
Chief Executive Officer

Sears, Roebuck and Co. at a Glance

Sears, Roebuck and Co. is a leading North American retailer of apparel, home and automotive products, and services. The company serves families across the United States through its 858 Full-line department stores, more than 2,100 specialized retail locations, and a variety of online offerings accessible through the company's Web site, **www.sears.com.** Sears also is the nation's number one credit provider among retailers.

RETAIL

Full-line Stores located primarily in the best malls in the nation:
Full assortment of appliances, electronics and home improvement products and services.
Complete selection of fashionable, quality apparel and accessories for the whole family at value prices.
Exclusive Sears brands such as Kenmore, Craftsman, DieHard, Fieldmaster, Crossroads and TKS Basics—all backed by the Sears guarantee.
Leading national brands such as Nike, Maytag and Sony.
Sears Hardware and Orchard Supply Hardware stores, featuring Craftsman tools, a wide assortment of national brands and other home repair products.
Sears locally owned Dealer Stores, bringing to smaller communities and urban centers appliances, electronics, lawn and garden merchandise, hardware, automobile batteries and exclusive Sears brands such as Kenmore, Craftsman and DieHard.
The Great Indoors, focusing on the four main rooms of the house—kitchen, bedroom, bathroom and great room—and serving as a one-stop resource for home decorating and remodeling.
Sears Auto Centers and NTB National Tire & Battery stores offering brand name tires, DieHard batteries and related services.

SERVICES

Reliable home services including parts, repairs, product installation and services, HVAC, carpeting, pest control and cabinet refacing; service contracts that provide annual maintenance checks as well as repair and replacement coverage.
Marketing channels that include specialty catalogs, telemarketing and direct mail.
Direct marketing of goods and services such as merchandise, insurance and club memberships.
Online solutions for the home, including online scheduling of product repair services and instant credit applications, the largest consumer parts site, Tool Territory with 120 brands, and the largest online appliance store.

CREDIT

Credit provider to more than 60 million customer households through the Sears Card, the largest proprietary credit card in the retail industry.

SEARS CANADA

Sears Canada, a majority-owned subsidiary and Canada's largest department store chain.
Offers retail, services and credit products similar to those offered in Sears domestic operations.

Consolidated Statements of Income

millions, except per common share data	1999	1998	1997
Revenues			
Merchandise sales and services	$36,728	$36,957	$36,649
Credit revenues	4,343	4,618	4,925
Total revenues	41,071	41,575	41,574
Costs and expenses			
Cost of sales, buying and occupancy	27,212	27,444	26,985
Selling and administrative	8,418	8,384	8,394
Provision for uncollectible accounts	871	1,287	1,532
Depreciation and amortization	848	830	785
Interest	1,268	1,423	1,409
Reaffirmation charge			475
Restructuring and impairment costs	41	352	
Total costs and expenses	38,658	39,720	39,580
Operating income	2,413	1,855	1,994
Other income, net	6	28	144
Income before income taxes, minority interest and extraordinary loss	2,419	1,883	2,138
Income taxes	904	766	912
Minority interest	62	45	38
Income before extraordinary loss	1,453	1,072	1,188
Extraordinary loss on early extinguishment of debt, net of tax		24	
Net income	$ 1,453	$ 1,048	$ 1,188
Earnings per common share – basic:			
Income before extraordinary loss	$ 3.83	$ 2.76	$ 3.03
Extraordinary loss		0.06	
Net income	$ 3.83	$ 2.70	$ 3.03
Earnings per common share – diluted:			
Income before extraordinary loss	$ 3.81	$ 2.74	$ 2.99
Extraordinary loss		0.06	
Net income	$ 3.81	$ 2.68	$ 2.99

See accompanying notes.

198

Management's Analysis of Consolidated Operations

Sears, Roebuck and Co. and its consolidated subsidiaries ("the Company") is a multiline retailer providing a wide array of merchandise and services in the United States, Puerto Rico and Canada. Operating results for the Company are reported for four domestic segments and one international segment. The domestic segments include the Company's operations in the United States and Puerto Rico.

The Company's segments are defined as follows:

Retail – consisting of:

> Full-line Stores – 858 Full-line stores, averaging 88,000 selling square feet, located primarily in the best malls in the nation and offering:

— Softlines – A complete selection of fashionable, quality apparel and accessories for the whole family, plus cosmetics, fine jewelry and home fashions, at value prices; includes leading national brands as well as exclusive Sears brands such as Canyon River Blues, Fieldmaster, Crossroads, TKS Basics and Circle of Beauty.

— Hardlines – A full assortment of appliances, electronics and home improvement products and services; includes major national brands as well as exclusive Sears brands such as Kenmore, Craftsman, WeatherBeater and DieHard.

> Specialty Stores – More than 2,100 specialty stores, located primarily in freestanding, off-the-mall locations or high-traffic neighborhood shopping centers.

— Hardware Stores – 267 neighborhood hardware stores under the Sears Hardware and Orchard Supply Hardware names, averaging 20,000 to 40,000 selling square feet, that carry Craftsman tools, a wide assortment of national brands and other home repair products.

— Dealer Stores – 738 independently-owned stores, averaging 5,000 selling square feet, that offer appliances, electronics, lawn and garden merchandise, hardware and automobile batteries in smaller communities and carry exclusive Sears brands such as Craftsman, Kenmore and DieHard.

— Contract Sales – Showrooms dedicated to appliance and home improvement products for commercial customers.

— The Great Indoors – Two prototype stores for home decorating and remodeling, averaging 100,000 selling square feet, dedicated to the four main rooms of the house: kitchen, bedroom, bathroom and great room.

— Automotive Stores – 798 Sears Auto Centers and 310 NTB National Tire & Battery stores that offer tires, DieHard and other brands of batteries, and related services. Auto Stores also included the Parts Group, which sold automotive parts through Parts America and Western Auto Stores until November 2, 1998, when the Company sold the Parts Group.

— Homelife Furniture Stores – included in 1997, 1998 and 1999 until January 30, 1999, when the Company sold Homelife.

Services – consisting of:

> Home Services, which provides service contracts, product installation and repair services, major home improvements and other home services such as pest control and carpet cleaning.

> Direct Response, consisting of direct-response marketing, which markets insurance (credit protection, life and health), clubs and services memberships, merchandise through specialty catalogs, and impulse and continuity merchandise.

Credit – which manages the Company's portfolio of credit card receivables arising from purchases of merchandise and services from domestic operations. The domestic credit card receivables portfolio consists primarily of Sears Card and Sears Premier Card account balances.

Corporate – includes activities that are of an overall holding company nature, primarily consisting of administrative activities and the Sears Online investment initiatives related to selling merchandise via the Company Web sites, the costs of which are not allocated to the Company's businesses.

International – consisting of retail, services, credit and corporate operations similar to the Company's domestic operations. International operations are conducted in Canada through Sears, Canada Inc. ("Sears Canada"), a majority owned subsidiary. International operations were also conducted through Sears, Roebuck de Mexico, S.A. de C.V. ("Sears Mexico"), a 75.5% owned subsidiary until March 1997, when the Company sold 60% of the outstanding shares of Sears Mexico.

Throughout management's analysis of consolidated operations and financial condition, certain prior year information has been reclassified to conform with the current year presentation. All references to earnings per share relate to diluted earnings per common share.

Management's Analysis of Consolidated Operations (CONTINUED)

RESULTS OF OPERATIONS

Consolidated

Net income in 1999 increased 38.6% to $1.45 billion, or $3.81 per share, from $1.05 billion, or $2.68 per share for 1998. The results of operations for 1999, 1998, and 1997 were affected by certain noncomparable items. The effects of these noncomparable items on net income and earnings per share are summarized as follows:

millions, except per share data	1999		1998		1997	
	AFTER-TAX	EARNINGS PER SHARE	AFTER-TAX	EARNINGS PER SHARE	AFTER-TAX	EARNINGS PER SHARE
Net income excluding noncomparable items	$1,482	$ 3.89	$1,300	$ 3.32	$1,303	$ 3.27
Restructuring charge for NTB and Corporate staff reductions	(29)	(0.08)				
Sale of Homelife			(21)	(0.05)		
Sale of Western Auto			(243)	(0.62)		
Extraordinary loss on debt extinguishment			(24)	(0.06)		
SFAS No. 125 accounting			36	0.09	136	0.35
Reaffirmation charge					(320)	(0.80)
Sale of Advantis					91	0.23
Sale of Sears Mexico					(36)	(0.09)
Postretirement life insurance					37	0.09
Parts America conversion					(23)	(0.06)
Net income as reported	$1,453	$ 3.81	$1,048	$ 2.68	$1,188	$ 2.99

Description of Noncomparable Items

In the third quarter of 1999 the Company implemented certain cost reduction strategies resulting in a $46 million pretax charge ($29 million after-tax). Of the $46 million charge, $25 million related to the closing of 33 automotive stores and $21 million related to severance costs for headquarters staff reductions of approximately 450 employees. The Company anticipates annual savings of approximately $40 million (pretax) related to these cost reduction efforts.

On November 18, 1998, the Company entered into an agreement to sell its Homelife furniture business for $100 million in cash, a $10 million note receivable and a 19% ownership interest in the new Homelife business. The Company recorded a loss of $33 million ($21 million after-tax) in the fourth quarter of 1998 related to this transaction. The sale was completed on January 30, 1999.

On November 2, 1998, the Company completed an Agreement and Plan of Merger of Western Auto, a wholly owned subsidiary, and Advance Auto Parts whereby Sears exchanged its interest in Western Auto for $175 million in cash and approximately 40% equity ownership interest in the resulting combined company. Based upon the terms of the sale, the Company recorded a pretax loss of $319 million ($243 million after-tax) in 1998.

On October 2, 1998, the Company prepaid debt with a face value of $300 million, which was due in May 2000. The transaction generated an extraordinary loss of $37 million ($24 million after-tax). The loss resulted primarily from the write-off of the related unamortized discount.

In 1997, the Company implemented Statement of Financial Accounting Standards ("SFAS") No. 125, which changed the way the Company accounted for securitizations. SFAS No. 125 accounting provided incremental operating income of $58 million in 1998 and $222 million in 1997 ($36 million and $136 million, respectively, after-tax).

The 1997 reaffirmation charge of $475 million ($320 million after-tax) represents the cost of the settlement of lawsuits and investigations which alleged that the Company had violated the United States Bankruptcy Code and consumer protection laws in various states through activities related to certain debt reaffirmation agreements and other related matters. There are no further open matters with respect to the reaffirmation charge taken in 1997.

In 1997, the Company sold to IBM its 30% equity interest in Advantis, a joint venture between IBM and the Company. The sale resulted in a pretax gain of $150 million ($91 million after-tax) recorded in other income.

In 1997, the Company sold 60% of the outstanding shares of Sears Mexico to Grupo Carso S.A. de C.V. The sale was recorded in the first quarter of 1997 and resulted in a pretax loss of $21 million reflected in other income and tax expense of $15 million, for an after-tax loss of $36 million.

The Company changed its postretirement life insurance benefit plan in 1997 by eliminating retiree life insurance benefits for all active associates not retired by December 31, 1997. This plan change resulted in a one-time pretax curtailment gain of $61 million ($37 million after-tax) recorded as a reduction of selling and administrative expense.

Management's Analysis of Consolidated Operations (CONTINUED)

The majority of the Western Auto stores were converted to the Parts America format in 1997 and, as a result, the Company recorded a pretax charge of $38 million ($23 million after-tax) for this initiative.

Analysis of Consolidated Results Excluding Noncomparable Items

Net income in 1999, excluding noncomparable items, was $1.48 billion or $3.89 per share, an increase of 17.2% over comparable 1998 per share earnings of $3.32. The improvement was the result of better performance in the Retail, Credit, and International segments and the reduction of shares outstanding, partially offset by a decline in Services

results and higher Corporate expenses including investments in Sears Online.

In 1998, net income excluding noncomparable items was $1.30 billion or $3.32 per share, an increase of 1.5% over comparable 1997 per share earnings of $3.27. The improved profitability of the Credit and Services segments, coupled with strong International performance, a reduction of shares outstanding, and a lower effective tax rate was largely offset by a decline in Retail results.

Reportable Segments

Segment operating income as reported and excluding noncomparable items is as follows:

millions	1999			1998			1997		
	EXCLUDING NON-COMPARABLE ITEMS	EFFECT OF NON-COMPARABLE ITEMS	AS REPORTED	EXCLUDING NON-COMPARABLE ITEMS	EFFECT OF NON-COMPARABLE ITEMS	AS REPORTED	EXCLUDING NON-COMPARABLE ITEMS	EFFECT OF NON-COMPARABLE ITEMS	AS REPORTED
Retail	$ 866	$(25)	$ 841	$ 734	$(352)	$ 382	$ 928	$ 23	$ 951
Services	329		329	375		375	361		361
Credit	1,347		1,347	1,086	58	1,144	1,005	(253)	752
Corporate	(301)	(21)	(322)	(211)		(211)	(212)		(212)
Domestic operating income	2,241	(46)	2,195	1,984	(294)	1,690	2,082	(230)	1,852
International	218		218	165		165	142		142
Total operating income	$2,459	$(46)	$2,413	$2,149	$(294)	$1,855	$2,224	$(230)	$1,994

Retail

Retail store revenues as reported, operating income excluding noncomparable items, and related information are as follows:

millions, except number of stores and Retail store revenues per selling square foot	1999	1998	1997
Full-line Stores revenues	$23,798	$23,140	$22,839
Specialty Stores revenues	5,977	7,289	7,247
Total Retail revenues[1]	$29,775	$30,429	$30,086
Operating income excluding noncomparable items	$ 866	$ 734	$ 928
Number of Full-line Stores	858	845	833
Number of Specialty Stores	2,153	2,198	2,697
Total Retail stores	3,011	3,043	3,530
Retail store revenues per selling square foot[2]	$ 325	$ 317	$ 318
Comparable store sales percentage increase [3]	1.8%	1.1%	2.3%

[1] The Company's 1997 fiscal year included 53 weeks, compared to 52 weeks in 1999 and 1998. Excluding the 53rd week in 1997, total retail revenues increased 3.0% in 1998.

[2] 1997 revenues per square foot calculation excludes the 53rd week.

[3] Includes licensed businesses operating within the Full-line stores.

Retail revenues decreased 2.1% in 1999 to $29.78 billion from $30.43 billion in 1998. Excluding the exited businesses, Western Auto and Homelife, retail revenues increased 3.2% in 1999. Revenues in 1999 and 1998 included 52 weeks compared to 53 weeks in 1997.

Full-line Stores revenues increased 2.8% in 1999, benefiting from the net addition of 13 Full-line Stores as 19 stores were opened and 6 were closed. The Full-line Stores increase was led by solid revenue performance in hardlines merchandise as comparable store sales increased in 1999. Hardlines revenue increases in home appliances, electronics and home improvement were partially offset by a decline in home office merchandise sales. Apparel sales were strong in women's special sizes, infant's and toddler's, fine jewelry, home fashions, and cosmetics and fragrances but were offset by results in dresses, footwear, junior's, boy's, girl's and men's apparel.

Specialty Store revenues decreased to $5.98 billion in 1999 from $7.29 billion in 1998 due primarily to the sale of Western Auto and Homelife. Excluding the exited businesses, specialty retail revenues increased 4.7% in 1999. The strong revenue performance in Hardware and Dealer Stores was partially offset by a decline in Auto Stores revenues.

The revenue increase in Hardware and Dealer Stores in 1999 resulted from the addition of new stores and strong comparable store sales increases. During 1999, the Company opened two net new Hardware Stores and 85 net new Dealer

Management's Analysis of Consolidated Operations (CONTINUED)

Stores. The Contract Sales business and The Great Indoors also produced revenue gains as the Company continued to expand these businesses.

The Auto Stores 1999 revenues were below management's expectations and declined from 1998 levels. Comparable store sales decreased and the Company closed 33 NTB stores in the third quarter of 1999. As of year-end, the Company operated 798 Sears Auto Centers and 310 NTB stores.

Retail revenues increased 1.1% in 1998 to $30.43 billion from $30.09 billion in 1997. 1998 included 52 weeks of revenue compared to 53 weeks in 1997.

Full-line Stores revenues increased 1.3% in 1998 as the Company added 12 net new Full-line Stores. In 1998, apparel sales gains were led by increases in women's special sizes, fine jewelry and cosmetics and fragrances, partially offset by weak sales of dresses, juniors, boy's and men's apparel. Hardlines merchandise had a solid revenue increase in 1998 led by strong sales growth in home appliances and electronics merchandise, partially offset by a decline in home improvement and home office merchandise sales.

Specialty Store revenues increased slightly to $7.29 billion in 1998 from $7.25 billion in 1997 as strong performance in Hardware and Dealer stores was offset by a decline in Auto Stores revenue. Auto Stores revenues declined in 1998 from 1997 as comparable store sales decreased from prior year levels, Western Auto had only 10 months of sales in 1998, and sales were affected by the relatively mild winter weather.

In addition to revenue performance, gross margin, selling and administrative expenses, and depreciation and amortization are important elements in determining Retail operating income. The following discussion of Retail gross margin, selling and administrative expense, and depreciation and amortization excludes the effect of noncomparable items to provide a more meaningful comparison between years. The noncomparable items that affected the Retail segment operating income were the restructuring costs related to the closing of 33 NTB stores in 1999, the losses related to the sales of Western Auto and Homelife in 1998, and the Parts America conversion and the postretirement life insurance curtailment in 1997.

Retail gross margin as a percentage of Retail revenues was flat in 1999 compared to 1998. While the first three quarters of 1999 reflected unfavorable gross margin rates compared to 1998, in the fourth quarter, gross margin rates rebounded in both hardlines and apparel, lifting the retail gross margin rate for the full year to a level consistent with 1998. In 1998, Retail gross margin as a percentage of Retail revenues declined 90 basis points from 1997. In 1998, the decline was due to higher promotional activity driven by a competitive retail environment.

Retail selling and administrative expense as a percentage of Retail revenues improved 50 basis points in 1999 from 1998. The improvement was primarily driven by lower marketing expenses and improvements related to the exit of the Western Auto and Homelife businesses which had higher cost structures. In 1998, Retail selling and administrative expense as a percentage of Retail revenues improved 40 basis points from 1997. In 1998, the improvement was primarily due to leveraging payroll and other employee-related costs.

Retail depreciation and amortization expense decreased 1.8% in 1999 from 1998 and increased 5.0% in 1998 compared to 1997. The slight decrease in 1999 reflects the absence of depreciation and amortization from the exited businesses of Homelife and Western Auto. The increase in 1998 reflects the continuation of the Company's store remodeling program and the growth in the number of Specialty Stores in operation.

Services

Services revenues and operating income as reported are as follows:

millions	1999	1998	1997
Revenues	$3,078	$3,113	$3,073
Operating income	$ `329	$ `375	$ `361

Services revenues, generated primarily by the Home Services business, declined 1.1% in 1999. Home Services revenues were down 1.6% due primarily to a decline in the home improvement business. Direct Response revenues increased 1.9% in 1999 from 1998 as the clubs and services business improved while insurance and other merchandise revenues were relatively flat.

In 1998, Services revenues increased 1.3% primarily due to an 8.5% increase in revenues from Direct Response. All categories of Direct Response products showed improved revenue results in 1998, including clubs and services, insurance and specialty catalogs. In 1998 Home Services revenues were flat as an increase in installation services was offset by a slight decline in the home improvement business and the 53rd week included in 1997.

Services gross margin as a percentage of Services revenues increased 20 basis points in 1999 from 1998. While gross margin rates were relatively flat in both the Home Services and Direct Response businesses, a shift in revenue towards the higher margin Direct Response business caused the overall margin rate to increase. In addition, included in the improved gross margin are the costs related to the exit of a Home Services licensed business relationship which adversely affected the Services gross margin rate by 65 basis points. In 1998, Services gross margin as a percentage of revenues improved 100 basis points from 1997, primarily due to improved profitability of the service contracts portfolio within the Home Services business.

Services selling and administrative expense as a percentage of Services revenues increased 130 basis points in 1999 from 1998. The increase was primarily due to higher payroll, insurance and marketing costs. In 1998, Services selling and administrative expense as a percentage of Services revenues increased 50 basis points from 1997 due to increased infrastructure investments.

Services depreciation and amortization expense increased 16.3% in 1999 from 1998 and 16.7% in 1998 compared to 1997. These increases reflect both infrastructure investments and recent acquisitions.

Management's Analysis of Consolidated Operations (CONTINUED)

Overall, while operating income for both Home Services and Direct Response decreased in 1999, the majority of the decrease came from the home improvement division of the Home Services business. Direct Response continued to provide a significant portion of the operating income for the Services segment in 1999.

Credit

Domestic Credit revenues and operating income are as follows:

millions	1999	1998	1997
Credit revenues	$4,085	$4,369	$4,649
Operating income excluding noncomparable items	$1,347	$1,086	$1,005
Noncomparable items:			
SFAS No. 125		58	222
Reaffirmation charge			(475)
Operating income as reported	$1,347	$1,144	$ ·752

Operating income as reported was $1.35 billion in 1999, an increase of $203 million over the 1998 level. Although credit revenue decreased during 1999, operating income favorability resulted from a lower provision for uncollectible accounts as the quality of the portfolio improved due to improved risk management techniques and investments made in the collection process. Increases in SG&A were more than offset by lower interest expense.

In 1998, the primary reason for the $392 million increase in reported operating income in the Credit segment compared to 1997 was the $475 million reaffirmation charge which adversely affected 1997 results.

In 1999, Credit revenues decreased 6.5% to $4.09 billion. The decrease in Credit revenues was attributable to a lower level of average owned credit card receivables and lower retained interest assets. In 1998, Credit revenues decreased 6.0% to $4.37 billion, reflecting lower average owned receivable balances, and the 53rd week of revenues contained in 1997.

A summary of certain Credit information for the managed portfolio is as follows:

	1999	1998	1997
Sears Card as a % of sales[1]	47.9%	51.6%	55.1%
Average account balance (dollars)	$ 1,121	$ 1,076	$ 1,058
Average managed credit card receivables (millions)	$26,593	$27,922	$27,150

[1] Sears Card as a % of sales includes Full-line Stores, Specialty Stores, Home Services, and Retail Outlet Stores.

The percentage of merchandise sales and services transacted with the Sears Card in 1999 declined to 47.9% compared to 51.6% in 1998, due to a greater preference for other payment methods, including cash, check and third-party credit cards.

Credit selling and administrative expense increased 9.0% in 1999 from the 1998 amount. This increase was primarily attributable to increased investment in credit collection efforts, enhanced risk management systems, the TSYS conversion costs and the launch of the Sears Premier Card. In 1998, selling and administrative expense increased 7.7% from the 1997 level primarily due to increased collection and risk management activities and litigation costs.

Domestic provision for uncollectible accounts and related information is as follows:

millions	1999	1998	1997
Provision for uncollectible accounts	$ ·837	$ 1,261	$ 1,493
Net credit charge-offs to average managed credit card receivables[1][2]	6.44%	7.35%	6.48%
Delinquency rates at year-end[3]	7.55%	6.82%	7.00%
Owned credit card receivables	$17,068	$17,443	$19,386
Allowance for uncollectible owned accounts	$ ·725	$ ·942	$ 1,077

[1] In 1998, the net credit charge-off rate includes the effect of the conversion of 12% of the accounts to the new credit system ("TSYS") in the fourth quarter of 1998. The effect on the charge-off rate was not material. In 1999, 38% of the accounts were converted in March and 50% in April. Balances are generally charged-off earlier under the TSYS system than under the previously used proprietary system.

[2] The following table sets forth the quarterly net credit charge-off rates for the managed portfolio for 1999, 1998 and 1997. Although the 1998 annual charge-off rate was higher than 1997, 1997 was a year of rapid deterioration in the charge-off rate while 1998 showed considerable improvement. In 1999, the charge-off rate continued to improve even though the Company converted to the TSYS operating system, which generally charges-off accounts earlier than under the proprietary system previously used. The net charge-off rate is affected by seasonality, periodic sales of uncollectible accounts to third parties, bankruptcy trends and other general economic trends.

	Q1	Q2	Q3	Q4	Annual Rate
1997	4.97%	5.69%	6.87%	7.76%	6.48%
1998	8.12%	7.37%	7.20%	6.74%	7.35%
1999	7.09%	7.11%	6.39%	5.20%	6.44%

[3] Delinquency rates in 1998 and 1997 were calculated based on the company's proprietary credit system. Under the Company's proprietary credit system, an account was generally considered delinquent when its cumulative past due balance was three or more times the scheduled minimum monthly payment. The 1998 delinquency rate was for the 88% of the managed accounts that had not been converted to TSYS. For the TSYS accounts, which represented 12% of the managed accounts at year-end 1998, the delinquency rate was 9.28%. For TSYS accounts, the aging methodology is based on the number of completed billing cycles during which a customer has failed to make a required payment. Therefore, under TSYS, accounts are considered delinquent when a customer has failed to make a payment in each of the last three or more billing cycles. The 1999 year-end delinquency rate is based on the TSYS methodology.

Management's Analysis of Consolidated Operations (CONTINUED)

The delinquency rates for accounts that had been converted to TSYS were as follows on a quarterly basis through 1999:

January 2, 1999 (12% converted)	9.28%
April 3, 1999 (50% converted)	8.07%
July 3, 1999 (100% converted)	7.29%
October 2, 1999 (100% converted)	7.57%
January 1, 2000 (100% converted)	7.58%

In 1999, the domestic provision for uncollectible accounts decreased $424 million to $837 million. The decrease is attributable to lower average owned credit card receivable balances and improvement in portfolio quality during the year. As shown in the table above, delinquency rates on a TSYS basis declined from year-end 1998, when delinquencies were at 9.28%, to 7.58% at the end of 1999. In addition, the net charge-off rate for 1999 decreased to 6.44% from 7.35% in 1998. The allowance for doubtful accounts at year-end is $725 million, or 4.26% of on-book receivables as compared to 5.44% at the prior year-end.

In 1998, the provision for uncollectible accounts decreased 15.5% from 1997. The decrease was primarily attributable to favorable trends in delinquency rates, charge-off experience and bankruptcy filings, as well as lower owned credit card receivable balances and one less week of provision expense in 1998 compared to 1997 due to the effect of the 53rd week. As of January 2, 1999, the allowance was $942 million compared to $1.08 billion at January 3, 1998. The $135 million decrease in the allowance for uncollectible accounts related to the improvement in portfolio quality and the reduction in owned credit card receivable balances. The owned credit card receivables decreased $1.94 billion during 1998 primarily due to the transfer of credit card receivables from Sears to a securitization Master Trust to provide receivable balances for future securitizations. Receivables transferred to the securitization Master Trust in 1998 were classified as retained interest in transferred credit card receivables in the balance sheet, and were transferred net of the related $106 million allowance balance.

Interest expense from the domestic segments is included in the Credit segment discussion because the majority of the Company's domestic interest expense is allocated to the Credit segment. Generally, the domestic interest expense that is not allocated to the Credit segment is allocated to the Retail segment and is not a significant cost relative to costs of sales, buying and occupancy, selling and administrative expense, and depreciation and amortization expense in the Retail segment.

Domestic interest expense is combined with the funding cost on receivables sold through securitizations to represent total funding costs. The Company uses credit card receivable securitizations as a significant funding source and therefore, for purposes of this analysis, the interest paid on securitizations

is considered a funding cost. The total domestic funding costs are as follows:

millions	1999	1998	1997
Domestic segments interest expense[1]	$1,168	$1,318	$1,290
Domestic funding cost of securitized receivables	419	433	437
Total domestic funding costs	$1,587	$1,751	$1,727

[1] Credit segment interest expense was $1,116, $1,244 and $1,259 for 1999, 1998 and 1997, respectively.

Total domestic funding costs decreased 9.4% in 1999 to $1.59 billion. The decrease in funding costs reflects the lower level of average managed credit card receivable balances and a lower funding rate environment. In 1998, the increase in funding costs reflects higher funding requirements due to a higher average managed credit card receivable portfolio, higher inventory levels and capital spending and share repurchases partially offset by a lower funding rate.

Corporate

Corporate expenses increased $111 million in 1999 compared to 1998. The increase is primarily attributable to investment spending for the Sears Online initiative and the $21 million restructuring charge related to staff reductions in the third quarter of 1999. In addition, increased spending on information systems and higher performance-based incentive costs drove Corporate expenses higher in 1999. In 1998, Corporate selling and administrative expense decreased $1 million compared to 1997 due to targeted cost control efforts.

International

International revenues and operating income are as follows:

millions	1999	1998	1997
Merchandise sales and services	$3,875	$3,415	$3,490
Credit revenues	258	249	276
Total revenues	$4,133	$3,664	$3,766
Operating income	$ 218	$ 165	$ 142

International operations include the results of Sears Canada for all periods presented and the results of Sears Mexico through the first quarter of 1997, when the Company sold its majority interest.

International revenues were $4.13 billion in 1999, a 12.8% increase from revenues of $3.66 billion in 1998. International revenues increased as Sears Canada experienced favorable results across all formats including Full-line stores, dealer stores, furniture stores, catalog, and credit. Comparable store sales were strong throughout the year. In 1998, revenues decreased 2.7% from 1997 due to the inclusion of $100 million of revenues related to Sears Mexico in the prior year. Sears Canada had strong retail and catalog sales performance

Management's Analysis of Consolidated Operations (CONTINUED)

in 1998 compared to 1997. However, the favorable performance was partially offset by the negative effects of a weaker Canadian dollar.

International gross margin as a percentage of International merchandise sales and services increased 130 basis points in 1999 from 1998 primarily due to a sharper focus on the management of the cost of goods sold. In 1998, gross margin as a percentage of merchandise sales and services decreased 30 basis points from 1997 primarily due to increased buying costs.

International selling and administrative expense as a percentage of total revenues was relatively flat in 1999 compared to 1998 as payroll, benefits and other related costs kept pace with the higher sales levels. In 1998, International selling and administrative expense as a percentage of total International revenues improved 90 basis points from 1997. The selling and administrative rate improvement was primarily due to leveraging payroll and other employee related costs.

International operating income improved $53 million in 1999 compared to 1998. Operating income improved $23 million in 1998 compared to 1997. The improvement in both years is due to revenue growth resulting from the aggressive growth strategy in the furniture and dealer store networks and renovations of Full-line stores.

On December 30, 1999 Sears Canada acquired T. Eaton Company for $66 million. The acquisition included trademarks, leases on 16 stores and certain tax net operating loss carryforwards.

Other Income

Consolidated other income consists of:

millions	1999	1998	1997
Gain on sale of Advantis	$	$	$150
Loss on sale of Sears Mexico			(21)
Gain on sales of property and investments	10	20	7
Miscellaneous	4	8	8
Total	$ 6	$28	$144

Income Tax Expense

Consolidated income tax expense as a percentage of pretax income was 37.4% in 1999, 40.7% in 1998 and 42.7% in 1997. The decrease in the effective tax rate in 1999 from 1998 is a result of the unusually high effective rate in 1998 caused by certain non-tax deductible expenses related to the sale of Western Auto. Excluding the effect of the Western Auto sale, the Company's consolidated effective tax rate would have been 38.2% in 1998. The 1997 tax rate was increased by certain non-tax deductible items related to the reaffirmation charge and the first quarter sale of Sears Mexico. Excluding these significant items, the consolidated effective tax rate would have been 39.9% in 1997. Excluding significant items in both 1998 and 1997, the decrease in 1998 income tax expense as a percentage of pretax income compared to 1997 was due to favorable resolution of tax audit issues as well as a reduction in domestic taxes on international operations.

Market Risk

The Company's outstanding debt securities and off-balance sheet derivatives are subject to repricing risk. The Company's policy is to manage interest rate risk through the strategic use of fixed and variable rate debt and interest rate derivatives. All debt securities and off-balance sheet derivatives are considered non-trading. At year-end 1999 and 1998, 23% and 27%, respectively, of the funding portfolio was variable rate (including current maturities of fixed-rate long-term debt that will reprice in the next 12 months and the effect of off-balance sheet derivative financial instruments, such as interest rate swaps). Based on the Company's funding portfolio as of year-end 1999 and 1998, which totaled $24.6 billion and $26.3 billion, respectively, a 100 basis point change in interest rates would affect annual pretax funding cost by approximately $56 million and $70 million, respectively. The calculation assumes the funding portfolio balance at year-end remains constant for an annual period and that the 100 basis point change occurs at the beginning of the annual period.

Inflation

The moderate rate of inflation over the past three years has not had a significant effect on the Company's sales and profitability.

Outlook

In 2000, the Company expects operating income improvement in its Retail, Services, Credit and International segments and expects earnings per share to benefit from a reduction in shares outstanding due to its $1.5 billion share repurchase program. The Company anticipates low double-digit earnings per share growth, excluding non-comparable items, for the full year of 2000.

Cautionary Statement Regarding Forward-Looking Information

Certain statements made in this Annual Report including the Chairman's Letter are forward-looking statements made in reliance on the safe harbor provisions of the Private Securities Litigation Reform Act of 1995. As such, they involve risks and uncertainties that could cause actual results to differ materially. The Company's forward-looking statements are based on assumptions about many important factors, including competitive conditions in the retail industry; changes in consumer confidence and spending; acceptance of new products; the ability of the Company to successfully implement its promotional plan and cost control strategy; success of technological advances; general United States economic conditions, such as higher interest rates; and normal business uncertainty. In addition, the Company typically earns a disproportionate share of its operating income in the fourth quarter due to holiday buying patterns, which are difficult to forecast with certainty. While the Company believes that its assumptions are reasonable, it cautions that it is impossible to predict the impact of such factors which could cause actual results to differ materially from predicted results. The Company intends the forward-looking statements in this annual report to speak only at the time of its release and does not undertake to update or revise these projections as more information becomes available.

Consolidated Balance Sheets

millions, except per share data	1999	1998
Assets		
Current assets		
Cash and cash equivalents	$ ˙729	$ ˙495
Retained interest in transferred credit card receivables	3,144	4,294
Credit card receivables	18,793	18,946
Less allowance for uncollectible accounts	760	974
Net credit card receivables	18,033	17,972
Other receivables	404	397
Merchandise inventories	5,069	4,816
Prepaid expenses and deferred charges	579	506
Deferred income taxes	709	791
Total current assets	28,667	29,271
Property and equipment		
Land	370	395
Buildings and improvements	5,837	5,530
Furniture, fixtures and equipment	5,209	4,871
Capitalized leases	496	530
Gross property and equipment	11,912	11,326
Less accumulated depreciation	5,462	4,946
Total property and equipment, net	6,450	6,380
Deferred income taxes	367	572
Other assets	1,470	1,452
Total assets	$36,954	$37,675
Liabilities		
Current liabilities		
Short-term borrowings	$ 2,989	$ 4,624
Current portion of long-term debt and capitalized lease obligations	2,165	1,414
Accounts payable and other liabilities	6,992	6,732
Unearned revenues	971	928
Other taxes	584	524
Total current liabilities	13,701	14,222
Long-term debt and capitalized lease obligations	12,884	13,631
Postretirement benefits	2,180	2,346
Minority interest and other liabilities	1,350	1,410
Total liabilities	30,115	31,609
Commitments and contingent liabilities		
Shareholders' equity		
Common shares ($.75 par value per share,		
1,000 shares authorized, 369.1 and 383.5 shares outstanding)	323	323
Capital in excess of par value	3,554	3,583
Retained earnings	5,952	4,848
Treasury stock — at cost	(2,569)	(2,089)
Deferred ESOP expense	(134)	(175)
Accumulated other comprehensive income	(287)	(424)
Total shareholders' equity	6,839	6,066
Total liabilities and shareholders' equity	$36,954	$37,675

See accompanying notes.

206

Management's Analysis of Consolidated Financial Condition

ANALYSIS OF CONSOLIDATED FINANCIAL CONDITION

The Company's significant financial capacity and flexibility are exemplified by the quality and liquidity of its assets and by its ability to access multiple sources of capital.

The owned credit card receivables balance of $18.79 billion excludes credit card receivables transferred to a securitization Master Trust ("Trust"). Through its subsidiary, SRFG, Inc., the Company sells securities backed by a portion of the receivables in the Trust to provide funding. In addition to the receivables in the Trust which back securities sold to third parties, the Company transfers additional receivables to the Trust in accordance with the terms of the securitization transactions and to have receivables readily available for future securitizations.

A summary of these balances at year-end is as follows:

millions	1999	1998	1997
Domestic:			
Managed credit card receivables	$26,785	$28,357	$28,945
Securitized balances sold	(6,579)	(6,626)	(6,404)
Retained interest in transferred credit card receivables[1]	(3,175)	(4,400)	(3,316)
Other customer receivables	37	112	161
Domestic owned credit card receivables	17,068	17,443	19,386
International owned credit card receivables	1,725	1,503	1,570
Consolidated owned credit card receivables	$18,793	$18,946	$20,956

[1] The 1999 and 1998 retained interest amounts are shown before reserves of $31 million and $106 million, respectively, related to the transfer of credit card receivables into the Master Trust in 1998.

The credit card receivable balances are geographically diversified within the United States and Canada. The Company grants retail consumer credit based on the use of proprietary and commercially available credit histories and scoring models. The Company promptly recognizes uncollectible accounts and maintains an adequate allowance for uncollectible accounts to reflect losses inherent in the owned portfolio as of the balance sheet date.

Inventories are primarily valued on the last-in, first-out or LIFO method. Inventories would have been $595 million higher if valued on the first-in, first-out or FIFO method at January 1, 2000. Inventories on a FIFO basis totaled $5.66 billion at January 1, 2000, compared to $5.50 billion at January 2, 1999. The increase in inventory levels is primarily due to additional inventory needed to support new Full-line stores, new Specialty Stores, and the growth of Sears Canada. The sale of Homelife partially offset some of the general increase in inventory levels.

Consolidated Statements of Cash Flows

millions	1999	1998	1997
Cash flows from operating activities			
Net income	$ 1,453	$ 1,048	$ 1,188
Adjustments to reconcile net income to net cash provided by			
(used in) operating activities			
Depreciation, amortization and other noncash items	908	907	807
Extraordinary loss on early extinguishment of debt		37	
Provision for uncollectible accounts	871	1,287	1,532
Restructuring, impairments and sale of businesses	46	352	(129)
(Gain) loss on sales of property and investments	(10)	(20)	7
Change in (net of acquisitions):			
Deferred income taxes	356	178	273
Retained interest in transferred credit card receivables	1,150	(978)	(1,056)
Credit card receivables	(873)	423	(2,285)
Merchandise inventories	(305)	(167)	(475)
Other operating assets	(150)	(65)	(160)
Other operating liabilities	251	88	(258)
Net cash provided by (used in) operating activities	3,697	3,090	(556)
Cash flows from investing activities			
Acquisition of businesses, net of cash acquired	(68)	(34)	(138)
Proceeds from sales of property and investments	118	220	394
Purchases of property and equipment	(1,033)	(1,212)	(1,328)
Net cash used in investing activities	(983)	(1,026)	(1,072)
Cash flows from financing activities			
Proceeds from long-term debt	1,491	2,686	3,920
Repayments of long-term debt	(1,516)	(3,375)	(3,299)
(Decrease) increase in short-term borrowings, primarily 90 days or less	(1,653)	(576)	1,834
Termination of interest rate swap agreements			(633)
Repayments of ESOP note receivable	57	23	16
Common shares purchased	(570)	(528)	(170)
Common shares issued for employee stock plans	61	126	103
Dividends paid to shareholders	(355)	(278)	(441)
Net cash (used in) provided by financing activities	(2,485)	(1,922)	1,330
Effect of exchange rate changes on cash and cash equivalents	5	5	4
Net increase (decrease) in cash and cash equivalents	234	137	(302)
Balance at beginning of year	495	358	660
Balance at end of year	$ 729	$ 495	$ 358

See accompanying notes.

Management's Analysis of Consolidated Financial Condition (CONTINUED)

Capital Resources

Total net funding for the Company at January 1, 2000, was $24.62 billion compared with $26.30 billion at January 2, 1999. The decrease in net funding is primarily due to a decrease in domestic managed credit card receivable balances

at year-end 1999 compared to year-end 1998. Net year-end funding, including debt reflected on the balance sheet and investor certificates related to credit card receivables sold through securitizations, is as follows:

millions	1999	% OF TOTAL	1998	% OF TOTAL	1997	% OF TOTAL
Short-term borrowings	$ 2,989	12.2%	$ 4,624	17.6%	$ 5,208	19.1%
Long-term debt and capitalized lease obligations	15,049	61.1%	15,045	57.2%	15,632	57.4%
Securitized balances sold	6,579	26.7%	6,626	25.2%	6,404	23.5%
Total funding	$24,617	100.0%	$26,295	100.0%	$27,244	100.0%

In 1999, the Company reduced the percentage of short-term borrowings and increased fixed-rate, longer-term debt and securitization funding in its funding mix as interest rate conditions were favorable in the term debt markets. The Company accesses a variety of capital markets to preserve flexibility and diversify its funding sources. The broad access to capital markets also allows the Company to effectively manage liquidity and repricing risk. Liquidity risk is the measure of the Company's ability to fund maturities and provide for the operating needs of its businesses. Repricing risk is the effect on net income from changes in interest rates. The Company's cost of funds is affected by a variety of general economic conditions, including the level and volatility of interest rates. To aid in the management of repricing risk, the Company uses off-balance sheet financial instruments, such as interest rate swaps. The Company has policies that centrally govern the use of such off-balance sheet financial instruments.

The ratings of the Company's debt securities as of January 1, 2000, appear in the table below:

	Moody's Investors Services, Inc.	Standard & Poor's	Duff & Phelps Credit Rating Co.	Fitch IBCA, Inc.
Unsecured long-term debt	A3	A-	A	A
Unsecured commercial paper	P-2	A-2	D-1	F-1
Term securitization	Aaa	AAA	AAA	AAA

On February 24, 2000, the Duff & Phelps Credit Rating Co. changed its ratings on the Company's debt securities from A, D-1 and AAA, to A-, D-1- and AAA, respectively.

The Company utilizes Sears Roebuck Acceptance Corp. ("SRAC"), a wholly owned subsidiary, to issue commercial paper, to maintain a medium-term note program, and to issue intermediate and long-term underwritten debt. SRAC issued term debt securities totaling $1.1 billion in 1999. SRAC commercial paper outstanding was $2.68 billion and $4.24 billion at January 1, 2000, and January 2, 1999, respectively. SRAC commercial paper is supported by $5.06 billion of syndicated

credit agreements, $875 million of which expires in 2002 and $4.185 billion of which expires in 2003. The weighted average interest rate on SRAC fixed rate term debt issued in 1999 was 6.44% compared to 6.43% in 1998. The following securities were issued during 1999:

> $750 million of 6.25%, 10-year underwritten notes, at a yield of 6.43%
> $250 million of variable rate medium term notes, with an average term of 1.8 years; and
> $99 million of fixed rate medium term notes, with an average coupon of 6.51% and an average term of 4.3 years.

The Company, through its subsidiary SRFG, Inc., securitizes domestic credit card receivables to access intermediate-term funding in a cost-effective manner. In 1999, the Company issued $1.4 billion of fixed-rate term certificates through securitizations, compared to $985 million in 1998. As of January 1, 2000, there were $6.58 billion of investor certificates outstanding that were backed by sold domestic credit card receivables.

Capital Spending

The Company has an ongoing capital expenditure program to renovate and update its Full-line Stores. In addition, the Company has added more Full-line and Specialty Stores. Capital expenditures during the past three years are as follows:

millions	1999	1998	1997
Full-line Stores, primarily remodeling and expansion efforts	$ 673	$ 672	$ 812
Specialty Stores	114	241	320
Other – distribution / support	246	299	196
Total capital expenditures	$1,033	$1,212	$1,328

The Company plans capital expenditures of $1.2 billion for 2000, which includes the opening of approximately 10 Full-line Stores, and more than 175 Specialty Stores. The Company may also pursue selective strategic acquisitions.

Consolidated Statements of Shareholders' Equity

dollars in millions / shares in thousands	Common Shares Outstanding	Common Stock	Capital in Excess of Par Value	Retained Earnings	Treasury Stock	Deferred ESOP Expense	Accumulated Other Comprehensive Income	Total Shareholders' Equity	Total Comprehensive Income
Balance, beginning of year 1997	391,394	$323	$3,618	$3,330	$(1,655)	$(230)	$(441)	$4,945	
Net income				1,188				1,188	$1,188
Other comprehensive income:									
Currency translation							(7)	(7)	(7)
Reclassification adjustment for loss included in net income							87	87	87
Minimum pension liability, net of tax of $34							60	60	60
Total comprehensive income									$1,318
Dividends to shareholders ($0.92 per share)				(360)				(360)	
Stock options exercised and other changes	2,936		(20)		123			103	
Shares repurchased	(3,442)				(170)			(170)	
ESOP expense recognized						26		26	
Balance, end of year 1997	390,888	$323	$3,598	$4,158	$(1,702)	$(204)	$(311)	$5,862	
Net income				1,048				1,048	$1,048
Other comprehensive income:									
Currency translation							(31)	(31)	(31)
Minimum pension liability, net of tax of $45							(82)	(82)	(82)
Total comprehensive income									$ '935
Dividends to shareholders ($0.92 per share)				(353)				(353)	
Stock options exercised and other changes	3,263		(15)		141			126	
Shares repurchased	(10,643)				(528)			(528)	
ESOP expense recognized						29		29	
Balance, end of year 1998	383,508	$323	$3,583	$4,848	$(2,089)	$(175)	$(424)	$6,066	
Net income				1,453				1,453	$1,453
Other comprehensive income:									
Currency translation							14	14	14
Minimum pension liability, net of tax of $57							104	104	104
Unrealized gain on securities held, net of tax of $11							19	19	19
Total comprehensive income									$1,590
Dividends to shareholders ($0.92 per share)				(349)				(349)	
Stock options exercised and other changes	2,041		(29)		90			61	
Shares repurchased	(16,421)				(570)			(570)	
ESOP expense recognized						41		41	
Balance, end of year 1999	369,128	$323	$3,554	$5,952	$(2,569)	$(134)	$(287)	$6,839	

See accompanying notes.

Management's Analysis of Consolidated Financial Condition (CONTINUED)

Share Repurchases

During 1999, the Company repurchased 16.4 million shares of its common stock for $570 million under its February 1998 share repurchase program related to employee stock-based incentive plans and its March 1999 $1.5 billion repurchase plan. As of the end of 1999, the Company has the capacity to repurchase $1.04 billion of shares under the March 1999 $1.5 billion repurchase plan.

Liquidity

Based upon the expected cash flow to be generated from future operations and the Company's ability to cost-effectively access multiple sources of funding, the Company believes sufficient resources will be available to maintain its planned level of operations, capital expenditures, dividends and share repurchases in the foreseeable future.

Year 2000

Year 2000 compliance is the ability of information systems to properly recognize and process dates and date-sensitive information including the year 2000 and beyond (commonly referred to as Year 2000 or Y2K). Year 2000 compliance is critical to the Company because the Company and many of its merchandise vendors and service providers are highly reliant on information systems to operate their businesses.

The Company used both internal and external resources to complete its Year 2000 compliance initiatives. The Year 2000 efforts of the Company's credit and bank operations were also subject to regulatory review.

The Company did not experience any significant Y2K problems. All Sears facilities opened as planned, systems were available on time and data centers, networks and infrastructure were operational continuously.

As of January 1, 2000, the Company's total costs (including external costs and the costs of internal personnel) related to its Year 2000 effort are approximately $62 million, all of which the Company (including Sears Canada) has incurred. In addition, the Company has accelerated the planned development of new systems with improved business functionality to replace systems that were not Year 2000 compliant, including the Company's new payroll processing system. These systems cost approximately $80 million, all of which the Company has incurred as of January 1, 2000. The Company funded Year 2000 costs with cash flows from operations.

Notes to Consolidated Financial Statements

NOTE >1> SUMMARY OF SIGNIFICANT ACCOUNTING POLICIES

Basis of Presentation

The consolidated financial statements include the accounts of Sears, Roebuck and Co. and all majority-owned domestic and international companies ("the Company"). Investments in companies in which the Company exercises significant influence, but not control, are accounted for using the equity method of accounting. Investments in companies in which the Company has less than a 20% ownership interest, and does not exercise significant influence, are accounted for at cost.

The preparation of financial statements in conformity with generally accepted accounting principles requires management to make estimates and assumptions that affect the reported amounts of assets and liabilities and disclosure of contingent assets and liabilities at the date of the financial statements and the reported amounts of revenues and expenses during the reporting period. Actual results could differ from these estimates.

Certain reclassifications have been made in the 1998 and 1997 financial statements to conform with the current year presentation.

Fiscal Year

The Company's fiscal year ends on the Saturday nearest December 31. Unless otherwise stated, references to years in this report relate to fiscal years rather than to calendar years.

Fiscal year	ENDED	WEEKS
1999	January 1, 2000	52
1998	January 2, 1999	52
1997	January 3, 1998	53

Merchandise Sales and Services

Revenues from merchandise sales and services are net of estimated returns and allowances and exclude sales tax. Included in merchandise sales and services are gross revenues of licensees of $1.69, $1.74 and $1.85 billion for 1999, 1998 and 1997, respectively. In December 1999 the Securities and Exchange Commission (SEC) issued Staff Accounting Bulletin No. 101, "Revenue Recognition in Financial Statements", which effectively changes previous guidance related to the recording of licensed business revenues for retail companies. In the year 2000, the Company will change its method of recording licensed business revenue. This change will reduce reported revenue and reported expenses, but have no impact on operating income.

Service Contracts

The Company sells extended service contracts with terms of coverage generally between 12 and 36 months. Revenues and incremental direct acquisition costs from the sale of these contracts are deferred and amortized over the lives of the contracts. Costs related to performing the services under the contracts are expensed as incurred.

Store Preopening Expenses

Costs associated with the opening of new stores are expensed as incurred.

Earnings Per Common Share

Basic earnings per common share is computed by dividing net income available to common shareholders by the weighted average number of common shares outstanding. Diluted earnings per common share also includes the dilutive effect of potential common shares (dilutive stock options) outstanding during the period.

Cash and Cash Equivalents

Cash equivalents include all highly liquid investments with maturities of three months or less at the date of purchase.

Retained Interest in Transferred Credit Card Receivables

As part of its domestic credit card securitizations, the Company transfers credit card receivables to a Master Trust ("Trust") in exchange for certificates representing undivided interests in such receivables. Effective January 3, 1998, the Company reclassified, for all periods presented, its retained interest in transferred credit card receivables to a separate balance sheet account and presented the related charge-offs of transferred credit card receivables as a reduction of credit revenues. Subsequent to January 3, 1998, amounts transferred from the Company's credit card portfolio to the Trust become securities upon transfer. Accounts are transferred net of the related allowance for uncollectible accounts and income is recognized generally on an effective yield basis over the collection period of the transferred balances. The retained interest consists of investor certificates held by the Company and the seller's certificate, which represents both contractually required seller's interest and excess seller's interest in the credit card receivables in the Trust. The contractually required seller's interest represents the dollar amount of credit card receivables that, according to the terms of the Company's securitization agreements, must be included in the Trust in addition to the amount of receivables which back the securities sold to third parties. The excess seller's interest is the dollar amount of receivables that exist in the Trust to provide for future securitizations, but is not contractually required to be in the Trust. Retained interests are as follows:

millions	1999	1998	1997
Investor certificates held by the Company	$ `960	$ `920	$ `545
Contractually required seller's interest	760	764	697
Excess seller's interest	1,455	2,716	2,074
Retained interest in transferred credit card receivables	$3,175[1]	$4,400[1]	$3,316

[1] The 1998 retained interest amount is shown before reserve of $106 million related to the transfers during 1998, $31 million of which remains at the 1999 year-end.

The Company intends to hold the investor certificates and contractually required seller's interest to maturity. The excess seller's interest is considered available for sale. Due to the revolving nature of the underlying credit card receivables, the carrying value of the Company's retained interest in transferred credit card receivables approximates fair value and is classified as a current asset.

Notes to Consolidated Financial Statements (CONTINUED)

Credit Card Receivables

Credit card receivables arise primarily under open-end revolving credit accounts used to finance purchases of merchandise and services offered by the Company. These accounts have various billing and payment structures, including varying minimum payment levels and finance charge rates. Based on historical payment patterns, the full receivable balance will not be repaid within one year.

Credit card receivables are shown net of an allowance for uncollectible accounts. The Company provides an allowance for uncollectible accounts based on impaired accounts, historical charge-off patterns and management judgement.

In 1997 and 1998 under the Company's proprietary credit system, uncollectible accounts were generally charged off automatically when the customer's past due balance was eight times the scheduled minimum monthly payment, except that accounts could be charged off sooner in the event of customer bankruptcy. However, in the fourth quarter of 1998, the Company converted 12% of its managed portfolio of credit card receivables to a new credit processing system. The remaining 88% of accounts on the proprietary credit system were then converted to the new system in the first and second quarters of 1999. Under the new system, the Company charges off an account automatically when a customer has failed to make a required payment in each of the eight billing cycles following a missed payment. Under both systems, finance charge revenue is recorded until an account is charged off, at which time uncollected finance charge revenue is recorded as a reduction of credit revenues.

The Company adopted Statement of Financial Accounting Standards ("SFAS") No. 125, "Accounting for Transfers and Servicing of Financial Assets and Extinguishments of Liabilities" in 1997. SFAS No. 125 requires that the Company recognize gains on its credit card securitizations which qualify as sales and that an allowance for uncollectible accounts not be maintained for receivable balances which are sold. Prior to adoption of SFAS No. 125, the Company maintained an allowance for uncollectible sold accounts as a recourse liability and did not recognize gains on securitizations. Accordingly, the adoption of SFAS No. 125 increased operating income by $58 million in 1998 and $222 million in 1997 versus the operating income that would have been recognized under the previous accounting method. In 1999, the effects of the change in accounting related to SFAS No. 125, compared to our previous accounting method, were not material.

Merchandise Inventories

Approximately 87% of merchandise inventories are valued at the lower of cost (using the last-in, first-out or "LIFO" method) or market using the retail method. To estimate the effects of inflation on inventories, the Company utilizes internally developed price indices.

The LIFO adjustment to cost of sales was a credit of $73, $34 and $17 million in 1999, 1998 and 1997, respectively. Partial liquidation of merchandise inventories valued under the LIFO method resulted in a credit of $2 million in 1997. No layer liquidation occurred in 1999 and 1998. If the first-in, first-out ("FIFO") method of inventory valuation had been used instead of the LIFO method, merchandise inventories would have been $595 and $679 million higher at January 1, 2000, and January 2, 1999, respectively.

Merchandise inventories of International operations, operations in Puerto Rico, and certain Sears Automotive Store formats, which in total represent approximately 13% of merchandise inventories, are recorded at the lower of cost or market based on the FIFO method.

Property and Equipment

Property and equipment is stated at cost less accumulated depreciation. Depreciation is provided principally by the straight-line method over the estimated useful lives of the related assets, generally 2 to 10 years for furniture, fixtures and equipment, and 15 to 50 years for buildings and building improvements.

Long-Lived Assets

Long-lived assets, identifiable intangibles and goodwill related to those assets are reviewed for impairment whenever events or changes in circumstances indicate that the carrying amount of such assets may not be recoverable.

Goodwill

Included in other assets is the excess of purchase price over net assets of businesses acquired ("goodwill"), which is amortized using the straight-line method over periods ranging from 10 to 40 years. The Company periodically assesses the recoverability of the carrying value and the appropriateness of the remaining life of goodwill.

Advertising

Costs for newspaper, television, radio and other media advertising are expensed the first time the advertising occurs. The total cost of advertising charged to expense was $1.63, $1.67 and $1.59 billion in 1999, 1998 and 1997, respectively.

Direct-Response Marketing

The Company direct markets insurance (credit protection, life and health), clubs and services memberships, merchandise through specialty catalogs, and impulse and continuity merchandise. For insurance and clubs and services, deferred revenue is recorded when the member is billed (upon expiration of any free trial period), and revenue is recognized over the insurance or membership period. For specialty catalog, impulse and continuity merchandise, revenue is recognized when merchandise is shipped.

Membership acquisition and renewal costs, which primarily relate to membership solicitations, are capitalized since such direct-response advertising costs result in future economic benefits. Such costs are amortized over the shorter of the program's life or five years, primarily in proportion to when revenues are recognized. For specialty catalogs, costs are amortized over the life of the catalog, not to exceed one year. The consolidated balance sheets include deferred direct-response advertising costs of $180 and $131 million at January 1, 2000, and January 2, 1999, respectively. The current portion is included in prepaid expenses and deferred charges, the long term portion in other assets.

Notes to Consolidated Financial Statements (CONTINUED)

Off-Balance Sheet Financial Instruments

The Company utilizes various off-balance sheet financial instruments to manage the interest rate and foreign currency risk associated with its borrowings. The counterparties to these instruments generally are major financial institutions with credit ratings of single-A or better.

Interest rate swap agreements modify the interest characteristics of a portion of the Company's debt. Any differential to be paid or received is accrued and is recognized as an adjustment to interest expense in the statement of income. The related accrued receivable or payable is included in other assets or liabilities. The fair values of the swap agreements are not recognized in the financial statements.

Gains or losses on terminations of interest rate swaps are deferred and amortized to interest expense over the remaining life of the original swap period to the extent the related debt remains outstanding.

Financial instruments used as hedges must be effective at reducing the type of risk associated with the exposure being hedged and must be designated as hedges at inception of the hedge contract. Accordingly, changes in market values of financial instruments must be highly correlated with changes in market values of the underlying items being hedged. Any financial instrument designated but ineffective as a hedge would be marked to market and recognized in earnings immediately.

Effect of New Accounting Standards

In June 1998, the Financial Accounting Standards Board issued SFAS No. 133, "Accounting for Derivative Instruments and Hedging Activities." In May 1999, the FASB voted to delay the adoption of SFAS No. 133 by one year. This statement is now required to be adopted in years beginning after June 15, 2000. The Company is currently evaluating the effect this statement might have on the consolidated financial position and results of operations of the Company.

NOTE >2> DISPOSITION OF BUSINESSES

On November 18, 1998, the Company entered into an agreement to exchange its interest in the Homelife furniture business for $100 million in cash, a $10 million note receivable and a 19% equity ownership in the new Homelife business. The Company recorded a pretax charge of $33 million ($21 million after-tax) in the fourth quarter of 1998 related to this transaction. The sale was completed on January 30, 1999.

On November 2, 1998, the Company completed an Agreement and Plan of Merger of Western Auto, a wholly owned subsidiary, and Advance Auto Parts, whereby Sears exchanged its interest in Western Auto for $175 million in cash and approximately 40% equity ownership in the resulting combined company. Based on the terms of the sale, the Company recorded a pretax charge of $319 million ($243 million after-tax) in 1998 related to this transaction. In the fourth quarter of 1999, certain estimates of remaining liabilities under the terms of the transaction were revised, resulting in $5 million of pretax income being recorded in the restructuring and impairment line of the income statement.

NOTE >3> RESTRUCTURING CHARGES

The Company implemented certain cost-reduction strategies during the third quarter of 1999 resulting in a $46 million pretax restructuring charge. Of the $46 million charge, $25 million relates to the closing of 33 automotive stores in three geographic markets and $21 million relates to severance costs for headquarters staff reductions of approximately 450 employees. The staff reductions and the closing of the 33 stores both occurred during the third quarter of 1999. Of the $25 million charge for the 33 closed stores, approximately $3 million relates to severance costs, $21 million is to reduce the carrying value of the closed store assets to their estimated fair value, less costs to sell, and $1 million is for other related costs. As of January 1, 2000, future cash payments to settle restructuring obligations approximate $16 million, which is expected to be paid primarily in the year 2000. The Company paid $20 million of the restructuring costs during the fourth quarter of 1999 resulting in a restructuring reserve balance of $26 million as of January 1, 2000.

NOTE >4> INCOME TAXES

Income before income taxes, minority interest and extraordinary loss is as follows:

millions	1999	1998	1997
Domestic	$2,189	$1,704	$2,018
Foreign	230	179	120
Total	$2,419	$1,883	$2,138

Federal, state and foreign taxes are as follows:

millions	1999	1998	1997
Current			
Federal	$414	$472	$468
State	24	41	75
Foreign	110	74	97
Total	548	587	640
Deferred			
Federal	332	159	256
State	40	15	18
Foreign	(16)	5	(2)
Total	356	179	272
Income tax provision	$904	$766	$912

A reconciliation of the statutory federal income tax rate to the effective rate is as follows:

	1999	1998	1997
Statutory federal income tax rate	35.0%	35.0%	35.0%
State income taxes, net of federal income tax benefit	1.7	1.9	2.9
Reaffirmation charge			1.3
Sale of Sears Mexico			1.3
Sale of Western Auto		2.3	
Other	0.7	1.5	2.2
Effective income tax rate	37.4%	40.7%	42.7%

Notes to Consolidated Financial Statements (CONTINUED)

Deferred taxes based upon differences between the financial statement and tax bases of assets and liabilities and available tax carryforwards consists of:

millions	1999	1998
Deferred tax assets:		
Unearned service contract income	$ ˙429	$ ˙417
Allowance for uncollectible accounts	320	448
State income taxes	149	125
Postretirement benefit liability	933	974
Minimum pension liability	108	165
Loss carryforward acquired	136	
Other deferred tax assets	478	565
Total deferred tax assets	2,553	2,694
Deferred tax liabilities:		
Property and equipment	421	399
Prepaid pension	53	78
LIFO	109	123
Deferred gain	279	235
Deferred revenue	137	73
Deferred swap termination loss	173	182
Other deferred tax liabilities	305	241
Total deferred tax liabilities	1,477	1,331
Net deferred taxes	$1,076	$1,363

Management believes that the realization of the deferred tax assets is more likely than not, based on the expectation that the Company will generate the necessary taxable income in future periods and, accordingly, no valuation reserve has been provided. Tax benefits from loss carryforwards will expire by 2006.

U.S. income and foreign withholding taxes were not provided on certain unremitted earnings of international affiliates which the Company considers to be permanent investments. The cumulative amount of unremitted income for which income taxes have not been provided totaled $479 million at January 1, 2000. If these earnings were to be remitted, taxes of $133 million would be due.

Income taxes of $327, $366 and $886 million were paid in 1999, 1998 and 1997, respectively.

NOTE >5> BENEFIT PLANS

Expenses for retirement and savings-related benefit plans were as follows:

millions	1999	1998	1997
Sears 401(k)			
Profit Sharing Plan	$ ˙37	$ ˙31	$ 33
Pension plans	89	88	106
Postretirement benefits	(46)	(38)	(41)
Other plans			6
Total	$ ˙80	$ ˙81	$104

Sears 401(k) Profit Sharing Plan

Most domestic employees are eligible to become members of the Sears 401(k) Profit Sharing Plan ("the Plan"). Under the terms of the Plan, the Company matches a portion of the employee contributions. In 1998 and 1997, the Company matching contribution was based on 6% of consolidated income, as defined, for the participating companies and was limited to 70% of eligible employee contributions. In 1999 and future periods, the Plan has been changed and the Company match is now fixed at 70% of eligible employee contributions. The Company's matching contributions were $77, $75 and $71 million in 1999, 1998 and 1997, respectively.

The Plan includes an Employee Stock Ownership Plan ("the ESOP") to prefund a portion of the Company's anticipated contribution. The Company provided the ESOP with a loan that was used to purchase Sears common shares in 1989. In June 1998, the ESOP refinanced the loan and extended its maturity to 2024. The purchased shares represent deferred compensation expense, which is presented as a reduction of shareholders' equity and recognized as expense when the shares are allocated to employees to fund the Company contribution. The per share cost of Sears common shares purchased by the ESOP in 1989 was $15.27. The Company uses the ESOP shares to fund the Company contribution, which thereby reduces expense.

The ESOP loan bears interest at 6.1% (9.2% prior to refinancing) and is repaid from dividends on the ESOP shares and additional cash payments provided by the Company. The Company has contributed cash to the ESOP annually in the amount equal to the ESOP's required interest and principal payments on the loan, less dividends received on the ESOP shares. The cash payments amounted to $57, $24 and $23 million in 1999, 1998 and 1997, respectively. The balance of the ESOP loan was $210 and $267 million at January 1, 2000 and January 2, 1999, respectively. Cash on hand in the ESOP at January 1, 2000 was $4 million.

The reported expense is determined as follows:

millions	1999	1998	1997
Interest expense			
recognized by ESOP	$ ˙13	$ ˙21	$ ˙27
Less dividends			
on ESOP shares	(17)	(19)	(21)
Cost of shares allocated			
to employees and			
plan expenses	41	29	26
Sears 401(k) Profit			
Sharing Plan expense	$ ˙37	$ ˙31	$ ˙33

At December 31, 1999, total committed to be released, allocated and remaining unallocated ESOP shares were 2.7, 14.4 and 8.8 million, respectively. All ESOP shares are considered outstanding in the calculation of earnings per share.

Notes to Consolidated Financial Statements (CONTINUED)

Retirement Benefit Plans

Certain domestic full-time and part-time employees are eligible to participate in noncontributory defined benefit plans after meeting age and service requirements. Substantially all Canadian employees are eligible to participate in contributory defined benefit plans. Pension benefits are based on length of service, compensation and, in certain plans, Social Security or other benefits. Funding for the various plans is determined using various actuarial cost methods. The Company uses October 31 as the measurement date for determining pension plan assets and obligations.

In addition to providing pension benefits, the Company provides certain medical and life insurance benefits for retired employees. Employees may become eligible for medical benefits if they retire in accordance with the Company's established retirement policy and are continuously insured under the Company's group medical plans or other approved plans for 10 or more years immediately prior to retirement. The Company shares the cost of the retiree medical benefits with retirees based on years of service. Generally, the Company's share of these benefit costs will be capped at the Company contribution calculated during the first year of retirement. The Company's postretirement benefit plans are not funded. The Company has the right to modify or terminate these plans.

The change in benefit obligation, change in plan assets, funded status, reconciliation to amounts recognized in the consolidated balance sheets and weighted average assumptions are as follows:

millions	PENSION BENEFITS		POSTRETIREMENT BENEFITS	
	1999	1998	1999	1998
Change in benefit obligation:				
Beginning balance	$2,872	$2,824	$`1,180	$`1,270
Benefits earned during the period	95	78	5	7
Interest cost	192	184	74	84
Actuarial loss (gain)	(16)	104	(205)	(22)
Benefits paid	(337)	(302)	(123)	(136)
Foreign exchange impact	22	(38)	2	4
Plan amendments		22	1	
Disposition of Western Auto				(19)
Other	2			
Ending balance	$2,830	$2,872	$ 934	$`1,180
Change in plan assets at fair value:				
Beginning balance	$2,560	$2,710	$	$
Actual return on plan assets	368	176		
Company contributions	50	46	123	136
Benefits paid	(337)	(302)	(123)	(136)
Foreign exchange impact	28	(64)		
Other	2	(6)		
Ending balance	$2,671	$2,560	$	$
Funded status of the plan:	$ (159)	$ (312)	$ `(934)	$(1,180)
Unrecognized net loss (gain)	410	600	(578)	(396)
Unrecognized prior service benefit	(21)	(25)	(668)	(770)
Net amount recognized	$ `230	$ `263	$(2,180)	$(2,346)
Amounts recognized in the balance sheet consist of:				
Prepaid benefit cost	$ `171	$ `164	$	$
Accrued benefit liability	(244)	(365)	(2,180)	(2,346)
Accumulated other comprehensive income	303	464		
Net amount recognized	$ `230	$ `263	$(2,180)	$(2,346)

	PENSION BENEFITS			POSTRETIREMENT BENEFITS		
	1999	1998	1997	1999	1998	1997
Weighted average assumptions:						
Discount rate	8.00%	7.25%	7.25%	8.00%	7.25%	7.25%
Return on plan assets	9.50%	9.50%	9.50%	NA	NA	NA
Rate of compensation increases	4.00%	4.00%	4.00%	NA	NA	NA

Notes to Consolidated Financial Statements (CONTINUED)

The components of net periodic benefit cost are as follows:

millions	PENSION BENEFITS			POSTRETIREMENT BENEFITS		
	1999	1998	1997	1999	1998	1997
Components of net periodic benefit cost:						
Benefits earned during the period	$ `95	$ `78	$ `74	$ `5	$ `7	$ 13
Interest cost	192	184	190	74	84	105
Expected return on plan assets	(228)	(220)	(203)			
Amortization of unrecognized net prior service benefit	3	8	6	(102)	(103)	(68)
Amortization of unrecognized transitional asset		9	(10)			
Recognized net loss (gain)	34	47	52	(23)	(26)	(30)
Elimination of postretirement life insurance for active associates						(61)
Other	1	16	14			
Net periodic benefit cost	$ `89	$ `88	$`106	$ (46)	$ (38)	$`(41)

The projected benefit obligation, accumulated benefit obligation and fair value of plan assets for the pension plans with accumulated benefit obligations in excess of plan assets were $2,236, $2,110 and $1,866 million, respectively, at January 1, 2000, and $2,309, $2,210 and $1,845 million, respectively, at January 2, 1999. The provisions of SFAS No. 87, "Employers' Accounting for Pensions," require the recognition of a minimum pension liability for each defined benefit plan for which the accumulated benefit obligation exceeds plan assets. The minimum pension liability, net of tax, was $195 million at January 1, 2000 and $299 million at January 2, 1999, and is included in accumulated other comprehensive income as a reduction of shareholders' equity.

In 1997, the Company announced changes to its postretirement life insurance benefit plan. Retiree life insurance benefits were eliminated for all active associates not retired by December 31, 1997. This plan change resulted in a one-time pretax gain of $61 million. In connection with the elimination of retirement life insurance benefits for all active associates, the Company also announced the reduction in life insurance over a 10-year period to a maximum coverage of $5,000 for all post-1977 retirees.

The weighted average health care cost trend rate used in measuring the postretirement benefit expense in 2000 is 6.0% for pre-65 retirees and 7.5% for post-65 retirees. For 2001 and beyond, the trend rates are 5.0% for pre-65 retirees and 6.5% for post-65 retirees. A one percentage point change in the assumed health care cost trend rate would have the following effects:

millions	ONE PERCENTAGE POINT INCREASE	ONE PERCENTAGE POINT DECREASE
Effect on total service and interest cost components	$ 3	$ (2)
Effect on postretirement benefit obligation	$16	$(14)

NOTE >6> BORROWINGS

Short-term borrowings consist of:

millions	1999	1998
Commercial paper	$2,824	$4,463
Bank loans	95	91
Promissory note	70	70
Other loans		
Total short-term borrowings	$2,989	$4,624
Weighted average interest rate at year end	6.0%	5.3%
Weighted average interest rate at year end, including effects of swaps	7.1%	6.3%

At January 1, 2000, SRAC's credit facilities totaled $5.06 billion in syndicated credit agreements. Sears Canada had credit agreements totaling $553 million. These syndicated and other credit agreements provide for loans at prevailing interest rates and mature at various dates through April 2003. The Company pays commitment fees in connection with these credit agreements.

The Company had interest rate swap agreements that established fixed rates on $1.52 billion and $1.50 billion of short-term variable rate debt at January 1, 2000 and January 2, 1999, respectively, resulting in weighted average interest rates of 6.7% and 6.8%, respectively. The weighted average maturity of agreements in effect on January 1, 2000, was approximately 14 years.

Notes to Consolidated Financial Statements (CONTINUED)

Long-term debt is as follows:

millis ISSUE	1999	1998
Sears, Roebuck and Co.		
6.25% Notes, due through 2004	$ ˙300	$ ˙500
8.2% Extendable Notes, due 1999		31
9.375% Debentures, due 2011	300	300
5.57% to 10.0% Medium-Term		
Notes, due 2000 to 2021	1,215	1,550
Sears Roebuck Acceptance Corp.		
6.125% to 7.51% Notes,		
due 2000 to 2038	5,827	5,084
5.53% to 7.26% Medium-Term		
Notes, due 2000 to 2013	5,716	5,976
Sears DC Corp.		
8.54% to 9.26% Medium-Term		
Notes, due 2001 to 2012	213	332
Sears Canada Inc.		
6.55% to 11.70% Debentures,		
due 2000 to 2007	305	392
Sears Canada Receivables Trust		
5.04% to 9.18% Receivables		
Trusts, due 2001 to 2006	735	405
Capitalized Lease Obligations	417	453
Other Notes and Mortgages	21	22
	15,049	15,045
Less current maturities	2,165	1,414
Total long-term debt	$12,884	$13,631

On October 2, 1998, the Company prepaid its 6% debentures with a face value of $300 million, which were due in May 2000. The transaction generated an extraordinary loss of $37 million and a related income tax benefit of $13 million, resulting in an after-tax loss of $24 million. The loss resulted primarily from the write-off of the related unamortized discount. The debt was refinanced with the issuance of commercial paper.

As of January 1, 2000, long-term debt maturities for the next five years are as follows:

millions	
2000	$2,165
2001	2,458
2002	1,654
2003	2,540
2004	862

The Company paid interest of $1.2, $1.3 and $1.4 billion in 1999, 1998 and 1997, respectively. Interest capitalized was $5, $5 and $3 million in 1999, 1998 and 1997, respectively.

NOTE >7> LEASE AND SERVICE AGREEMENTS

The Company leases certain stores, office facilities, warehouses, computers and transportation equipment.

Operating and capital lease obligations are based upon contractual minimum rates and, for certain stores, amounts in excess of these minimum rates are payable based upon specified percentages of sales. Contingent rent is accrued over the lease term, provided that the achievement of the specified sales level that triggers the contingent rental is probable. Certain leases include renewal or purchase options. Operating lease rentals were $399, $431 and $439 million, including contingent rentals of $52, $55 and $57 million in 1999, 1998 and 1997, respectively.

Minimum lease obligations, excluding taxes, insurance and other expenses payable directly by the Company, for leases in effect as of January 1, 2000, are as follows:

millions	CAPITAL LEASES	OPERATING LEASES
2000	$ 66	$ ˙352
2001	60	303
2002	56	253
2003	56	224
2004	54	195
After 2004	714	1,092
Total minimum payments	$1,006	$2,419
Less imputed interest	589	
Present value of		
minimum lease payments	417	
Less current maturities	16	
Long-term obligations	$ 401	

The Company has committed to purchase data and voice networking and information processing services of at least $216 million annually through 2004 from a third-party provider. Total expenses incurred by the Company for these services during 1999, 1998 and 1997 were $318, $355 and $361 million, respectively. The Company may also be responsible for certain stores leases that have been assigned.

NOTE >8> FINANCIAL INSTRUMENTS

In the normal course of business, the Company invests in various financial assets, incurs various financial liabilities and enters into agreements involving off-balance sheet financial instruments. The Company's financial assets and liabilities are recorded in the consolidated balance sheets at historical cost, which approximates fair value.

To determine fair value, credit card receivables are valued by discounting estimated future cash flows. The estimated cash flows reflect the historical cardholder payment experience and are discounted at market rates. Long-term debt is valued based on quoted market prices when available or discounted cash flows, using interest rates currently available to the Company on similar borrowings.

Notes to Consolidated Financial Statements (CONTINUED)

The Company is a party to off-balance sheet financial instruments to manage interest rate and foreign currency risk. These financial instruments involve, to varying degrees, elements of market, credit, foreign exchange and interest rate risk in excess of amounts recognized in the balance sheet. In certain transactions, the Company may require collateral or other security to support the off-balance sheet financial instruments with credit risk.

Debt-related

The Company had the following off-balance sheet financial instruments related to its outstanding borrowings at the end of 1999 and 1998:

millions	1999 CONTRACT OR NOTIONAL AMOUNT	FAIR VALUE	CARRYING VALUE
Interest rate swap agreements:			
Pay floating rate, receive fixed rate	$ ·83	$ ·	$
Pay fixed rate, receive floating rate	1,517	148	
Foreign currency hedge agreements	9	₫	

millions	1998 CONTRACT OR NOTIONAL AMOUNT	FAIR VALUE	CARRYING VALUE
Interest rate swap agreements:			
Pay floating rate, receive fixed rate	$ ·805	$ ·9	$
Pay fixed rate, receive floating rate	1,499	(176)	
Foreign currency hedge agreements	10	₫	

The Company uses interest rate swaps to manage the interest rate risk associated with its borrowings and to manage the Company's allocation of fixed and variable-rate debt. For pay floating rate, receive fixed rate swaps, the Company paid a weighted average rate of 5.21% and received a weighted average rate of 6.87% in 1999. For pay fixed rate, receive floating rate swaps, the Company paid a weighted average rate of 6.68% and received a weighted average rate of 5.21% in 1999. The fair values of interest rate swaps are based on prices quoted from dealers. If a counterparty fails to meet the terms of a swap agreement, the Company's exposure is limited to the net amount that would have been received, if any, over the agreement's remaining life.

Maturity dates of the off-balance sheet financial instruments outstanding at January 1, 2000 are as follows:

	Notional amount		
millions	1 YEAR	2-5 YEARS	OVER 5 YEARS
Interest rate swap agreements	$283	$173	$1,144
Foreign currency hedge agreements	5	4	

During 1997, the Company paid $633 million to terminate interest rate swaps. The deferred loss related to these terminations was $415 million and $441 million at January 1, 2000, and January 2, 1999, respectively, and is being amortized over the remaining lives of the original swap periods.

Credit-related

The Company had outstanding domestic securitized credit card receivables sold of $6.58 and $6.63 billion at January 1, 2000, and January 2, 1999, respectively, for which the Company's credit risk exposure is contractually limited to the investor certificates held by the Company.

Other

The Company had a financial guaranty of $89 million at January 1, 2000. This guaranty represents a commitment by the Company to guarantee the performance of certain municipal bonds issued in connection with the Company's headquarters building. No amounts were accrued in the balance sheet for any potential loss associated with this guaranty at January 1, 2000, and January 2, 1999.

NOTE >9> SIGNIFICANT GROUP CONCENTRATIONS OF CREDIT RISK

The Company grants credit to customers throughout North America. The five states and the respective receivable balances in which the Company had the largest amount of managed credit card receivables were as follows:

millions	1999	% OF BALANCE	1998	% OF BALANCE
California	$2,778	10.4%	$2,946	10.4%
Texas	2,127	7.9%	2,285	8.1%
Florida	1,943	7.3%	2,069	7.3%
New York	1,592	5.9%	1,689	6.0%
Pennsylvania	1,364	5.1%	1,457	5.1%

NOTE >10> LEGAL PROCEEDINGS

The Company remains a party to two cases arising from the Company's purchase of garments produced under allegedly illegal labor conditions on the island of Saipan in the Commonwealth of the Northern Marianas Islands. The two actions were filed on January 13, 1999, the first on behalf of ten "Doe" plaintiffs in the United States District Court for the Central District of California against eighteen domestic

Notes to Consolidated Financial Statements (CONTINUED)

clothes retailers and eleven foreign clothing suppliers (which case subsequently was transferred to the United States District Court for the District of Hawaii), and the second by various interest groups, purportedly on behalf of the general public of the State of California, in the San Francisco County Superior Courts. Plaintiffs in the suits seek various injunctive relief, damages (including punitive and treble damages), restitution and disgorgement of profits, interest, and attorney fees and costs. On February 23, 2000, the Company entered into a settlement agreement with the plaintiffs that provides for the dismissal of both cases with respect to the Company. While continuing to deny plaintiffs' claims and contentions, the Company agreed to an immaterial one-time cash payment to the plaintiffs. The Company further agreed that following the effective date of the agreement, it would only purchase garments produced in Saipan from factories that adhere to the terms of a monitoring program provided for in the settlement agreement. The settlement of the cases is subject to the final approval of both courts. In the event that the settlement is not approved and the cases continue against the Company, their consequences are not presently determinable, but in the opinion of the management of the Company, the ultimate liability is not expected to have a material effect on the results of operations, financial position, liquidity or capital resources of the Company.

The Company is subject to various other legal and governmental proceedings, many involving routine litigation incidental to the business. Other matters contain allegations that are nonroutine and involve compensatory, punitive or treble damage claims in very large amounts, as well as other types of relief. The consequences of these matters are not presently determinable but, in the opinion of management of the Company after consulting with legal counsel, the ultimate liability in excess of reserves currently recorded is not expected to have a material effect on annual results of operations, financial position, liquidity or capital resources of the Company.

NOTE >11> OTHER INCOME

In 1997, the Company sold its 30% equity interest in Advantis, a joint venture between IBM and the Company, to IBM. This transaction resulted in a pretax gain of $150 million and is recorded in other income.

Also in 1997, the Company completed the sale of 60% of the outstanding shares of Sears, Roebuck de Mexico, S.A. de C.V. to Grupo Carso S.A. de C.V. The sale resulted in a pretax loss of $21 million and is reflected in other income.

NOTE >12> EARNINGS PER SHARE

The following table sets forth the computations of basic and diluted earnings per share:

millions, except per share data	1999	1998	1997
Net income available to common shareholders[1]	$1,453	$1,048	$1,188
Average common shares outstanding	379.2	388.6	391.6
Earnings per share - basic	$ 3.83	$ 2.70	$ 3.03
Dilutive effect of stock options	1.8	3.1	6.2
Average common and common equivalent shares outstanding	381.0	391.7	397.8
Earnings per share - diluted	$ 3.81	$ 2.68	$ 2.99

[1] Income available to common shareholders is the same for purposes of calculating basic and diluted EPS.

In each period, certain options were excluded from the computation of diluted earnings per share because they would have been antidilutive. At January 1, 2000, January 2, 1999 and January 3, 1998, options to purchase 11.9, 5.2 and 4.7 million shares of stock at prices ranging from $40 to $64, $52 to $64 and $47 to $64 per share were excluded from the 1999, 1998 and 1997 calculations, respectively.

NOTE >13> SHAREHOLDERS' EQUITY

Dividend Payments

Under terms of indentures entered into in 1981 and thereafter, the Company cannot take specified actions, including the declaration of cash dividends, that would cause its unencumbered assets, as defined, to fall below 150% of its liabilities, as defined. At January 1, 2000, approximately $4.5 billion could be paid in dividends to shareholders under the most restrictive indentures.

Share Repurchase Program

On February 3, 1998, the Board of Directors extended, for an additional two years, the common share repurchase program which is used to acquire shares for distribution in connection with the expected exercise of stock options, the grant of restricted shares and the exchange of deferred shares under the Company's stock plans. The program authorized the Company to acquire up to 20 million Sears common shares on the open market. By the end of the first quarter of 1999, all 20 million common shares authorized to be purchased under this repurchase program had been acquired.

On March 10, 1999, the Board of Directors approved a common share repurchase program to acquire up to $1.5 billion of the Company's common shares by December 31, 2001. The shares are to be purchased on the open market or through privately negotiated transactions. As of January 1, 2000, approximately 14.0 million common shares have been acquired under this repurchase program at a cost of approximately $464 million.

Notes to Consolidated Financial Statements (CONTINUED)

NOTE >14> STOCK-BASED COMPENSATION

Stock Option Plans

Options to purchase common stock of the Company have been granted to employees under various plans at prices equal to the fair market value of the stock on the dates the options were granted. Generally, options vest over a three- or four-year period and become exercisable either in equal, annual installments over the vesting period, or at the end of the vesting period. Options generally expire in 10 or 12 years.

Additionally, certain options were granted in 1997 and 1999 with performance-based features that required the Company's share price to reach specified targets at three- and five-year intervals from the grant date to be earned. In February 1999, the Company extended the period of time allowed to meet the specified targets for the 1997 grants by one year. The Company had 1.1 million, 1.2 million, and 1.4 million performance-based options outstanding at the end of 1999, 1998 and 1997, respectively. Subject to the satisfaction of the performance-based features, these performance-based options vest 50% in year six, 25% in year seven and 25% in year eight from the time of grant. The Company did not recognize compensation expense in 1999, 1998 or 1997 related to these options because the exercise price exceeded the Company share price at each year end.

The Company measures compensation cost under Accounting Principles Board Opinion No. 25, "Accounting for Stock Issued to Employees," and no compensation cost has been recognized for its fixed stock option plans. In accordance with SFAS No. 123, "Accounting for Stock-Based Compensation," the fair value of each option grant is estimated on the date of grant using the Black-Scholes option-pricing model. The following assumptions were used during the respective years to estimate the fair value of options granted:

	1999	1998	1997
Dividend yield	2.16%	1.81%	1.59%
Expected volatility	29%	29%	29%
Risk-free interest rate	5.03%	5.82%	6.19%
Expected life of options	6 years	6 years	6 years

Had compensation cost for the Company's stock option plans been determined using the fair value method under SFAS No. 123, the Company's net income and earnings per share would have been reduced to the pro forma amounts indicated below:

millions, except earnings per share	1999	1998	1997
Net income — as reported	$1,453	$1,048	$1,188
Net income — pro forma	1,414	1,023	1,174
Earnings per share — basic			
As reported	3.83	2.70	3.03
Pro forma	3.73	2.63	3.00
Earnings per share — diluted			
As reported	3.81	2.68	2.99
Pro forma	3.71	2.61	2.95

Changes in stock options are as follows:

shares in thousands	1999 SHARES	1999 WEIGHTED AVERAGE EXERCISE PRICE	1998 SHARES	1998 WEIGHTED AVERAGE EXERCISE PRICE	1997 SHARES	1997 WEIGHTED AVERAGE EXERCISE PRICE
Beginning balance	15,251	$39.93	15,155	$34.16	14,389	$25.00
Granted	5,668	40.89	4,171	55.73	4,165	58.23
Exercised	(1,084)	22.76	(2,671)	25.00	(2,832)	23.67
Canceled or expired	(1,309)	51.11	(1,404)	52.98	(567)	31.17
Ending balance	18,526	$40.44	15,251	$39.93	15,155	$34.16
Reserved for future grant at year-end	5,337		9,979		12,840	
Exercisable	7,844	$27.92	8,217	$25.43	7,524	$23.89
Fair value of options granted during the year		$13.35		$18.61		$17.98

Notes to Consolidated Financial Statements (CONTINUED)

The following table summarizes information about stock options outstanding at January 1, 2000:

shares in thousands	OPTIONS OUTSTANDING				OPTIONS EXERCISABLE	
RANGE OF EXERCISE PRICES	NUMBER OUTSTANDING AT 01/01/00	WEIGHTED AVG. REMAINING CONTRACTUAL LIFE IN YEARS		WEIGHTED AVG. EXERCISE PRICE	NUMBER EXERCISABLE AT 01/01/00	WEIGHTED AVG. EXERCISE PRICE
$10.00 to $20.00	1,336	4.4		$16.41	1,336	$16.41
20.01 to 30.00	4,229	6.5		24.24	4,224	24.23
30.01 to 40.00	1,103	8.8		31.97	989	31.94
40.01 to 50.00	7,239	8.3		42.94	1,177	48.08
50.01 to 64.00	4,619	8.0		60.31	118	55.81
$10.00 to $64.00	18,526	7.7		$40.44	7,844	$27.92

Associate Stock Purchase Plan

On May 8, 1997, the shareholders approved the Company's Associate Stock Ownership Plan ("ASOP"). The ASOP allows eligible employees the right to elect to use up to 10% of their eligible compensation to purchase Sears common stock on a quarterly basis at the lower of 85% of the fair market value at the beginning or end of each calendar quarter. The maximum number of shares of Sears common stock available under the ASOP is 10 million. The first purchase period began January 1, 1998. There were 0.6 million shares issued under the ASOP in 1998 and 0.7 million shares issued in 1999.

NOTE >15> SUMMARY OF SEGMENT DATA

The Company is a multiline retailer providing a wide array of merchandise and services, and no single product or service accounted for a significant percentage of the Company's consolidated revenue. The Company has four domestic segments, which include the Company's operations in the United States and Puerto Rico, and one international segment. The domestic segments are Retail, Services, Credit and Corporate.

The Retail segment includes the operating results of the Company's Full-line Stores and Specialty Stores; and the Services segment includes the operating results of the Company's Home Services and Direct Response businesses. These businesses have been aggregated into their respective reportable segments based on the management reporting structure and their similar economic characteristics, customers and distribution channels.

A general description of the merchandise and services offered in each segment follows:

Retail

Full-line Stores, which are located principally in shopping malls, sell apparel, home fashions and hardlines merchandise. Specialty Stores, consisting of Hardware, Dealer, The Great Indoors, Auto, Contract Sales, and Homelife furniture stores sell hardlines, home fashions, auto products and furniture. The Homelife furniture stores were sold on January 30, 1999.

Services

Associates and third-party licensee partners of the Company provide product repair services, extended warranty service contracts and home improvement products. Direct Response consists of direct-response marketing, which markets insurance (credit protection, life and health), clubs and service memberships, merchandise through specialty catalogs, and impulse and continuity merchandise.

Credit

The Credit business manages the Company's portfolio of credit card receivables arising from purchases of merchandise and services from domestic operations.

Corporate

The Corporate segment includes activities that are of a holding-company nature, primarily consisting of administrative activities and the Sears Online investment initiatives related to selling merchandise via the Company Web site, the costs of which are not allocated to the Company's businesses.

International

The International segment consists of retail, credit, services and corporate operations similar to the Company's domestic operations. International operations are conducted in Canada through Sears Canada, Inc., a 54.6% owned subsidiary. International operations were also conducted in Mexico through Sears, Roebuck de Mexico, S.A. de C.V. ("Sears Mexico") until March 29, 1997, when the Company sold 60% of the outstanding shares of Sears Mexico. Thereafter, Sears Mexico's results are no longer included in the Company's consolidated results.

The segments do not record intersegment revenues and expenses. External revenues and expenses are allocated between the applicable segments.

The domestic segments participate in a centralized funding program. Interest expense is allocated to the Credit segment based on its funding requirements assuming a 9-to-1 debt to equity ratio. Funding includes debt reflected on the balance sheet and investor certificates related to credit card receivables sold through securitizations. Services is allocated interest income based on the after-tax cash flow it generates through the sale of service contracts. The remainder of net domestic interest expense is reported in the Retail segment.

The Company's segments are evaluated on a pretax basis, and a stand-alone income tax provision is not calculated for the individual segments. The Company includes its deferred income taxes within the Corporate segment. The other accounting policies of the segments are substantially the same as those described in the Company's summary of significant accounting policies footnote

222

Notes to Consolidated Financial Statements (CONTINUED)

millions	RETAIL	SERVICES	CREDIT	INTERNATIONAL	CORPORATE	CONSOLIDATED
1999						
Revenue	$29,775	$3,078	$ 4,085	$4,133	$ ·	$41,071
Depreciation and						
amortization expense	659	57	14	76	42	848
Interest revenue		59				59
Interest expense	111		1,116	100		1,327
Operating income (expense)	841	329	1,347	218	(322)	2,413
Equity in net income						
of investees accounted						
for by the equity method	(4)			9		5
Noncomparable items—						
income (expense), pretax	(25)				(21)	(46)
Total assets	10,130	1,087	20,622	3,324	1,791	36,954
Capital expenditures	711	81	39	143	59	1,033
1998						
Revenue	$30,429	$3,113	$ 4,369	$3,664	$ ·	$41,575
Depreciation and						
amortization expense	671	49	13	64	33	830
Interest revenue		59				59
Interest expense	133		1,244	105		1,482
Operating income (expense)	382	375	1,144	165	(211)	1,855
Equity in net income						
of investees accounted						
for by the equity method				5		5
Noncomparable items—						
income (expense), pretax	(352)		58		(37)	(331)
Total assets	10,046	943	21,605	2,816	2,265	37,675
Capital expenditures	934	50	18	91	119	1,212
1997						
Revenue	$30,086	$3,073	$ 4,649	$3,766	$ ·	$41,574
Depreciation and						
amortization expense	639	42	13	60	31	785
Interest revenue		61				61
Interest expense	92		1,259	119		1,470
Operating income (expense)	951	361	752	142	(212)	1,994
Equity in net income						
of investees accounted						
for by the equity method				6		6
Noncomparable items—						
income (expense), pretax	23		(253)	(21)	150	(101)
Total assets	10,732	753	22,250	2,801	2,164	38,700
Capital expenditures	1,114	51	9	108	46	1,328

Noncomparable items in 1999 were:

Retail:	Restructuring charge for NTB store closings
Corporate:	Corporate staff reductions

Noncomparable items in 1998 were:

Retail:	Impairment loss related to the sales of Western Auto and Homelife
Credit:	SFAS No. 125 accounting
Corporate:	Extraordinary loss on debt extinguishment

Noncomparable items in 1997 were:

Retail:	Postretirement life insurance curtailment, partially offset by the Parts America conversion
Credit:	Reaffirmation charge, partially offset by SFAS No. 125 accounting
International:	Loss on the sale of Sears Mexico
Corporate:	Gain on the sale of Advantis

Management's Report

The financial statements, financial analyses and all other information were prepared by management, which is responsible for their integrity and objectivity. Management believes the financial statements, which require the use of certain estimates and judgments, fairly and accurately reflect the financial position and operating results of Sears, Roebuck and Co. ("the Company") in accordance with generally accepted accounting principles. All financial information is consistent with the financial statements.

Management maintains a system of internal controls that it believes provides reasonable assurance that, in all material respects, assets are maintained and accounted for in accordance with management's authorizations and transactions are recorded accurately in the books and records. The concept of reasonable assurance is based on the premise that the cost of internal controls should not exceed the benefits derived. To assure the effectiveness of the internal control system, the organizational structure provides for defined lines of responsibility and delegation of authority. The Company's formally stated and communicated policies demand of employees high ethical standards in their conduct of its business. These policies address, among other things, potential conflicts of interest; compliance with all domestic and foreign laws, including those related to financial disclosure; and the confidentiality of proprietary information. As a further enhancement of the above, the Company's comprehensive internal audit program is designed for continual evaluation of the adequacy and effectiveness of its internal controls and measures adherence to established policies and procedures.

Deloitte & Touche LLP, independent certified public accountants, have audited the financial statements of the Company, and their report is presented below. Their audit also includes a study and evaluation of the Company's control environment, accounting systems and control procedures to the extent necessary to conclude that the financial statements present fairly the Company's financial position and results of operations. The independent accountants and internal auditors advise management of the results of their audits, and make recommendations to improve the system of internal controls. Management evaluates the audit recommendations and takes appropriate action.

The Audit Committee of the Board of Directors is comprised entirely of directors who are not employees of the Company. The committee reviews audit plans, internal control reports, financial reports and related matters and meets regularly with the Company's management, internal auditors and independent accountants. The independent accountants and the internal auditors advise the committee of any significant matters resulting from their audits and have free access to the committee without management being present.

Arthur C. Martinez
Chairman, President and Chief Executive Officer

Julian C. Day
Executive Vice President and Chief Operating Officer

Jeffrey N. Boyer
Chief Financial Officer

Independent Auditors' Report

**To the Shareholders and Board of Directors
Sears, Roebuck and Co.**

We have audited the accompanying Consolidated Balance Sheets of Sears, Roebuck and Co. as of January 1, 2000 and January 2, 1999, and the related Consolidated Statements of Income, Shareholders' Equity, and Cash Flows for each of the three years in the period ended January 1, 2000. These financial statements are the responsibility of the Company's management. Our responsibility is to express an opinion on these financial statements based on our audits.

We conducted our audits in accordance with generally accepted auditing standards. Those standards require that we plan and perform the audit to obtain reasonable assurance about whether the financial statements are free of material misstatement. An audit includes examining, on a test basis, evidence supporting the amounts and disclosures in the financial statements. An audit also includes assessing the accounting principles used and significant estimates made by management, as well as evaluating the overall financial statement presentation. We believe that our audits provide a reasonable basis for our opinion.

In our opinion, such consolidated financial statements present fairly, in all material respects, the financial position of Sears, Roebuck and Co. as of January 1, 2000 and January 2, 1999, and the results of its operations and its cash flows for each of the three years in the period ended January 1, 2000 in conformity with generally accepted accounting principles.

Deloitte & Touche LLP
Chicago, Illinois
February 7, 2000

Five-Year Summary of Consolidated Financial Data

millions, except per common share and shareholder data	1999	1998	1997	1996	1995
Operating results					
Revenues	$ 41,071	$ 41,575	$ 41,574	$ 38,064	$ 34,835
Costs and expenses	38,658	39,720	39,580	35,981	33,130
Operating income	2,413	1,855	1,994	2,083	1,705
Other income, net	6	28	144	30	27
Income before income taxes, minority					
interest and extraordinary loss	2,419	1,883	2,138	2,113	1,732
Income taxes	904	766	912	834	703
Income from continuing operations	1,453	1,072	1,188	1,271	1,025
Income from discontinued operations					776
Extraordinary loss		24			
Net income	1,453	1,048	1,188	1,271	1,801
Financial position					
Retained interest in transferred					
credit card receivables	$ 3,144	$ 4,294	$ 3,316	$ 2,260	$ 5,579
Credit card receivables, net	18,033	17,972	19,843	19,303	14,527
Merchandise inventories	5,069	4,816	5,044	4,646	4,033
Property and equipment, net	6,450	6,380	6,414	5,878	5,077
Total assets	36,954	37,675	38,700	36,167	33,130
Short-term borrowings	2,989	4,624	5,208	3,533	5,349
Long-term debt	15,049	15,045	15,632	14,907	11,774
Total debt	18,038	19,669	20,840	18,440	17,123
Percent of debt to equity	264%	324%	356%	373%	391%
Shareholders' equity	$ 6,839	$ 6,066	$ 5,862	$ 4,945	$ 4,385
Shareholders' common share investment					
Book value per common share	$ 18.53	$ 15.82	$ 15.00	$ 12.63	$ 10.40
Shareholders	220,749	233,494	235,336	243,986	256,624
Average common and					
equivalent shares outstanding	381	392	398	399	394
Earnings per common share – diluted					
Income from continuing operations	$ 3.81	$ 2.74	$ 2.99	$ 3.12	$ 2.53
Income from discontinued operations					1.97
Extraordinary loss		.06			
Net income	$ 3.81	$ 2.68	$ 2.99	$ 3.12	$ 4.50
Cash dividends declared					
per common share	$ .92	$ .92	$ .92	$ .92	$ 1.26
Cash dividend payout percent	24.1%	34.3%	30.8%	29.5%	28.0%
Market price –					
per common share (high-low)	53³/₁₆ – 26¹¹/₁₆	65 – 39¹/₁₆	65qf – 38ef	53uk – 38qf	60 – 30
Closing market price at December 31	30ek	42qs	45qf	46	39
Price/earnings ratio (high-low)	14 – 7	24 – 15	22 – 13	17 – 12	16 – 12

Operating results and financial position reflect the 1995 dispositions of Allstate and Homart as discontinued operations.

The percent of debt to equity is calculated using equity from continuing operations.

The 1995 price/earnings ratio was calculated on a continuing operations basis.

Stock prices have not been restated to reflect the Allstate distribution.

Certain prior year information has been reclassified to conform with current year presentation.

1996 and 1995 have not been restated to reflect the licensed business reclassification for Sears Canada.

Quarterly Results (UNAUDITED)

millions, except per common share data	First Quarter		Second Quarter		Third Quarter		Fourth Quarter		Year	
	1999	1998	1999	1998	1999	1998	1999	1998	1999	1998
Revenues	$9,037	$9,233	$9,992	$10,314	$9,538	$9,803	$12,504	$12,225	$41,071	$41,575
Operating income	245	222	564	566	383	173	1,221	894	2,413	1,855
Net income	146	133	331	336	236	44	740	535	1,453	1,048
Earnings per common share – diluted	0.38	0.34	0.86	0.85	0.62	0.11	1.98	1.39	3.81	2.68
Excluding impact of noncomparable items										
Operating income	245	188	564	537	429	478	1,221	946	2,459	2,149
Net income	146	112	331	318	265	298	740	572	1,482	1,300
Earnings per common share – diluted	$ 0.38	$ 0.28	$ 0.86	$ 0.80	$ 0.69	$ 0.76	$ 1.98	$ 1.48	$ 3.89	$ 3.32

1999 noncomparable items consist of restructuring charges related to the headquarters staff reduction and the sale of 33 Auto Stores, both of which occurred in the third quarter.

1998 noncomparable items consist of impairment charges related to the sale of Western Auto and Homelife, an extraordinary loss on the early extinguishment of debt and the impact of SFAS No. 125 accounting.

The fourth quarter pretax LIFO adjustments were credits of $103 and $64 million in 1999 and 1998, compared with charges of $30 million for the first nine months of the respective years.

Total of quarterly earnings per common share may not equal the annual amount because net income per common share is calculated independently for each quarter.

Certain quarterly information has been reclassified to conform with year-end presentation.

Common Stock Market Information and Dividend Highlights (UNAUDITED)

dollars	First Quarter		Second Quarter		Third Quarter		Fourth Quarter		Year	
	1999	1998	1999	1998	1999	1998	1999	1998	1999	1998
Stock price range										
High	47qk	59uk	53³/₁₆	65	47ek	63⁹/₁₆	35qs	50ef	53³/₁₆	65
Low	39¹/₁₆	42qs	41tk	55¹/₁₆	29ek	40⁹/₁₆	26¹¹/₁₆	39¹/₁₆	26¹¹/₁₆	39¹/₁₆
Close	44¹¹/₁₆	58qf	47¹¹/₁₆	62¹/₁₆	32ef	41uk	30ek	42qs	30ek	42qs
Cash dividends declared	0.23	0.23	0.23	0.23	0.23	0.23	0.23	0.23	0.92	0.92

Stock price ranges are for the New York Stock Exchange (trading symbol – S), which is the principal market for the Company's common stock.

The number of registered common shareholders at February 29, 2000 was 219,149.

In addition to the New York Stock Exchange, the Company's common stock is listed on the following exchanges: Chicago; Pacific, San Francisco; London, England; Amsterdam, The Netherlands; Swiss, EBS; and Dusseldorf, Germany.

Executive Officers

ARTHUR C. MARTINEZ

60, chairman, president and chief executive officer since 1995. Chairman and chief executive officer of the former Merchandise Group, 1992-1995. M.B.A., 1965, Harvard University; B.S., 1960, Polytechnic University.

M. SHAN ATKINS

42, executive vice president, Strategic Initiatives since September 1999. Senior vice president–Corporate Strategy, April, 1999; vice president/general merchandising manager, Lawn & Garden 1998-1999; vice president-strategy, Merchandise Planning Office, Imports 1996-1998. Vice president and partner of Bain & Company, 1982-1996. M.B.A., 1983 Harvard Business School; Bachelor of Commerce, 1979, Queens University.

JEFFREY N. BOYER

41, chief financial officer since September 1999. Vice president and controller, 1998-1999; vice president, finance–Full-line Stores, 1996-1998. Vice president, business development of The Pillsbury Co., 1995-1996 and vice president of Finance–general foods of Kraft General Foods, 1994-1995. B.S., 1980, University of Illinois; C.P.A., 1980, Illinois.

JAMES R. CLIFFORD

54, president and chief operating officer of Full-line Stores since 1998. Sears Canada, Inc.–president and chief operating officer, 1996-1998; senior vice president and chief financial officer, 1993-1996. M.B.A., 1971, Seattle University; B.B.A., 1968, Cleveland State.

MARK A. COHEN

51, president, Softlines, chief marketing officer since September 1999. Executive vice president–Marketing from January to August 1999. Senior vice president of Cosmetics, Accessories, Fine Jewelry, Footwear and Home Fashions,

1998-1999. Chairman and chief executive officer of Bradlees, Inc., 1994-1997. M.B.A., 1971 and B.A. Engineering, 1969, Columbia University.

MARY E. CONWAY

51, president, Stores since September 1999. President, Full-line Stores 1999; senior vice president, Northeast Region 1998-1999; region general manager 1993-1998. 1982, Beaver College; 1980, St. Joseph University.

JULIAN C. DAY

47, executive vice president and chief operating officer since September 1999. Executive vice president and chief financial officer, March 1999 to September 1999. Executive vice president and chief financial officer of Safeway, Inc. 1992-1998. M.B.A., 1979, London Business School; M.A., 1975 and B.A., 1974, Oxford University.

LYLE G. HEIDEMANN

54, president, Hardlines since 1999. Senior vice president, Appliances/ Electronics, 1998-1999; vice president, Appliances/Electronics, 1997-1998; vice president, general merchandise manager–Home Appliances, 1996-1997; divisional vice president, Lawn and Garden/Sporting Goods, 1992-1996. B.S., 1967, Northern Illinois University.

ANASTASIA D. KELLY

50, executive vice president, general counsel since September 1999. Executive vice president, general counsel and secretary, March 1999 to September 1999. Fanie Mae–senior vice president, general counsel and secretary, 1996-1999; senior vice president and general counsel, 1996 and senior vice president, deputy general 1995-1996. Partner, Wilmer, Cutler & Pickering, 1990-1995. J.D., 1981, George Washington University National Law Center; B.A., 1971, Trinity College.

ALAN J. LACY

46, president, Services since September 1999, president of Sears Credit from 1997 until 1999 (additionally as chief financial officer from 1998 to 1999), and chief financial officer, from 1995 until 1997. Executive vice president and chief financial officer 1995-1997; senior vice president of Finance of the former Merchandise Group 1994-1995. Vice president of Financial Services and Systems of Philip Morris Companies Inc. and president of Philip Morris Capital Corporation, 1993-1994. M.B.A., 1977, Emory University; B.S., 1975, Georgia Institute of Technology.

GERALD N. MILLER

52, senior vice president and chief information officer since 1998. Vice president of Logistics Information Systems 1995-1998; senior systems, director 1994-1995. Vice president of Information Technology of Bergen Brunswig Corporation, 1987-1994. B.S.–Finance, 1970, Long Beach State.

WILLIAM G. PAGONIS

58, executive vice president, Logistics since 1994. Senior vice president, 1993-1994. Retired Lieutenant General, U.S. Army. M.B.A., 1970 and B.S., 1964, Pennsylvania State University.

JOHN T. SLOAN

48, executive vice president, Human Resources since 1999. Senior vice president, Human Resources, 1998-1999. Vice president–Human Resources, Full-line stores, 1996-1998. Senior vice president of administration of Tribune Company, 1993-1996. M.B.A., 1976, Fordham University; B.S., 1974, Cornell University.

Board of Directors

a.

b.

c.

d.

e.

f.

g.

h.

i.

j.

k.

Committee Membership:
1. Audit Committee
2. Compensation Committee
3. Executive Committee
4. Nominating Committee
* Chairman of Committee

ARTHUR C. MARTINEZ 3*   a.
60, chairman, president and chief executive officer since 1995;
chairman and chief executive officer of the former Merchandise
Group 1992-1995. Vice chairman and director of Saks Fifth Avenue
1990-1992. Director, Pepsi Co., Inc. Sears director since 1995.

RICHARD C. NOTEBAERT 1,4   b.
52, chairman, president and chief executive officer of Ameritech
Corporation from 1994 until his retirement in December 1999;
president and chief operating officer 1993-1994; vice chairman
1993. Sears director since 1996.

HALL ADAMS, JR. 1,4   c.
66, chairman and chief executive officer of Leo Burnett
Company, Inc. from 1987 until his retirement in 1992.
Director, The Dun & Bradstreet Corporation and McDonald's
Corporation. Sears director since 1993.

BRENDA C. BARNES 1,2*,3,4   d.
46, Interim president, chief operating officer, Starwood Hotels
and Resorts since November 1999; former president and chief
executive officer of PepsiCola North America 1996-1998;
chief operating officer of PepsiCola North America 1994-1996.
Director, Avon Products, Inc.; Lucas Digital Ltd. and Lucas Arts
Entertainment Company; Starwood Hotels & Resorts; and The New
York Times Company. Sears director since 1997.

HUGH B. PRICE 1,4   e.
58, president and chief executive officer of the National Urban
League since 1994; vice president of Rockefeller Foundation
1988-1994. Director, Bell Atlantic Corporation, New England
Telephone & Telegraph Co. and New York Telephone Company.
Sears director since 1997.

WARREN L. BATTS 1*,3,4   f.
67, chairman and chief executive officer of Tupperware Corporation
from 1996-1997; chairman of Premark International, Inc. from
1996-1997; chairman and chief executive officer of Premark
1986-1996. Director, The Allstate Corporation; Cooper Industries,
Inc.; Derby Cycle Corporation and Sprint Corporation.
Sears director since 1986.

PATRICK G. RYAN 2,4   g.
62, chairman and chief executive officer of Aon Corporation since
1990; president and chief executive officer from August 1982 through
April 1999. Director, Tribune Company. Sears director since 1997.

ALSTON D. CORRELL, JR. 1,2   h.
58, chairman, chief executive officer and president of Georgia-Pacific
Corporation since 1993; president and chief operating officer
1991-1993. Director, Sun Trust Banks, Inc. and The Southern
Company. Sears director since 1996.

DOROTHY A. TERRELL 1,2   i.
54, president, services group and senior vice president, worldwide
sales, Natural MicroSystems Corporation since 1998; president of
SunExpress, Inc. and corporate executive officer of Sun Microsystems,
Inc. 1991-1997. Director, General Mills, Inc.; Herman Miller, Inc.;
and Massachusetts Technology Development Corporation.
Sears director since 1995.

MICHAEL A. MILES 2,3,4*   j.
60, chairman and chief executive officer of Phillip Morris
Companies Inc. from 1991-1994. Director, The Allstate Corporation;
Dell Computer Corporation, Interpublic Group of Companies,
Morgan Stanley, Dean Witter, Discover & Co. and Time Warner Inc.
Sears director since 1992.

W. JAMES FARRELL 1,2   k.
57, chairman and chief executive officer of Illinois Tool Works Inc.
since 1996; chief executive officer, 1995; executive vice president
1983-1994. Director, The Allstate Corporation and The Quaker Oats
Company. Sears director since 1999.

Company Information

TAKEDA

ANNUAL REPORT 1999

Year ended March 31, 1999

Net Sales Breakdown
(¥ Billion)

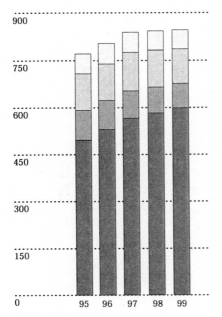

- ■ Pharmaceuticals
- ■ Bulk Vitamin & Food
- ☐ Chemical Products
- ☐ Agro Products and Others

Overseas Sales
(¥ Billion; %)

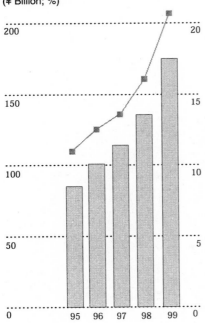

- ☐ Overseas Sales
- ■ Percentage of Net Sales

Consolidated Sales and Income

The business environment surrounding the Takeda Group grew more severe during fiscal 1998, the year ended March 31, 1999, due to the effects of global credit instability and the Asian economic crisis. In the pharmaceutical industry, Takeda's principal business, a succession of large-scale mergers and acquisitions, especially by major companies in Europe and the United States, combined with borderless markets to usher in an era of intense competition.

Amid these trends, the Takeda Group, which aims to be an R&D-driven international enterprise, is developing its global operations and drawing on the strengths of each group company to improve consolidated financial results and raise the value of the Company.

During fiscal 1998, Takeda continued to make rapid strides in its global business. We established our own marketing company in the United States and filed a New Drug Application for diabetes treatment AD-4833 (pioglitazone hydrochloride) in Europe and the United States.

The tough business environment in Japan continued during fiscal 1998 with no sign of economic recovery. Overseas, however, market conditions for ethical drugs were favorable, particularly in the United States. As a result, both net sales and income increased compared with the previous fiscal year.

Net sales increased 0.3 percent to ¥844.6 billion (US$6,980 million) as increased sales of ethical drugs in overseas markets offset a decrease in domestic sales. Net sales to customers outside Japan totaled ¥175.2 billion (US$1,448 million), a year-on-year increase of 29.1 percent, and accounted for 20.7 percent of total net sales, an increase of 4.6 percentage points from fiscal 1997.

In income categories, operating income increased 7.0 percent to ¥142.2 billion (US$1,175 million), reflecting Takeda's success in expanding sales of high-value-added products and other factors. U.S. affiliate TAP Holdings Inc., accounted for by the equity method, achieved growth in sales of the proton pump inhibitor lansoprazole (U.S. brand name: *Prevacid*), an international strategic product, which contributed strongly to a 9.3 percent increase in income before income taxes and minority interests to ¥182.1 billion (US$1,505 million). As a result, net income increased 12.4 percent to ¥91.7 billion (US$758 million).

Net income per share was ¥103.52 (US$0.86), ¥10.55 higher than in the prior fiscal year. Furthermore, return on shareholders' equity increased to 10.6 percent from 10.3 percent. Takeda increased cash dividends per share to ¥29.00 (US$0.24) from ¥21.25 in fiscal 1997.

Segment Information

The Company's operations, as explained in Note 12 of

233

the Notes to Consolidated Financial Statements, are classified into four business segments: Pharmaceuticals, Bulk Vitamin and Food, Chemical Products and Other.

Pharmaceuticals

In keeping with its goal of being an R&D-driven international enterprise, Takeda focused efforts in its pharmaceutical business on creating and developing original new drugs for the global market. At the same time, the Company moved quickly to expand its marketing bases in the United States and Europe.

In the United States, the world's largest market for pharmaceuticals, we established our second marketing base, Takeda Pharmaceuticals America, Inc., in May 1998. In Europe, we established Takeda Europe Research & Development Centre Ltd. in September 1998 in the United Kingdom, where regulatory affairs for the European pharmaceutical market are centered.

In January 1999 in the United States, and in March 1999 in Europe, we filed a New Drug Application for diabetes treatment AD-4833 (pioglitazone hydrochloride). AD-4833, our newest international strategic product, was launched in August 1999 under the brand name *Actos* in the United States.

Following introductions in the United States and Europe, in June 1999 we began sales of hypertension treatment *Blopress* in Japan.

In Japan, where policies to contain healthcare costs make market expansion difficult, Takeda successfully expanded sales of core products such as *Leuplin*, a luteinizing hormone-releasing hormone (LH-RH) analog, and *Basen*, a disaccharidase inhibitor for preventing postprandial hyperglycemia in diabetes mellitus. However, factors such as the withdrawal from the market of *Avan*, a brain-energy metabolism enhancer, resulted in a decrease in domestic pharmaceutical sales.

Outside Japan, sales of lansoprazole (brand name: *Prevacid*) in the United States contributed strongly to overseas results.

Total net sales of the Pharmaceuticals business therefore increased 2.9 percent, to ¥597.5 billion (US$4,938 million), and operating income from this business increased 8.2 percent to ¥132.7 billion (US$1,097 million). The Pharmaceuticals business thus increased its weighting in the overall business of the Takeda Group.

Bulk Vitamin and Food

In April 1998, the U.S. manufacturing and marketing subsidiaries merged to bolster earnings potential in the North American market. However, price declines for vitamin C and *Ribotide* led to a decrease of 5.4 percent in Bulk Vitamin and Food business sales to ¥78.3 billion (US$647 million).

Although the Bulk Vitamin and Food business posted an operating loss of ¥0.6 billion (US$5 million), this represented an improvement of ¥0.4 billion over the prior fiscal year, in part due to better performance at subsidiary Takeda Food Products, Ltd.

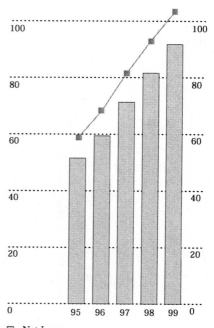

Net Income and Net Income per Share
(¥ Billion; ¥)

■ Net Income
━■ Net Income per Share

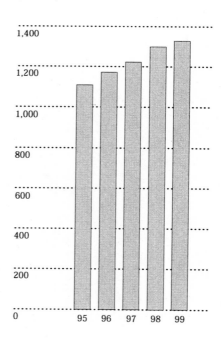

Total Assets
(¥ Billion)

234

Chemical Products

The Chemical Products business, which includes the Life-Environment business, further developed its overseas presence in fiscal 1998 with the acquisition of activated carbon manufacturer Davao Central Chemical Corporation in the Philippines. However, the economic slump in Japan reduced demand related to housing and automobiles. Consequently, sales in the Chemical Products business declined 6.0 percent to ¥110.5 billion (US$913 million), and operating income fell 13.4 percent to ¥6.8 billion (US$56 million).

Other Businesses

In the Agro business, sales of agricultural chemicals and animal health products decreased due to weak domestic demand. As a result, net sales of other businesses decreased 4.2 percent to ¥58.2 billion (US$481 million), and operating income dropped 8.1 percent to ¥3.2 billion (US$26 million).

Financial Position and Liquidity

As of March 31, 1999, total assets were ¥1,326.9 billion (US$10,966 million), an increase of 2.4 percent from a year earlier resulting primarily from an increase in marketable securities and investment securities. Total liabilities, the sum of current and long-term liabilities, decreased 11.1 percent to ¥389.7 billion (US$3,221 million) as conversion into shares of an issue of 1.9 percent unsecured convertible bonds due in 1998 reduced the current portion of long-term debt and income taxes payable decreased.

Higher retained earnings resulted in a 9.4 percent increase in shareholders' equity to ¥907.3 billion (US$7,498 million), which accounted for 68.4 percent of total assets, compared to 64.0 percent at March 31, 1998. Shareholders' equity per share increased ¥76.79 from a year earlier to ¥1,020.35 (US$8.43).

Net cash provided by operating activities decreased ¥4.0 billion to ¥104.9 billion (US$867 million). This decrease in cash flow occurred despite increased net income as accrued expenses and income taxes payable decreased.

Net cash used in investing activities increased ¥96.6 billion from the previous fiscal year to ¥169.3 billion (US$1,399 million). This was due mainly to an increase in purchases of marketable securities.

Net cash used in financing activities increased ¥3.2 billion to ¥22.8 billion (US$189 million), primarily because of the increase in cash dividends paid for the fiscal year.

Cash and cash equivalents at the end of the year decreased ¥85.9 billion to ¥313.7 billion (US$2,593 million) from a year earlier.

Takeda will continue working to improve results and deploy capital efficiently in order to maintain a sound financial structure.

Year 2000 (Y2K) Issue

Takeda recognizes the Y2K issue as a critical management concern, and has charged a director with responsibility for ensuring that Takeda and its group companies deal with it effectively. To prevent a material adverse impact caused by external entities such as suppliers on its business operations, the Company is also working to ensure their Y2K readiness. Remediation and replacement of information systems and equipment have been progressing according to plan, with remediation and replacement of all critical systems scheduled for completion in September 1999. The Company has also prepared a comprehensive contingency plan detailing responses to foreseeable risks. Expenses related to Y2K remediation are not expected to have a material impact on the operations or results of the Takeda Group.

Legal Proceedings

The Company's 100-percent-owned subsidiary, Takeda Vitamin & Food USA, Inc. (TVFU), which manufactures and sells vitamin bulks in the U.S.A., submitted the documents regarding its vitamin business to the U.S. Department of Justice according to certain subpoena issued in May 1998.

The Company and TVFU are among co-defendants with other companies in class-action law suits brought in the U.S.A. by plaintiffs claiming that they suffered damages from an alleged conspiracy of price fixing and market allocations in the worldwide vitamins market.

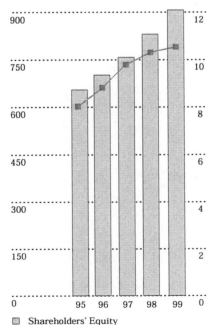

Shareholders' Equity & ROE
(¥ Billion; %)

☐ Shareholders' Equity
🔶 ROE (Return on Equity)

ELEVEN-YEAR SUMMARY OF SELECTED FINANCIAL DATA

Years ended March 31

	1999	1998	1997	1996
For the years ended March 31:				
Net sales	¥ 844,643	¥ 841,816	¥ 838,824	¥ 801,341
Operating income	142,220	132,952	127,350	112,707
Income before income taxes and minority interests	182,142	166,649	147,985	125,787
Income taxes	89,019	83,368	75,094	64,837
Minority interests	1,368	1,671	1,508	1,106
Net income	91,755	81,610	71,383	59,844
Capital investments	29,241	34,091	30,741	30,358
Depreciation and amortization	32,651	32,763	31,473	33,255
Research and development costs	77,487	79,039	71,754	68,006
Per share amounts (Yen and U.S. dollars)				
(See Note 11 to consolidated financial statements):				
Net income	¥103.52	¥92.97	¥81.52	¥68.35
Cash dividends	29.00	21.25	17.25	15.00
At March 31:				
Current assets	¥ 913,263	¥ 877,808	¥ 826,288	¥ 787,615
Property, plant and equipment	224,229	232,092	229,400	231,532
Investments and other assets	189,507	186,302	165,087	153,086
Total assets	1,326,999	1,296,202	1,220,775	1,172,233
Current liabilities	280,058	324,735	292,873	299,032
Long-term liabilities	109,705	113,920	144,198	147,825
Minority interests	29,863	28,166	26,565	25,467
Shareholders' equity	907,373	829,381	757,139	699,909
Number of shareholders	54,059	59,008	71,172	81,278
Number of employees	15,776	16,443	16,586	17,258

Notes: 1. The U.S. dollar amounts in this report represent translations of Japanese yen, for convenience only, at the rate of ¥121=US$1, the approximate exchange rate at March 31, 1999.

2. In the year ended March 31, 1995, 35 previously unconsolidated subsidiaries accounted for by the equity method were consolidated. As a result, the number of consolidated subsidiaries totaled 47 and 24 companies were accounted for by the equity method.

| | Millions of yen | | | | | | Thousands of U.S. dollars (Note 1) |
1995	1994	1993	1992	1991	1990	1989	1999
¥ 771,667	¥ 727,845	¥ 720,140	¥709,686	¥691,409	¥697,915	¥689,381	$ 6,980,521
95,285	88,434	76,675	67,963	70,297	78,145	87,931	1,175,372
107,145	103,210	93,029	85,727	104,998	92,767	97,297	1,505,306
54,424	54,520	43,827	50,603	58,902	54,849	57,173	735,694
1,291	1,064	1,168	1,288	1,607	1,057	1,270	11,306
51,430	47,626	48,034	33,836	44,489	36,861	38,854	758,306
36,337	42,965	37,953	39,627	45,726	38,179	29,032	241,661
29,768	27,922	27,508	26,199	23,718	21,185	17,805	269,843
67,159	62,934	62,277	59,742	53,388	51,163	45,336	640,388
¥58.74	¥54.43	¥54.98	¥38.74	¥50.98	¥42.28	¥44.77	$0.86
14.00	13.00	12.00	12.00	12.00	10.00	10.00	0.24
¥ 721,814	¥ 693,837	¥ 662,777	¥641,275	¥645,414	¥659,782	¥621,447	$ 7,547,628
241,506	210,236	196,441	188,145	182,200	163,221	123,343	1,853,132
147,428	148,350	147,427	149,134	135,385	129,854	141,846	1,566,174
1,110,748	1,052,423	1,006,645	978,554	962,999	952,857	886,636	10,966,934
275,636	271,498	249,853	261,689	273,902	304,478	277,677	2,314,529
157,323	145,657	158,628	158,081	155,422	151,436	147,296	906,653
24,666	21,407	20,508	19,484	18,342	16,846	12,606	246,802
653,123	613,861	577,656	539,300	515,333	480,097	449,057	7,498,950
87,897	89,384	88,446	89,349	87,329	82,282	72,873	
17,580	15,792	15,781	15,497	15,210	15,137	13,675	

Takeda Chemical Industries, Ltd. and Consolidated Subsidiaries

CONSOLIDATED BALANCE SHEETS

March 31, 1999 and 1998

	Millions of yen		Thousands of U.S. dollars (Note 1)
ASSETS	1999	1998	1999
Current assets:			
Cash and cash equivalents —			
Cash	¥ 39,213	¥ 36,980	$ 324,074
Time deposits	274,585	362,789	2,269,298
Total	313,798	399,769	2,593,372
Marketable securities (Note 3)	227,032	92,845	1,876,298
Notes and accounts receivable —			
Trade notes	61,173	69,342	505,562
Trade accounts	138,621	137,276	1,145,628
Due from unconsolidated subsidiaries and affiliates	28,859	26,946	238,504
Allowance for doubtful receivables and losses on sales returns	(3,775)	(4,010)	(31,198)
Total	224,878	229,554	1,858,496
Inventories (Note 4)	107,767	107,049	890,636
Deferred income taxes	28,180	37,367	232,893
Other current assets	11,608	11,224	95,933
Total current assets	913,263	877,808	7,547,628
Property, plant and equipment (Note 5):			
Land	39,603	40,029	327,298
Buildings and structures	229,146	225,402	1,893,769
Machinery and equipment	382,256	371,249	3,159,140
Construction in progress	6,887	12,156	56,917
Total	657,892	648,836	5,437,124
Accumulated depreciation	(433,663)	(416,744)	(3,583,992)
Net property, plant and equipment	224,229	232,092	1,853,132
Investments and other assets:			
Investments in and advances to unconsolidated subsidiaries and affiliates (Note 3)	73,764	81,846	609,620
Investment securities (Note 3)	50,058	40,596	413,702
Deferred income taxes	36,612	38,430	302,579
Other assets	29,073	25,430	240,273
Total investments and other assets	189,507	186,302	1,566,174
TOTAL	¥1,326,999	¥1,296,202	$10,966,934

See notes to consolidated financial statements.

	Millions of yen		Thousands of U.S. dollars (Note 1)
LIABILITIES AND SHAREHOLDERS' EQUITY	1999	1998	1999
Current liabilities:			
Bank loans (Note 5)	¥ 9,361	¥ 9,509	$ 77,364
Current portion of long-term debt (Note 5)	2,119	24,077	17,512
Notes and accounts payable —			
Trade notes	11,277	12,373	93,198
Trade accounts	80,154	78,287	662,430
Due to unconsolidated subsidiaries and affiliates	21,603	20,101	178,537
Total	113,034	110,761	934,165
Accrued expenses	68,464	76,014	565,818
Income taxes payable	38,698	54,902	319,818
Other current liabilities	48,382	49,472	399,852
Total current liabilities	280,058	324,735	2,314,529
Long-term liabilities:			
Long-term debt (Note 5)	9,858	10,896	81,471
Retirement benefits (Note 6)	93,961	96,909	776,537
Reserve for SMON compensation (Note 7)	5,886	6,115	48,645
Total long-term liabilities	109,705	113,920	906,653
Minority interests	29,863	28,166	246,802
Commitments and contingencies (Note 13)			
Shareholders' equity (Notes 8 and 14):			
Common stock — authorized, 2,400,000,000 shares;			
issued and outstanding shares with par value of ¥50 per share:			
March 31, 1999 — 889,272,395 shares			
March 31, 1998 — 878,991,506 shares	63,540	52,468	525,124
Additional paid-in capital	49,637	38,578	410,223
Legal reserve	14,250	12,804	117,769
Retained earnings	779,946	725,531	6,445,834
Total shareholders' equity	907,373	829,381	7,498,950
TOTAL	¥1,326,999	¥1,296,202	$10,966,934

Takeda Chemical Industries, Ltd. and Consolidated Subsidiaries

CONSOLIDATED STATEMENTS OF INCOME

Years ended March 31, 1999, 1998 and 1997

	Millions of yen			Thousands of U.S. dollars (Note 1)
	1999	1998	1997	1999
Net sales (Notes 3 and 12)	¥844,643	¥841,816	¥838,824	$6,980,521
Operating costs and expenses (Note 12):				
Cost of sales (Note 3)	435,787	443,292	449,228	3,601,546
Selling, general and administrative (Note 9)	266,636	265,572	262,246	2,203,603
Total	702,423	708,864	711,474	5,805,149
Operating income (Note 12)	142,220	132,952	127,350	1,175,372
Other income (expenses):				
Interest and dividend income	8,603	6,677	5,783	71,099
Interest expense	(1,059)	(1,808)	(2,257)	(8,752)
Equity in earnings of unconsolidated subsidiaries and affiliates	35,981	24,193	17,270	297,364
Gain on sale of investment in an affiliate	—	4,833	—	—
Loss on sales and disposals of property, plant and equipment	(332)	(666)	(37)	(2,744)
Exchange gains (losses)	(734)	1,328	968	(6,066)
Other — net	(2,537)	(860)	(1,092)	(20,967)
Total	39,922	33,697	20,635	329,934
Income before income taxes and minority interests	182,142	166,649	147,985	1,505,306
Income taxes (Note 10):				
Current	78,014	93,088	78,219	644,744
Deferred	11,005	(9,720)	(3,125)	90,950
Total	89,019	83,368	75,094	735,694
Income before minority interests	93,123	83,281	72,891	769,612
Minority interests	1,368	1,671	1,508	11,306
Net income	¥ 91,755	¥ 81,610	¥ 71,383	$ 758,306

	Yen			U.S. dollars (Note 1)
Amounts per common share (Note 11):				
Net income	¥103.52	¥92.97	¥81.52	$0.86
Cash dividends applicable to the year	29.00	21.25	17.25	0.24

See notes to consolidated financial statements.

Takeda Chemical Industries, Ltd. and Consolidated Subsidiaries

CONSOLIDATED STATEMENTS OF SHAREHOLDERS' EQUITY

Years ended March 31, 1999, 1998 and 1997

	Millions of yen			Thousands of U.S. dollars (Note 1)
	1999	1998	1997	1999
Common stock:				
Balance, beginning of year	¥ 52,468	¥ 48,948	¥ 48,942	$ 433,620
Shares issued upon conversion of debt	11,072	3,520	6	91,504
Balance, end of year	¥ 63,540	¥ 52,468	¥ 48,948	$ 525,124
Additional paid-in capital:				
Balance, beginning of year	¥ 38,578	¥ 35,063	¥ 35,057	$ 318,826
Increase due to conversion of debt	11,059	3,515	6	91,397
Balance, end of year	¥ 49,637	¥ 38,578	¥ 35,063	$ 410,223
Legal reserve:				
Balance, beginning of year	¥ 12,804	¥ 12,235	¥ 12,235	$ 105,818
Transfer from retained earnings	1,446	569	—	11,951
Balance, end of year	¥ 14,250	¥ 12,804	¥ 12,235	$ 117,769
Retained earnings:				
Balance, beginning of year	¥725,531	¥660,893	¥603,675	$5,996,124
Net income	91,755	81,610	71,383	758,306
Cash dividends paid; ¥24.75 ($0.20) — 1999,				
¥18.25 — 1998 and ¥15.75 — 1997 (per share)	(21,885)	(16,001)	(13,792)	(180,868)
Bonuses to directors and corporate auditors	(239)	(402)	(373)	(1,975)
Transfer to legal reserve	(1,446)	(569)	—	(11,951)
Effect on beginning retained earnings of changing from the equity method to the cost method of accounting for an investment in a certain former affiliate	(13,770)	—	—	(113,802)
Balance, end of year	¥779,946	¥725,531	¥660,893	$6,445,834

See notes to consolidated financial statements.

CONSOLIDATED STATEMENTS OF CASH FLOWS

Years ended March 31, 1999, 1998 and 1997

	Millions of yen			Thousands of U.S. dollars (Note 1)
	1999	1998	1997	1999
Operating activities:				
Net income	¥ 91,755	¥ 81,610	¥ 71,383	$ 758,306
Adjustments to reconcile net income to net cash provided by operating activities:				
Depreciation and amortization	32,651	32,763	31,473	269,843
Loss on sales and disposals of property, plant and equipment	332	666	37	2,744
Provision for deferred income taxes	11,005	(9,720)	(3,125)	90,950
Undistributed earnings of unconsolidated subsidiaries and affiliates	(7,998)	(16,370)	(16,252)	(66,099)
Gain on sale of investment in an affiliate	—	(4,833)	—	—
Changes in assets and liabilities, net of effects from consolidating a former affiliate (Note 2):				
Decrease in notes and accounts receivable	4,676	18,312	10,350	38,645
Decrease (increase) in inventories	(718)	(4,643)	802	(5,934)
Decrease (increase) in other current assets	(384)	342	1,458	(3,174)
Decrease (increase) in other assets	(4,853)	(13)	3,553	(40,107)
Increase (decrease) in notes and accounts payable	2,273	(6,784)	2,140	18,785
Increase (decrease) in accrued expenses	(7,550)	3,593	5,527	(62,397)
Increase (decrease) in income taxes payable	(16,204)	12,042	(111)	(133,917)
Increase (decrease) in other current liabilities	1,043	1,839	(13,175)	8,620
Decrease in liability for retirement benefits	(2,948)	(892)	(1,079)	(24,364)
Increase in minority interests	1,697	1,167	1,098	14,025
Other	202	(98)	(21)	1,669
Net cash provided by operating activities	104,979	108,981	94,058	867,595
Investing activities:				
Payment for purchases of property, plant and equipment	(28,932)	(33,936)	(31,745)	(239,107)
Proceeds from sales of property, plant and equipment	1,085	89	2,492	8,967
Payment for purchases of investment securities	(8,652)	(337)	(3,540)	(71,504)
Proceeds from sale of investment in an affiliate	—	5,488	—	—
Proceeds from sales of investment securities	1,199	1,350	911	9,909
Decrease (increase) in investments in and advances to unconsolidated subsidiaries and affiliates	184	(78)	17	1,521
Net increase in marketable securities	(134,187)	(40,191)	(13,175)	(1,108,984)
Cash paid for acquiring a majority interest in a former affiliate, net of cash and cash equivalents from consolidating this subsidiary	—	(5,078)	—	—
Net cash used in investing activities	(169,303)	(72,693)	(45,040)	(1,399,198)
Financing activities:				
Redemption of bonds	(215)	(500)	(600)	(1,777)
Proceeds from issuance of long-term debt	2,256	2,708	1,995	18,645
Repayment of long-term debt	(2,889)	(3,371)	(4,777)	(23,876)
Net increase (decrease) in bank loans	(148)	(2,438)	1,972	(1,223)
Dividends paid	(21,885)	(16,001)	(13,792)	(180,868)
Net cash used in financing activities	(22,881)	(19,602)	(15,202)	(189,099)
Effect of exchange rate changes (Note 2)	1,234	(274)	(1,907)	10,198
Net increase in cash and cash equivalents	(85,971)	16,412	31,909	(710,504)
Cash and cash equivalents, beginning of year	399,769	383,357	351,448	3,303,876
Cash and cash equivalents, end of year	¥313,798	¥399,769	¥383,357	$2,593,372
Additional cash flow information:				
Interest paid	¥ 1,061	¥ 1,779	¥ 2,452	$ 8,769
Income taxes paid	94,218	80,509	78,315	778,661
Noncash financing activity:				
Convertible debt converted into common stock	¥ 22,131	¥ 7,035	¥ 12	$ 182,901
Noncash investing activities:				
The Company acquired a majority of a certain affiliate in the year ended March 31, 1998 and included it in the consolidation (Note 2). In conjunction with the acquisition, liabilities were assumed as follows:				
Assets acquired	¥ —	¥ 6,054	¥ —	$ —
Investment eliminated	—	(723)	—	—
Cash paid to acquire a majority of the capital stock	—	(5,607)	—	—
Goodwill	—	4,885	—	—
Minority interests	—	(434)	—	—
Liabilities assumed	¥ —	¥ 4,175	¥ —	$ —
Effect on beginning retained earnings of changing from the equity method to the cost method of accounting for an investment in a certain former affiliate	¥ (13,770)	¥ —	¥ —	$ (113,802)

See notes to consolidated financial statements.

NOTES TO CONSOLIDATED FINANCIAL STATEMENTS

Years ended March 31, 1999, 1998 and 1997

Note 1

BASIS OF PRESENTING CONSOLIDATED FINANCIAL STATEMENTS

The accompanying consolidated financial statements are prepared from the consolidated financial statements issued for domestic reporting purposes in accordance with the provisions set forth in the Japanese Securities and Exchange Law. Takeda Chemical Industries, Ltd. (the "Company") and its domestic consolidated subsidiaries maintain their accounts and records in accordance with the provisions set forth in the Japanese Commercial Code and in conformity with generally accepted accounting principles and practices in Japan, which are different in certain respects as to application and disclosure requirements of International Accounting Standards, and its overseas subsidiaries and affiliates in conformity with those of the countries of their domicile.

In preparing the consolidated financial statements, certain reclassifications and rearrangements have been made to the consolidated financial statements issued domestically in Japan in order to present them in a form which is more familiar to readers outside Japan. Presentation of a consolidated statement of cash flows as an integral part of the basic financial statements is not required for domestic reporting purposes but is included herein for the convenience of readers. In addition, the accompanying notes include information which is not required under generally accepted accounting principles and practices in Japan but is presented herein as additional information.

The financial statements are stated in Japanese yen, the currency of the country in which the Company is incorporated and operates. The translations of Japanese yen amounts into U.S. dollar amounts are included solely for the convenience of readers outside Japan and have been made at the rate of ¥121 to US$1, the approximate rate of exchange at March 31, 1999. Such translations should not be construed as representations that the Japanese yen amounts could be converted into U.S. dollars at that or any other rate.

Note 2

SUMMARY OF SIGNIFICANT ACCOUNTING POLICIES

Principles of consolidation

The accompanying consolidated financial statements include the accounts of the Company and its significant subsidiaries (together the "Companies"). All significant intercompany balances and transactions are eliminated in consolidation.

During the fiscal year ended March 31, 1999, the Company established two new subsidiaries and acquired a majority interest of a certain affiliate (defined as ownership from 20% to 50%), previously accounted for by the cost method. During the fiscal year ended March 31, 1998, the Company established five new subsidiaries and acquired a majority interest of a certain affiliate, previously accounted for by the equity method. The consolidated financial statements include the balances of such subsidiaries and their operations and cash flows from the date of their inclusion in the consolidation.

During the fiscal year ended March 31, 1999, due to the decrease in ownership of a certain company, previously accounted for by the equity method, the former affiliate has been accounted for by the cost method and retained earnings at April 1, 1998 has been retroactively adjusted.

Cash and cash equivalents

In reporting cash flows, the Companies consider cash and time deposits with maturities of one year or less to be cash and cash equivalents. Such time deposits may be withdrawn on demand without diminution of principal.

Marketable securities and investments

Publicly traded marketable securities included in marketable and investment securities are carried at the lower of cost or market value applied on an individual basis. Cost is determined by the average method. Except for certain insignificant affiliates, the Company's investments in unconsolidated subsidiaries and affiliates are stated at their underlying net equity values after elimination of intercompany profits. Other securities are stated at cost except that appropriate write-downs are recorded for securities with values that have been permanently impaired.

Inventories

Merchandise and raw materials are stated at the lower of cost or market value and finished products and work-in-process are stated at cost. Cost is primarily determined by the average method.

Property, plant and equipment

Property, plant and equipment is stated at cost. Depreciation is primarily computed by the declining-balance method at rates based on the estimated useful lives of the assets.

Goodwill

The excess of the purchase price over net assets of a subsidiary acquired ("goodwill") is amortized on the straight-line method over five years. Goodwill at March 31, 1999 and 1998 were ¥2,929 million ($24,207 thousand) and ¥3,907 million, net of amortization of ¥1,956 million ($16,165 thousand) and ¥978 million, respectively.

Retirement benefits

The liability for retirement benefits is stated at an amount which would be required to be paid if all employees eligible under the Companies' retirement benefit plans voluntarily ter-

243

minated their employment as of the balance sheet date, less amounts funded under contributory and non-contributory trusteed pension plans. The liability includes retirement benefits for directors and corporate auditors of the Company, payments of which are subject to the approval of the shareholders.

Stock and bond issue costs
Stock and bond issue costs are charged to income as incurred.

Foreign currency transactions
Foreign currency amounts are translated into Japanese yen at the rates in effect at each balance sheet date for monetary current assets and current liabilities, and at historical rates for all other assets and liabilities, except for those covered by forward exchange contracts which are translated at the contracted rates. However, when there is a significant unrealized exchange loss related to long-term receivables and payables, such receivables and payables are translated into Japanese yen at the exchange rates in effect at the balance sheet date. Revenue and expense items denominated in foreign currencies are translated at historical rates. Exchange gains or losses are credited or charged to income as incurred. However, exchange gains or losses arising from the translation of long-term receivables or payables at forward contract rates are deferred and amortized over the terms of the related contracts.

Foreign currency financial statements
The financial statements of overseas subsidiaries and affiliates are translated into Japanese yen by the following principal methods as set forth by the Financial Accounting Standard on Foreign Currency Translation in Japan.

The balance sheet accounts of overseas subsidiaries and affiliates are translated into Japanese yen at the current exchange rates as of the balance sheet date except intercompany accounts and shareholders' equity, which are translated at historical rates. Revenue and expense accounts of overseas subsidiaries and affiliates are translated into Japanese yen at the average exchange rate for the year. Differences arising from such translation are included in other assets or liabilities.

Income taxes
Current income taxes are provided for based on amounts currently payable for each year. Deferred income taxes arising from timing differences in the recognition of income and expenses for tax and financial reporting purposes are reflected in the consolidated financial statements. Accrued income taxes on undistributed earnings of overseas subsidiaries and affiliates are also reflected in the consolidated financial statements. Accrued income taxes on the undistributed earnings of domestic subsidiaries and affiliates are not provided because dividends received from domestic companies are expected to be non-taxable.

At March 31, 1999, deferred tax assets were devalued at a new statutory tax rate, effective at the year end. The amount of devaluation of ¥8,009 million ($66,190 thousand) was charged to income for the year ended March 31, 1999.

Cash dividends
Cash dividends charged to retained earnings are those actually paid during the year and consist of year-end dividends for the preceding year and interim dividends for the current year.

Reclassifications
Certain reclassifications have been made to the consolidated financial statements for the year ended March 31, 1999. The consolidated financial statements for 1998 have been retroactively restated to conform to the 1999 presentation.

Note 3

MARKETABLE SECURITIES AND INVESTMENTS

Current marketable securities, which consisted principally of debt securities, approximated aggregate market value at March 31, 1999 and 1998. Information regarding non-current marketable equity and debt securities included in investment securities at March 31, 1999 and 1998 was as follows:

	Millions of yen		Thousands of U.S. dollars
	1999	1998	1999
Carrying value	¥ 35,221	¥ 33,707	$ 291,083
Aggregate market value	265,204	205,776	2,191,768
Gross unrealized gains	229,983	172,069	1,900,685

Investments in and advances to unconsolidated subsidiaries and affiliates at March 31, 1999 and 1998 consisted of the following:

	Millions of yen		Thousands of U.S. dollars
	1999	1998	1999
Investments at cost	¥11,577	¥13,835	$ 95,678
Equity in undistributed earnings	58,483	64,224	483,330
Total	70,060	78,059	579,008
Advances	3,704	3,787	30,612
Total	¥73,764	¥81,846	$609,620

At March 31, 1999 and 1998, the Company's investment in one affiliate (1999) and two affiliates (1998), recorded at ¥13,609 million ($112,471 thousand) and ¥29,334 million based on the equity method, had aggregate quoted market values of ¥12,377 million ($102,289 thousand) and ¥31,900 million, respectively.

Financial information with respect to unconsolidated subsidiaries and affiliates, which were recorded based on the equity method at March 31, 1999 and 1998 and for each of the three years ended March 31, 1999, is summarized as follows:

	Millions of yen		Thousands of U.S. dollars
	1999	1998	1999
Current assets	¥268,528	¥339,137	$2,219,240
Other assets	99,075	138,814	818,802
Total	367,603	477,951	3,038,042
Current liabilities	179,465	211,040	1,483,182
Other liabilities	18,689	31,631	154,455
Net assets	¥169,449	¥235,280	$1,400,405

	Millions of yen			Thousands of U.S. dollars
	1999	1998	1997	1999
Net sales	¥613,588	¥639,777	¥590,096	$5,070,975
Net income	72,404	53,146	40,178	598,380

Sales to and purchases from unconsolidated subsidiaries and affiliates were as follows:

	Millions of yen			Thousands of U.S. dollars
	1999	1998	1997	1999
Sales	¥128,708	¥109,862	¥105,948	$1,063,702
Purchases	65,401	58,124	58,384	540,504

Note 4

INVENTORIES

Inventories at March 31, 1999 and 1998 consisted of the following:

	Millions of yen		Thousands of U.S. dollars
	1999	1998	1999
Finished products and merchandise	¥ 54,413	¥ 53,051	$449,694
Work-in-process	36,393	35,816	300,768
Raw materials	16,961	18,182	140,174
Total	¥107,767	¥107,049	$890,636

Note 5

BANK LOANS AND LONG-TERM DEBT

Bank loans consisted of short-term bank loans represented by notes, generally due in one year. The Companies obtain financing by discounting notes and export drafts with banks. Such discounted notes and drafts and the related contingent liabilities were not included in the balance sheets but are disclosed as contingent liabilities (see Note 13).

The weighted average annual interest rates of short-term bank loans and discounted notes and export drafts at March 31, 1999 and 1998 were 1.8% and 2.1%, respectively.

Long-term debt at March 31, 1999 and 1998 consisted of the following:

	Millions of yen		Thousands of U.S. dollars
	1999	1998	1999
1.9% unsecured convertible bonds due 1998	¥ —	¥22,347	$ —
Unsecured loans from banks and financial institutions due through 2023 with interest ranging from 1.4% to 6.7%	1,582	2,266	13,074
Secured bonds due through 2004 with interest ranging from 1.6% to 4.9%	1,300	1,200	10,744
Collateralized loans from financial institutions due through 2015 with interest ranging from 0.7% to 6.7%	9,095	9,160	75,165
Total	11,977	34,973	98,983
Less current portion	2,119	24,077	17,512
Total	¥ 9,858	¥10,896	$81,471

The annual maturities of long-term debt were as follows:

Year ending March 31	Millions of yen	Thousands of U.S. dollars
2000	¥ 2,119	$17,512
2001	6,133	50,686
2002	1,588	13,124
2003	1,101	9,099
2004	210	1,736
2005 and thereafter	826	6,826
Total	¥11,977	$98,983

At March 31, 1999, assets pledged as collateral for long-term debt were as follows:

	Millions of yen	Thousands of U.S. dollars
Property, plant and equipment, net of accumulated depreciation	¥12,332	$101,917

As is customary in Japan, security must be given if requested by a lending bank. Banks have the right to offset cash deposited with them against any debt or obligation that becomes due or, in case of default and certain other specified events, against all other debt payable to the banks. None of the lenders has ever exercised this right against the Companies' obligations.

Note 6

RETIREMENT BENEFITS

Employees of the Companies terminating their employment either voluntarily or upon reaching the mandatory retirement age are entitled to severance payments based on the rate of pay at the time of termination, length of service and certain other factors. The Company has a contributory trusteed pension plan which is interrelated with the Japanese government social welfare program which consists of a basic portion requiring employee and employer contributions, plus an additional portion established by the Company. The Company and certain consolidated subsidiaries also have non-contributory trusteed pension plans. A portion of the above retirement benefits is funded under such pension plans.

At March 31, 1999 and 1998, the assets of the pension plans amounted to ¥116,919 million ($966,273 thousand) and ¥109,587 million, respectively.

Charges to income with respect to retirement benefits for the years ended March 31, 1999, 1998 and 1997 were ¥15,615 million ($129,050 thousand), ¥15,300 million and ¥22,268 million, respectively.

Note 7

RESERVE FOR SMON COMPENSATION

The Company was co-defendant with the Japanese government and other pharmaceutical companies in legal actions in Japan. The plaintiffs claimed that a certain medicine, a product of one of the co-defendants, which was distributed by the Company, was a cause of SMON, a neurological disease affecting the plaintiffs.

Compromise settlements have been made with all the plaintiffs through December 25, 1996.

The Company has made a provision in the accompanying consolidated financial statements for estimated future medical treatment payments over the remaining lives of the parties entitled under the compromise settlements.

Note 8

SHAREHOLDERS' EQUITY

Under the Japanese Commercial Code (the "Code"), at least 50% of the issue price of new shares, with the minimum of the par value thereof, is required to be designated as stated capital.

Under the Code, the Company is required to appropriate and set aside as a legal reserve an amount at least equal to 10% of the amounts paid as an appropriation of retained earnings, including dividends and other distributions, until such reserve equals 25% of stated capital. This reserve is not available for dividends but may be used to eliminate or reduce a deficit by resolution of the shareholders or may be transferred to common stock by resolution of the Board of Directors.

The Company may transfer portions of additional paid-in capital to common stock by resolution of the Board of Directors. The Company may also transfer portions of unappropriated retained earnings, available for dividends, to common stock by resolution of the shareholders.

Under the Code, the amount legally available for dividends is based upon retained earnings as recorded on the books of the Company. At March 31, 1999, retained earnings available for future dividends amounted to ¥556,414 million ($4,598,463 thousand) subject to legal reserve requirements.

Note 9

RESEARCH AND DEVELOPMENT COSTS

Research and development costs are charged to income as incurred. Research and development costs for the years ended March 31, 1999, 1998 and 1997 were ¥77,487 million ($640,388 thousand), ¥79,039 million and ¥71,754 million, respectively.

Note 10

INCOME TAXES

The effective income tax rates of the Companies differed from the statutory tax rate for the following reasons:

	1999	1998	1997
Statutory tax rate	47.7%	51.4%	51.4%
Expenses not deductible for tax purposes	2.2	2.9	3.4
Loss in subsidiaries	1.3	0.6	0.7
Equity in earnings of unconsolidated subsidiaries and affiliates	(6.6)	(4.5)	(4.6)
Non-taxable dividend income	(0.3)	(0.4)	(0.3)
Tax credits primarily for research and development costs	(0.2)	(0.2)	(0.7)
Effect of statutory tax rate change (see Note 2)	4.4	—	—
Other — net	0.4	0.2	0.8
Effective tax rate	48.9%	50.0%	50.7%

Deferred income taxes consisted of the following:

	Millions of yen			Thousands of U.S. dollars
	1999	1998	1997	1999
Expenses recorded on books of account but not currently deductible for tax purposes	¥(1,976)	¥(9,468)	¥(5,687)	$(16,331)
Accrued enterprise tax, deductible when paid	1,901	(1,661)	(62)	15,711
Accrued income taxes on undistributed earnings of overseas subsidiaries and affiliates	2,605	3,104	3,343	21,529
Elimination of intercompany profits	466	(1,695)	(719)	3,851
Effect of statutory tax rate change (see Note 2)	8,009	—	—	66,190
Total	¥11,005	¥(9,720)	¥(3,125)	$ 90,950

Note 11

AMOUNTS PER COMMON SHARE

The computations of net income per common share were based on the weighted average number of shares outstanding. The average number of common shares used in the computations was 886,393 thousand shares, 877,766 thousand shares and 875,700 thousand shares for the years ended March 31, 1999, 1998 and 1997, respectively.

The effect of the dilution on net income per common share, assuming full conversion of outstanding convertible bonds at the beginning of each year (or at the time of issuance, if after the beginning of the year) with applicable adjustment for related interest expense, net of tax, would be immaterial.

Cash dividends per common share are the amounts applicable to the respective years, including dividends to be paid after the end of the year.

SEGMENT INFORMATION

The Companies' operations are classified into four business segments: pharmaceuticals, bulk vitamin and food, chemical products, and other. The pharmaceuticals segment is composed of those operations involved in the production and sale of ethical and over-the-counter pharmaceuticals and reagents. The bulk vitamin and food segment consists of operations principally involved in the production and sale of vitamins, beverages and food additives. The chemical products segment is involved in the production and sale of polyurethane, polyester resins, their

compounds and activated carbon. The other segment mainly consists of agro products, real estate management and warehousing operations. The agro products operations include the production and sale of agricultural chemicals such as insecticides, herbicides and fungicides, and animal health products such as veterinary medicines for pets, feed additives and medicines for fisheries. Summarized financial information by business segment for years ended March 31, 1999, 1998 and 1997 is as follows:

| | Millions of yen | | | | | | Thousands of U.S. dollars | |
| | Net sales | | | Operating income | | | Net sales | Operating income |
	1999	1998	1997	1999	1998	1997	1999	1999
Pharmaceuticals	¥597,552	¥580,692	¥565,834	¥132,794	¥122,674	¥119,453	$4,938,446	$1,097,471
Bulk vitamin and food	78,307	82,776	87,505	(695)	(1,191)	(2,271)	647,165	(5,744)
Chemical products	110,573	117,611	122,340	6,860	7,922	6,895	913,826	56,694
Other	58,211	60,737	63,145	3,261	3,547	3,273	481,084	26,951
Consolidated	¥844,643	¥841,816	¥838,824	¥142,220	¥132,952	¥127,350	$6,980,521	$1,175,372

There were no significant intersegment sales. General corporate administrative expenses are generally allocated among the segments in proportion to their operating expenses. Income and expenses not allocated to business segments include other

income and expense items such as interest and dividend income, interest expense, and equity in earnings of unconsolidated subsidiaries and affiliates.

| | Millions of yen | | | | | | Thousands of U.S. dollars | | |
| | Identifiable assets | | Depreciation and amortization | | Capital expenditures | | Identifiable assets | Depreciation and amortization | Capital expenditures |
	1999	1998	1999	1998	1999	1998	1999	1999	1999
Pharmaceuticals	¥ 502,238	¥ 464,380	¥20,098	¥19,771	¥19,101	¥24,043	$ 4,150,727	$166,099	$157,860
Bulk vitamin and food	65,979	68,592	3,919	4,410	1,506	1,966	545,281	32,388	12,446
Chemical products	123,597	118,532	6,383	6,398	6,603	7,207	1,021,463	52,752	54,570
Other	69,948	70,573	2,251	2,184	2,031	875	578,083	18,604	16,785
	761,762	722,077	32,651	32,763	29,241	34,091	6,295,554	269,843	241,661
Corporate	565,237	574,125	—	—	—	—	4,671,380	—	—
Consolidated	¥1,326,999	¥1,296,202	¥32,651	¥32,763	¥29,241	¥34,091	$10,966,934	$269,843	$241,661

Corporate assets are principally cash and cash equivalents, marketable securities and investment securities.

For fiscal years beginning on and after April 1, 1997, the

Company is required to disclose geographic data for net sales to customers outside Japan, as follows:

| | Millions of yen | | | Thousands of U.S. dollars | Percentage of consolidated net sales | | |
| | Net sales to customers outside Japan | | | Net sales to customers outside Japan | | | |
	1999	1998	1997	1999	1999	1998	1997
North America	¥ 82,717	¥ 53,753	—	$ 683,612	9.7%	6.4%	—
Europe	58,895	47,923	—	486,736	7.0	5.7	—
Other	33,649	34,035	—	278,090	4.0	4.0	—
Total	¥175,261	¥135,711	¥114,153	$1,448,438	20.7%	16.1%	13.6%

Note 13

COMMITMENTS AND CONTINGENCIES

Commitments outstanding at March 31, 1999 for the purchase of property, plant and equipment amounted to approximately ¥7,579 million ($62,636 thousand).

At March 31, 1999, contingent liabilities were as follows:

	Millions of yen	Thousands of U.S. dollars
Loans guaranteed	¥12,610	$104,215
Notes and export drafts discounted	711	5,876

Note 14

SUBSEQUENT EVENT

On June 29, 1999, the shareholders of the Company approved payment of a year-end cash dividend of ¥16.25 ($0.13) per share to holders of record at March 31, 1999 totaling ¥14,450 million ($119,421 thousand) and bonuses to directors and corporate auditors of ¥182 million ($1,504 thousand).

INDEPENDENT AUDITORS' REPORT

Tohmatsu & Co.
Osaka Kokusai Building
3-13, Azuchimachi 2-chome
Chuo-ku, Osaka 541-0052
Japan

Telephone: (06)6261-1381
Facsimile: (06)6261-1238

To the Board of Directors and Shareholders of
  Takeda Chemical Industries, Ltd.:

We have examined the consolidated balance sheets of Takeda Chemical Industries, Ltd. and consolidated subsidiaries as of March 31, 1999 and 1998, and the related consolidated statements of income, shareholders' equity, and cash flows for each of the three years in the period ended March 31, 1999, all expressed in Japanese yen. Our examinations were made in accordance with auditing standards, procedures and practices generally accepted and applied in Japan and, accordingly, included such tests of the accounting records and such other auditing procedures as we considered necessary in the circumstances.

In our opinion, the consolidated financial statements referred to above present fairly the financial position of Takeda Chemical Industries, Ltd. and consolidated subsidiaries as of March 31, 1999 and 1998, and the results of their operations and their cash flows for each of the three years in the period ended March 31, 1999, in conformity with accounting principles and practices generally accepted in Japan applied on a consistent basis.

Our examinations also comprehended the translation of Japanese yen amounts into U.S. dollar amounts and, in our opinion, such translation has been made in conformity with the basis stated in Note 1. Such U.S. dollar amounts are presented solely for the convenience of readers outside Japan.

Deloitte Touche Tohmatsu

June 29, 1999

Texaco
Annual Report 1999

Management's Discussion and Analysis (MD&A)

INTRODUCTION

We use the MD&A to explain Texaco's operating results and general financial condition. A table of financial highlights that provides a financial picture of the company is followed by four main sections: Industry Review, Results of Operations, Analysis of Income by Operating Segments and Other Items.

Industry Review — we discuss the economic factors that affected our industry in 1999. We also provide our near-term outlook for the industry.

Results of Operations — we explain changes in consolidated revenues, costs, expenses and income taxes. Summary schedules, showing results before and after special items, complete this section. Special items are significant benefits or charges outside the scope of normal operations.

Analysis of Income by Operating Segments — we discuss the performance of our operating segments: Exploration and Production (Upstream), Refining, Marketing and Distribution (Downstream) and Global Gas and Power. We also discuss Other Business Units and our Corporate/Non-operating results.

Other Items section includes:

> Liquidity and Capital Resources: How we manage cash, working capital and debt and other actions to provide financial flexibility

> Reorganizations, Restructurings and Employee Separation Programs: A discussion of our reorganizations and other cost-cutting initiatives

> Capital and Exploratory Expenditures: Our program to invest in the business, especially in projects aimed at future growth

> Environmental Matters: A discussion about our expenditures relating to protection of the environment

> New Accounting Standards: A description of a new accounting standard to be adopted

> Euro Conversion: The status of our program to adapt to the euro currency

> Year 2000 (Y2K): A discussion of how we successfully dealt with the Y2K issue

Our discussions in the MD&A and other sections of this Annual Report contain forward-looking statements that are based upon our best estimate of the trends we know about or anticipate. Actual results may be different from our estimates. We have described in our 1999 Annual Report on Form 10-K the factors that could change these forward-looking statements.

FINANCIAL HIGHLIGHTS

(Millions of dollars, except per share and ratio data)	1999	1998	1997
Revenues	$ 35,691	$ 31,707	$ 46,667
Income before special items and cumulative effect of accounting change	$ 1,214	$ 894	$ 1,894
Special items	(37)	(291)	770
Cumulative effect of accounting change	—	(25)	—
Net income	$ 1,177	$ 578	$ 2,664
Diluted income per common share *(dollars)*			
Income before special items and cumulative effect of accounting change	$ 2.21	$ 1.59	$ 3.45
Special items	(.07)	(.55)	1.42
Cumulative effect of accounting change	—	(.05)	—
Net income	$ 2.14	$ .99	$ 4.87
Cash dividends per common share *(dollars)*	$ 1.80	$ 1.80	$ 1.75
Total assets	$ 28,972	$ 28,570	$ 29,600
Total debt	$ 7,647	$ 7,291	$ 6,392
Stockholders' equity	$ 12,042	$ 11,833	$ 12,766
Current ratio	1.05	1.07	1.07
Return on average stockholders' equity*	10.0%	4.9%	23.5%
Return on average capital employed before special items*	8.3%	6.5%	13.0%
Return on average capital employed*	8.1%	5.0%	17.3%
Total debt to total borrowed and invested capital	37.5%	36.8%	32.3%

*Returns for 1998 exclude the cumulative effect of accounting change (see Note 2 to the financial statements).

INDUSTRY REVIEW

Introduction

International petroleum market conditions changed dramatically during 1999. Over the first few months, crude oil prices were very weak. While economic activity and oil demand were beginning to show signs of increasing, oil supplies were excessive. Then, in April, the Organization of Petroleum Exporting Countries (OPEC) along with other oil producing countries cut output sharply. Oil prices increased and remained strong over the balance of the year.

> **For 1999, WTI crude oil prices averaged $19.31 per barrel, or 34% above the 1998 average.**

Average Price Per Barrel of West Texas Intermediate (WTI) Crude Oil
(Dollars)

$0	$4	$8	$12	$16	$20	$24

Prices in 1999 recovered from historically low levels in 1998.

The increase in crude oil prices boosted revenues from crude oil operations. However, higher crude oil costs, together with other factors such as excess gasoline and distillate stocks, tended to hurt the financial performance of refineries in most markets.

Review of 1999

After slowing sharply in 1998 due to a severe global economic crisis, the rate of world economic growth increased last year. Growth accelerated from a meager 2.3% in 1998 to 2.9% in 1999.

Economic activity varied among regions. The U.S. economy continued to grow at a strong pace with low inflation, due in part to a technology-led surge in labor productivity. Economic expansion in Western Europe also picked up in the second half of the year, benefiting from increased domestic demand and the favorable impact of a weak euro currency on exports.

World economic expansion was reinforced by the beginning of economic recovery in Asia. Several of the key economies in the Asian region, including South Korea, Malaysia, the Philippines, Singapore and Thailand sustained solid economic upturns in 1999. Other regional economies, such as Hong Kong, also turned around. Similarly, Japan, the world's second largest economy, showed signs of emerging from its worst downturn in the post-war period. This improvement was due to extraordinarily low interest rates and increased government spending. However, consumer demand had yet to recover.

The Latin American region, which was hard hit earlier in the year, also began to grow again toward year-end. This renewed growth was propelled by turnarounds in Brazil, Mexico, Argentina and Chile. Moreover, world commodity prices started to rebound from the low levels which resulted from the 1998 economic crisis. This, in turn, spurred economic growth in other areas, particularly the oil producing countries of the Middle East and Africa. In addition, the Russian economy turned upward after many years of decline. This improvement was due to factors such as higher oil prices, increased agricultural output and the substitution of domestically produced goods for imports.

This rebound in economic activity led to a significant increase in the demand for petroleum products worldwide. During 1999, consumption averaged 75.5 million barrels per day (BPD), a 1.3 million BPD, or 1.7% gain over the prior year. This growth, however, was not evenly distributed among regions.

> In the more advanced economies, oil demand rose by 700,000 BPD, boosted by the U.S. and to a lesser extent by Japan

> In the less developed countries, Asian oil demand recovered from its 1998 slump and rose by 500,000 BPD, while growth in Latin America exceeded 100,000 BPD

> Demand in Eastern Europe rose by 100,000 BPD but was offset by an equal decline in the former Soviet Union

> In other regions, demand registered no growth

Demand growth alone may have been insufficient to boost prices. Consequently, OPEC and some non-OPEC producers agreed to cut production. Oil output from these countries, which had been cut twice during 1998, was scaled back further during the early part of 1999 by an additional 1.8 million BPD — bringing the total reduction to a significant 4 million BPD.

Average OPEC Crude Oil Production (Excluding Iraq)
(Millions of barrels a day)

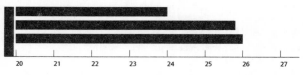

20	21	22	23	24	25	26	27

OPEC reduced production dramatically since 1998.

The production curtailment and the resultant tightening balance between supply and demand caused the price of crude oil to soar from its depressed 1998 and early 1999 levels. The market price of West Texas Intermediate (WTI) averaged $19.31 per barrel, an increase of 34% from the prior year. During the final months of 1999, oil prices reached their highest levels in several years and continued to increase in early 2000.

Near-Term Outlook

We expect global economic expansion to accelerate from 2.9% in 1999 to a 3.7% gain this year, reflecting several factors:

> Continued, but slower, gains in the United States as the Federal Reserve moves to moderate growth by raising interest rates

> Continued economic expansion in Western Europe

> Further strengthening in the developing world, particularly the developing nations of Asia and Latin America

> Continued low growth in Russia

On the other hand, the outlook for the large Japanese economy remains clouded by the apparent inability of the economy to grow without strong government spending. Private demand must eventually substitute for government spending if the recovery is to be sustained. Furthermore, Japanese export growth could be jeopardized by a pronounced appreciation in the value of the yen. Accordingly, we expect the Japanese economy to register only minimal growth this year.

With the increase in global economic activity, the demand for crude oil will be greater. An increase in worldwide oil consumption of about 1.6 million BPD is expected. Non-OPEC production should recover considerably and may boost output to levels close to the one million BPD mark. OPEC may therefore choose to relax its quotas and increase production.

The crude oil price outlook is highly uncertain. In the past, high crude oil prices have often encouraged OPEC to increase production sharply, causing prices to drop. Higher petroleum demand and a potential weakening in crude oil costs could benefit downstream margins.

RESULTS OF OPERATIONS

Revenues

Our consolidated worldwide revenues were $35.7 billion in 1999, $31.7 billion in 1998 and $46.7 billion in 1997. Our revenues benefited from higher commodity prices, especially crude oil in the second half of 1999. We also benefited from higher refined product sales volumes in 1999. The decrease in 1998 resulted largely from the accounting for Equilon, a downstream joint venture in the United States we formed in January 1998. Under accounting rules, the significant revenues of the operations we contributed to this joint venture are no longer included in our consolidated revenues. Revenues, costs and expenses of the joint venture are reported net as "equity in income of affiliates" in our income statement.

Sales Revenues – Price/Volume Effects

Our sales revenues were higher in 1999 due to an increase of 38% in our realized crude oil prices. Crude oil and natural gas liquids production, however, was 5% lower, due to natural field declines and asset sales in the U.S. and temporary operating problems in the U.K.

Sales revenues from petroleum products increased in 1999 led by higher prices and stronger international volumes. Volume growth for marine fuel sales benefited from our joint venture with Chevron formed late in 1998.

Our volumes of natural gas sold in 1999 decreased in the U.S. due to lower production and reduced sales of purchased gas. Internationally, we withdrew from the U.K. retail gas marketing business.

Our sales revenues decreased in 1998 due to historically low crude oil, natural gas and refined product prices. Partly offsetting the decline in prices were higher liquids production and sales volumes.

Other Revenues

Other revenues include our equity in the income of affiliates, income from asset sales and interest income. Results for 1999 were lower than 1998 due to reduced interest income on notes and marketable securities and lower asset sales. Equity in income of affiliates in 1999 was consistent with 1998 results. Lower downstream margins in the Caltex Asia-Pacific Region and Motiva's U.S. East and Gulf Coast areas depressed results. However, we realized higher refining margins in Equilon's West Coast operating areas. We also benefited from stronger crude oil prices in our Indonesian producing affiliate.

Results for 1998 show a decrease in other revenues from 1997. Equity in income of affiliates decreased in 1998, mostly due to a decline in Caltex' results. This decline was partly offset by the inclusion of results for Equilon. Income from asset sales was also lower in 1998.

Our share of special charges by our affiliates included in other revenues amounted to $153 million in 1999 and $159 million in 1998. In 1999, these major special charges included refinery asset write-downs in the U.S. and a loss on the sale of an interest in a Japanese affiliate. These charges were reduced by inventory valuation benefits in the U.S. and abroad, as well as tax revaluation benefits in Korea. The 1998 special charges included inventory valuation adjustments, net U.S. alliance formation costs and Caltex restructuring charges.

In 1997, special gains included $416 million from upstream asset sales in the U.K. North Sea and Myanmar.

Costs and Expenses

Costs and expenses from operations were $33.3 billion in 1999, $30.5 billion in 1998 and $42.9 billion in 1997. Higher prices and product volumes increased our cost of goods sold in 1999. While costs have increased, reflecting world oil prices, operating expenses declined in 1999. This improvement reflects our continued emphasis on cost containment and operational efficiency. Similar to the discussion of revenue above, the decrease in both costs and expenses for 1998 is largely due to the accounting treatment for Equilon.

Special items recorded by our subsidiaries increased costs and operating expenses by $121 million in 1999, $382 million in 1998 and $136 million in 1997. Major special items in 1999 included inventory valuation benefits in subsidiaries, which reversed similar charges recorded in 1998 when commodity prices were very depressed. The year 1998 also included higher asset write-downs and employee separation costs.

Asset write-downs in 1999, which increased depreciation, depletion and amortization expense by $87 million, resulted mainly from impairments in our global gas and power segment and our corporate center. Asset write-downs in 1998, which increased depreciation, depletion and amortization expense by $150 million, resulted from impairments primarily in our upstream operations. These and other asset impairments we have recognized since initially applying the provisions of SFAS 121 have been driven by specific events. These include the sale of properties or downward revisions in underground reserve quantities. Impairments have not resulted from changes in prices used to calculate future revenues. In performing our impairment reviews of assets not held for sale, we use our best judgment in estimating future cash flows. This includes our outlook of commodity prices based on our view of supply and demand forecasts and other economic indicators.

Special charges in 1997 were principally for asset write-downs and royalty litigation issues.

Interest expense for 1999 and 1998 increased due mostly to higher average debt levels after a slight decrease in 1997.

During 1999 we kept tight control over expenses. Our success is illustrated by the chart below.

Cash Expenses Per Barrel
(Dollars)

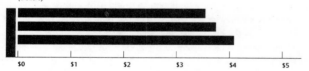

| $0 | $1 | $2 | $3 | $4 | $5 |

Tight expense control led to a 5% per barrel reduction in 1999.

> **In 1999, we realized $743 million in pre-tax cost savings and synergy capture, exceeding our year-end 2000 target of $650 million, a full year ahead of schedule. We have identified other opportunities that should capture an additional $400 million in savings by 2001.**

Income Taxes

Income tax expense was $602 million in 1999, $98 million in 1998 and $663 million in 1997. The increase in 1999 is mostly due to higher income from international producing operations. These areas are generally high tax jurisdictions. The year 1997 included a $488 million benefit from an IRS settlement.

Income Summary Schedules

The following schedules show after-tax results before and after special items and before the cumulative effect of accounting change. A full discussion of special items is included in our Analysis of Income by Operating Segments.

Income (loss)

(Millions of dollars)	1999	1998	1997
Income before special items and cumulative effect of accounting change	$ 1,214	$ 894	$ 1,894
Special items:			
Inventory valuation adjustments	152	(142)	—
Write-downs of assets	(157)	(93)	(41)
Reorganizations, restructurings and employee separation costs	(74)	(144)	—
Gains (losses) on major asset sales	(62)	20	367
Tax benefits on asset sales	40	43	—
Tax issues	106	25	480
Royalty issues	(30)	—	(36)
Environmental issues	(12)	—	—
Total special items	(37)	(291)	770
Income before cumulative effect of accounting change	$ 1,177	$ 603	$ 2,664

The following schedule further details our results:

Income (loss)

(Millions of dollars)	Before Special Items			After Special Items		
	1999	1998	1997	1999	1998	1997
Exploration and production (upstream)						
United States	$ 666	$ 381	$ 1,038	$ 652	$ 301	$ 990
International	386	181	479	360	129	812
Total	1,052	562	1,517	1,012	430	1,802
Refining, marketing and distribution (downstream)						
United States	287	276	312	208	221	325
International	338	503	524	370	332	508
Total	625	779	836	578	553	833
Global gas and power	21	(33)	(46)	(14)	(16)	(46)
Total	1,698	1,308	2,307	1,576	967	2,589
Other business units	(3)	(2)	2	(3)	(2)	2
Corporate/Non-operating	(481)	(412)	(415)	(396)	(362)	73
Income before cumulative effect of accounting change	$ 1,214	$ 894	$ 1,894	$ 1,177	$ 603	$ 2,664

ANALYSIS OF INCOME BY OPERATING SEGMENTS

Upstream

In our upstream business, we explore for, find, produce and sell crude oil, natural gas liquids and natural gas.

Our upstream operations benefited from improved crude oil prices during 1999. The following discussion will focus on how the improved price environment and other business factors affected our earnings. The U.S. results for 1998 and 1997 include some minor Canadian operations which were sold at the end of 1998.

United States Upstream

(Millions of dollars, except as indicated)	1999	1998	1997
Operating income before special items	$ 666	$ 381	$ 1,038
Special items:			
Write-downs of assets	—	(51)	(31)
Employee separation costs	(11)	(29)	—
Gains on major asset sales	18	—	26
Royalty issues	(30)	—	(36)
Tax issues	9	—	(7)
Total special items	(14)	(80)	(48)
Operating income	$ 652	$ 301	$ 990
Selected Operating Data:			
Net production			
Crude oil and NGL *(thousands of barrels a day)*	395	433	396
Natural gas available for sale *(millions of cubic feet a day)*	1,462	1,679	1,706
Average realized crude price *(dollars per barrel)*	$ 14.70	$ 10.60	$ 17.34
Average realized natural gas price *(dollars per MCF)*	$ 2.18	$ 2.00	$ 2.37
Exploratory expenses *(millions of dollars)*	$ 234	$ 257	$ 189
Production costs *(dollars per barrel)*	$ 4.01	$ 4.07	$ 3.94
Return on average capital employed before special items	10.5%	6.0%	20.9%
Return on average capital employed	10.3%	4.7%	20.0%

WHAT HAPPENED IN THE UNITED STATES?

Business Factors

PRICES We benefited from higher prices in 1999, which improved earnings by $342 million. Our average realized crude oil price increased by 39% to $14.70 per barrel. This follows a 39% decrease in 1998 when crude prices plummeted to over 20 year lows in the fourth quarter. Crude oil prices recovered in 1999 as OPEC and several non-OPEC producers implemented cutbacks in production. These production cutbacks, coupled with increasing demand in improving global economies, led to a decline in worldwide inventory levels. Our average realized natural gas price in 1999 increased 9% to $2.18 per thousand cubic feet (MCF). This follows a 16% decrease in 1998.

PRODUCTION Our production declined by 10% in 1999. This decrease was due to natural field declines, asset sales and reduced investment in mature properties consistent with our focus on capital efficiency. In 1998 our production increased by 5%. This was due to our acquisition of heavy oil producer Monterey Resources in November 1997, new production in the Gulf of Mexico and higher production from our Kern River field in California.

> **Our capital expenditures in 1999 reflect our shift in upstream strategy to pursue high-margin, high-impact projects rather than multiple projects with incremental potential.**

U.S. Finding and Development Cost Per Barrel of Oil Equivalent
(Dollars)

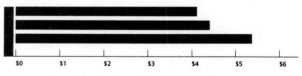

We continue to reduce our per barrel finding and development costs.

EXPLORATORY EXPENSES We expensed $234 million on exploratory activity in 1999. This included a $100 million write-off of investments in the Fuji and McKinley prospects in the Gulf of Mexico. These prospects, initially drilled between 1995 and 1998, were determined to be non-commercial in the fourth quarter of 1999 after appraisal drilling. Our exploratory expenses in 1998 were $257 million, 36% higher than 1997.

Other Factors

Our cash operating expenses decreased in 1999 by 10%. This was a result of cost savings from the restructuring of our worldwide upstream organization. Our production costs per barrel increased in 1998 and then decreased slightly in 1999. Our 1999 production cost per barrel benefited from cost savings but were negatively impacted by production declines of 10%.

U.S. Production Costs Per Barrel
(Dollars)

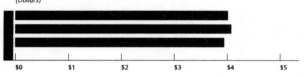

Cost savings initiatives lowered our per barrel production costs in 1999.

Special Items

Our results for 1999 included a $30 million charge for the settlement of crude oil royalty valuation issues on federal lands and an $11 million charge for employee separation costs. The employee separation costs result from the expansion of our 1998 program. Results for 1998 included a charge for employee separation costs of $29 million. See the section entitled, *Reorganizations, Restructurings and Employee Separation Programs* on page 26 for additional information. During 1999, we also recorded an $18 million gain on asset sales in California and a $9 million production tax refund.

Results for 1998 also included asset write-downs of $51 million for impaired properties in Louisiana and Canada. The impaired Louisiana property represents an unsuccessful enhanced recovery project. We determined in the fourth quarter of 1998 that the carrying value of this property exceeded future undiscounted cash flows. Fair value was determined by discounting expected future cash flows. The Canadian properties were impaired following our decision in October 1998 to exit the upstream business in Canada. These properties were written down to their sales price with the sale closing in December 1998.

Results for 1997 included a charge of $31 million for asset write-downs and a gain of $26 million from the sale of gas properties in Canada. We also recorded charges of $36 million for royalty issues and $7 million for tax issues.

260

International Upstream

(Millions of dollars, except as indicated)	1999	1998	1997
Operating income before special items	$ 386	$ 181	$ 479
Special items:			
Write-downs of assets	—	(42)	(10)
Employee separation costs	(2)	(10)	—
Gains on major asset sales	—	—	328
Tax issues	(24)	—	15
Total special items	(26)	(52)	333
Operating income	$ 360	$ 129	$ 812
Selected Operating Data:			
Net production			
Crude oil and NGL *(thousands of barrels a day)*	490	497	437
Natural gas available for sale *(millions of cubic feet a day)*	537	548	471
Average realized crude price *(dollars per barrel)*	$ 15.23	$ 11.20	$ 17.64
Average realized natural gas price *(dollars per MCF)*	$ 1.34	$ 1.63	$ 1.66
Exploratory expenses *(millions of dollars)*	$ 267	$ 204	$ 282
Production costs *(dollars per barrel)*	$ 4.37	$ 3.74	$ 4.30
Return on average capital employed before special items	10.3%	5.8%	17.5%
Return on average capital employed	9.6%	4.1%	29.7%

WHAT HAPPENED IN THE INTERNATIONAL AREAS?

Business Factors

PRICES Our earnings increased by $327 million in 1999 due to the rebound in crude oil prices. Our average crude oil price increased by 36% to $15.23 per barrel. The 1999 recovery in crude oil prices was due to worldwide production cutbacks and improved demand. This improvement follows a decline of 37% in 1998. The trend of lower crude oil prices began in late 1997 and continued throughout 1998 with prices dropping to over 20 year lows in the fourth quarter. Our average realized natural gas price in 1999 declined to $1.34 per MCF, a decrease of 18%. This follows a decrease of 2% in 1998.

> **Our international average realized crude oil price in 1999 was $15.23 per barrel, an increase of 36%.**

PRODUCTION Our production in 1999 declined slightly. We experienced some declines in the U.K. North Sea due to operating problems. In Indonesia we had lower production volumes as higher prices reduced our lifting entitlements for cost recovery under a production sharing agreement. We also experienced lower gas production in Latin America. These declines were partially offset by increased production in the Partitioned Neutral Zone as a result of increased drilling activity and further development of the Karachaganak field in the Republic of Kazakhstan. Our production increased 14% in 1998 due to a full year's production in the U.K. North Sea from the Captain and Erskine fields and new production from the Galley field. Production also grew in the Partitioned Neutral Zone.

International Net Proved Reserves
(Millions of barrels of oil equivalent)

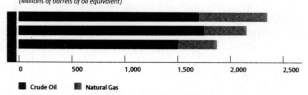

■ Crude Oil   ■ Natural Gas

Net proved reserves increased due to the Malampaya and Karachaganak projects.

EXPLORATORY EXPENSES We expensed $267 million on exploratory activity in 1999, an increase of 31%. This included about $50 million for an unsuccessful exploratory well in a new offshore area of Trinidad. Also included is $30 million of prior year drilling expenditures in Thailand, which we wrote off in 1999 after we determined the prospect to be non-commercial. In 1999, our main focus areas were in Nigeria and Brazil. Our exploratory expenses were $204 million in 1998, a decrease of 28%.

Other Factors

Our 1999 cash operating expenses decreased by 3% as a result of continuing cost savings initiatives and the restructuring of our worldwide upstream organization. Our production costs were $4.37 per barrel, an increase of 17%. This increase reflects lower production in Indonesia due to lower entitlement liftings for cost recovery as a result of higher prices.

International Upstream Capital and Exploratory Expenditures
(Billions of dollars)

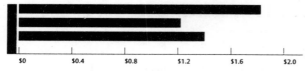

$0	$0.4	$0.8	$1.2	$1.6	$2.0

The growth in international upstream investments shows our focus on high-impact projects.

Special Items

Our results for 1999 included a $24 million charge for prior years' tax issues in the U.K. and a $2 million charge for employee separation costs. The employee separation costs result from the expansion of our 1998 program. Results for 1998 included a charge for employee separation costs of $10 million. See the section entitled, *Reorganizations, Restructurings and Employee Separation Programs* on page 26 for additional information.

Results for 1998 also included a write-down of $42 million for the impairment of our investment in the Strathspey field in the U.K. North Sea. The Strathspey impairment was caused by a downward revision in the fourth quarter of 1998 of the estimated volume of the field's proved reserves. Fair value was determined by discounting expected future cash flows.

Results for 1997 included a $10 million charge for asset write-downs and gains on asset sales of $328 million. These sales included a 15% interest in the Captain field in the U.K. and investments in an Australian pipeline system and the company's Myanmar operations. Also, 1997 included a $15 million prior period tax benefit.

LOOKING FORWARD IN THE WORLDWIDE UPSTREAM

We intend to continue to cost-effectively explore for, develop and produce crude oil and natural gas reserves by focusing on high-margin, high-impact projects. In an effort to boost long-term upstream profitability, we are selling producing properties that no longer fit our business strategy. The cash proceeds from these sales will be reinvested into major upstream projects that offer higher returns. In 2000 we plan to sell producing properties totaling about 100,000 barrels per day of production in the U.S., offshore Trinidad and in the U.K. North Sea. As a result, beginning in 2001 we expect worldwide production to increase by two to three percent annually over the next three to five years. In addition to California, our growth areas of focus include:

> Philippines — where in 1999 we acquired a 45% interest in the Malampaya Deep Water Natural Gas Project. This added 140 million BOE to our proved reserve base and increased our international gas reserves by 30%. Our share of production is anticipated to reach 240 MMCF per day by 2003

> West Africa — where in 1999 we announced the major Agbami oil discovery offshore Nigeria

> U.S. Gulf of Mexico — where we hold both exploration and production acreage and saw the June 1999 start-up of our Gemini Project

> Venezuela — where in 1999 we increased our interest from 20% to 30% in the Hamaca Oil Project

> Kazakhstan — where we hold interests in the Karachaganak and North Buzachi Projects

> Brazil — where in 1999 we signed an agreement with Petrobras, Brazil's national oil company, to become an equity partner in the Campos and Santos exploration and the Frade development areas offshore Brazil and successfully bid on three high potential offshore exploration blocks in Brazil's First License Round

As we implement these growth plans, we will continue to lower our per barrel operating costs through additional cost-savings initiatives.

> **Our investment in the Malampaya gas project added 140 million BOE to our proved oil and gas reserve base, representing a 30% increase in our international gas reserves.**

Downstream

In our downstream business, we refine, transport and sell crude oil and products, such as gasoline, fuel oil and lubricants.

Our U.S. downstream includes our share of operations in Equilon and Motiva. The Equilon area includes western and midwestern refining and marketing operations, and nationwide trading, transportation and lubricants activities. Our 1999 and 1998 results in this area are our share of the earnings of our joint venture with Shell, Equilon, which began operations on January 1, 1998. We have a 44% interest in Equilon. Results for 1997 are for our subsidiary operations in this same area. The Motiva area includes eastern and Gulf Coast refining and marketing operations. Our results for 1999 and the last half of 1998 are our share of the earnings of our joint venture with Shell and Saudi Refining, Inc., Motiva, which began operations on July 1, 1998. We have a 32.5% interest in Motiva. Results for the first half of 1998 and the year 1997 are for our 50% share of our joint venture with Saudi Refining, Inc., Star.

Internationally, our wholly-owned downstream operations are reported separately as Latin America and West Africa and Europe. We also have a 50% interest in a joint venture with Chevron, Caltex, which operates in Africa, Asia, Australia, the Middle East and New Zealand.

In the U.S. and international operations, we also have other businesses, which include aviation and marine product sales, lubricants marketing and other refined product trading activity.

United States Downstream

(Millions of dollars, except as indicated)	1999	1998	1997
Operating income before special items	$ 287	$ 276	$ 312
Special items:			
Write-downs of assets	(76)	—	—
Inventory valuation adjustments	8	(34)	—
Reorganizations, restructurings and employee separation costs	(11)	(21)	—
Gains on major asset sales	—	—	13
Total special items	(79)	(55)	13
Operating income	$ 208	$ 221	$ 325
Selected Operating Data:			
Refinery input (thousands of barrels a day)	671	698	747
Refined product sales (thousands of barrels a day)	1,377	1,203	1,022
Return on average capital employed before special items	11.3%	9.6%	9.8%
Return on average capital employed	8.2%	7.7%	10.2%

WHAT HAPPENED IN THE UNITED STATES?

Equilon These operations contributed $288 million to our 1999 operating earnings before special items. We achieved higher earnings in 1999 from improved West Coast refining margins as a result of industry refinery outages earlier in the year. We also benefited from improved utilization of the Martinez refinery, strong transportation results from higher throughput and realization of cost savings and synergies. These include improved efficiency of work processes, reduction of supply costs, sharing best practices, capitalizing on logistical and trading opportunities and greater utilization of proprietary pipelines. These improved results in 1999 were partly offset by operating problems at the Puget Sound refinery earlier in the year and weak marketing margins as pump prices lagged behind increases in gasoline spot prices. Our sales volumes improved in 1999 due to increased trading activity.

The 1998 earnings were flat when compared with 1997. Strong transportation and lubricants earnings as well as cost and expense reductions were offset by the effects of significant downtime at certain refineries, lower margins and interest expense. Refined product sales volumes increased. This included 4% growth in Texaco-branded gasoline sales.

> **Our share of the U.S. affiliates' pre-tax cost savings and synergy capture was $326 million in 1999.**

Motiva These operations contributed only $12 million to our 1999 operating income before special items. Our 1999 results were lower than 1998. They were negatively impacted by weak refining and marketing margins on the East and Gulf Coasts due to the inability to pass along rising crude costs and high industry-wide refined product inventory levels. These weaknesses were partly offset by improved refinery reliability and cost savings and synergies that were achieved by Motiva. These include reduction of fuel additive supply costs, improved efficiency of work processes, improved asset utilization and sharing best practices.

The 1998 earnings were lower due to refinery downtime coupled with lower refining margins. Refined product sales were higher as a result of our joint venture and an increase in Texaco-branded gasoline sales. The year 1997 benefited from improved Gulf Coast refining margins.

Special Items
Results for 1999 and 1998 included net special charges of $79 million and $55 million, representing our share of special items recorded by our U.S. alliances. Results for 1997 included a gain of $13 million from the sale of our credit card business.

The 1999 charge included $76 million for the write-downs of assets to their estimated sales values by Equilon for the intended sales of its El Dorado and Wood River refineries. Equilon completed the sale of the El Dorado refinery to Frontier Oil Corporation in November 1999, and is continuing to seek a purchaser for the Wood River refinery.

Our 1999 results also included an inventory valuation benefit of $8 million due to higher 1999 inventory values. This follows a 1998 charge of $34 million to reflect lower market prices on December 31, 1998 for inventories of crude oil and refined products. We value inventories at the lower of cost or market, after initially recording at cost. Inventory valuation adjustments are reversed when prices recover and the associated physical units of inventory are sold.

Our 1999 and 1998 results included net charges of $11 million and $21 million for reorganizations, restructurings and employee separation costs. The 1999 charge represents dismantling expenses at a closed refinery, an adjustment to the Anacortes refinery sale and employee separation costs from the expansion of Equilon's and Motiva's 1998 separation programs. The 1998 net charge was for U.S.

alliance formation issues. This net charge included $52 million for employee separation costs and $45 million for write-downs of closed facilities and surplus equipment to their net realizable value. These facilities included a refinery in Texas, lubricant plants in various states, a sales terminal in Louisiana and research facilities and equipment in Texas and New York. Also included in net charges were gains of $76 million from the Federal Trade Commission-mandated sale of the Anacortes refinery and Plantation pipeline.

International Downstream

(Millions of dollars, except as indicated)	1999	1998	1997
Operating income before special items	$ 338	$ 503	$ 524
Special items:			
Inventory valuation adjustments	144	(108)	—
Write-downs of assets	(23)	—	—
Reorganizations, restructurings and employee separation costs	(41)	(63)	—
Losses on major asset sales	(80)	—	—
Tax issues	32	—	(16)
Total special items	32	(171)	(16)
Operating income	$ 370	$ 332	$ 508
Selected Operating Data:			
Refinery input (thousands of barrels a day)	820	832	804
Refined product sales (thousands of barrels a day)	1,844	1,685	1,563
Return on average capital employed before special items	5.6%	8.2%	9.2%
Return on average capital employed	6.1%	5.4%	8.9%

WHAT HAPPENED IN THE INTERNATIONAL AREAS?

Latin America and West Africa Our operations in Latin America and West Africa contributed 66% of our 1999 operating income before special items. Results in 1999 were lower than 1998 as they reflected a squeeze on refining margins as escalating crude costs outpaced product price increases. Our results were also adversely affected by depressed marketing margins and lower volumes in Brazil due to poor economic conditions and related currency devaluation. Partially offsetting these conditions was an overall 7% increase in refined product sales volume led by our Caribbean and Central American operations. In 1998, earnings increased due to higher refined product sales volumes from service station acquisitions and the expansion of our industrial customer base.

Europe Our European operations contributed 26% of our 1999 operating income before special items. Results for 1999 were lower due to poor refining margins. Product price increases failed to keep pace with escalating crude costs. A 6% increase in refined product sales volumes helped to offset the squeeze on margins. In 1998, earnings increased significantly from improved refining and marketing margins. Additionally, during 1998 we grew our refined product sales volumes by increasing retail outlets and obtaining new commercial business.

Caltex Our results for Caltex in 1999 before special items were $28 million. These results were lower than 1998. Results were adversely affected by depressed refining and marketing margins. This was caused by the inability to recover rapidly escalating crude oil costs in the marketplace and product oversupply. These declines were partially offset by an inventory drawdown benefit and gains from the sale of marketable securities. There were also lower currency losses from reduced volatility and generally improved economic conditions. In 1998, our results for Caltex were $156 million lower than 1997. This was mainly due to negative currency impacts of $204 million. Excluding currency effects, our results for Caltex improved in 1998 due to higher margins and volumes.

In the Caltex area, most of our operations have a net liability exposure, which creates currency losses when foreign currencies strengthen against the U.S. dollar and currency gains when these currencies weaken against the U.S. dollar. Effective October 1, 1997, Caltex changed the functional currency used to account for operations in Korea and Japan to the U.S. dollar.

International Refined Product Sales
(Thousands of barrels a day)

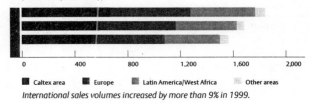

| 0 | 400 | 800 | 1,200 | 1,600 | 2,000 |

■ Caltex area   ■ Europe   ▦ Latin America/West Africa   ▨ Other areas

International sales volumes increased by more than 9% in 1999.

Special Items

Results for 1999 included net special benefits of $32 million. Results for 1998 and 1997 included net special charges of $171 million and $16 million. Special items relating to Caltex represent our 50 percent share.

Results for 1999 included inventory valuation benefits of $144 million due to higher 1999 inventory values. This follows a 1998 charge of $108 million to reflect lower market prices on December 31, 1998 for inventories of crude oil and refined products, as well as additional charges recorded in prior years. We value inventories at the lower of cost or market, after initially recording at cost. Inventory valuation adjustments are reversed when prices recover and the associated physical units of inventory are sold.

Results for 1999 included a charge of $23 million for the write-downs of assets. These write-downs on properties to be disposed of include $10 million for marketing assets in our subsidiary in Poland and $13 million for assets in our Caltex operations.

Our 1999 results included a $9 million charge for employee separation costs for our subsidiaries operating in Europe and Latin America. These costs resulted from the expansion of our 1998 program. Results for 1998 included a charge for employee separation costs of $20 million. See the section entitled, *Reorganizations, Restructurings and Employee Separation Programs* on page 26 for additional information.

Results for 1999 also included charges of $80 million related to our share of the Caltex loss on the sale of its equity interest in Koa Oil Company, Limited, including deferred currency translation net losses. Additionally, our results for 1999 included a Caltex Korean tax benefit of $54 million due to asset revaluation and $22 million for prior year tax charges in the U.K. Results for 1997 included a charge of $16 million primarily for a European deferred tax adjustment.

Results for 1999 and 1998 included other charges of $32 million and $43 million, representing our share of a Caltex reorganization program. The 1999 charge represented continued expenses related to the 1998 program. The 1998 charge resulted from their decision to structure their organization along functional lines and to reduce costs by establishing a shared service center in the Philippines. In implementing this change, Caltex also relocated its headquarters from Dallas to Singapore. About $35 million of the 1998 charge relates to severance and other retirement benefits for about 200 employees not

relocating, write-downs of surplus furniture and equipment and other costs. The balance of the charge is for severance costs in other affected areas and amounts spent in relocating employees to the new shared service center.

LOOKING FORWARD IN THE WORLDWIDE DOWNSTREAM

We intend to do the following in our worldwide downstream:

> Reduce our exposure to refining

> Continue to achieve lower costs and capture synergies

> Focus on business opportunities in areas of trading, transportation and lubricants

> Pursue marketing growth opportunities in selected areas

Global Gas and Power

(Millions of dollars, except as indicated)	**1999**	1998	1997
Operating income (loss) before special items	**$ 21**	$ (33)	$ (46)
Special items:			
Write-downs of assets	**(32)**	—	—
Employee separation costs	**(3)**	(3)	—
Gain on major asset sale	**—**	20	—
Total special items	**(35)**	17	—
Operating loss	**$ (14)**	$ (16)	$ (46)
Natural gas sales *(millions of cubic feet a day)*	**3,134**	3,764	3,452
Net power sales *(gigawatt hours)*	**4,353**	4,395	4,185

Global Gas and Power includes marketing of natural gas and natural gas liquids, gas processing plants, pipelines, power generation plants, gasification licensing and equity plants, and our hydrocarbons-to-liquids and fuel cell technology units. Gasification is a proprietary technology that converts low value hydrocarbons into useful synthesis gas for the chemical, refining and power industries. During 1999, responsibility for these activities was combined under a single senior executive, forming the Global Gas and Power segment. Prior period information has been restated to reflect this change.

Our gas marketing operating results in 1999 benefited from improved natural gas liquids margins. Our 1999 results also included gains on normal asset sales and lower operating expenses. The asset sales included our interest in a U.K. retail gas marketing operation and the sale of a U.S. gas gathering pipeline.

Results for 1998 were adversely affected by losses associated with our start-up wholesale and retail marketing activities in the U.K. We exited the U.K. wholesale gas marketing business in October 1998. Weak natural gas and natural gas liquids margins in the U.S. also contributed to the poor results. Milder than normal temperatures reduced demand and squeezed margins.

Our operating results for the power and gasification business in 1999 benefited from higher gasification licensing revenues and cogeneration income. This was partially offset by lower margins from Indonesian geothermal activities and the non-recurring recoupment of development costs in 1998. The lower Indonesian geothermal margins are due to higher costs and lower revenues caused by regional economic weakness.

Special Items
Results for both 1999 and 1998 included charges of $3 million for employee separation costs. The 1999 charge resulted from the expansion of our 1998 program. See the section entitled, *Reorganizations, Restructurings and Employee Separation Programs* on page 26 for additional information.

Our 1999 results also included charges of $32 million for asset write-downs from the impairment of certain gas plants in Louisiana. We determined in the fourth quarter of 1999 that as a result of declining gas volumes available for processing, the carrying value of these plants exceeded future undiscounted cash flows. Fair value was determined by discounting expected future cash flows. Our 1998 results also included a gain of $20 million on the sale of an interest in our Discovery pipeline affiliate.

LOOKING FORWARD IN GLOBAL GAS AND POWER
We believe there is great promise with emerging gas and power technologies. Accordingly, we are pursuing opportunities utilizing gasification, hydrocarbons-to-liquids and fuel cell technologies. We continue to develop power projects in conjunction with our exploration, production and refining needs. Our future plans include:

> Developing power projects where significant reserves of natural gas require commercialization

> Expanding our gasification technology to commercialize this environmentally friendly technology

> Using our technology to develop opportunities in the fuel cell and hydrocarbons-to-liquids businesses

Effective March 1, 2000, we will form a joint venture with a subsidiary of Enron Corp. to combine the companies' intrastate pipeline and storage businesses in southeast Louisiana.

Other Business Units

(Millions of dollars)	1999	1998	1997
Operating income (loss)	$ (3)	$ (2)	$ 2

Our other business units mainly include our insurance operations. There were no significant items in our three-year results.

Corporate/Non-operating

(Millions of dollars)	1999	1998	1997
Results before special items	$ (481)	$ (412)	$ (415)
Special items:			
Write-downs of assets	(26)	—	—
Employee separation costs	(6)	(18)	—
Tax benefits on asset sales	40	43	—
Tax issues	89	25	488
Environmental issues	(12)	—	—
Total special items	85	50	488
Total Corporate/Non-operating	$ (396)	$ (362)	$ 73

Corporate/Non-operating
Corporate/Non-operating includes our corporate center and financing activities. The year 1999 reflects higher interest expense resulting from increases in debt levels. Results for 1998 included lower overhead and tax expense. Higher interest income was mostly offset by interest expense from higher average debt levels.

Special Items
Results for 1999 included tax benefits of $89 million. These are associated with favorable determinations in the fourth quarter on prior years' tax issues. Results for 1999 and 1998 included tax benefits of $40 million and $43 million from the sales of interests in a subsidiary. Additionally, results for 1998 included a benefit of $25 million to adjust for prior years' federal tax liabilities. The year 1997 included a tax benefit of $488 million from an IRS settlement.

Our 1999 results also included a $6 million charge for employee separation costs. These costs resulted from the expansion of our 1998 program. Results for 1998 included a charge for employee separations of $18 million. See the section entitled, *Reorganizations, Restructurings and Employee Separation Programs* on page 26 for additional information.

We also recorded in 1999 charges of $12 million for environmental issues and $26 million for the impairment of assets and related disposal costs. The assets write-downs resulted from our joint plan with state and local agencies to convert for third-party industrial use idle facilities, formerly used in research activities. The facilities and equipment were written down to their appraised values.

OTHER ITEMS
Liquidity and Capital Resources
INTRODUCTION The Statement of Consolidated Cash Flows on page 37 reports the changes in cash balances for the last three years, and summarizes the inflows and outflows of cash between operating, investing and financing activities. Our cash requirements are met by cash from operations, supplemented by outside borrowings and the proceeds from the sale of non-strategic assets.

The main components of cash flows are:

INFLOWS *Cash from operating activities* represents net income adjusted for non-cash charges or credits, such as depreciation, depletion and amortization, and changes in working capital and other balances. Cash from operating activities excludes exploratory expenses, which we show as a cash outflow from investing activities. Operating cash flows for 1999 of $3,169 million benefited from higher commodity prices and our expense reduction programs. For more detailed insight into our financial and operational results, see Analysis of Income by Operating Segments on the preceding pages.

New borrowings in 1999 reflect a net increase of $290 million compared to a net increase of $1,052 million in 1998. During the year, we borrowed $1,668 million from our existing "shelf" registration, including $1,268 million under our medium-term note program. We decreased our commercial paper by $518 million during the year, to $1,099 million at year-end. See Note 9 to the financial statements for total outstanding debt, including 1999 borrowings.

After December 31, 1999, we issued an additional $530 million under our medium-term note program to refinance existing short-term debt. As a result, our total remaining capacity under our "shelf" registration is $1,445 million, covering possible issuances of both debt and equity securities.

> **We maintain strong credit ratings and access to global financial markets providing us flexibility to borrow funds at low capital costs.**

Our senior debt is rated A+ by Standard & Poor's Corporation and A1 by Moody's Investors Service. Our U.S. commercial paper is rated A-1 by Standard & Poor's and Prime-1 by Moody's. These ratings denote high quality investment grade securities. Our debt has an average maturity of 10 years and a weighted average interest rate of 7.0%. We also maintain $2.05 billion in revolving credit facilities, which remain unused, to provide liquidity and to support our commercial paper program.

Other net cash inflows in 1999 represent proceeds from the sale of non-strategic assets of $321 million, net sales/maturities of investment instruments of $346 million and the collection of notes receivable from an affiliate of $101 million.

OUTFLOWS *Capital and exploratory expenditures (Capex)* were $2,957 million in 1999 — The section on page 27 describes in more detail the uses of our Capex dollars.

Payments of dividends were $1,047 million in 1999 — $964 million to common, $28 million to preferred and $55 million to shareholders who hold a minority interest in Texaco subsidiary companies.

The following year-end table reflects our key financial indicators:

(Millions of dollars, except as indicated)	1999	1998	1997
Current ratio	**1.05**	1.07	1.07
Total debt	**$ 7,647**	$ 7,291	$ 6,392
Average years debt maturity	**10**	10	11
Average interest rates	**7.0%**	7.0%	7.2%
Minority interest in subsidiary companies	**$ 710**	$ 679	$ 645
Stockholders' equity	**$ 12,042**	$ 11,833	$ 12,766
Total debt to total borrowed and invested capital	**37.5%**	36.8%	32.3%

OUTLOOK We consider our financial position to be sufficiently strong to meet our anticipated future financial requirements. Our financial policies and procedures afford us flexibility to meet the changing landscape of our financial environment. Cash required to service debt maturities in 2000 is projected to be $1,450 million. However, we intend to refinance these maturities.

In 2000, we feel our *cash from operating activities* and *cash proceeds from asset sales,* coupled with our *borrowing* capacity, will allow us to meet our *Capex* program. Additionally, we will continue to provide a sustained return to our shareholders in the form of dividends.

MANAGING MARKET RISK We are exposed to the following types of market risks:

> The price of crude oil, natural gas and petroleum products

> The value of foreign currencies in relation to the U.S. dollar

> Interest rates

We use contracts such as futures, swaps and options in managing our exposure to these risks. We have written policies that govern our use of these instruments and limit our exposure to market and counterparty risks. These arrangements do not expose us to material adverse effects. See Notes 9, 14 and 15 to the financial statements and Supplemental Market Risk Disclosures on page 63 for additional information.

Reorganizations, Restructurings and Employee Separation Programs
In the fourth quarter of 1998, we announced that we were reorganizing several of our operations and implementing other cost-cutting initiatives. The principal units affected were our worldwide upstream; our international downstream, principally our marketing operations in the United Kingdom and Brazil and our refining operations in Panama; global gas marketing, now included as part of our global gas and power operating segment; and our corporate center. We accrued $115 million ($80 million, net of tax) for employee separations, curtailment

costs and special termination benefits associated with these announced restructurings in the fourth quarter of 1998. During the second quarter of 1999, we expanded the employee separation programs and recorded an additional provision of $48 million ($31 million, net of tax). For the most part, separation accruals are shown as operating expenses in the Statement of Consolidated Income.

The following table identifies each of our four restructuring initiatives. It provides the provision recorded in the fourth quarter of 1998 and the additional provision recorded in the second quarter of 1999. It also shows the deductions made through December 31, 1999 and the remaining obligations as of December 31, 1999. These deductions include cash payments of $124 million and transfers to long-term obligations of $12 million. We will pay the remaining obligations in future periods in accordance with plan provisions.

(Millions of dollars)	Provision Recorded in 1998	Provision Recorded in 1999	Deductions made through December 31, 1999	Remaining Obligations as of December 31, 1999
Worldwide upstream	$ 56	$ 20	$ (71)	$ 5
International downstream	25	13	(26)	12
Global gas and power	5	4	(7)	2
Corporate center	29	11	(32)	8
Total	$ 115	$ 48	$ (136)	$ 27

At the time we initially announced these programs, we estimated that over 1,400 employee reductions would result. Employee reductions of 800 in worldwide upstream, 300 in international downstream, 100 in global gas and power and 200 in our corporate center were expected. During the second quarter of 1999, we expanded the program by almost 1,100 employees, comprised of 600 employees in worldwide upstream, 250 employees in international downstream, 100 employees in global gas and power and 150 employees in our corporate center. Through December 31, 1999, employee reductions totaled 1,375 in worldwide upstream, 518 in international downstream, 165 in global gas and power, and 404 in our corporate center.

As a result of our reorganizations and restructurings, we captured significant annual pre-tax cost and expense savings and synergies. We captured $236 million in worldwide upstream, $44 million in international downstream, $32 million in global gas and power and $59 million in our corporate center. These savings include lower people-related and operating expenses.

Additionally, our major affiliates have also captured significant annual pre-tax cost and expense savings and synergies, as a result of their own reorganizations. Our share of these savings from our U.S. downstream joint ventures, Equilon and Motiva, was $326 million, representing lower people-related expenses and reductions in cash operating expenses due to efficiencies. We realized $19 million in annual pre-tax cost savings, representing our share of the Caltex reorganization. These savings represent lower people-related expenses. We also captured $27 million in annual pre-tax cost reductions from our worldwide Fuel and Marine Marketing joint venture with Chevron, representing our share of reductions in operating costs and expenses due to efficiencies.

Capital and Exploratory Expenditures
1999 ACTIVITY Worldwide capital and exploratory expenditures, including our share of affiliates, were $3.9 billion for 1999, $4.0 billion for 1998 and $5.9 billion for 1997. The year 1997 included the $1.4 billion acquisition of Monterey Resources Inc., a producing company with operations primarily in California. Texaco's 1999 expenditures include acquisitions of and increased ownership interests in upstream projects. Expenditures were geographically and functionally split as follows:

Capital and Exploratory Expenditures — Geographical
(Billions of dollars)

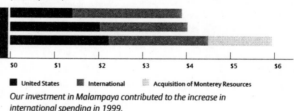

■ United States   ■ International   ▨ Acquisition of Monterey Resources

Our investment in Malampaya contributed to the increase in international spending in 1999.

Capital and Exploratory Expenditures — Functional
(Billions of dollars)

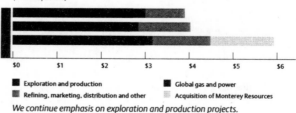

■ Exploration and production   ■ Global gas and power
■ Refining, marketing, distribution and other   ▨ Acquisition of Monterey Resources

We continue emphasis on exploration and production projects.

EXPLORATION AND PRODUCTION Significant areas of investment included:

> Exploration and development work in West Africa where we announced the major Agbami oil discovery offshore Nigeria in 1999

> Acquisition of a 45% interest in the Malampaya Deep Water Natural Gas Project in the Philippines

> Increased ownership interest in the Venezuelan Hamaca Oil Project from 20% to 30%

> Development work in Kazakhstan on the Karachaganak and North Buzachi fields

> Acquisition of exploration leases in the Brazilian Campos and Santos Basins

REFINING, MARKETING AND DISTRIBUTION AND OTHER Investment activities included:

> Reduced spending by Equilon and Motiva on refining

> Increased service station construction and renovation in the Caribbean

> Increased global gasification and power projects

The following table details our capital and exploratory expenditures:

(Millions of dollars)	1999 U.S.	1999 Inter-national	1999 Total	1998 U.S.	1998 Inter-national	1998 Total	1997 U.S.	1997 Inter-national	1997 Total
Exploration and production									
Exploratory expenses	$ 234	$ 267	$ 501	$ 257	$ 204	$ 461	$ 189	$ 282	$ 471
Capital expenditures	666	1,556	2,222	1,179	1,015	2,194	2,854*	1,095	3,949*
Total exploration and production	900	1,823	2,723	1,436	1,219	2,655	3,043	1,377	4,420
Refining, marketing and distribution	379	487	866	431	717	1,148	427	848	1,275
Global gas and power	103	176	279	124	61	185	149	34	183
Other	18	7	25	29	2	31	50	2	52
Total	$ 1,400	$ 2,493	$ 3,893	$ 2,020	$ 1,999	$ 4,019	$ 3,669	$ 2,261	$ 5,930
Total, excluding affiliates	$ 1,012	$ 2,051	$ 3,063	$ 1,528	$ 1,496	$ 3,024	$ 3,421	$ 1,718	$ 5,139

*Capital expenditures for 1997 include $1,448 million for the acquisition of Monterey Resources Inc.

2000 AND BEYOND

Spending for the year 2000 is expected to rise to $4.7 billion, an increase of $800 million over 1999 levels. In the upstream, spending is being allocated to our large impact producing projects in West Africa, Venezuela, Kazakhstan, the Philippines and the U.K. North Sea. Major exploration programs are underway in our key focus areas of Nigeria, Brazil and the deepwater Gulf of Mexico. International marketing will increase spending in the rapidly growing Caribbean area. Modest increases in spending are also anticipated for our international refinery system, particularly the Pembroke refinery in Wales. However, refining expenditures are generally being held at maintenance levels. Our global gas and power business is growing and has identified additional power generation and gasification projects as well as natural gas business opportunities.

Environmental Matters

The cost of compliance with federal, state and local environmental laws in the U.S. and international countries continues to be substantial. Using definitions and guidelines established by the American Petroleum Institute, our 1999 environmental spending was $633 million. This includes our equity share in the environmental expenditures of our major affiliates, Equilon, Motiva and the Caltex Group of Companies. The following table provides our environmental expenditures for the past three years:

(Millions of dollars)	1999	1998	1997
Capital expenditures	$ 118	$ 175	$ 162
Non-capital:			
Ongoing operations	391	495	538
Remediation	98	93	79
Restoration and abandonment	26	44	46
Total environmental expenditures	$ 633	$ 807	$ 825

CAPITAL EXPENDITURES

Our spending for capital projects in 1999 was $118 million. These expenditures were made to comply with clean air and water regulations as well as waste management requirements. Worldwide capital expenditures projected for 2000 and 2001 are $91 million and $121 million.

ONGOING OPERATIONS

In 1999, environmental expenses charged to current operations were $391 million. These expenses related largely to the production of cleaner-burning gasoline and the management of our environmental programs.

REMEDIATION

Remediation Costs and Liabilities Our worldwide remediation expenditures in 1999 were $98 million. This included $12 million spent on the remediation of Superfund waste sites. At the end of 1999, we had liabilities of $391 million for the estimated cost of our known environmental liabilities. This includes $46 million for the cleanup of Superfund waste sites. We have accrued for these remediation liabilities based on currently available facts, existing technology and presently enacted laws and regulations. It is not possible to project overall costs beyond amounts disclosed due to the uncertainty surrounding future developments in regulations or until new information becomes available.

Superfund Sites Under the Comprehensive Environmental Response, Compensation and Liability Act (CERCLA), the U.S. Environmental Protection Agency (EPA) and other regulatory agencies have identified us as a potentially responsible party (PRP) for cleanup of Superfund waste sites. We have determined that we may have potential exposure, though limited in most cases, at 178 Superfund waste sites. Of these sites, 104 are on the EPA's National Priority List. Under Superfund, liability is joint and several, that is, each PRP at a site can be held liable individually for the entire cleanup cost of the site. We are, however, actively pursuing the sharing of Superfund costs with other identified PRPs. The sharing of these costs is on the basis of weight, volume and toxicity of the materials contributed by the PRP.

RESTORATION AND ABANDONMENT COSTS AND LIABILITIES

Expenditures in 1999 for restoration and abandonment of our oil and gas producing properties amounted to $26 million. At year-end 1999, accruals to cover the cost of restoration and abandonment were $911 million.

We make every reasonable effort to fully comply with applicable governmental regulations. Changes in these regulations as well as our continuous re-evaluation of our environmental programs may result in additional future costs. We believe that any mandated future costs would be recoverable in the marketplace, since all companies within our industry would be facing similar requirements. However, we do not believe that such future costs would be material to our financial position or to our operating results over any reasonable period of time.

New Accounting Standards

In June 1998, the Financial Accounting Standards Board (FASB) issued SFAS 133, "Accounting for Derivative Instruments and Hedging Activities." SFAS 133 establishes new accounting rules and disclosure requirements for most derivative instruments and hedge transactions. In June 1999, the FASB issued SFAS 137, which deferred the effective date of SFAS 133. We will adopt SFAS 133 effective January 1, 2001 and are currently assessing the effects of adoption.

Euro Conversion

On January 1, 1999, 11 of the 15 member countries of the European Union established fixed conversion rates between their existing currencies and one common currency — the euro. The euro began trading on world currency exchanges at that time and may be used in business transactions. On January 1, 2002, new euro-denominated bills and coins will be issued, and legacy currencies will be completely withdrawn from circulation by June 30 of that year.

Prior to introduction of the euro, our operating subsidiaries affected by the euro conversion completed computer systems upgrades and fiscal and legal due diligence to ensure our euro readiness. Computer systems have been adapted to ensure that all our operating subsidiaries have the capability to comply with necessary business requirements and customer/supplier preferences. Legal due diligence was conducted to ensure post-euro continuity of contracts, and fiscal reviews were completed to ensure compatibility with our banking relationships. We, therefore, experienced no major impact on our current business operations as a result of the introduction of the euro.

We continue to review our marketing and operational policies and procedures to ensure our ability to continue to successfully conduct all aspects of our business in this new, price-transparent market. We believe that the euro conversion will not have a material adverse impact on our financial condition or results of operations.

Year 2000 (Y2K)

We encountered no major operating or other problems due to the Y2K issue. The Y2K issue concerned the inability of some information and technology-based operating systems to properly recognize and process date-sensitive information beyond December 31, 1999. Since we began addressing this issue in 1995, we assessed over 45,000 systems for potential problems. By November 1, 1999, we completed modifying or upgrading all of our critical and essential systems and gained assurances that our major affiliates were prepared for the Y2K rollover. We also completed our review of critical suppliers and customers, developed contingency plans, and established an Early Alert System to monitor the Y2K status of our key facilities around the world during the rollover.

During the year 1999 and the first few weeks of 2000, we spent about $22 million on Y2K issues, bringing our total spent since 1995 to $59 million. We do not anticipate expending additional funds on Y2K related activities.

Description of Significant Accounting Policies

PRINCIPLES OF CONSOLIDATION

The consolidated financial statements consist of the accounts of Texaco Inc. and subsidiary companies in which we hold direct or indirect voting interest of more than 50%. Intercompany accounts and transactions are eliminated.

The U.S. dollar is the functional currency of all our operations and substantially all of the operations of affiliates accounted for on the equity method. For these operations, translation effects and all gains and losses from transactions not denominated in the functional currency are included in income currently, except for certain hedging transactions. The cumulative translation effects for the equity affiliates using functional currencies other than the U.S. dollar are included in the currency translation adjustment in stockholders' equity.

USE OF ESTIMATES

In preparing Texaco's consolidated financial statements in accordance with generally accepted accounting principles, management is required to use estimates and judgment. While we have considered all available information, actual amounts could differ from those reported as assets and liabilities and related revenues, costs and expenses and the disclosed amounts of contingencies.

REVENUES

We recognize revenues for crude oil, natural gas and refined product sales at the point of passage of title specified in the contract. We record revenues on forward sales where cash has been received to deferred income until title passes.

CASH EQUIVALENTS

We generally classify highly liquid investments with a maturity of three months or less when purchased as cash equivalents.

INVENTORIES

We value inventories at the lower of cost or market, after initially recording at cost. For virtually all inventories of crude oil, petroleum products and petrochemicals, cost is determined on the last-in, first-out (LIFO) method. For other merchandise inventories, cost is generally on the first-in, first-out (FIFO) method. For materials and supplies, cost is at average cost.

INVESTMENTS AND ADVANCES

We use the equity method of accounting for investments in certain affiliates owned 50% or less, including corporate joint ventures, limited liability companies and partnerships. Under this method, we record equity in the pre-tax income or losses of limited liability companies and partnerships, and equity in the net income or losses of corporate joint-venture companies currently in Texaco's revenues, rather than when realized through dividends or distributions.

We record the net income of affiliates accounted for at cost in net income when realized through dividends.

We account for investments in debt securities and in equity securities with readily determinable fair values at fair value if classified as available-for-sale.

PROPERTIES, PLANT AND EQUIPMENT AND DEPRECIATION, DEPLETION AND AMORTIZATION

We follow the "successful efforts" method of accounting for our oil and gas exploration and producing operations.

We capitalize as incurred the lease acquisition costs of properties held for oil, gas and mineral production. We expense as incurred exploratory costs other than wells. We initially capitalize exploratory wells, including stratigraphic test wells, pending further evaluation of whether economically recoverable proved reserves have been found. If such reserves are not found, we charge the well costs to exploratory expenses. For locations not requiring major capital expenditures, we record the charge within one year of well completion. We capitalize intangible drilling costs of productive wells and of development dry holes, and tangible equipment costs. Also capitalized are costs of injected carbon dioxide related to development of oil and gas reserves.

We base our evaluation of impairment for properties, plant and equipment intended to be held on comparison of carrying value against undiscounted future net pre-tax cash flows, generally based on proved developed reserves. If an impairment is identified, we adjust the asset's carrying amount to fair value. We generally account for assets to be disposed of at the lower of net book value or fair value less cost to sell.

We amortize unproved oil and gas properties, when individually significant, by property using a valuation assessment. We generally amortize other unproved oil and gas properties on an aggregate basis over the average holding period, for the portion expected to be nonproductive. We amortize productive properties and other tangible and intangible costs of producing activities principally by field. Amortization is based on the unit-of-production basis by applying the ratio of produced oil and gas to estimated recoverable proved oil and gas reserves. We include estimated future restoration and abandonment costs in determining amortization and depreciation rates of productive properties.

We apply depreciation of facilities other than producing properties generally on the group plan, using the straight-line method, with composite rates reflecting the estimated useful life and cost of each class of property. We depreciate facilities not on the group plan individually by estimated useful life using the straight-line method. We exclude estimated salvage value from amounts subject to depreciation. We amortize capitalized non-mineral leases over the estimated useful life of the asset or the lease term, as appropriate, using the straight-line method.

We record periodic maintenance and repairs at manufacturing facilities on the accrual basis. We charge to expense normal maintenance and repairs of all other properties, plant and equipment as incurred. We capitalize renewals, betterments and major repairs that materially extend the useful life of properties and record a retirement of the assets replaced, if any.

When capital assets representing complete units of property are disposed of, we credit or charge to income the difference between the disposal proceeds and net book value.

ENVIRONMENTAL EXPENDITURES

When remediation of a property is probable and the related costs can be reasonably estimated, we accrue the expenses of environmental remediation costs and record them as liabilities. Recoveries or reimbursements are recorded as an asset when receipt is assured. We expense or capitalize other environmental expenditures, principally maintenance or preventive in nature, as appropriate.

DEFERRED INCOME TAXES

We determine deferred income taxes utilizing a liability approach. The income statement effect is derived from changes in deferred income taxes on the balance sheet. This approach gives consideration to the future tax consequences associated with differences between financial accounting and tax bases of assets and liabilities. These differences relate to items such as depreciable and depletable properties, exploratory and intangible drilling costs, non-productive leases, merchandise inventories and certain liabilities. This approach gives immediate effect to changes in income tax laws upon enactment.

We reduce deferred income tax assets by a valuation allowance when it is more likely than not (more than 50%) that a portion will not be realized. Deferred income tax assets are assessed individually by type for this purpose. This process requires the use of estimates and judgment, as many deferred income tax assets have a long potential realization period.

We do not make provision for possible income taxes payable upon distribution of accumulated earnings of foreign subsidiary companies and affiliated corporate joint-venture companies when such earnings are deemed to be permanently reinvested.

ACCOUNTING FOR CONTINGENCIES

Certain conditions may exist as of the date financial statements are issued, which may result in a loss to the company, but which will only be resolved when one or more future events occur or fail to occur. Such contingent liabilities are assessed by the company's management and legal counsel. The assessment of loss contingencies necessarily involves an exercise of judgment and is a matter of opinion. In assessing loss contingencies related to legal proceedings that are pending against the company or unasserted claims that may result

in such proceedings, the company's legal counsel evaluates the perceived merits of any legal proceedings or unasserted claims as well as the perceived merits of the amount of relief sought or expected to be sought therein.

If the assessment of a contingency indicates that it is probable that a material liability had been incurred and the amount of the loss can be estimated, then the estimated liability would be accrued in the company's financial statements. If the assessment indicates that a potentially material liability is not probable, but is reasonably possible, or is probable but cannot be estimated, then the nature of the contingent liability, together with an estimate of the range of possible loss if determinable and material, would be disclosed.

Loss contingencies considered remote are generally not disclosed unless they involve guarantees, in which case the nature of the guarantee would be disclosed. However, in some instances in which disclosure is not otherwise required, the company may disclose contingent liabilities of an unusual nature which, in the judgment of management and its legal counsel, may be of interest to stockholders or others.

STATEMENT OF CONSOLIDATED CASH FLOWS

We present cash flows from operating activities using the indirect method. We exclude exploratory expenses from cash flows of operating activities and apply them to cash flows of investing activities. On this basis, we reflect all capital and exploratory expenditures as investing activities.

Statement of Consolidated Income

(Millions of dollars) For the years ended December 31	1999	1998	1997
Revenues			
Sales and services (includes transactions with significant affiliates of $4,839 million in 1999, $4,169 million in 1998 and $3,633 million in 1997)	$ 34,975	$ 30,910	$ 45,187
Equity in income of affiliates, interest, asset sales and other	716	797	1,480
Total revenues	35,691	31,707	46,667
Deductions			
Purchases and other costs (includes transactions with significant affiliates of $1,691 million in 1999, $1,669 million in 1998 and $2,178 million in 1997)	27,442	24,179	35,230
Operating expenses	2,319	2,508	3,251
Selling, general and administrative expenses	1,186	1,224	1,755
Exploratory expenses	501	461	471
Depreciation, depletion and amortization	1,543	1,675	1,633
Interest expense	504	480	412
Taxes other than income taxes	334	423	520
Minority interest	83	56	68
	33,912	31,006	43,340
Income before income taxes and cumulative effect of accounting change	1,779	701	3,327
Provision for income taxes	602	98	663
Income before cumulative effect of accounting change	1,177	603	2,664
Cumulative effect of accounting change	—	(25)	—
Net income	$ 1,177	$ 578	$ 2,664
Net Income per Common Share (dollars)			
Basic:			
Income before cumulative effect of accounting change	$ 2.14	$ 1.04	$ 4.99
Cumulative effect of accounting change	—	(.05)	—
Net income	$ 2.14	$ .99	$ 4.99
Diluted:			
Income before cumulative effect of accounting change	$ 2.14	$ 1.04	$ 4.87
Cumulative effect of accounting change	—	(.05)	—
Net income	$ 2.14	$ .99	$ 4.87
Average Number of Common Shares Outstanding (for computation of earnings per share) (thousands)			
Basic	535,369	528,416	522,234
Diluted	537,860	528,965	542,570

See accompanying notes to consolidated financial statements.

Consolidated Balance Sheet

(Millions of dollars) As of December 31	1999	1998
Assets		
Current Assets		
Cash and cash equivalents	$ 419	$ 249
Short-term investments – at fair value	29	22
Accounts and notes receivable (includes receivables from significant affiliates of $585 million in 1999 and $694 million in 1998), less allowance for doubtful accounts of $27 million in 1999 and $28 million in 1998	4,060	3,955
Inventories	1,182	1,154
Deferred income taxes and other current assets	273	256
Total current assets	5,963	5,636
Investments and Advances	6,426	7,184
Net Properties, Plant and Equipment	15,560	14,761
Deferred Charges	1,023	989
Total	$ 28,972	$ 28,570
Liabilities and Stockholders' Equity		
Current Liabilities		
Notes payable, commercial paper and current portion of long-term debt	$ 1,041	$ 939
Accounts payable and accrued liabilities (includes payables to significant affiliates of $61 million in 1999 and $395 million in 1998)		
Trade liabilities	2,585	2,302
Accrued liabilities	1,203	1,368
Estimated income and other taxes	839	655
Total current liabilities	5,668	5,264
Long-Term Debt and Capital Lease Obligations	6,606	6,352
Deferred Income Taxes	1,468	1,644
Employee Retirement Benefits	1,184	1,248
Deferred Credits and Other Non-current Liabilities	1,294	1,550
Minority Interest in Subsidiary Companies	710	679
Total	16,930	16,737
Stockholders' Equity		
Market auction preferred shares	300	300
ESOP convertible preferred stock	—	428
Unearned employee compensation and benefit plan trust	(306)	(334)
Common stock – shares issued: 567,576,504 in 1999; 567,606,290 in 1998	1,774	1,774
Paid-in capital in excess of par value	1,287	1,640
Retained earnings	9,748	9,561
Other accumulated non-owner changes in equity	(119)	(101)
	12,684	13,268
Less – Common stock held in treasury, at cost	642	1,435
Total stockholders' equity	12,042	11,833
Total	$ 28,972	$ 28,570

See accompanying notes to consolidated financial statements.

Statement of Consolidated Stockholders' Equity

	Shares	Amount	Shares	Amount	Shares	Amount
(Shares in thousands; amounts in millions of dollars)		1999		1998		1997
Preferred Stock						
par value $1; shares authorized – 30,000,000						
Market Auction Preferred Shares (Series G, H, I and J) –						
liquidation preference of $250,000 per share						
Beginning and end of year	1	$ 300	1	$ 300	1	$ 300
Series B ESOP Convertible Preferred Stock						
Beginning of year	649	389	693	416	720	432
Redemptions	(587)	(352)	—	—	—	—
Retirements	(62)	(37)	(44)	(27)	(27)	(16)
End of year	—	—	649	389	693	416
Series F ESOP Convertible Preferred Stock						
Beginning of year	53	39	56	41	57	42
Redemptions	(53)	(39)	—	—	—	—
Retirements	—	—	(3)	(2)	(1)	(1)
End of year	—	—	53	39	56	41
Unearned Employee Compensation						
(related to ESOP and restricted stock awards)						
Beginning of year		(94)		(149)		(175)
Awards		(18)		(36)		(16)
Amortization and other		46		91		42
End of year		(66)		(94)		(149)
Benefit Plan Trust						
(common stock)						
Beginning of year	9,200	(240)	9,200	(240)	8,000	(203)
Additions	—	—	—	—	1,200	(37)
End of year	9,200	(240)	9,200	(240)	9,200	(240)
Common Stock						
par value $3.125; shares authorized – 850,000,000						
Beginning of year	567,606	1,774	567,606	1,774	548,587	1,714
Monterey acquisition	(29)	—	—	—	19,019	60
End of year	567,577	1,774	567,606	1,774	567,606	1,774
Common Stock Held in Treasury, at Cost						
Beginning of year	32,976	(1,435)	25,467	(956)	21,191	(628)
Redemption of Series B and						
Series F ESOP Convertible						
Preferred Stock	(16,180)	699	—	—	—	—
Purchases of common stock	—	—	9,572	(551)	7,423	(410)
Transfer to benefit plan trust	—	—	—	—	(1,200)	37
Other – mainly employee benefit plans	(2,327)	94	(2,063)	72	(1,947)	45
End of year	14,469	$ (642)	32,976	$ (1,435)	25,467	$ (956)

See accompanying notes to consolidated financial statements.

(Continued on next page.)

Statement of Consolidated Stockholders' Equity

(Millions of dollars)	1999	1998	1997
Paid-in Capital in Excess of Par Value			
Beginning of year	$ 1,640	$ 1,688	$ 630
Redemption of Series B and Series F ESOP			
Convertible Preferred Stock	(308)	—	—
Monterey acquisition	(2)	—	1,091
Treasury stock transactions relating to investor services plan			
and employee compensation plans	(43)	(48)	(33)
End of year	1,287	1,640	1,688
Retained Earnings			
Balance at beginning of year	9,561	9,987	8,292
Add:			
Net income	1,177	578	2,664
Tax benefit associated with dividends on unallocated			
ESOP Convertible Preferred Stock and Common Stock	2	3	4
Deduct: Dividends declared on			
Common stock			
($1.80 per share in 1999 and 1998			
and $1.75 per share in 1997)	964	952	918
Preferred stock			
Series B ESOP Convertible Preferred Stock	17	38	40
Series F ESOP Convertible Preferred Stock	2	4	4
Market Auction Preferred Shares (Series G, H, I and J)	9	13	11
Balance at end of year	9,748	9,561	9,987
Other Accumulated Non-owner Changes in Equity			
Currency translation adjustment			
Beginning of year	(107)	(105)	(65)
Change during year	8	(2)	(40)
End of year	(99)	(107)	(105)
Minimum pension liability adjustment			
Beginning of year	(24)	(16)	—
Change during year	1	(8)	(16)
End of year	(23)	(24)	(16)
Unrealized net gain on investments			
Beginning of year	30	26	33
Change during year	(27)	4	(7)
End of year	3	30	26
Total other accumulated non-owner changes in equity	(119)	(101)	(95)
Stockholders' Equity			
End of year (including preceding page)	$ 12,042	$ 11,833	$ 12,766

See accompanying notes to consolidated financial statements.

Statement of Consolidated Non-owner Changes in Equity

(Millions of dollars)	1999	1998	1997
Net Income	**$ 1,177**	$ 578	$ 2,664
Other Non-owner Changes in Equity:			
Currency translation adjustment			
Reclassification to net income of realized loss on sale of affiliate	**17**	—	—
Other unrealized net change during period	**(9)**	(2)	(40)
Total	**8**	(2)	(40)
Minimum pension liability adjustment			
Before income taxes	**1**	(16)	(21)
Income taxes	**—**	8	5
Total	**1**	(8)	(16)
Unrealized net gain on investments			
Net gain (loss) arising during period			
Before income taxes	**12**	35	22
Income taxes	**(2)**	(11)	(9)
Reclassification to net income of net realized (gain) or loss			
Before income taxes	**(48)**	(31)	(29)
Income taxes	**11**	11	9
Total	**(27)**	4	(7)
Total other non-owner changes in equity	**(18)**	(6)	(63)
Total non-owner changes in equity	**$ 1,159**	$ 572	$ 2,601

See accompanying notes to consolidated financial statements.

Statement of Consolidated Cash Flows

(Millions of dollars) For the years ended December 31	1999	1998	1997
Operating Activities			
Net income	$ 1,177	$ 578	$ 2,664
Reconciliation to net cash provided by (used in) operating activities			
Cumulative effect of accounting change	—	25	—
Depreciation, depletion and amortization	1,543	1,675	1,633
Deferred income taxes	(140)	(152)	451
Exploratory expenses	501	461	471
Minority interest in net income	83	56	68
Dividends from affiliates, greater than (less than) equity in income	233	224	(370)
Gains on asset sales	(87)	(109)	(558)
Changes in operating working capital			
Accounts and notes receivable	(637)	125	718
Inventories	(28)	(51)	(56)
Accounts payable and accrued liabilities	382	16	(856)
Other – mainly estimated income and other taxes	130	(205)	(64)
Other – net	12	(99)	(186)
Net cash provided by operating activities	3,169	2,544	3,915
Investing Activities			
Capital and exploratory expenditures	(2,957)	(3,101)	(3,628)
Proceeds from asset sales	321	282	1,036
Sales (purchases) of leasehold interests	(23)	25	(503)
Purchases of investment instruments	(432)	(947)	(1,102)
Sales/maturities of investment instruments	778	1,118	1,096
Collection of note/formation payments from U.S. affiliate	101	612	—
Other – net	—	—	(57)
Net cash used in investing activities	(2,212)	(2,011)	(3,158)
Financing Activities			
Borrowings having original terms in excess of three months			
Proceeds	2,353	1,300	507
Repayments	(1,080)	(741)	(637)
Net increase (decrease) in other borrowings	(983)	493	628
Purchases of common stock	—	(579)	(382)
Dividends paid to the company's stockholders			
Common	(964)	(952)	(918)
Preferred	(28)	(53)	(55)
Dividends paid to minority stockholders	(55)	(52)	(81)
Net cash used in financing activities	(757)	(584)	(938)
Cash and Cash Equivalents			
Effect of exchange rate changes	(30)	(11)	(19)
Increase (decrease) during year	170	(62)	(200)
Beginning of year	249	311	511
End of year	$ 419	$ 249	$ 311

See accompanying notes to consolidated financial statements.

Notes to Consolidated Financial Statements

NOTE 1 SEGMENT INFORMATION

We are presenting below information about our operating segments for the years 1999, 1998 and 1997, according to Statement of Financial Accounting Standards 131, "Disclosures about Segments of an Enterprise and Related Information," which we adopted in 1998. Due to the formation in 1999 of our Global Gas and Power segment, prior period information has been restated.

We determined our operating segments based on differences in the nature of their operations, geographic location and internal management reporting. The composition of segments and measure of segment profit are consistent with that used by our Executive Council in making strategic decisions. The Executive Council is headed by the Chairman and Chief Executive Officer and includes, among others, the Senior Vice Presidents having oversight responsibility for our business units.

Operating Segments 1999

(Millions of dollars)	Sales and Services Outside	Sales and Services Inter-segment	Sales and Services Total	After-tax Profit (Loss)	Income Tax Expense (Benefit)	DD&A Expense	Other Non-cash Items	Capital Expenditures	Assets at Year-End
Exploration and production									
United States	$ 2,166	$ 1,547	$ 3,713	$ 652	$ 299	$ 758	$ 167	$ 670	$ 8,696
International	2,684	924	3,608	360	545	451	30	1,273	5,333
Refining, marketing and distribution									
United States	3,579	18	3,597	208	73	3	78	3	3,714
International	22,114	75	22,189	370	101	220	132	375	8,542
Global gas and power	4,422	117	4,539	(14)	(8)	65	10	161	1,297
Segment totals	$ 34,965	$ 2,681	37,646	1,576	1,010	1,497	417	2,482	27,582
Other business units			32	(3)	(2)	1	—	—	365
Corporate/Non-operating			6	(396)	(406)	45	(1)	21	1,430
Intersegment eliminations			(2,709)	—	—	—	—	—	(405)
Consolidated			$ 34,975	$ 1,177	$ 602	$ 1,543	$ 416	$ 2,503	$ 28,972

Operating Segments 1998

(Millions of dollars)	Sales and Services Outside	Sales and Services Inter-segment	Sales and Services Total	After-tax Profit (Loss)	Income Tax Expense (Benefit)	DD&A Expense	Other Non-cash Items	Capital Expenditures	Assets at Year-End
Exploration and production									
United States	$ 1,712	$ 1,659	$ 3,371	$ 301	$ 34	$ 892	$ 1	$ 1,200	$ 8,699
International	2,020	695	2,715	129	132	513	18	901	4,345
Refining, marketing and distribution									
United States	2,612	29	2,641	221	88	29	230	1	4,066
International	19,805	106	19,911	332	130	204	135	396	8,214
Global gas and power	4,748	76	4,824	(16)	4	15	45	122	1,119
Segment totals	$ 30,897	$ 2,565	33,462	967	388	1,653	429	2,620	26,443
Other business units			50	(2)	—	1	3	—	381
Corporate/Non-operating			5	(362)	(290)	21	(67)	30	1,945
Intersegment eliminations			(2,607)	—	—	—	—	—	(199)
Consolidated, before cumulative effect of accounting change			$ 30,910	$ 603	$ 98	$ 1,675	$ 365	$ 2,650	$ 28,570

Operating Segments 1997

(Millions of dollars)	Sales and Services			After-tax Profit (Loss)	Income Tax Expense (Benefit)	DD&A Expense	Other Non-cash Items	Capital Expenditures	Assets at Year-End
	Outside	Inter-segment	Total						
Exploration and production									
United States	$ 365	$ 4,149	$ 4,514	$ 990	$ 487	$ 783	$ 281	$ 1,349	$ 8,769
International	2,565	693	3,258	812	566	442	104	901	4,107
Refining, marketing and distribution									
United States	16,984	250	17,234	325	172	178	169	262	5,668
International	20,009	362	20,371	508	117	173	(166)	482	7,908
Global gas and power	5,260	247	5,507	(46)	(6)	15	63	113	1,178
Segment totals	$ 45,183	$ 5,701	50,884	2,589	1,336	1,591	451	3,107	27,630
Other business units			64	2	2	1	3	—	431
Corporate/Non-operating			4	73	(675)	41	242	52	2,030
Intersegment eliminations			(5,765)	—	—	—	—	—	(491)
Consolidated			$ 45,187	$ 2,664	$ 663	$ 1,633	$ 696	$ 3,159	$ 29,600

Our exploration and production segments explore for, find, develop and produce crude oil and natural gas. The United States segment in 1998 and 1997 included minor operations in Canada. Our refining, marketing and distribution segments process crude oil and other feedstocks into refined products and purchase, sell and transport crude oil and refined petroleum products. The global gas and power segment includes the U.S. natural gas operations, which purchases natural gas and natural gas products from our exploration and production operations and third parties for resale. It also operates natural gas processing plants and pipelines in the United States. Also included in this segment are our power generation, gasification, hydrocarbons-to-liquids and fuel cell technology operations. This segment sold its U.K. wholesale gas business in 1998 and its U.K. retail gas marketing business in 1999. Other business units include our insurance operations and investments in undeveloped mineral properties. None of these units is individually significant in terms of revenue, income or assets.

You are encouraged to read Note 5 — *Investments and Advances*, beginning on page 41, which includes information about our affiliates and the formation of the Equilon and Motiva alliances in 1998.

Corporate and non-operating includes the assets, income and expenses relating to cash management and financing activities, our corporate center and other items not directly attributable to the operating segments.

We apply the same accounting policies to each of the segments as we do in preparing the consolidated financial statements. Intersegment sales and services are generally representative of market prices or arms-length negotiated transactions. Intersegment receivables are representative of normal trade balances. Other non-cash items principally include deferred income taxes, the difference between cash distributions and equity in income of affiliates, and non-cash charges and credits associated with asset sales. Capital expenditures are presented on a cash basis, excluding exploratory expenses.

The countries in which we have significant sales and services and long-lived assets are listed below. Sales and services are based on the origin of the sale. Long-lived assets include properties, plant and equipment and investments in foreign producing operations where the host governments own the physical assets under terms of the operating agreements.

(Millions of dollars)	Sales and Services			Long-lived assets at December 31		
	1999	1998	1997	1999	1998	1997
United States	$ 9,733	$ 8,184	$ 21,657	$ 8,630	$ 8,757	$ 11,437
International – Total	$ 25,242	$ 22,726	$ 23,530	$ 7,109	$ 6,250	$ 5,876
Significant countries included above:						
Brazil	2,404	3,175	3,175	326	301	266
Netherlands	1,955	1,636	1,901	246	257	250
United Kingdom	9,211	7,529	6,862	2,275	2,257	2,384

NOTE 2 ADOPTION OF NEW ACCOUNTING STANDARDS

SFAS 128 — During 1997, we adopted SFAS 128, "Earnings per Share." Our basic and diluted net income per common share under SFAS 128 were approximately the same as under the comparable prior basis of reporting.

SFAS 130, 131 and 132 — In 1998, Texaco adopted SFAS 130, 131 and 132. SFAS 130, "Reporting Comprehensive Income," requires that we report all items classified as comprehensive income under its provisions as separate components within a financial statement. SFAS 131, "Disclosures about Segments of an Enterprise and Related Information," requires the reporting of certain income, revenue, expense and asset data about operating segments of public enterprises. Operating segments are based upon a company's internal management structure. SFAS 131 also requires data for revenues and long-lived assets by major countries of operation. SFAS 132, "Employer's Disclosures about Pensions and Other Postretirement Benefits," requires disclosure of new information on changes in plan benefit obligations and fair values of plan assets.

SOP 98-5 — Effective January 1, 1998, Caltex, our affiliate, adopted Statement of Position 98-5, "Reporting on the Costs of Start-Up Activities," issued by the American Institute of Certified Public Accountants. This Statement requires that the costs of start-up activities and organization costs, as defined, be expensed as incurred. The cumulative effect of adoption on Texaco's net income for 1998 was a net loss of $25 million. This Statement was adopted by Texaco and our other affiliates effective January 1, 1999. The effect was not significant.

NOTE 3 INCOME PER COMMON SHARE

Basic net income per common share is net income less preferred stock dividend requirements divided by the average number of common shares outstanding. Diluted net income per common share assumes issuance of the net incremental shares from stock options and full conversion of all dilutive convertible securities at the later of the beginning of the year or date of issuance. Common shares held by the benefit plan trust are not considered outstanding for purposes of net income per common share.

(Millions, except per share amounts) For the years ended December 31	1999			1998			1997		
	Income	Shares	Per Share	Income	Shares	Per Share	Income	Shares	Per Share
Basic net income:									
Income before cumulative effect of accounting change	$ 1,177			$ 603			$ 2,664		
Less: Preferred stock dividends	(29)			(54)			(56)		
Income before cumulative effect of accounting change, for basic income per share	$ 1,148	535.4	$ 2.14	$ 549	528.4	$ 1.04	$ 2,608	522.2	$ 4.99
Effect of dilutive securities:									
ESOP Convertible preferred stock	—	—		—	—		34	19.3	
Stock options and restricted stock	3	2.5		—	.4		—	.8	
Convertible debentures	—	—		1	.2		—	.3	
Income before cumulative effect of accounting change, for diluted income per share	$ 1,151	537.9	$ 2.14	$ 550	529.0	$ 1.04	$ 2,642	542.6	$ 4.87

NOTE 4 INVENTORIES

(Millions of dollars) As of December 31	1999	1998
Crude oil	$ 141	$ 116
Petroleum products and other	857	839
Materials and supplies	184	199
Total	$ 1,182	$ 1,154

At December 31, 1999, the excess of estimated market value over the carrying value of inventories was $136 million. The carrying value of inventories at December 31, 1998 is net of a valuation allowance of $99 million to adjust from cost to market value. This valuation allowance was reversed in 1999 as market prices increased and the associated physical units of inventory were sold.

NOTE 5 INVESTMENTS AND ADVANCES

We account for our investments in affiliates, including corporate joint ventures and partnerships owned 50% or less, on the equity method. Our total investments and advances are summarized as follows:

(Millions of dollars) As of December 31	1999	1998
Affiliates accounted for on the equity method		
Exploration and production		
United States	$ 243	$ 230
International		
CPI	454	452
Other	14	24
	711	706
Refining, marketing and distribution		
United States		
Equilon	1,953	2,266
Motiva	686	896
International		
Caltex	1,685	1,747
Other	234	210
	4,558	5,119
Global gas and power	281	188
Other affiliates	13	3
Total	5,563	6,016
Miscellaneous investments, long-term receivables, etc., accounted for at:		
Fair value	138	470
Cost, less reserve	725	698
Total	$ 6,426	$ 7,184

Our equity in the net income of affiliates is adjusted to reflect income taxes for limited liability companies and partnerships whose income is directly taxable to us:

(Millions of dollars) For the years ended December 31	1999	1998	1997
Equity in net income (loss)			
Exploration and production			
United States	$ 53	$ 37	$ 40
International			
CPI	139	107	171
Other	—	(12)	—
	192	132	211
Refining, marketing and distribution			
United States			
Equilon	142	199	—
Motiva	(3)	22	—
Star	—	(3)	95
Other	—	—	48
International			
Caltex	11	(36)	252
Other	27	15	20
	177	197	415
Global gas and power	6	(11)	(11)
Other affiliates	—	—	1
Total	$ 375	$ 318	$ 616
Dividends received	$ 716	$ 709	$ 332

The undistributed earnings of these affiliates included in our retained earnings were $2,613 million, $2,846 million and $3,096 million as of December 31, 1999, 1998 and 1997.

Caltex Group

We have investments in the Caltex Group of Companies, owned 50% by Texaco and 50% by Chevron Corporation. The Caltex group consists of P.T. Caltex Pacific Indonesia (CPI), American Overseas Petroleum Limited and subsidiary and Caltex Corporation and subsidiaries (Caltex). This group of companies is engaged in the exploration for and production, transportation, refining and marketing of crude oil and products in Africa, Asia, Australia, the Middle East and New Zealand.

Results for the Caltex Group in 1998 include an after-tax charge of $50 million (Texaco's share $25 million) for the cumulative effect of accounting change. See Note 2 for additional information.

Equilon Enterprises LLC

Effective January 1, 1998, Texaco and Shell Oil Company formed Equilon Enterprises LLC (Equilon), a Delaware limited liability company. Equilon is a joint venture that combined major elements of the companies' western and midwestern U.S. refining and marketing businesses and their nationwide trading, transportation and lubricants businesses. We own 44% and Shell Oil Company owns 56% of Equilon.

The carrying amounts at January 1, 1998, of the principal assets and liabilities of the businesses we contributed to Equilon were $.2 billion of net working capital assets, $2.8 billion of net properties, plant and equipment and $.2 billion of debt. These amounts were reclassified to investment in affiliates accounted for by the equity method.

In April 1998, we received $463 million from Equilon, representing reimbursement of certain capital expenditures incurred prior to the formation of the joint venture. In July 1998, we received $149 million from Equilon for certain specifically identified assets transferred for value to Equilon. In February 1999, we received $101 million from Equilon for the payment of notes receivable.

Motiva Enterprises LLC
Effective July 1, 1998, Texaco, Shell and Saudi Aramco formed Motiva Enterprises LLC (Motiva), a Delaware limited liability company. Motiva is a joint venture that combined Texaco's and Saudi Aramco's interests and major elements of Shell's eastern and Gulf Coast U.S. refining and marketing businesses. Texaco's and Saudi Aramco's interest in these businesses were previously conducted by Star Enterprise (Star), a joint-venture partnership owned 50% by Texaco and 50% by Saudi Refining, Inc., a corporate affiliate of Saudi Aramco. Texaco and Saudi Refining, Inc., each owns 32.5% and Shell owns 35% of Motiva.

The investment in Motiva at date of formation approximated the previous investment in Star. The Motiva investment and previous Star investment are recorded as investment in affiliates accounted for on the equity method.

The following table provides summarized financial information on a 100% basis for the Caltex Group, Equilon, Motiva, Star and all other affiliates that we account for on the equity method, as well as Texaco's total share of the information. The net income of all limited liability companies and partnerships is net of estimated income taxes. The actual income tax liability is reflected in the accounts of the respective members or partners and is not shown in the following table.

Motiva's and Star's assets at the respective balance sheet dates include the remaining portion of the assets which were originally transferred from Texaco to Star at the fair market value on the date of formation of Star. Our investment and equity in the income of Motiva and Star, as reported in our consolidated financial statements, reflect the remaining unamortized historical carrying cost of the assets transferred to Star at formation of Star. Additionally, our investments in Motiva and Star include adjustments for contractual arrangements on the formation of Star, principally involving contributed inventories.

(Millions of dollars)	Equilon	Motiva	Caltex Group	Other Affiliates	Total Texaco's Share
1999					
Gross revenues	$ 29,398	$ 12,196	$ 14,915	$ 2,895	$ 25,650
Income (loss) before income taxes	$ 347	$ (69)	$ 780	$ 348	$ 679
Net income (loss)	$ 226	$ (45)	$ 390	$ 232	$ 375
As of December 31:					
Current assets	$ 4,209	$ 1,271	$ 2,705	$ 801	$ 3,796
Non-current assets	7,208	5,307	7,604	2,230	9,321
Current liabilities	(5,636)	(1,278)	(3,395)	(736)	(4,916)
Non-current liabilities	(735)	(2,095)	(2,639)	(792)	(2,638)
Net equity	$ 5,046	$ 3,205	$ 4,275	$ 1,503	$ 5,563

(Millions of dollars)	Equilon	Motiva	Star	Caltex Group	Other Affiliates	Total Texaco's Share
1998						
Gross revenues	$ 22,246	$ 5,371	$ 3,190	$ 11,505	$ 2,541	$ 20,021
Income (loss) before income taxes and cumulative effect of accounting change	$ 502	$ 78	$ (128)	$ 519	$ 170	$ 662
Net income (loss)	$ 326	$ 51	$ (83)	$ 143	$ 84	$ 318
As of December 31:						
Current assets	$ 2,640	$ 1,481		$ 1,974	$ 687	$ 2,769
Non-current assets	7,752	5,257		7,684	2,021	9,313
Current liabilities	(4,044)	(1,243)		(2,839)	(727)	(3,924)
Non-current liabilities	(382)	(1,667)		(2,421)	(672)	(2,142)
Net equity	$ 5,966	$ 3,828		$ 4,398	$ 1,309	$ 6,016

(Millions of dollars)	Star	Caltex Group	Other Affiliates	Total Texaco's Share
1997				
Gross revenues	$ 7,758	$ 15,699	$ 4,028	$ 13,312
Income before income taxes	$ 301	$ 1,210	$ 605	$ 940
Net income	$ 196	$ 846	$ 400	$ 616
As of December 31:				
Current assets	$ 1,042	$ 2,521	$ 947	$ 1,965
Non-current assets	3,260	7,193	3,607	6,324
Current liabilities	(769)	(2,991)	(1,032)	(2,270)
Non-current liabilities	(1,072)	(2,131)	(2,022)	(2,198)
Net equity	$ 2,461	$ 4,592	$ 1,500	$ 3,821

NOTE 6 PROPERTIES, PLANT AND EQUIPMENT

	Gross		Net	
(Millions of dollars) As of December 31	1999	1998	1999	1998
Exploration and production				
United States	$ 21,565	$ 21,991	$ 7,822	$ 7,945
International	8,835	7,554	3,804	2,950
Total	30,400	29,545	11,626	10,895
Refining, marketing and distribution				
United States	33	75	22	27
International	4,575	4,487	3,107	3,055
Total	4,608	4,562	3,129	3,082
Global gas and power	748	660	317	267
Other	771	727	488	517
Total	$ 36,527	$ 35,494	$ 15,560	$ 14,761
Capital lease amounts included above	$ 152	$ 264	$ 3	$ 79

Accumulated depreciation, depletion and amortization totaled $20,967 million and $20,733 million at December 31, 1999 and 1998. Interest capitalized as part of properties, plant and equipment was $28 million in 1999, $21 million in 1998 and $20 million in 1997.

In 1999, 1998 and 1997, we recorded pre-tax charges of $87 million, $150 million and $63 million for the write-downs of impaired assets. These charges were recorded to depreciation, depletion and amortization expense.

1999

In our global gas and power operating segment, pre-tax asset write-downs from the impairment of certain gas plants in Louisiana were $49 million. We determined in the fourth quarter that, as a result of declining gas volumes available for processing, the carrying value of these plants exceeded future undiscounted cash flows. Fair value was determined by discounting expected future cash flows.

Pre-tax asset write-downs of $28 million included in corporate resulted from our joint plan with state and local agencies to convert for third-party industrial use idle facilities, formerly used in research activities. The facilities and equipment were written down to their appraised values. An additional $10 million was recorded to bring certain marketing assets of our subsidiary in Poland to be disposed of to their appraised value.

1998

In the U.S. exploration and production operating segment, pre-tax asset write-downs for impaired properties in Louisiana and Canada were $64 million. The Louisiana property represents an unsuccessful enhanced recovery project. We determined in the fourth quarter of 1998 that the carrying value of this property exceeded future undiscounted cash flows. Fair value was determined by discounting expected future cash flows. Canadian properties were impaired following our decision in October 1998 to exit the upstream business in Canada. These properties were written down to their sales price with the sale closing in December 1998.

In the international exploration and production operating segment, the pre-tax asset write-down for the impairment of our investment in the Strathspey field in the U.K. North Sea was $58 million. The Strathspey impairment was caused by a downward revision in the fourth quarter of the estimated volume of the field's proved reserves. Fair value was determined by discounting expected future cash flows.

In the U.S. downstream operating segment, the pre-tax asset write-downs for the impairment of surplus facilities and equipment held for sale and not transferred to the Equilon joint venture was $28 million. Fair value was determined by an independent appraisal.

1997

In our U.S. exploration and producing operating segment, pre-tax asset write-downs for impaired properties in Louisiana and Canada were $48 million. The Louisiana impairment resulted from the write-downs of gas plants due to insufficient contract volumes and the Canadian impairment resulted from unsuccessful enhanced recovery projects and downward revisions to underground reserves.

In our international exploration and producing operating segment, pre-tax asset write-downs of $15 million for impaired properties in the U.K. North Sea were caused by downward revisions to underground reserves.

Fair values were based on expected future discounted cash flows.

NOTE 7 FOREIGN CURRENCY

Currency translations resulted in pre-tax losses of $47 million in 1999, $80 million in 1998 and $59 million in 1997. After applicable taxes, 1999 included a gain of $25 million compared to a loss of $94 million in 1998 and a gain of $154 million in 1997.

The after-tax currency gain in 1999 related principally to balance sheet translation. After-tax currency impacts for years 1998 and 1997 were largely due to currency volatility in Asia. In 1998, our Caltex affiliate incurred significant currency-related losses due to the strengthening of the Korean won and Japanese yen against the U.S. dollar. In contrast, those currencies weakened against the U.S. dollar in 1997, which resulted in significant currency-related gains.

Results for 1997 through 1999 were also impacted by the effect of currency rate changes on deferred income taxes denominated in British pounds. This results in gains from strengthening of the U.S. dollar and losses from weakening of the U.S. dollar. These effects were gains of $8 million in 1999, losses of $5 million in 1998 and gains of $28 million in 1997.

Effective October 1, 1997, Caltex changed the functional currency for its operations in its Korean and Japanese affiliates to the U.S. dollar.

Currency translation adjustments shown in the separate stockholders' equity account result from translation items pertaining to certain affiliates of Caltex. For 1999, we recorded unrealized losses of $9 million from these adjustments. In addition, we reversed an existing $17 million deferred loss due to the sale by Caltex of its investment in Koa Oil Company, Limited. As a result, a $17 million loss was recorded in Texaco's net income as part of the loss on this sale. For years 1998 and 1997, currency translation losses recorded to stockholders' equity were $2 million and $40 million.

NOTE 8 TAXES

(Millions of dollars)	1999	1998	1997
Federal and other income taxes			
Current			
U.S. Federal	$ 100	$ (45)	$ (538)
Foreign	678	283	689
State and local	(36)	12	61
Total	742	250	212
Deferred			
U.S.	(120)	(104)	457
Foreign	(20)	(48)	(6)
Total	(140)	(152)	451
Total income taxes	602	98	663
Taxes other than income taxes			
Oil and gas production	64	70	127
Property	69	108	139
Payroll	91	119	125
Other	110	126	129
Total	334	423	520
Import duties and other levies			
U.S.	34	36	53
Foreign	6,937	6,843	5,414
Total	6,971	6,879	5,467
Total direct taxes	7,907	7,400	6,650
Taxes collected from consumers	2,097	2,148	3,370
Total all taxes	$ 10,004	$ 9,548	$ 10,020

The deferred income tax assets and liabilities included in the Consolidated Balance Sheet as of December 31, 1999 and 1998 amounted to $198 million and $205 million, as net current assets and $1,468 million and $1,644 million, as net non-current liabilities. The table that follows shows deferred income tax assets and liabilities by category:

	(Liability) Asset	
(Millions of dollars) As of December 31	1999	1998
Depreciation	$ (991)	$ (1,079)
Depletion	(383)	(429)
Intangible drilling costs	(881)	(726)
Other deferred tax liabilities	(691)	(686)
Total	(2,946)	(2,920)
Employee benefit plans	548	532
Tax loss carryforwards	599	641
Tax credit carryforwards	495	368
Environmental liabilities	123	116
Other deferred tax assets	711	639
Total	2,476	2,296
Total before valuation allowance	(470)	(624)
Valuation allowance	(800)	(815)
Total	$ (1,270)	$ (1,439)

The preceding table excludes certain potential deferred income tax asset amounts for which possibility of realization is extremely remote.

The valuation allowance relates principally to upstream operations in Denmark. The related deferred income tax assets result from tax loss carryforwards and book versus tax asset basis differences for a hydrocarbon tax. Loss carryforwards from this tax are generally determined by individual field and, in that case, are not usable against other fields' taxable income.

The following schedule reconciles the differences between the U.S. Federal income tax rate and the effective income tax rate excluding the cumulative effect of accounting change in 1998:

	1999	1998	1997
U.S. Federal income tax rate assumed to be applicable	35.0%	35.0%	35.0%
IRS settlement	—	—	(14.7)
Net earnings and dividends attributable to affiliated corporations accounted for on the equity method	(3.8)	(7.0)	(4.7)
Aggregate earnings and losses from international operations	14.4	10.4	6.2
U.S. tax adjustments	(5.0)	(8.7)	(.3)
Sales of stock of subsidiaries	(2.2)	(6.1)	—
Energy credits	(3.8)	(11.7)	(1.4)
Other	(.8)	2.1	(.2)
Effective income tax rate	33.8%	14.0%	19.9%

The year 1997 included a $488 million benefit resulting from an IRS settlement.

For companies operating in the United States, pre-tax earnings before the cumulative effect of an accounting change aggregated $484 million in 1999, $194 million in 1998 and $1,527 million in 1997. For companies with operations located outside the United States, pre-tax earnings on that basis aggregated $1,295 million in 1999, $507 million in 1998 and $1,800 million in 1997.

Income taxes paid, net of refunds, amounted to $600 million, $430 million and $285 million in 1999, 1998 and 1997.

The undistributed earnings of subsidiary companies and of affiliated corporate joint-venture companies accounted for on the equity method, for which deferred U.S. income taxes have not been provided

at December 31, 1999, amounted to $1,708 million and $2,187 million. The corresponding amounts at December 31, 1998 were $1,328 million and $2,226 million. Determination of the unrecognized U.S. deferred income taxes on these amounts is not practicable.

For the years 1999, 1998 and 1997, no loss carryforward benefits were recorded for U.S. Federal income taxes. For the years 1999, 1998 and 1997, the tax benefits recorded for loss carryforwards were $54 million, $30 million and $31 million in foreign income taxes.

At December 31, 1999, we had worldwide tax basis loss carryforwards of approximately $1,647 million, including $941 million which do not have an expiration date. The remainder expire at various dates through 2019.

Foreign tax credit carryforwards available for U.S. Federal income tax purposes amounted to approximately $245 million at December 31, 1999, expiring at various dates through 2004. Alternative minimum tax and other tax credit carryforwards available for U.S. Federal income tax purposes were $461 million at December 31, 1999, of which $357 million have no expiration date. The remaining credits expire at various dates through 2014. The credits that are not utilized by the expiration dates may be taken as deductions for U.S. Federal income tax purposes. For the year 1999, we recorded tax credit carryforwards of $68 million for U.S. Federal income tax purposes.

NOTE 9 SHORT-TERM DEBT, LONG-TERM DEBT, CAPITAL LEASE OBLIGATIONS AND RELATED DERIVATIVES
Notes Payable, Commercial Paper and Current Portion of Long-term Debt

(Millions of dollars) As of December 31	1999	1998
Notes payable to banks and others with originating terms of one year or less	$ 1,251	$ 368
Commercial paper	1,099	1,617
Current portion of long-term debt and capital lease obligations		
Indebtedness	734	991
Capital lease obligations	7	13
	3,091	2,989
Less short-term obligations intended to be refinanced	2,050	2,050
Total	$ 1,041	$ 939

The weighted average interest rate of commercial paper and notes payable to banks at December 31, 1999 and 1998 was 5.9%.

Long-term Debt and Capital Lease Obligations

(Millions of dollars) As of December 31	1999	1998
Long-Term Debt		
3-1/2% convertible notes due 2004	$ 203	$ 204
5.5% note due 2009	397	—
5.7% notes due 2008	201	201
6% notes due 2005	299	299
6-7/8% notes due 1999	—	200
6-7/8% debentures due 2023	196	196
7.09% notes due 2007	150	150
7-1/2% debentures due 2043	198	198
7-3/4% debentures due 2033	199	199
8% debentures due 2032	148	147
8-1/4% debentures due 2006	150	150
8-3/8% debentures due 2022	198	198
8-1/2% notes due 2003	200	199
8-5/8% debentures due 2010	150	150
8-5/8% debentures due 2031	199	199
8-5/8% debentures due 2032	199	199
8-7/8% debentures due 2021	150	150
9% notes due 1999	—	200
9-3/4% debentures due 2020	250	250
Medium-term notes, maturing from 2000 to 2043 (7.0%)	757	543
Revolving Credit Facility, due 1999-2002 – variable rate (5.9%)	—	309
Pollution Control Revenue Bonds, due 2012 – variable rate (3.5%)	166	166
Other long-term debt:		
Texaco Inc. – Guarantee of ESOP Series F loan – variable rate (6.6%)	—	2
U.S. dollars (6.6%)	369	335
Other currencies (9.4%)	472	394
Total	5,251	5,238
Capital Lease Obligations (see Note 10)	46	68
	5,297	5,306
Less current portion of long-term debt and capital lease obligations	741	1,004
	4,556	4,302
Short-term obligations intended to be refinanced	2,050	2,050
Total long-term debt and capital lease obligations	$ 6,606	$ 6,352

The percentages shown for variable-rate debt are the interest rates at December 31, 1999. The percentages shown for the categories "Medium-term notes" and "Other long-term debt" are the weighted average interest rates at year-end 1999. Where applicable, principal amounts shown in the preceding schedule include unamortized premium or discount. Interest paid, net of amounts capitalized, amounted to $480 million in 1999, $474 million in 1998 and $395 million in 1997.

At December 31, 1999, we had revolving credit facilities with commitments of $2.05 billion with syndicates of major U.S. and international banks. These facilities are available as support for our issuance of commercial paper as well as for working capital and other general corporate purposes. We had no amounts outstanding under these facilities at year-end 1999. We pay commitment fees on these facilities. The banks reserve the right to terminate the credit facilities upon the occurrence of certain specific events, including a change in control.

At December 31, 1999, our long-term debt included $2.05 billion of short-term obligations scheduled to mature during 2000, which we have both the intent and the ability to refinance on a long-term basis through the use of our $2.05 billion revolving credit facilities.

Contractual annual maturities of long-term debt, including sinking fund payments and potential repayments resulting from options that debtholders might exercise, for the five years subsequent to December 31, 1999 are as follows (in millions):

2000	2001	2002	2003	2004
$ 734	$ 135	$ 191	$ 273	$ 31

Debt-related Derivatives

We seek to maintain a balanced capital structure that provides financial flexibility and supports our strategic objectives while achieving a low cost of capital. This is achieved by balancing our liquidity and interest rate exposures. We manage these exposures primarily through long-term and short-term debt on the balance sheet. In managing our exposure to interest rates, we seek to balance the benefit of the lower cost of floating rate debt, with its inherent increased risk, with fixed rate debt having less market risk. To achieve this objective, we also use off-balance sheet derivative instruments, primarily interest rate swaps, to manage identifiable exposures on a non-leveraged, non-speculative basis.

Summarized below are the carrying amounts and fair values of our debt and debt-related derivatives at December 31, 1999 and 1998. Our use of derivatives during the periods presented was limited to interest rate swaps, where we either paid or received the net effect of a fixed rate versus a floating rate (commercial paper or LIBOR) index at specified intervals, calculated by reference to an agreed notional principal amount.

(Millions of dollars) As of December 31	1999	1998
Notes Payable and Commercial Paper:		
Carrying amount	$ 2,350	$ 1,985
Fair value	2,348	1,985
Related Derivatives –		
Payable (Receivable):		
Carrying amount	$ —	$ —
Fair value	(13)	17
Notional principal amount	$ 300	$ 300
Weighted average maturity *(years)*	7.3	8.3
Weighted average fixed pay rate	6.42%	6.42%
Weighted average floating		
receive rate	6.42%	5.32%
Long-Term Debt, including		
current maturities:		
Carrying amount	$ 5,251	$ 5,238
Fair value	5,225	5,842
Related Derivatives –		
Payable (Receivable):		
Carrying amount	$ (19)	$ (4)
Fair value	55	(9)
Notional principal amount	$ 1,294	$ 449
Weighted average maturity *(years)*	5.8	8.4
Weighted average fixed receive rate	5.69%	6.24%
Weighted average floating pay rate	6.10%	5.03%
Unamortized net gain on		
terminated swaps		
Carrying amount	$ 4	$ 5

Excluded from this table is an interest rate and equity swap with a notional principal amount of $200 million entered into in 1997, related to the 3-1/2% notes due 2004. We pay a floating rate and receive a fixed rate. Also, the counterparty assumes all exposure for the potential equity-based cash redemption premium on the notes. The fair value of this swap was not significant at year-end 1999 and 1998.

During 1999, floating rate pay swaps having an aggregate notional principal amount of $30 million were amortized or matured. We initiated $875 million of new floating rate pay swaps in connection with certain of the 1999 debt issuances. There was no activity in fixed rate pay swaps during 1999.

Fair values of debt are based upon quoted market prices, as well as rates currently available to us for borrowings with similar terms and maturities. We estimate the fair value of swaps as the amount that would be received or paid to terminate the agreements at year-end, taking into account current interest rates and the current creditworthiness

of the swap counterparties. The notional amounts of derivative contracts do not represent cash flow and are not subject to credit risk.

Amounts receivable or payable based on the interest rate differentials of derivatives are accrued monthly and are reflected in interest expense as a hedge of interest on outstanding debt. Gains and losses on terminated swaps are deferred and amortized over the life of the associated debt or the original term of the swap, whichever is shorter.

NOTE 10 LEASE COMMITMENTS AND RENTAL EXPENSE

We have leasing arrangements involving service stations, tanker charters, crude oil production and processing equipment and other facilities. We reflect amounts due under capital leases in our balance sheet as obligations, while we reflect our interest in the related assets as properties, plant and equipment. The remaining lease commitments are operating leases, and we record payments on such leases as rental expense.

As of December 31, 1999, we had estimated minimum commitments for payment of rentals (net of non-cancelable sublease rentals) under leases which, at inception, had a non-cancelable term of more than one year, as follows:

(Millions of dollars)	Operating Leases	Capital Leases
2000	$ 134	$ 9
2001	93	9
2002	416	8
2003	50	7
2004	54	7
After 2004	315	14
Total lease commitments	$ 1,062	$ 54
Less interest		8
Present value of total capital		
lease obligations		$ 46

Operating lease commitments for 2002 include a $304 million residual value guarantee of leased production facilities if we do not renew the lease.

Rental expense relative to operating leases, including contingent rentals based on factors such as gallons sold, is provided in the table below. Such payments do not include rentals on leases covering oil and gas mineral rights.

(Millions of dollars)	1999	1998	1997
Rental expense			
Minimum lease rentals	$ 218	$ 208	$ 270
Contingent rentals	6	—	3
Total	224	208	273
Less rental income on			
properties subleased			
to others	54	50	78
Net rental expense	$ 170	$ 158	$ 195

NOTE 11 EMPLOYEE BENEFIT PLANS

Texaco Inc. and certain of its non-U.S. subsidiaries sponsor various benefit plans for active employees and retirees. The costs of the savings, health care and life insurance plans relative to employees' active service are shared by the company and its employees, with Texaco's costs for these plans charged to expense as incurred. In addition, accruals for employee benefit plans are provided principally for the unfunded costs of various pension plans, retiree health and life insurance benefits, incentive compensation plans and for separation benefits payable to employees.

Employee Stock Ownership Plans (ESOP)

We recorded ESOP expense of $3 million in 1999, $1 million in 1998 and $2 million in 1997. Our contributions to the Employees Thrift Plan of Texaco Inc. and the Employees Savings Plan of Texaco Inc. amounted to $3 million in 1999, $1 million in 1998 and $2 million in 1997. These plans are designed to provide participants with a benefit of approximately 6% of base pay, as well as any benefits earned under the current employee Performance Compensation Program. In December 1999, we made a $27 million advanced company ESOP allocation for the period December 1999 through November 2000 to participants of the Employees Thrift Plan.

During the year, we called the Series B and Series F Convertible Preferred Stock and converted them into Texaco common stock, with future ESOP allocations being made in common stock. Following this conversion, we paid $12 million in dividends. Dividends on the preferred and common ESOP shares used to service debt of the plans are tax deductible to the company.

In 1999, 1998 and 1997, we paid $19 million, $42 million and $44 million in dividends on Series B and Series F stock. The trustee applied the dividends to fund interest payments which amounted to $2 million, $5 million and $7 million for 1999, 1998 and 1997, as well as to reduce principal on the ESOP loans. The Savings Plan ESOP loan was satisfied in January 1999. In November 1998 and December 1997, a portion of the original Thrift Plan ESOP loan was refinanced through a company loan. The refinancing will extend the ESOP for a period of up to six years.

We include in our long-term debt the plans' original ESOP loans guaranteed by Texaco Inc. As the ESOP repays the original and refinanced ESOP loans, we reduce the remaining ESOP-related unearned employee compensation included as a component of stockholders' equity.

Benefit Plan Trust

We have established a benefit plan trust for funding company obligations under some of our benefit plans. At year-end 1999, the trust contained 9.2 million shares of treasury stock. We intend to continue to pay our obligations under our benefit plans. The trust will use the shares, proceeds from the sale of such shares and dividends on such shares to pay benefits only to the extent that we do not pay such benefits. The trustee will vote the shares held in the trust as instructed by the trust's beneficiaries. The shares held by the trust are not considered outstanding for earnings per share purposes until distributed or sold by the trust in payment of benefit obligations.

Termination Benefits

In the fourth quarter of 1998, we announced we were restructuring several of our operations. The principal units affected were our worldwide upstream; our international downstream, principally our marketing operations in the United Kingdom and Brazil and our refining operations in Panama; our global gas marketing operations, now included as part of our global gas and power segment; and our corporate center. In 1998, we recorded an after-tax charge of $80 million for employee separations, curtailment costs and special termination benefits associated with our restructuring. The charge was comprised of $88 million of operating expenses, $27 million of selling, general and administrative expenses and $35 million in related income tax benefits. We initially estimated that over 1,400 employee reductions worldwide would occur. In the second quarter of 1999, we expanded the employee separation programs and recorded an after-tax charge of $31 million to cover an additional 1,100 employee reductions. The charge was comprised of $36 million of operating expenses, $12 million of selling, general and administrative expenses and $17 million in related income tax benefits. The restructuring programs were completed during 1999. Through December 31, 1999, under these programs we have separated 2,462 employees and paid $124 million of benefits and transferred $12 million to long-term obligations. The remaining benefits of $27 million will be paid in future periods in accordance with plan provisions.

We recorded an after-tax charge of $56 million in the fourth quarter of 1996 to cover the costs of employee separations, including employees of affiliates, as a result of a company-wide realignment and consolidation of our operations. We recorded an adjustment of $6 million in the fourth quarter of 1997 to increase the accrual from the previous amount. The program was completed by the end of 1997 with the reduction of approximately 920 employees. During 1999 we paid $4 million of benefits under this program. The remaining benefits of $8 million will be paid in future periods in accordance with plan provisions.

Pension Plans

We sponsor pension plans that cover the majority of our employees. Generally, these plans provide defined pension benefits based on years of service and final average pay. Pension plan assets are principally invested in equity and fixed income securities and deposits with insurance companies.

Effective October 1, 1999, the Retirement Plan was changed to provide improved early retirement benefits and/or lump sum options availability, for vested employees who terminate before age 55. Pensions are now based on a new point system (age plus service) which pays graduated pensions to terminating members.

Total worldwide expense for all employee pension plans of Texaco, including pension supplementations and smaller non-U.S.

plans, was $41 million in 1999 and $92 million in 1998 and 1997.

The following data are provided for principal U.S. and non-U.S. plans:

| | Pension Benefits | | | | Other U.S. Benefits | |
| | 1999 | | 1998 | | | |
(Millions of dollars) As of December 31	U.S.	Int'l	U.S.	Int'l	1999	1998
Changes in Benefit (Obligations)						
Benefit (obligations) at January 1	$ (1,884)	$ (979)	$ (1,769)	$ (835)	$ (773)	$ (756)
Service cost	(46)	(25)	(60)	(21)	(6)	(9)
Interest cost	(113)	(82)	(117)	(86)	(49)	(50)
Amendments	(29)	(23)	—	(3)	12	—
Actuarial gain/(loss)	(16)	(26)	(191)	(117)	59	8
Employee contributions	(3)	(1)	(4)	(3)	(14)	(12)
Benefits paid	63	62	64	70	66	56
Curtailments/settlements	364	(2)	193	—	12	(7)
Special termination benefits	—	—	(12)	—	—	(3)
Currency adjustments	—	96	—	16	—	—
Acquisitions/joint ventures	—	—	12	—	60	—
Benefit (obligations) at December 31	$ (1,664)	$ (980)	$ (1,884)	$ (979)	$ (633)	$ (773)
Changes in Plan Assets						
Fair value of plan assets at January 1	$ 1,826	$ 1,028	$ 1,702	$ 900	$ —	$ —
Actual return on plan assets	236	151	293	142	—	—
Company contributions	15	26	90	32	52	44
Employee contributions	3	1	4	3	14	12
Expenses	(7)	—	(6)	(2)	—	—
Benefits paid	(63)	(62)	(64)	(70)	(66)	(56)
Currency adjustments	—	(74)	—	23	—	—
Curtailments/settlements	(364)	—	(176)	—	—	—
Acquisitions/joint ventures	—	—	(17)	—	—	—
Fair value of plan assets at December 31	$ 1,646	$ 1,070	$ 1,826	$ 1,028	$ —	$ —
Funded Status of the Plans						
Obligation (greater than) less than assets	$ (18)	$ 90	$ (58)	$ 49	$ (633)	$ (773)
Unrecognized net transition asset	(7)	(1)	(14)	(14)	—	—
Unrecognized prior service cost	85	63	68	52	(7)	4
Unrecognized actuarial (gain)/loss	(161)	(17)	(93)	4	(143)	(92)
Net (liability)/asset recorded in Texaco's Consolidated Balance Sheet	$ (101)	$ 135	$ (97)	$ 91	$ (783)	$ (861)
Net (liability)/asset recorded in Texaco's Consolidated Balance Sheet consists of:						
Prepaid benefit asset	$ 84	$ 373	$ 72	$ 346	$ —	$ —
Accrued benefit liability	(231)	(246)	(215)	(268)	(783)	(861)
Intangible asset	23	8	23	12	—	—
Other accumulated non-owner equity	23	—	23	1	—	—
Net (liability)/asset recorded in Texaco's Consolidated Balance Sheet	$ (101)	$ 135	$ (97)	$ 91	$ (783)	$ (861)
Assumptions as of December 31						
Discount rate	8.0%	8.1%	6.75%	9.5%	8.0%	6.75%
Expected return on plan assets	10.0%	8.8%	10.0%	8.4%	—	—
Rate of compensation increase	4.0%	5.2%	4.0%	6.1%	4.0%	4.0%
Health care cost trend rate	—	—	—	—	4.0%	4.0%

(Millions of dollars) As of December 31	Pension Benefits						Other U.S. Benefits		
	1999		1998		1997		1999	1998	1997
	U.S.	Int'l	U.S.	Int'l	U.S.	Int'l	1999	1998	1997
Components of Net Periodic Benefit Expenses									
Service cost	$ 46	$ 25	$ 60	$ 21	$ 54	$ 17	$ 6	$ 9	$ 6
Interest cost	113	82	117	86	117	85	49	50	49
Expected return on plan assets	(140)	(81)	(136)	(79)	(132)	(66)	—	—	—
Amortization of transition asset	(6)	(12)	(4)	(10)	(5)	(8)	—	—	—
Amortization of prior service cost	11	13	11	7	10	6	—	—	—
Amortization of (gain)/loss	4	(2)	6	(2)	3	—	(1)	(4)	(5)
Curtailments/settlements	(15)	2	6	—	—	—	(12)	1	—
Special termination charges	—	—	8	—	—	—	—	2	—
Net periodic benefit expenses	$ 13	$ 27	$ 68	$ 23	$ 47	$ 34	$ 42	$ 58	$ 50

For pension plans with accumulated obligations in excess of plan assets, the projected benefit obligation and the accumulated benefit obligation were $410 million and $379 million as of December 31, 1999, and $414 million and $383 million as of December 31, 1998. The fair value of plan assets for both years was $0.

In connection with the formation of Equilon, effective January 1, 1998, we transferred to Equilon pension benefit obligations of $12 million and related plan assets of $17 million.

Other U.S. Benefits

We sponsor postretirement plans in the U.S. that provide health care and life insurance for retirees and eligible dependents. Effective October 1, 1999, we introduced an age and service point schedule for eligible participants. Our U.S. health insurance obligation is our fixed dollar contribution. The plans are unfunded, and the costs are shared by us and our employees and retirees. Certain of the company's non-U.S. subsidiaries have postretirement benefit plans, the cost of which is not significant to the company.

As a result of the transfer of employees to the downstream alliances effective April 1, 1999, $58 million of postretirement benefit obligations were also transferred.

For measurement purposes, the fixed dollar contribution is expected to increase by 4% per annum for all future years. A change in our fixed dollar contribution has a significant effect on the amounts we report. A 1% change in our contributions would have the following effects:

(Millions of dollars)	1-Percentage Point Increase	1-Percentage Point Decrease
Effect on annual total of service and interest cost components	$ 4	$ (4)
Effect on postretirement benefit obligation	$ 38	$ (34)

NOTE 12 STOCK INCENTIVE PLAN

Under our Stock Incentive Plan, stock options, restricted stock and other incentive award forms may be granted to executives, directors and key employees to provide motivation to enhance the company's success and increase shareholder value. The maximum number of shares that may be awarded as stock options or restricted stock under the plan is 1% of the common stock outstanding on December 31 of the previous year. The following table summarizes the number of shares at December 31, 1999, 1998 and 1997 available for awards during the subsequent year:

(Shares) As of December 31	1999	1998	1997
To all participants	15,646,336	12,677,325	9,607,506
To those participants not officers or directors	2,020,621	1,967,715	2,362,273
Total	17,666,957	14,645,040	11,969,779

Restricted shares granted under the plan contain a performance element which must be satisfied in order for all or a specified portion of the shares to vest. Restricted performance shares awarded in each year under the plan were as follows:

	1999	1998	1997
Shares	278,402	334,798	281,174
Weighted average fair value	$ 62.78	$ 61.59	$ 55.09

Stock options granted under the plan extend for 10 years from the date of grant and vest over a two year period at a rate of 50% in the first year and 50% in the second year. The exercise price cannot be less than the fair market value of the underlying shares of common stock on the date of the grant. The plan provides for restored options. This feature enables a participant who exercises a stock option by exchanging previously acquired common stock or who has shares withheld by us to satisfy tax withholding obligations, to receive new options equal to the number of shares exchanged or withheld. The restored options are fully exercisable six months after the date of grant and the exercise price is the fair market value of the common stock on the day the restored option is granted.

We apply APB Opinion 25 in accounting for our stock-based compensation programs. Stock-based compensation expense recognized in connection with the plan was $19 million in 1999, $17 million in 1998 and $18 million in 1997. Had we accounted for our plan using the accounting method recommended by SFAS 123, net income and earnings per share would have been the pro forma amounts below:

	1999	1998	1997
Net income *(Millions of dollars)*			
As reported	$ 1,177	$ 578	$ 2,664
Pro forma	$ 1,107	$ 524	$ 2,621
Earnings per share *(dollars)*			
Basic — as reported	$ 2.14	$ .99	$ 4.99
— pro forma	$ 2.01	$ .89	$ 4.91
Diluted — as reported	$ 2.14	$ .99	$ 4.87
— pro forma	$ 2.01	$ .89	$ 4.79

We used the Black-Scholes model with the following assumptions to estimate the fair market value of options at date of grant:

	1999	1998	1997
Expected life	2 yrs.	2 yrs.	2 yrs.
Interest rate	5.4%	5.4%	6.0%
Volatility	29.1%	22.5%	18.6%
Dividend yield	3.0%	3.0%	3.0%

Option award activity during 1999, 1998 and 1997 is summarized in the following table:

	1999		1998		1997	
(Stock options)	Shares	Weighted Average Exercise Price	Shares	Weighted Average Exercise Price	Shares	Weighted Average Exercise Price
Outstanding January 1	11,616,049	$ 59.48	10,071,307	$ 53.31	9,436,406	$ 42.73
Granted	2,015,741	62.78	2,388,593	61.56	2,084,902	55.06
Exercised	(8,163,386)	59.24	(7,732,978)	53.18	(9,533,861)	44.86
Restored	7,448,018	64.55	6,889,941	60.77	8,103,502	55.32
Canceled	(819,284)	64.48	(814)	78.08	(19,642)	51.43
Outstanding December 31	12,097,138	62.98	11,616,049	59.48	10,071,307	53.31
Exercisable December 31	6,358,652	$ 62.57	5,945,445	$ 58.93	3,197,262	$ 51.21
Weighted average fair value of options granted during the year		$ 11.21		$ 8.48		$ 6.92

The following table summarizes information on stock options outstanding at December 31, 1999:

		Options Outstanding			Options Exercisable	
Exercisable Price Range (per share)	Shares	Weighted Average Remaining Life	Weighted Average Exercise Price		Shares	Weighted Average Exercise Price
$ 25.36 – 31.84	20,323	2.4 yrs.	$ 29.32		20,323	$ 29.32
$ 32.47 – 78.08	12,076,815	6.3 yrs.	$ 63.04		6,338,329	$ 62.67
$ 25.36 – 78.08	12,097,138	6.3 yrs.	$ 62.98		6,358,652	$ 62.57

NOTE 13 PREFERRED STOCK AND RIGHTS

Series B ESOP Convertible Preferred Stock

At December 31, 1998, the outstanding shares of Series B ESOP Convertible Preferred Stock (Series B) were held by an ESOP. Dividends on each share of Series B were cumulative and payable semiannually at the rate of $57 per annum.

On June 30, 1999, after we called the Series B for redemption, each share of Series B was converted into 25.736 shares, or 15.1 million shares in total, of common stock.

Series D Junior Participating Preferred Stock and Rights

In 1989, we declared a dividend distribution of one Right for each outstanding share of common stock. This was adjusted to one-half Right when we declared a two-for-one stock split in 1997. In 1998, our shareholders approved the extension of the Rights until May 1, 2004. Unless we redeem the Rights, the Rights will be exercisable only after a person(s) acquires, obtains the right to acquire or commences a tender offer that would result in that person(s) acquiring 20% or more of the outstanding common stock other than pursuant to a Qualifying Offer. A Qualifying Offer is an all-cash, fully financed tender offer for all outstanding shares of common stock which remains open for 45 days, which results in the acquiror owning a majority of the company's voting stock, and in which the acquiror agrees to purchase for cash all remaining shares of common stock. The Rights entitle holders to purchase from the company units of Series D Junior Participating Preferred Stock (Series D). In general, each Right entitles the holder to acquire shares of Series D, or in certain cases common stock, property or other securities, at a formula value equal to two times the exercise price of the Right.

We can redeem the Rights at one cent per Right at any time prior to 10 days after the Rights become exercisable. Until a Right becomes exercisable, the holder has no additional voting or dividend rights and it will not have any dilutive effect on the company's earnings. We have reserved and designated 3 million shares as Series D for issuance upon exercise of the Rights. At December 31, 1999, the Rights are not exercisable.

Series F ESOP Convertible Preferred Stock

At December 31, 1998, the outstanding shares of Series F ESOP Convertible Preferred Stock (Series F) were held by an ESOP. Dividends on each share of Series F were cumulative and payable semiannually at the rate of $64.53 per annum.

On February 16, 1999, after we called the Series F for redemption, each share of Series F was converted into 20 shares, or 1.1 million shares in total, of common stock.

Market Auction Preferred Shares

There are 1,200 shares of cumulative variable rate preferred stock, called Market Auction Preferred Shares (MAPS) outstanding. The MAPS are grouped into four series (300 shares each of Series G, H, I and J) of $75 million each, with an aggregate value of $300 million.

The dividend rates for each series are determined by Dutch auctions conducted at seven-week or longer intervals.

During 1999, the annual dividend rate for the MAPS ranged between 3.59% and 4.36% and dividends totaled $9 million ($7,713, $7,772, $7,989 and $7,935 per share for Series G, H, I and J).

For 1998, the annual dividend rate for the MAPS ranged between 3.96% and 4.50% and dividends totaled $13 million ($11,280, $11,296, $11,227 and $11,218 per share for Series G, H, I and J). For 1997, the annual dividend rate for the MAPS ranged between 3.88% and 4.29% and dividends totaled $11 million ($9,689, $9,650, $9,675 and $9,774 per share for Series G, H, I and J).

We may redeem the MAPS, in whole or in part, at any time at a liquidation preference of $250,000 per share, plus premium, if any, and accrued and unpaid dividends thereon.

The MAPS are non-voting, except under limited circumstances.

NOTE 14 FINANCIAL INSTRUMENTS

We utilize various types of financial instruments in conducting our business. Financial instruments encompass assets and liabilities included in the balance sheet, as well as derivatives which are principally off-balance sheet.

Derivatives are contracts whose value is derived from changes in an underlying commodity price, interest rate or other item. We use derivatives to reduce our exposure to changes in foreign exchange rates, interest rates and crude oil, petroleum products and natural gas prices. Our written policies restrict our use of derivatives to protecting existing positions and committed or anticipated transactions. On a limited basis, we may use commodity-based derivatives to establish a position in anticipation of future movements in prices or margins. Derivative transactions expose us to counterparty credit risk. We place contracts only with parties whose credit-worthiness has been pre-determined under credit policies and limit the dollar exposure to any counterparty. Therefore, risk of counterparty non-performance and exposure to concentrations of credit risk are limited.

CASH AND CASH EQUIVALENTS Fair value approximates cost as reflected in the Consolidated Balance Sheet at December 31, 1999 and 1998 because of the short-term maturities of these instruments. Cash equivalents are classified as held-to-maturity. The amortized cost of cash equivalents at December 31, 1999 includes $67 million of time deposits and $165 million of commercial paper. Comparable amounts at year-end 1998 were $72 million and $109 million.

SHORT-TERM AND LONG-TERM INVESTMENTS Fair value is primarily based on quoted market prices and valuation statements obtained from major financial institutions. At December 31, 1999, our available-for-sale securities had an estimated fair value of $167 million, including gross unrealized gains of $11 million and losses of $6 million. At December 31, 1998, our available-for-sale securities had an estimated fair value of $492 million, including gross unrealized gains of $40 million and losses of $8 million. The available-for-sale securities consist primarily of debt securities issued by U.S. and foreign governments and corporations. The majority of these investments mature within five years.

Proceeds from sales of available-for-sale securities were $750 million in 1999, $1,011 million in 1998 and $1,040 million in 1997. These sales resulted in gross realized gains of $45 million in 1999, $53 million in 1998 and $48 million in 1997, and gross realized losses of $13 million, $22 million and $19 million.

The estimated fair value of other long-term investments qualifying as financial instruments but not included above, for which it is practicable to estimate fair value, approximated the December 31, 1999 and 1998 carrying values of $465 million and $331 million.

SHORT-TERM DEBT, LONG-TERM DEBT AND RELATED DERIVATIVES Refer to Note 9 for additional information about debt and related derivatives outstanding at December 31, 1999 and 1998.

FORWARD EXCHANGE AND OPTION CONTRACTS As an international company, we are exposed to currency exchange risk. To hedge against adverse changes in foreign currency exchange rates, we will enter into forward and option contracts to buy and sell foreign currencies. Shown below in U.S. dollars are the notional amounts of outstanding forward exchange contracts to buy and sell foreign currencies.

(Millions of dollars)	Buy	Sell
Australian dollars	$ 251	$ 37
British pounds	1,161	145
Danish kroner	245	39
Euro	264	40
New Zealand dollars	145	—
Other European currencies	56	11
Total at December 31, 1999	$ 2,122	$ 272
Total at December 31, 1998	$ 2,953	$ 883

Market risk exposure on these contracts is essentially limited to currency rate movements. At year-end 1999, there were $10 million of unrealized gains and $30 million of unrealized losses related to these contracts. At year-end 1998, there were $8 million of unrealized gains and $19 million of unrealized losses.

We use forward exchange contracts to buy foreign currencies primarily to hedge the net monetary liability position of our European, Australian and New Zealand operations and to hedge portions of significant foreign currency capital expenditures and lease commitments. These contracts generally have terms of 60 days or less. Contracts that hedge foreign currency monetary positions are marked-to-market monthly. Any resultant gains and losses are included in income currently as other costs. At year-end 1999 and 1998, hedges of foreign currency commitments principally involved capital projects requiring expenditure of British pounds and Danish kroner. The percentages of planned capital expenditures hedged at year-end were: British pounds – 90% in 1999 and 54% in 1998; Danish kroner – 94% in 1999 and 40% in 1998. Realized gains and losses on hedges of foreign currency commitments are initially recorded to deferred charges. Subsequently, the amounts are applied to the capitalized project cost on a percentage-of-completion basis, and are then amortized over the lives of the applicable projects. At year-end 1999 and 1998, net hedging gains of $17 million and $50 million, respectively, had yet to be amortized.

We sell foreign currencies under a separately managed program to hedge the value of our investment portfolio denominated in foreign currencies. Our strategy is to hedge the full value of this portion of our investment portfolio and to close out forward contracts upon the sale or maturity of the corresponding investments. We value these contracts at market based on the foreign exchange rates in effect on the balance sheet dates. We record changes in the value of these contracts as part of the carrying amount of the related investments. We record related gains and losses, net of applicable income taxes, to stockholders' equity until the underlying investments are sold or mature.

PREFERRED SHARES OF SUBSIDIARIES Refer to Note 15 regarding derivatives related to subsidiary preferred shares.

PETROLEUM AND NATURAL GAS HEDGING We hedge a portion of the market risks associated with our crude oil, natural gas and petroleum product purchases, sales and exchange activities to reduce price exposure. All hedge transactions are subject to the company's corporate risk management policy which sets out dollar, volumetric and term limits, as well as to management approvals as set forth in our delegations of authorities.

We use established petroleum futures exchanges, as well as "over-the-counter" hedge instruments, including futures, options, swaps and other derivative products. In carrying out our hedging programs, we analyze our major commodity streams for fixed cost, fixed revenue and margin exposure to market price changes. Based on this corporate risk profile, forecasted trends and overall business objectives, we determine an appropriate strategy for risk reduction.

Hedge positions are marked-to-market for valuation purposes. Gains and losses on hedge transactions, which offset losses and gains on the underlying "cash market" transactions, are recorded to deferred income or charges until the hedged transaction is closed, or until the anticipated future purchases, sales or production occur. At that time, any gain or loss on the hedging contract is recorded to operating revenues as an increase or decrease in margins, or to inventory, as appropriate. Derivative transactions not designated as hedging a specific position or transaction are adjusted to market at each balance sheet date. Gains and losses are included in operating income.

At December 31, 1999 and 1998, there were open derivative commodity contracts required to be settled in cash, consisting mostly of basis swaps related to location differences in prices. Notional contract amounts, excluding unrealized gains and losses, were $6,604 million and $4,397 million at year-end 1999 and 1998. These amounts principally represent future values of contract volumes over the remaining duration of outstanding swap contracts at the respective dates. These contracts hedge a small fraction of our business activities, generally for the next twelve months. Unrealized gains and losses on contracts outstanding at year-end 1999 were $195 million and $132 million, respectively. At year-end 1998, unrealized gains and losses were $161 million and $140 million, respectively.

NOTE 15 OTHER FINANCIAL INFORMATION, COMMITMENTS AND CONTINGENCIES

Environmental Liabilities

Texaco Inc. and subsidiary companies have financial liabilities relating to environmental remediation programs which we believe are sufficient for known requirements. At December 31, 1999, the balance sheet includes liabilities of $246 million for future environmental remediation costs. Also, we have accrued $803 million for the future cost of restoring and abandoning existing oil and gas properties.

We have accrued for our probable environmental remediation liabilities to the extent reasonably measurable. We based our accruals for these obligations on technical evaluations of the currently available facts, interpretation of the regulations and our experience with similar sites. Additional accrual requirements for existing and new remediation sites may be necessary in the future when more facts are known. The potential also exists for further legislation which may provide limitations on liability. It is not possible to project the overall costs or a range of costs for environmental items beyond that disclosed above. This is due to uncertainty surrounding future developments, both in relation to remediation exposure and to regulatory initiatives. We believe that such future costs will not be material to our financial position or to our operating results over any reasonable period of time.

Preferred Shares of Subsidiaries

Minority holders own $602 million of preferred shares of our subsidiary companies, which is reflected as minority interest in subsidiary companies in the Consolidated Balance Sheet.

MVP Production Inc., a subsidiary, has variable rate cumulative preferred shares of $75 million owned by one minority holder. The shares have voting rights and are redeemable in 2003. Dividends on these shares were $4 million in 1999, 1998 and 1997.

Texaco Capital LLC, another subsidiary, has three classes of preferred shares, all held by minority holders. The first class is 14 million shares totaling $350 million of Cumulative Guaranteed Monthly Income Preferred Shares, Series A (Series A). The second class is 4.5 million shares totaling $112 million of Cumulative Adjustable Rate Monthly Income Preferred Shares, Series B (Series B).

The third class, issued in Canadian dollars, is 3.6 million shares totaling $65 million of Deferred Preferred Shares, Series C (Series C). Texaco Capital LLC's sole assets are notes receivable from Texaco Inc. The payment of dividends and payments on liquidation or redemption with respect to Series A, Series B and Series C are guaranteed by Texaco Inc.

The fixed dividend rate for Series A is 6-7/8% per annum. The annual dividend rate for Series B averaged 5.0% for 1999, 5.1% for 1998 and 5.9% for 1997. The dividend rate on Series B is reset quarterly per contractual formula. Dividends on Series A and Series B are paid monthly. Dividends on Series A for 1999, 1998 and 1997 totaled $24 million for each year. Annual dividends on Series B totaled $6 million for both 1999 and 1998 and $7 million for 1997.

Series A and Series B are redeemable under certain circumstances at the option of Texaco Capital LLC (with Texaco Inc.'s consent) in whole or in part at $25 per share plus accrued and unpaid dividends to the date fixed for redemption.

Dividends on Series C at a rate of 7.17% per annum, compounded annually, will be paid at the redemption date of February 28, 2005, unless earlier redemption occurs. Early redemption may result upon the occurrence of certain specific events.

We have entered into an interest rate and currency swap related to Series C preferred shares. The swap matures in the year 2005. Over the life of the interest rate swap component of the contract, we will make LIBOR-based floating rate interest payments based on a notional principal amount of $65 million. Canadian dollar interest will accrue to us at a fixed rate applied to the accreted notional principal amount, which was Cdn. $87 million at the inception of the swap.

The currency swap component of the transaction calls for us to exchange at contract maturity date $65 million for Cdn. $170 million, representing Cdn. $87 million plus accrued interest. The carrying amount of this contract represents the Canadian dollar accrued interest receivable by us. At year-end 1999 and 1998, the carrying amounts of this swap, which approximated fair value, were $20 million and $16 million, respectively.

Series A, Series B and Series C preferred shares are non-voting, except under limited circumstances.

The above preferred stock issues currently require annual dividend payments of approximately $34 million. We are required to redeem $75 million of this preferred stock in 2003, $65 million (plus accreted dividends of $59 million) in 2005, $112 million in 2024 and $350 million in 2043. We have the ability to extend the required redemption dates for the $112 million and $350 million of preferred stock beyond 2024 and 2043.

Pending Award

In July 1999, the Governing Council of the United Nations Compensation Commission (UNCC) approved an award to Saudi Arabian Texaco Inc. (SAT), a wholly-owned subsidiary of Texaco Inc., of about $505 million, plus unspecified interest, for damages sustained as a result of Iraq's invasion of Kuwait in 1990. Payments to SAT are subject to income tax in Saudi Arabia at an applicable tax rate of 85%. SAT is party to a concession agreement with the Kingdom of Saudi Arabia covering the Partitioned Neutral Zone in Southern Kuwait and Northern Saudi Arabia.

The UNCC funds compensation awards by retaining 30% of Iraqi oil sales revenue under an agreement with Iraq. We do not know when we will receive this award since the timing of payments by the UNCC depends on several factors, including the total amount of all compensation awards, the ability of Iraq to produce and sell oil, the price of Iraqi oil and the duration of U.N. trade sanctions on Iraq. This award will be recognized in income when collection is assured.

Financial Guarantees

We have guaranteed the payment of certain debt, lease commitments and other obligations of third parties and affiliate companies. These guarantees totaled $716 million and $797 million at December 31, 1999 and 1998. The year-end 1999 and 1998 amounts include $336 million and $387 million of operating lease commitments of Equilon, our affiliate.

Exposure to credit risk in the event of non-payment by the obligors is represented by the contractual amount of these instruments. No loss is anticipated under these guarantees.

On December 22, 1999, our 50% owned affiliate, Caltex Corporation (Caltex), settled an excise tax claim with the United States Internal Revenue Service (IRS) for $65 million. The IRS claim related to sales of crude oil by Caltex to Japanese customers beginning in 1980. The original claim was for $292 million in excise taxes, $140 million in penalties and $1.6 billion in interest. In order to litigate this claim, Caltex had arranged for a letter of credit for $2.5 billion. Pursuant to an agreement with the IRS in May 1999, the letter of credit was reduced to $200 million. The letter of credit, which Texaco and its 50% partner, Chevron Corporation, had severally guaranteed, was terminated upon settlement. Resolution of this matter had no significant impact on reported results.

Throughput Agreements

Texaco Inc. and certain of its subsidiary companies previously entered into certain long-term agreements wherein we committed to ship through affiliated pipeline companies and an offshore oil port sufficient volume of crude oil or petroleum products to enable these affiliated companies to meet a specified portion of their individual debt obligations, or, in lieu thereof, to advance sufficient funds to enable these affiliated companies to meet these obligations. In 1998, we assigned the shipping obligations to Equilon, our affiliate, but Texaco remains responsible for deficiency payments on virtually all of these agreements. Additionally, Texaco has entered into long-term purchase commitments with third parties for take or pay gas transportation. At December 31, 1999 and 1998, our maximum exposure to loss was estimated to be $445 million and $500 million.

However, based on our right of counterclaim against Equilon and unaffiliated third parties in the event of non-performance, our net exposure was estimated to be $173 million and $195 million at December 31, 1999 and 1998.

No significant losses are anticipated as a result of these obligations.

Litigation

Texaco and approximately 50 other oil companies are defendants in 17 purported class actions. The actions are pending in Texas, New Mexico, Oklahoma, Louisiana, Utah, Mississippi and Alabama. The plaintiffs allege that the defendants undervalued oil produced from properties leased from the plaintiffs by establishing artificially low selling prices. They allege that these low selling prices resulted in the defendants underpaying royalties or severance taxes to them. Plaintiffs seek to recover royalty underpayments and interest. In some cases plaintiffs also seek to recover severance taxes and treble and punitive damages. Texaco and 24 other defendants have executed a settlement agreement with most of the plaintiffs that will resolve many of these disputes. The federal court in Texas gave final approval to the settlement in April 1999 and the matter is now pending before the U.S. Fifth Circuit Court of Appeal.

Texaco has reached an agreement with the federal government to resolve similar claims. The claims of various state governments remain unresolved.

It is impossible for us to ascertain the ultimate legal and financial liability with respect to contingencies and commitments. However, we do not anticipate that the aggregate amount of such liability in excess of accrued liabilities will be materially important in relation to our consolidated financial position or results of operations.

Report of Management

We are responsible for preparing Texaco's consolidated financial statements in accordance with generally accepted accounting principles. In doing so, we must use judgment and estimates when the outcome of events and transactions is not certain. Information appearing in other sections of this Annual Report is consistent with the financial statements.

Texaco's financial statements are based on its financial records. We rely on Texaco's internal control system to provide us reasonable assurance these financial records are being accurately and objectively maintained and the company's assets are being protected. The internal control system comprises:

> Corporate Conduct Guidelines requiring all employees to obey all applicable laws, comply with company policies and maintain the highest ethical standards in conducting company business,

> An organizational structure in which responsibilities are defined and divided, and

> Written policies and procedures that cover initiating, reviewing, approving and recording transactions.

We require members of our management team to formally certify each year that the internal controls for their business units are operating effectively.

Texaco's internal auditors review and report on the effectiveness of internal controls during the course of their audits. Arthur Andersen LLP, selected by the Audit Committee and approved by stockholders, independently audits Texaco's financial statements. Arthur Andersen LLP assesses the adequacy and effectiveness of Texaco's internal controls when determining the nature, timing and scope

of their audit. We seriously consider all suggestions for improving Texaco's internal controls that are made by the internal and independent auditors.

The Audit Committee is comprised of six directors who are not employees of Texaco. This Committee reviews and evaluates Texaco's accounting policies and reporting practices, internal auditing, internal controls, security and other matters. The Committee also evaluates the independence and professional competence of Arthur Andersen LLP and reviews the results and scope of their audit. The internal and independent auditors have free access to the Committee to discuss financial reporting and internal control issues.

Peter I. Bijur
Chairman of the Board and Chief Executive Officer

Patrick J. Lynch
Senior Vice President and Chief Financial Officer

George J. Batavick
Comptroller

Report of Independent Public Accountants

To the Stockholders, Texaco Inc.:

We have audited the accompanying consolidated balance sheet of Texaco Inc. (a Delaware corporation) and subsidiary companies as of December 31, 1999 and 1998, and the related statements of consolidated income, cash flows, stockholders' equity and non-owner changes in equity for each of the three years in the period ended December 31, 1999. These financial statements are the responsibility of the company's management. Our responsibility is to express an opinion on these financial statements based on our audits.

We conducted our audits in accordance with auditing standards generally accepted in the United States. Those standards require that we plan and perform the audit to obtain reasonable assurance about whether the financial statements are free of material misstatement. An audit includes examining, on a test basis, evidence supporting the amounts and disclosures in the financial statements. An audit also includes assessing the accounting principles used and significant estimates made by management, as well as evaluating the overall

financial statement presentation. We believe that our audits provide a reasonable basis for our opinion.

In our opinion, the financial statements referred to above present fairly, in all material respects, the financial position of Texaco Inc. and subsidiary companies as of December 31, 1999 and 1998, and the results of their operations and their cash flows for each of the three years in the period ended December 31, 1999 in conformity with accounting principles generally accepted in the United States.

Arthur Andersen LLP
February 24, 2000
New York, N.Y.

297

Supplemental Oil and Gas Information

The following pages provide information required by Statement of Financial Accounting Standards No. 69, Disclosures about Oil and Gas Producing Activities.

Table I – Net Proved Reserves

The reserve quantities include only those quantities that are recoverable based upon reasonable estimates from sound geological and engineering principles. As additional information becomes available, these estimates may be revised. Also, we have a large inventory of potential hydrocarbon resources that we expect will increase our reserve base as future investments are made in exploration and development programs.

> Proved *developed* reserves are reserves that we expect to be recovered through existing wells with existing equipment and operating methods.

> Proved *undeveloped* reserves are reserves that we expect to be recovered from new wells on undrilled acreage, or from existing wells where a relatively major expenditure is required for completion of development.

Table I

**Net Proved Reserves of
Crude Oil and Natural Gas Liquids**
(Millions of Barrels)

Net Proved Reserves of Natural Gas
(Billions of Cubic Feet)

	Consolidated Subsidiaries					Equity Affiliate – Other East	World-wide	Consolidated Subsidiaries					Equity Affiliate – Other East	World-wide
	United States	Other West	Europe	Other East	Total			United States	Other West	Europe	Other East	Total		
Developed reserves	1,100	50	165	418	1,733	354	2,087	3,360	893	452	96	4,801	136	4,937
Undeveloped reserves	222	6	232	48	508	109	617	368	138	509	4	1,019	17	1,036
As of December 31, 1996	1,322	56	397	466	2,241	463	2,704	3,728	1,031	961	100	5,820	153	5,973
Discoveries & extensions	107	13	34	61	215	4	219	692	26	92	346	1,156	2	1,158
Improved recovery	15	—	65	—	80	18	98	7	—	22	—	29	5	34
Revisions	55	3	11	100	169	22	191	228	75	41	(22)	322	19	341
Net purchases (sales)	413	(2)	(31)	(8)	372	—	372	10	(118)	(7)	(310)	(425)	—	(425)
Production	(145)	(5)	(45)	(66)	(261)	(56)	(317)	(643)	(96)	(81)	(2)	(822)	(17)	(839)
Total changes	445	9	34	87	575	(12)	563	294	(113)	67	12	260	9	269
Developed reserves	1,374	54	210	463	2,101	354	2,455	3,379	792	576	110	4,857	145	5,002
Undeveloped reserves	393	11	221	90	715	97	812	643	126	452	2	1,223	17	1,240
As of December 31, 1997*	1,767	65	431	553	2,816	451	3,267	4,022	918	1,028	112	6,080	162	6,242
Discoveries & extensions	70	2	8	32	112	1	113	599	6	47	98	750	1	751
Improved recovery	136	—	16	3	155	156	311	4	—	7	—	11	3	14
Revisions	46	(15)	22	55	108	137	245	152	(12)	(6)	34	168	10	178
Net purchases (sales)	(38)	—	—	26	(12)	—	(12)	(39)	—	—	250	211	—	211
Production	(157)	(4)	(58)	(71)	(290)	(61)	(351)	(633)	(92)	(112)	(17)	(854)	(25)	(879)
Total changes	57	(17)	(12)	45	73	233	306	83	(98)	(64)	365	286	(11)	275
Developed reserves	1,415	39	246	490	2,190	456	2,646	3,345	688	615	374	5,022	135	5,157
Undeveloped reserves	409	9	173	108	699	228	927	760	132	349	103	1,344	16	1,360
As of December 31, 1998*	1,824	48	419	598	2,889	684	3,573	4,105	820	964	477	6,366	151	6,517
Discoveries & extensions	**66**	**11**	**23**	**23**	**123**	**2**	**125**	**442**	**7**	**93**	**42**	**584**	**5**	**589**
Improved recovery	**34**	**—**	**2**	**29**	**65**	**52**	**117**	**4**	**—**	**2**	**235**	**241**	**1**	**242**
Revisions	**11**	**—**	**36**	**72**	**119**	**(132)**	**(13)**	**285**	**193**	**7**	**427**	**912**	**3**	**915**
Net purchases (sales)	**(9)**	**—**	**—**	**23**	**14**	**—**	**14**	**(81)**	**—**	**—**	**712**	**631**	**—**	**631**
Production	**(144)**	**(4)**	**(53)**	**(75)**	**(276)**	**(60)**	**(336)**	**(550)**	**(79)**	**(104)**	**(27)**	**(760)**	**(26)**	**(786)**
Total changes	**(42)**	**7**	**8**	**72**	**45**	**(138)**	**(93)**	**100**	**121**	**(2)**	**1,389**	**1,608**	**(17)**	**1,591**
Developed reserves	**1,361**	**39**	**261**	**545**	**2,206**	**316**	**2,522**	**3,388**	**865**	**557**	**787**	**5,597**	**131**	**5,728**
Undeveloped reserves	**421**	**16**	**166**	**125**	**728**	**230**	**958**	**817**	**76**	**405**	**1,079**	**2,377**	**3**	**2,380**
As of December 31, 1999*	**1,782**	**55**	**427**	**670**	**2,934**	**546**	**3,480**	**4,205**	**941**[a]	**962**	**1,866**	**7,974**[a]	**134**	**8,108**[a]
*Includes net proved NGL reserves														
As of December 31, 1997	246	—	71	—	317	4	321							
As of December 31, 1998	250	—	68	22	340	6	346							
As of December 31, 1999	**250**	**—**	**74**	**134**	**458**	**1**	**459**							

(a) Additionally, there is approximately 489 BCF of natural gas in Other West which will be available from production during the period 2005-2016 under a long-term purchase associated with a service agreement.

The following chart summarizes our experience in finding new quantities of oil and gas to replace our production. Our reserve replacement performance is calculated by dividing our reserve additions by our production. Our additions relate to new discoveries, existing reserve extensions, improved recoveries and revisions to previous reserve estimates. The chart excludes oil and gas quantities from purchases and sales.

	Worldwide	United States	International
Year 1999	111%	99%	124%
Year 1998	166%	144%	191%
Year 1997	167%	132%	212%
3-year average	148%	126%	174%
5-year average	138%	115%	166%

Table II – Standardized Measure

The standardized measure provides a common benchmark among those companies that have exploration and producing activities. This measure may not necessarily match our view of the future cash flows from our proved reserves.

The standardized measure is calculated at a 10% discount. Future revenues are based on year-end prices for oil and gas. Future production and development costs are based on current year costs. Extensive judgment is used to estimate the timing of production and future costs over the remaining life of the reserves. Future income taxes are calculated using each country's statutory tax rate.

Our inventory of potential hydrocarbon resources, which may become proved in the future, are excluded. This could significantly impact our standardized measure in the future.

Table II – Standardized Measure of Discounted Future Net Cash Flows

(Millions of dollars)	United States	Other West	Europe	Other East	Total	Equity Affiliate – Other East	Worldwide
As of December 31, 1999							
Future cash inflows from sale of oil & gas, and service fee revenue	$ 45,281	$ 2,668	$ 11,875	$ 16,890	$ 76,714	$ 7,646	$ 84,360
Future production costs	(10,956)	(913)	(2,264)	(2,946)	(17,079)	(2,254)	(19,333)
Future development costs	(3,853)	(239)	(1,749)	(1,956)	(7,797)	(767)	(8,564)
Future income tax expense	(8,304)	(758)	(2,428)	(7,665)	(19,155)	(2,340)	(21,495)
Net future cash flows before discount	22,168	758	5,434	4,323	32,683	2,285	34,968
10% discount for timing of future cash flows	(10,816)	(327)	(1,985)	(2,243)	(15,371)	(887)	(16,258)
Standardized measure of discounted future net cash flows	$ 11,352	$ 431	$ 3,449	$ 2,080	$ 17,312	$ 1,398	$ 18,710
As of December 31, 1998							
Future cash inflows from sale of oil & gas, and service fee revenue	$ 23,147	$ 1,657	$ 6,581	$ 4,816	$ 36,201	$ 4,708	$ 40,909
Future production costs	(10,465)	(605)	(2,574)	(2,551)	(16,195)	(1,992)	(18,187)
Future development costs	(4,055)	(142)	(1,695)	(761)	(6,653)	(803)	(7,456)
Future income tax expense	(2,583)	(419)	(715)	(1,023)	(4,740)	(967)	(5,707)
Net future cash flows before discount	6,044	491	1,597	481	8,613	946	9,559
10% discount for timing of future cash flows	(2,626)	(244)	(644)	(167)	(3,681)	(391)	(4,072)
Standardized measure of discounted future net cash flows	$ 3,418	$ 247	$ 953	$ 314	$ 4,932	$ 555	$ 5,487
As of December 31, 1997							
Future cash inflows from sale of oil & gas, and service fee revenue	$ 34,084	$ 2,305	$ 9,395	$ 7,690	$ 53,474	$ 5,182	$ 58,656
Future production costs	(10,980)	(807)	(2,854)	(2,303)	(16,944)	(1,840)	(18,784)
Future development costs	(4,693)	(132)	(1,809)	(749)	(7,383)	(476)	(7,859)
Future income tax expense	(5,512)	(652)	(898)	(3,445)	(10,507)	(1,519)	(12,026)
Net future cash flows before discount	12,899	714	3,834	1,193	18,640	1,347	19,987
10% discount for timing of future cash flows	(5,361)	(252)	(1,424)	(374)	(7,411)	(519)	(7,930)
Standardized measure of discounted future net cash flows	$ 7,538	$ 462	$ 2,410	$ 819	$ 11,229	$ 828	$ 12,057

Table III – Changes in the Standardized Measure
The annual change in the standardized measure is explained in this table by the major sources of change, discounted at 10%.

> *Sales & transfers, net of production costs* capture the current year's revenues less the associated producing expenses. The net amount reflected here correlates to Table VII for revenues less production costs.

> *Net changes in prices, production & development costs* are computed before the effects of changes in quantities. The beginning-of-the-year production forecast is multiplied by the net annual change in the unit sales price and production cost.

> *Discoveries & extensions* indicate the value of the new reserves at year-end prices, less related costs.

> *Development costs incurred during the period* capture the current year's development costs that are shown in Table V. These costs will reduce the previously estimated future development costs.

> *Accretion of discount* represents 10% of the beginning discounted future net cash flows before income tax effects.

> *Net change in income taxes* is computed as the change in present value of future income taxes.

Table III – Changes in the Standardized Measure

(Millions of dollars)	1999	1998	1997
		Worldwide Including Equity in Affiliate – Other East	
Standardized measure – beginning of year	$ 5,487	$ 12,057	$ 17,966
Sales of minerals-in-place	(352)	(160)	(79)
	5,135	11,897	17,887
Changes in ongoing oil and gas operations:			
Sales and transfers of produced oil and gas, net of production costs during the period	(4,230)	(3,129)	(4,921)
Net changes in prices, production and development costs	21,990	(11,205)	(14,632)
Discoveries and extensions and improved recovery, less related costs	1,821	728	2,681
Development costs incurred during the period	1,598	1,770	1,976
Timing of production and other changes	(517)	(1,170)	(969)
Revisions of previous quantity estimates	301	852	1,476
Purchases of minerals-in-place	895	48	449
Accretion of discount	881	1,916	3,027
Net change in discounted future income taxes	(9,164)	3,780	5,083
Standardized measure – end of year	$ 18,710	$ 5,487	$ 12,057

Table IV – Capitalized Costs
Costs of the following assets are capitalized under the "successful efforts" method of accounting. These costs include the activities of Texaco's upstream operations but exclude the crude oil marketing activities, geothermal and other non-producing activities. As a result, this table will not correlate to information in Note 6 to the financial statements.

> *Proved properties* include mineral properties with proved reserves, development wells and uncompleted development well costs.

> *Unproved properties* include leaseholds under exploration (even where hydrocarbons were found but not in sufficient quantities to be considered proved reserves) and uncompleted exploratory well costs.

> *Support equipment and facilities* include costs for seismic and drilling equipment, construction and grading equipment, repair shops, warehouses and other supporting assets involved in oil and gas producing activities.

> *The accumulated depreciation, depletion and amortization* represents the portion of the assets that have been charged to expense in prior periods. It also includes provisions for future restoration and abandonment activity.

Table IV – Capitalized Costs

(Millions of dollars)	United States	Other West	Europe	Other East	Total	Affiliate – Other East	Worldwide
		Consolidated Subsidiaries				Equity	
As of December 31, 1999							
Proved properties	$ 20,364	$ 304	$ 5,327	$ 2,273	$ 28,268	$ 1,085	$ 29,353
Unproved properties	983	139	50	619	1,791	335	2,126
Support equipment and facilities	441	267	37	529	1,274	975	2,249
Gross capitalized costs	21,788	710	5,414	3,421	31,333	2,395	33,728
Accumulated depreciation, depletion and amortization	(13,855)	(298)	(3,955)	(1,365)	(19,473)	(1,217)	(20,690)
Net capitalized costs	$ 7,933	$ 412	$ 1,459	$ 2,056	$ 11,860	$ 1,178	$ 13,038
As of December 31, 1998							
Proved properties	$ 20,601	$ 515	$ 4,709	$ 1,799	$ 27,624	$ 1,015	$ 28,639
Unproved properties	1,188	53	71	390	1,702	408	2,110
Support equipment and facilities	437	27	37	342	843	768	1,611
Gross capitalized costs	22,226	595	4,817	2,531	30,169	2,191	32,360
Accumulated depreciation, depletion and amortization	(14,140)	(277)	(3,381)	(1,253)	(19,051)	(1,119)	(20,170)
Net capitalized costs	$ 8,086	$ 318	$ 1,436	$ 1,278	$ 11,118	$ 1,072	$ 12,190

Table V – Costs Incurred

This table summarizes how much we spent to explore and develop our existing reserve base, and how much we spent to acquire mineral rights from others (classified as proved or unproved).

> *Exploration costs* include geological and geophysical costs, the cost of carrying and retaining undeveloped properties and exploratory drilling costs.

> *Development costs* include the cost of drilling and equipping development wells and constructing related production facilities for extracting, treating, gathering and storing oil and gas from proved reserves.

> *Exploration and development costs* may be capitalized or expensed, as applicable. Such costs also include administrative expenses and depreciation applicable to support equipment associated with these activities. As a result, the costs incurred will not correlate to *Capital and Exploratory Expenditures*.

On a worldwide basis, in 1999 we spent $4.37 for each BOE we added. Finding and development costs averaged $3.80 for the three-year period 1997-1999 and $3.88 per BOE for the five-year period 1995-1999.

Table V – Costs Incurred

(Millions of dollars)	United States	Other West	Europe	Other East	Total	Affiliate – Other East	Worldwide
		Consolidated Subsidiaries				Equity	
For the year ended December 31, 1999							
Proved property acquisition	$ 4	$ —	$ —	$ 481	$ 485	$ —	$ 485
Unproved property acquisition	39	25	—	27	91	—	91
Exploration	204	92	23	224	543	19	562
Development	698	97	319	301	1,415	183	1,598
Total	$ 945	$ 214	$ 342	$ 1,033	$ 2,534	$ 202	$ 2,736
For the year ended December 31, 1998							
Proved property acquisition	$ 27	$ —	$ —	$ 199	$ 226	$ —	$ 226
Unproved property acquisition	85	1	—	32	118	—	118
Exploration	417	92	65	277	851	19	870
Development	1,073	25	308	204	1,610	160	1,770
Total	$ 1,602	$ 118	$ 373	$ 712	$ 2,805	$ 179	$ 2,984
For the year ended December 31, 1997							
Proved property acquisition	$ 1,099*	$ —	$ —	$ —	$ 1,099	$ —	$ 1,099
Unproved property acquisition	527*	1	—	23	551	—	551
Exploration	480	15	59	234	788	18	806
Development	1,220	62	419	108	1,809	167	1,976
Total	$ 3,326	$ 78	$ 478	$ 365	$ 4,247	$ 185	$ 4,432

*Includes the acquisition of Monterey Resources on a net cost basis of $1,520 million, which is net of deferred income taxes amounting to $469 million and $245 million for the acquired proved and unproved properties, respectively.

Table VI – Unit Prices

Average sales prices are calculated using the gross revenues in Table VII. Average production costs equal producing (lifting) costs, other taxes and the depreciation, depletion and amortization of support equipment and facilities.

	Crude oil and NGL per barrel	Natural gas per thousand cubic feet	Crude oil and NGL per barrel	Natural gas per thousand cubic feet	Crude oil and NGL per barrel	Natural gas per thousand cubic feet		Average production costs (per composite barrel)	
				Average sales prices					
	1999		1998		1997		1999	1998	1997
United States	$ 16.56	$ 2.13	$ 10.14	$ 1.93	$ 16.32	$ 2.32	$ 4.01	$ 4.07	$ 3.94
Other West	14.12	.77	9.65	.92	14.40	1.03	2.87	1.86	2.80
Europe	17.42	1.99	11.73	2.42	18.41	2.42	6.15	5.24	5.58
Other East	15.33	.18	9.61	.38	16.87	1.89	3.45	3.65	4.11
Affiliate – Other East	13.24	—	9.81	—	14.89	—	3.95	2.68	3.76

Table VII – Results of Operations

Results of operations for exploration and production activities consist of all the activities within our upstream operations, except for crude oil marketing activities, geothermal and other non-producing activities. As a result, this table will not correlate to the *Analysis of Income by Operating Segments.*

> *Revenues* are based upon our production that is available for sale and excludes revenues from resale of third party volumes, equity earnings of certain smaller affiliates, trading activity and miscellaneous operating income. Expenses are associated with current year operations, but do not include general overhead and special items.

> *Production costs* consist of costs incurred to operate and maintain wells and related equipment and facilities. These costs also include taxes other than income taxes and administrative expenses.

> *Exploration costs* include dry hole, leasehold impairment, geological and geophysical expenses, the cost of retaining undeveloped leaseholds and administrative expenses. Also included are taxes other than income taxes.

> *Depreciation, depletion and amortization* includes the amount for support equipment and facilities.

> *Estimated income taxes* are computed by adjusting each country's income before income taxes for permanent differences related to the oil and gas producing activities, then multiplying the result by the country's statutory tax rate and adjusting for applicable tax credits.

Table VII – Results of Operations

(Millions of dollars)	Consolidated Subsidiaries					Equity Affiliate – Other East	Worldwide
	United States	Other West	Europe	Other East	Total		
For the year ended December 31, 1999							
Gross revenues from:							
Sales and transfers, including affiliate sales	$ 2,890	$ —	$ 617	$ 935	$ 4,442	$ 592	$ 5,034
Sales to unaffiliated entities	230	116	498	202	1,046	24	1,070
Production costs	(943)	(39)	(435)	(252)	(1,669)	(205)	(1,874)
Exploration costs	(243)	(97)	(21)	(154)	(515)	(17)	(532)
Depreciation, depletion and amortization	(794)	(22)	(336)	(134)	(1,286)	(109)	(1,395)
Other expenses	(92)	(15)	(1)	(53)	(161)	(3)	(164)
Results before estimated income taxes	1,048	(57)	322	544	1,857	282	2,139
Estimated income taxes	(312)	(8)	(114)	(457)	(891)	(143)	(1,034)
Net results	$ 736	$ (65)	$ 208	$ 87	$ 966	$ 139	$ 1,105
For the year ended December 31, 1998							
Gross revenues from:							
Sales and transfers, including affiliate sales	$ 2,570	$ —	$ 438	$ 571	$ 3,579	$ 454	$ 4,033
Sales to unaffiliated entities	218	120	509	122	969	28	997
Production costs	(1,066)	(35)	(400)	(250)	(1,751)	(150)	(1,901)
Exploration costs	(286)	(31)	(53)	(137)	(507)	(16)	(523)
Depreciation, depletion and amortization	(832)	(22)	(422)	(113)	(1,389)	(106)	(1,495)
Other expenses	(198)	—	(4)	(10)	(212)	(1)	(213)
Results before estimated income taxes	406	32	68	183	689	209	898
Estimated income taxes	(49)	(14)	(27)	(166)	(256)	(102)	(358)
Net results	$ 357	$ 18	$ 41	$ 17	$ 433	$ 107	$ 540
For the year ended December 31, 1997							
Gross revenues from:							
Sales and transfers, including affiliate sales	$ 3,492	$ —	$ 495	$ 934	$ 4,921	$ 610	$ 5,531
Sales to unaffiliated entities	312	165	499	178	1,154	43	1,197
Production costs	(986)	(57)	(323)	(249)	(1,615)	(192)	(1,807)
Exploration costs	(238)	(10)	(60)	(195)	(503)	(16)	(519)
Depreciation, depletion and amortization	(735)	(27)	(382)	(129)	(1,273)	(110)	(1,383)
Other expenses	(249)	—	—	(24)	(273)	9	(264)
Results before estimated income taxes	1,596	71	229	515	2,411	344	2,755
Estimated income taxes	(511)	(40)	(85)	(418)	(1,054)	(173)	(1,227)
Net results	$ 1,085	$ 31	$ 144	$ 97	$ 1,357	$ 171	$ 1,528

Supplemental Market Risk Disclosures

We use derivative financial instruments to hedge interest rate, foreign currency exchange and commodity market risks. Derivatives principally include interest rate and/or currency swap contracts, forward and option contracts to buy and to sell foreign currencies, and commodity futures, options, swaps and other instruments. We hedge only a portion of our risk exposures for assets, liabilities, commitments and future production, purchases and sales. We remain exposed on the unhedged portion of such risks.

The estimated sensitivity effects below assume that valuations of all items within a risk category will move in tandem. This cannot be assured for exposures involving interest rates, currency exchange rates, petroleum and natural gas. Users should realize that actual impacts from future interest rate, currency exchange and petroleum and natural gas price movements will likely differ from the disclosed impacts due to ongoing changes in risk exposure levels and concurrent adjustments of hedging derivative positions. Additionally, the range of variability in prices and rates is representative only of past fluctuations for each risk category. Past fluctuations in rates and prices may not necessarily be an indicator of probable future fluctuations.

Notes 9, 14 and 15 to the financial statements include details of our hedging activities, fair values of financial instruments, related derivatives exposures and accounting policies.

DEBT AND DEBT-RELATED DERIVATIVES

We had variable rate debt of approximately $2.8 billion and $2.7 billion at year-end 1999 and 1998, before effects of related interest rate swaps. Interest rate swap notional amounts at year-end 1999 increased by $845 million from year-end 1998.

Based on our overall interest rate exposure on variable rate debt and interest rate swaps at December 31, 1999 (including the interest rate and equity swap), a hypothetical two percentage points increase or decrease in interest rates would decrease or increase net income approximately $52 million.

CURRENCY FORWARD EXCHANGE AND OPTION CONTRACTS

During 1999, the net notional amount of open forward contracts decreased $220 million. This related mostly to a decrease in balance sheet monetary exposures.

The effect on fair value of our forward exchange contracts at year-end 1999 from a hypothetical 10% change in currency exchange rates would be an increase or decrease of approximately $185 million. This would be offset by an opposite effect on the related hedged exposures.

PETROLEUM AND NATURAL GAS HEDGING

In 1999, the notional amount of open derivative contracts increased by $2,207 million, mostly related to natural gas hedging.

For commodity derivatives outstanding at year-end 1999 that are permitted to be settled in cash or another financial instrument, the aggregate effect of a hypothetical 17% change in natural gas prices, a 13% change in crude oil prices and a 14% change in petroleum product prices would not be material to our consolidated financial position, net income or cash flows.

INVESTMENTS IN DEBT AND PUBLICLY TRADED EQUITY SECURITIES

We are subject to price risk on this unhedged portfolio of available-for-sale securities. During 1999, market risk exposure decreased by $325 million. At year-end 1999, a 10% appreciation or depreciation in debt and equity prices would change portfolio fair value by about $17 million. This assumes no fluctuations in currency exchange rates.

PREFERRED SHARES OF SUBSIDIARIES

We are exposed to interest rate risk on dividend requirements of Series B preferred shares of Texaco Capital LLC.

We are exposed to currency exchange risk on the Canadian dollar denominated Series C preferred shares of Texaco Capital LLC. We are exposed to offsetting currency exchange risk as well as interest rate risk on a swap contract used to hedge the Series C.

Based on the above exposures, a hypothetical two percentage points increase or decrease in the applicable variable interest rates and a hypothetical 10% appreciation or depreciation in the Canadian dollar exchange rate would not materially affect our consolidated financial position, net income or cash flows.

MARKET AUCTION PREFERRED SHARES (MAPS)

We are exposed to interest rate risk on dividend requirements of MAPS. A hypothetical two percentage points increase or decrease in interest rates would not materially affect our consolidated financial position or cash flows. There are no derivatives related to MAPS.

Selected Financial Data

Selected Quarterly Financial Data

(Millions of dollars)	First Quarter	Second Quarter	Third Quarter	Fourth Quarter 1999	First Quarter	Second Quarter	Third Quarter	Fourth Quarter 1998
Revenues								
Sales and services	$ 6,914	$ 8,116	$ 9,472	$ 10,473	$ 7,922	$ 7,729	$ 7,481	$ 7,778
Equity in income of affiliates, interest, asset sales and other	276	153	205	82	225	315	226	31
	7,190	8,269	9,677	10,555	8,147	8,044	7,707	7,809
Deductions								
Purchases and other costs	5,450	6,356	7,448	8,188	6,114	5,972	5,836	6,257
Operating expenses	559	550	544	666	580	645	593	690
Selling, general and administrative expenses	290	311	270	315	276	296	290	362
Exploratory expenses	130	80	72	219	141	90	93	137
Depreciation, depletion and amortization	361	365	356	461	388	375	409	503
Interest expense, taxes other than income taxes and minority interest	216	212	214	279	249	240	237	233
	7,006	7,874	8,904	10,128	7,748	7,618	7,458	8,182
Income (loss) before income taxes and cumulative effect of accounting change	184	395	773	427	399	426	249	(373)
Provision for (benefit from) income taxes	(15)	122	386	109	140	84	34	(160)
Income (loss) before cumulative effect of accounting change	199	273	387	318	259	342	215	(213)
Cumulative effect of accounting change	—	—	—	—	(25)	—	—	—
Net income (loss)	$ 199	$ 273	$ 387	$ 318	$ 234	$ 342	$ 215	$ (213)
Total non-owner changes in equity	$ 179	$ 271	$ 393	$ 316	$ 239	$ 344	$ 210	$ (221)
Net income (loss) per common share (dollars)								
Basic								
Income (loss) before cumulative effect of accounting change	$ .35	$ .50	$ .71	$ .58	$ .46	$ .62	$ .38	$ (.43)
Cumulative effect of accounting change	—	—	—	—	(.05)	—	—	—
Net income (loss)	$ .35	$ .50	$ .71	$ .58	$ .41	$ .62	$ .38	$ (.43)
Diluted								
Income (loss) before cumulative effect of accounting change	$ .35	$ .50	$ .71	$ .58	$ .46	$ .61	$ .38	$ (.43)
Cumulative effect of accounting change	—	—	—	—	(.04)	—	—	—
Net income (loss)	$ .35	$ .50	$ .71	$ .58	$ .42	$ .61	$ .38	$ (.43)

See accompanying notes to consolidated financial statements.

Five-Year Comparison of Selected Financial Data

(Millions of dollars)	1999	1998	1997	1996	1995
For the year:					
Revenues	$ 35,691	$ 31,707	$ 46,667	$ 45,500	$ 36,787
Net income before cumulative effect of accounting changes	$ 1,177	$ 603	$ 2,664	$ 2,018	$ 728
Cumulative effect of accounting changes	—	(25)	—	—	(121)
Net income	$ 1,177	$ 578	$ 2,664	$ 2,018	$ 607
Total non-owner changes in equity	$ 1,159	$ 572	$ 2,601	$ 1,863	$ 592
Net income per common share* *(dollars)*					
Basic					
Income before cumulative effect of accounting changes	$ 2.14	$ 1.04	$ 4.99	$ 3.77	$ 1.29
Cumulative effect of accounting changes	—	(.05)	—	—	(.24)
Net income	$ 2.14	$ .99	$ 4.99	$ 3.77	$ 1.05
Diluted					
Income before cumulative effect of accounting changes	$ 2.14	$ 1.04	$ 4.87	$ 3.68	$ 1.28
Cumulative effect of accounting changes	—	(.05)	—	—	(.23)
Net income	$ 2.14	$ .99	$ 4.87	$ 3.68	$ 1.05
Cash dividends per common share* *(dollars)*	$ 1.80	$ 1.80	$ 1.75	$ 1.65	$ 1.60
Total cash dividends paid on common stock	$ 964	$ 952	$ 918	$ 859	$ 832
At end of year:					
Total assets	$ 28,972	$ 28,570	$ 29,600	$ 26,963	$ 24,937
Debt and capital lease obligations					
Short-term	$ 1,041	$ 939	$ 885	$ 465	$ 737
Long-term	6,606	6,352	5,507	5,125	5,503
Total debt and capital lease obligations	$ 7,647	$ 7,291	$ 6,392	$ 5,590	$ 6,240

*Reflects two-for-one stock split effective September 29, 1997.

See accompanying notes to consolidated financial statements.

Texaco Inc. Board of Directors

PETER I. BIJUR
Chairman of the Board
and Chief Executive Officer
Texaco Inc.
White Plains, NY

A. CHARLES BAILLIE
Chairman and
Chief Executive Officer
Toronto-Dominion Bank
Toronto, Canada

MARY K. BUSH
President
Bush & Company
Washington, DC

EDMUND M. CARPENTER
President and
Chief Executive Officer
Barnes Group, Inc.
Bristol, CT

MICHAEL C. HAWLEY
Chairman of the Board and
Chief Executive Officer
The Gillette Company
Boston, MA

FRANKLYN G. JENIFER
President
The University of Texas at Dallas
Dallas, TX

SAM NUNN
Partner
King & Spalding
Atlanta, GA

CHARLES H. PRICE, II
Former Chairman
Mercantile Bank of
Kansas City
Kansas City, MO

CHARLES R. SHOEMATE
Chairman, President and
Chief Executive Officer
Bestfoods
Englewood Cliffs, NJ

ROBIN B. SMITH
Chairman and
Chief Executive Officer
Publishers Clearing House
Port Washington, NY

WILLIAM C. STEERE, JR.
Chairman and
Chief Executive Officer
Pfizer Inc.
New York, NY

THOMAS A. VANDERSLICE
Private Investor
Naples, FL

COMMITTEES OF THE BOARD

EXECUTIVE COMMITTEE
Peter I. Bijur, Chair
Edmund M. Carpenter
Franklyn G. Jenifer
Sam Nunn
Charles H. Price, II
Robin B. Smith
Thomas A. Vanderslice

COMMITTEE OF NON-MANAGEMENT DIRECTORS
Thomas A. Vanderslice, Chair
All non-management Directors

AUDIT COMMITTEE
Thomas A. Vanderslice, Chair
Michael C. Hawley
Franklyn G. Jenifer
Sam Nunn
Charles R. Shoemate
Robin B. Smith

COMMITTEE ON DIRECTORS AND BOARD GOVERNANCE
Robin B. Smith, Chair
Edmund M. Carpenter
Michael C. Hawley
Thomas A. Vanderslice

COMPENSATION COMMITTEE
William C. Steere, Jr., Chair
Edmund M. Carpenter
Michael C. Hawley
Charles H. Price, II
Charles R. Shoemate
Thomas A. Vanderslice

PUBLIC RESPONSIBILITY COMMITTEE
Franklyn G. Jenifer, Chair
A. Charles Baillie
Mary K. Bush
Michael C. Hawley
Sam Nunn
Robin B. Smith
William C. Steere, Jr.

FINANCE COMMITTEE
Peter I. Bijur, Chair
A. Charles Baillie
Mary K. Bush
Edmund M. Carpenter
Charles H. Price, II
William C. Steere, Jr.

PREFERRED STOCK COMMITTEE
Peter I. Bijur, Chair
Edmund M. Carpenter

Texaco Inc. Officers

PETER I. BIJUR
Chairman of the Board and
Chief Executive Officer

PATRICK J. LYNCH
Senior Vice President and
Chief Financial Officer

JOHN J. O'CONNOR
Senior Vice President
Worldwide Exploration &
Production

GLENN F. TILTON
Senior Vice President
Global Businesses

WILLIAM M. WICKER
Senior Vice President
Corporate Development

BRUCE S. APPELBAUM
Vice President
Worldwide Exploration &
New Ventures

EUGENE CELENTANO
Vice President
International Marketing &
Manufacturing

JAMES F. LINK
Vice President
Finance & Risk Management

JAMES R. METZGER
Vice President and
Chief Technology Officer

ROBERT C. OELKERS
Vice President
Worldwide Supply &
Trading Operations

DEVAL L. PATRICK
Vice President and
General Counsel

ELIZABETH P. SMITH
Vice President
Investor Relations &
Shareholder Services

ROBERT A. SOLBERG
Vice President
Worldwide Upstream
Commercial Development

JANET L. STONER
Vice President
Human Resources

MICHAEL N. AMBLER
General Tax Counsel

GEORGE J. BATAVICK
Comptroller

IRA D. HALL
Treasurer

MICHAEL H. RUDY
Secretary

CHANGES

> George J. Batavick was elected Comptroller of Texaco Inc.,
effective April 1, 1999.

> C. Robert Black, Senior Vice President of Texaco Inc., retired on
May 1, 1999, after 41 years of service.

> Stephen M. Turner, Senior Vice President of Texaco Inc., retired on
June 1, 1999, after 10 years of service.

> James F. Link was elected Vice President of Texaco Inc., effective
October 1, 1999.

> Claire S. Farley, Vice President of Texaco Inc., retired on
October 1, 1999, after 18 years of service.

> Ira D. Hall was elected Treasurer of Texaco Inc., effective
October 1, 1999.

> Kjestine M. Anderson, Secretary of Texaco Inc., retired on
December 31, 1999, after 20 years of service.

> Michael H. Rudy was elected Secretary of Texaco Inc., effective
January 1, 2000.

> Bruce S. Appelbaum was elected Vice President of Texaco Inc.,
effective March 1, 2000.

> Clarence P. Cazalot, Jr., Vice President of Texaco Inc., retired on
March 3, 2000, after 27 years of service.

Investor Information

COMMON STOCK — MARKET AND DIVIDEND INFORMATION:

Texaco Inc. common stock (symbol TX) is traded principally on the New York Stock Exchange. As of February 24, 2000, there were 198,698 shareholders of record. In 1999, Texaco's common stock price reached a high of 70^{1/16}$, and closed December 31, 1999, at 54^{5/16}$.

	Common Stock Price Range				Dividends	
	High	Low	High	Low		
	1999		1998		1999	1998
First Quarter	$ 59³⁄₁₆	$ 44⁹⁄₁₆	$ 65	$ 49¹⁄₁₆	$ .45	$ .45
Second Quarter	70¹⁄₁₆	55⅛	63¾	55¾	.45	.45
Third Quarter	68½	60⁵⁄₁₆	64⅞	55¼	.45	.45
Fourth Quarter	67³⁄₁₆	52⅜	63⅞	50¼	.45	.45

STOCK TRANSFER AGENT AND SHAREHOLDER COMMUNICATIONS

FOR INFORMATION ABOUT TEXACO OR ASSISTANCE WITH YOUR ACCOUNT, PLEASE CONTACT:

Texaco Inc.
Investor Services
2000 Westchester Avenue
White Plains, NY 10650-0001
Phone: 1-800-283-9785
Fax: (914) 253-6286
E-mail: invest@texaco.com

NY DROP AGENT

ChaseMellon Shareholder Services
120 Broadway – 13th Floor
New York, NY 10271
Phone: (212) 374-2500
Fax: (212) 571-0871

CO-TRANSFER AGENT

Montreal Trust Company
151 Front Street West – 8th Floor
Toronto, Ontario, Canada M5J 2N1
Phone: 1-800-663-9097
Fax: (416) 981-9507

SECURITY ANALYSTS AND INSTITUTIONAL INVESTORS SHOULD CONTACT:

Elizabeth P. Smith
Vice President, Texaco Inc.
Phone: (914) 253-4478
Fax: (914) 253-6269
E-mail: smithep@texaco.com

ANNUAL MEETING

Texaco Inc.'s Annual Stockholders Meeting will be held at Purchase College, The State University of New York, in Purchase, NY, on Wednesday, April 26, 2000. A formal notice of the meeting, together with a proxy statement and proxy form, is being mailed to stockholders with this report.

INVESTOR SERVICES PLAN

The company's Investor Services Plan offers a variety of benefits to individuals seeking an easy way to invest in Texaco Inc. common stock. Enrollment in the Plan is open to anyone, and investors may make initial investments directly through the company. The Plan features dividend reinvestment, optional cash investments, and custodial service for stock certificates. Open an account or access your registered shareholder account on the Internet through our new TexLink connection at www.texaco.com. Texaco's Investor Services Plan is an excellent way to start an investment program for family or friends. For a complete informational package, including a Plan prospectus, call 1-800-283-9785, e-mail at invest@texaco.com, or visit Texaco's Internet home page at www.texaco.com.

Westvāco
Annual Report 1999

FINANCIAL REVIEW

Management's discussion and analysis of
financial condition and results of operations

Analysis of operations

Sales of $2.8 billion for the fiscal year were down 2.9% from 1998, the result of a 4.3% decrease in price and product mix partially offset by a 1.4% improvement in the volume of shipments. Net income in 1999 was $111.2 million, or $1.11 per share, basic and diluted, a 15.8% decrease from 1998 earnings of $132.0 million, or $1.30 per share, basic and diluted. Earnings for the current year include a pretax restructuring charge of $80.5 million, or $.49 per share, basic and diluted, in connection with a business performance improvement plan and an income tax benefit of $15.0 million, or $.15 per share, basic and diluted, related to a release of deferred taxes, both recorded in the fourth quarter (see notes to the financial statements). The restructuring charge included $76.0 million for the writedown of fixed assets. We expect to obtain about $35 million in pretax annual savings from both operational efficiencies and from scaling back operations that no longer meet our financial or strategic objectives. We estimate these restructuring activities will be completed by the end of fiscal year 2000. The income tax benefit results from a business reorganization which reduced the company's deferred state income tax liability. Earnings for 1999 include an after-tax gain of $14.0 million, or $.14 per share, basic and diluted, from the sale of nonstrategic timberlands.

Sales for the year continued to be affected by weak pricing primarily due to global overcapacity combined with a strong U.S. dollar. During the second half of the year, pressures from lower-priced imported coated printing papers began to ease as demand increased for papers used in catalogue and direct mail applications. Late in the third quarter, the company announced a $60 per ton price increase for coated web-offset paper products, as well as increases on additional grades, including linerboard and bleached board. Export sales from the United States increased compared to 1998 and accounted for 18% of the

company's consolidated sales. Total sales outside of the United States, including sales of our foreign operating subsidiaries, accounted for approximately 24% of consolidated sales compared to 25% in the prior year. Gross profit margin for the year improved to 20% compared with 19% for the prior year, due mainly to cost improvement initiatives. Fiscal year 1999 operating results also benefited from an increase in noncash pension credits of $26.9 million, reflecting cumulative favorable investment returns on pension plan assets. We anticipate that earnings in fiscal year 2000 will benefit from a similar increase over fiscal year 1999.

Paper segment: Paper segment sales for the year of $1.03 billion increased marginally from the prior year, due to an increase in volume of 7.1% offset by a decrease in price and product mix of 6.8%. Markets for the company's paper products continue to be very competitive, resulting in net sales realizations being substantially below 1998 levels. Paper shipments for the fourth quarter of 1999 were up approximately 15% compared to the same prior year period. Late in the third quarter, the company announced the first price increase since 1996 for coated paper products. Operating profit for the paper segment for the year was $62.0 million, which decreased from $84.8 million for the prior year period, due mainly to lower sales prices.

Packaging segment: Packaging segment sales decreased 6.8% from the prior year to $1.46 billion in 1999, due to decreases in price and product mix of 5.3% and volume of 1.5%. Markets for the company's paperboard products continue to be very competitive, and our net sales realizations per ton were below 1998 levels. Operating profit for 1999 decreased 8.2% to $190.5 million primarily due to product pricing pressures which offset the company's progress in cost improvement initiatives. Promising trends in our packaging businesses include improved linerboard prices, increased sales of unbleached folding carton board and higher shipments in Brazil during the second half of the year compared to the first half. Rigesa, Ltda., our Brazilian subsidiary, accounted for 13% of 1999 packaging segment operating profit compared to 17% for the 1998 comparable period, due primarily to the 64% devaluation of the Brazilian real during the year, following the Brazilian government's decision to allow the real to float. In the local currency, Rigesa's sales for the year increased 12% compared to the year earlier period. We anticipate that the unsettled global economic conditions will continue to pose special challenges for our industry. During 1999, approximately 26% of packaging segment sales were made to the tobacco industry for packaging tobacco products compared to approximately 28% for 1998. Approximately 18% of segment sales were exported or used to produce products for export with the remaining 8% made for the domestic tobacco industry for sale in the United States. The current legal, regulatory and legislative pressures on the tobacco industry may have an adverse effect on packaging segment profitability. While we would expect to compensate for such an adverse effect by continuing growth in other consumer product markets, these alternatives may not, in the short run, fully offset any decline in profitability related to sales to the tobacco industry.

Chemicals segment: Chemicals segment sales for the year decreased 5.3% from 1998 to $314.5 million, due to favorable changes in price and product mix of 3.3% which were more than offset by a decrease in volume of 8.6%. Operating profit for the chemicals segment was $52.5 million compared to $53.2 million in the prior year.

Other items: Other income [expense] increased from the prior year due to the increased gains on the sales of timberlands in the current year. Interest expense increased 12% for the year compared to the prior year, due to the lower levels of capitalized interest in the current year and increased use of commercial paper. The effective tax rate for 1999 decreased to 24.9% compared to 35.4% in the prior year, principally due to the reduction in the deferred state income tax liability to reflect a lower effective state income rate, as described above.

In October 1999, Westvaco signed a definitive agreement to acquire Temple-Inland's bleached paperboard mill in Evadale, TX. The company will pay $575 million for the mill's fixed assets and approximately $50 million for working capital. The transaction is scheduled to close in December 1999.

On November 29, 1999, Westvaco signed a definitive agreement to acquire Mebane Packaging Group, a leading supplier of packaging for pharmaceutical products and personal care items. The sale is scheduled to close by the end of the first quarter of fiscal 2000.

Fiscal year 1998

Extremely challenging global business conditions were felt throughout our industry during our 1998 fiscal year. Asian markets were particularly challenging as a result of currency devaluations and reduced economic activity in the region. Sales of $2.9 billion for the fiscal year were down 3.2% from 1997, the result of decreases of 1.8% in the volume of shipments and 1.4% in price and product mix. Net income in 1998 was $132.0 million, or $1.30 per share, basic and diluted, a decline of 18.9% from $162.7 million, or $1.60 per share basic and $1.58 per share diluted, earned in 1997. Other principal factors contributing to our decline in earnings included a strike within our Envelope Division and difficult circumstances within our Consumer Packaging Division, which are discussed in the paper and packaging segment analyses, respectively. Despite stiff challenges resulting from turmoil in international markets and adverse currency valuations, export sales from the United States increased slightly compared to 1997 and represented approximately 17% of the company's consolidated sales for 1998. Sales outside of the United States, including sales of our foreign operating subsidiaries, accounted for approximately 25% of consolidated sales and were slightly below prior year levels. The marginal improvements in most international markets were more than offset by reduced business for our packaging operations in Brazil, where the government's austerity measures enacted last fall in response to the Asian crisis had sharply curtailed economic growth. Gross profit margin for the year was 19% in both 1998 and 1997. As discussed further below, the effect of weakened product pricing was largely offset by our cost improvement initiatives. Depreciation and amortization expense for the year increased 4.4% from the prior year, due to several important projects having been placed in service and the effect of acceleration of lives on replaced assets.

FINANCIAL REVIEW

Paper segment sales for the year decreased 2.8% to $1.03 billion, due to decreases in volume of .8% and in price and product mix of 2.0%. Operating profit for the paper segment for the year was $84.8 million which increased from $82.0 million for the prior year period due mainly to increased efforts in our cost improvement initiatives that were offset by the effect of the Envelope Division strike. In February 1998, six of the company's eight Envelope Division locations went on strike. The strike, which was settled in early March, reduced second quarter consolidated earnings by approximately $.05 per share and continued to adversely impact earnings for the balance of the year. During 1998, we completed the second major coated paper machine rebuild in two years at our mill in Luke, MD. The rebuilds reduced both 1997 and 1998 fiscal year earnings by approximately $.05 per share.

Packaging segment sales decreased 4.4% from the prior year to $1.57 billion, due to decreases in volume of 3.1% and price and product mix of 1.3%. Lower shipments of domestic commodity grade containerboard products and Brazilian corrugated boxes were marginally offset by improvements in our differentiated saturating kraft paper. Operating profit for the year decreased 9.2% from 1997, primarily due to product pricing pressures, from both manufacturing difficulties and marketing challenges. Together these combined to offset the company's progress in cost improvement initiatives. Rigesa accounted for 17% of packaging segment operating profit compared to 21% for the 1997 comparable period. The Brazilian government's financial reforms enacted in the fall of 1997 have sharply curtailed economic growth, which has reduced business for our packaging operations. Due to the decline in the rate of inflation in Brazil in recent years, effective November 1, 1997, the Brazilian real became the functional currency for the company's Brazilian operations and adjustments resulting from financial statement translations since then have been included in the shareholders' equity section of the balance sheet. The effect of this change did not have a significant impact on earnings for the period. During 1998, approximately 28% of packaging segment sales were made to the tobacco industry for packaging. Approximately 18% of segment sales were exported or used to produce products for export with the remaining 10% made for the domestic tobacco industry for sale in the United States. In the fourth quarter of 1998, a pretax charge of $5 million, or $.03 per share, was recorded, which was the result of operational changes to strengthen the Consumer Packaging Division. The charge reflects costs associated with announced terminations for approximately 240 employees and the writedown of certain assets.

Chemicals segment sales for the year increased 2.6% from 1997 to $332.1 million, due to favorable changes in price and product mix of 1.4% and volume of 1.2%. Operating profit for the chemicals segment increased 8.5% to a level of $53.2 million.

Other income [expense] decreased from the prior year, due to losses on the sales of plant and equipment reported in 1998 compared to gains in 1997. Interest expense increased 18.1% for the year compared to the prior year period, due to the issuance of sinking fund debentures in March and June 1997 and lower levels of capitalized interest in the current year. The effective tax rate for 1998 increased to 35.4% compared to 34.0% in the prior year, principally due to the decline in foreign earnings subject to lower tax rates.

Liquidity and capital resources

At October 31, 1999, the ratio of current assets to current liabilities was 1.7 compared to 1.6 and 2.0 in 1998 and 1997, respectively. The twelve-month average collection period for trade receivables was 34 days in 1999 compared to 35 days in 1998 and 32 days in 1997. Finished goods inventories decreased from prior year levels, reflecting the selective shutdown of paper machines to control inventory levels and improved fourth quarter shipments. Cash flows from operations were $413 million for 1999, compared to $407 million in 1998 and $391 million in 1997. Management believes that the company's ability to generate cash from operations and its capacity to issue short-term and long-term debt are adequate to fund working capital, capital spending and other needs in the foreseeable future.

New investment in plant and timberlands was $232 million for 1999, compared to $420 million in 1998 and $614 million in 1997. Cash payments for these investments totaled $229 million in 1999, $423 million in 1998 and $621 million in 1997. This planned lower level of capital spending follows

FINANCIAL REVIEW

the completion of several important initiatives that added significant support to our long-term strategy. At October 31, 1999, the funds required to complete all authorized capital projects were approximately $147 million. Capital expenditures for 2000 are expected to be approximately $250 million, including the expenditures at the Evadale, TX, mill after the acquisition, and will be used to support our current production capacity levels. The company may from time to time use outside sources as needed to finance future capital investments as it has in the past. The company had $15 million in commercial paper outstanding at October 31, 1999, compared to $80 million at October 31, 1998, and none at October 31, 1997. The company maintains a $500 million revolving credit agreement, and there was no borrowing under this arrangement during the current year period. The ratio of debt to total capital employed was 34% at October 31, 1999, 1998 and 1997. In 1997, the Board of Directors authorized the periodic repurchase of the company's common stock to satisfy issuances under its stock option plans. During 1999, 460,000 shares were purchased at a cost of $11 million and 466,169 shares were issued out of treasury to satisfy stock option exercises.

During the second quarter of 1999, the company completed the acquisition of an equity interest in a new consumer packaging business with a plant in Guangzhou, China. The company paid $22.7 million for a 45% interest in the Chinese operations. The investment was financed from operating cash flows.

As discussed earlier, the company signed two definitive agreements to acquire Temple-Inland's bleached paperboard mill and Mebane Packaging Group. In November 1999, the company issued $200 million of 6.85% five-year notes and $200 million of 7.10% ten-year notes to fund part of these purchases, with the remainder to be financed with short-term debt backed by a revolving credit facility which will be replaced with long-term debt as market conditions permit.

Environmental matters: In 1995, the company authorized removal of elemental chlorine from all of its pulp bleaching processes. This important initiative, completed during 1997 at a cost of approximately $110 million, represented a major step by Westvaco in addressing subsequent EPA regulations for the U.S. pulp and paper industry regarding air and water quality. These regulations, known as the Cluster Rule, were published in the Federal Register in April 1998. The company anticipates additional capital costs to comply with other parts of these new regulations over the next several years to be in the range of $100 million to $150 million which will also increase operating costs in the range of $3 million to $7 million annually. Environmental organizations are challenging the EPA regarding certain aspects of the Cluster Rule in the U.S. Court of Appeals. Westvaco and other companies are participating in that litigation. If the legal challenge by environmental organizations to the regulations is successful, the company could face additional compliance costs of up to $150 million over the next several years.

The company is currently named as a potentially responsible party with respect to the cleanup of a number of hazardous waste sites under the Comprehensive Environmental Response, Compensation, and Liability Act (CERCLA) and similar state laws. While joint and several liability is authorized under CERCLA, as a practical matter, remediation costs will be allocated among the waste generators and others involved. The company has accrued approximately $5 million for estimated potential cleanup costs based upon its close monitoring of ongoing activities and its past experience with these matters. In addition, the company is involved in the remediation of certain other than CERCLA sites and has accrued approximately $10 million for remediation of these sites.

Year 2000 *(as of mid-December 1999)*

Westvaco's six-phase base program aimed at identifying and eliminating the company's Year 2000 problems in high-risk areas was substantially complete by June 30, 1999. The six phases (inventory, assessment of business criticality, technical assessment of potential Year 2000 failures, remediation, testing and contingency planning) encompassed both information and noninformation technology systems. For both our domestic and foreign operations, the program included a review of all computer hardware and software, whether used directly to support business and manufacturing processes or embedded in components of machinery and other equipment.

FINANCIAL REVIEW

As the company's Year 2000 compliance efforts are an ongoing process, Westvaco has, where necessary, expanded and advanced its Year 2000 base program to enhance the company's level of readiness beyond the base program June 30 target date. With the goal of identifying and tracking any remaining tasks needing to be accomplished between now and December 31, the advanced program is designed to (1) review and properly archive all records associated with Year 2000 measures to date; (2) refine Westvaco's contingency plans after consulting with experts in the power and process manufacturing industries and reviewing procedures to be followed prior to and upon any computer-related system failure at Westvaco or at a utility serving Westvaco; (3) establish a communications center at Westvaco's Laurel, MD, data center to collect and disseminate all Year 2000-related information during key transition periods; and (4) identify and resolve open items by taking steps similar to those undertaken as part of the company's six-phase base program. Open items may include (a) newly reclassified, high-risk items, as well as medium- and low-risk items where remediation may have been planned but not yet completed; (b) components overlooked during the base program; (c) new components purchased subsequent to June 30, 1999 (excluding those acquired in connection with the Evadale, TX, mill and Mebane Packaging Group transactions discussed below); (d) storeroom items not included in the base program; and (e) key vendors and customers from whom Westvaco has not yet seen confirmation of readiness. The advanced program is progressing, yet significant work remains. Nevertheless, the company continues to be optimistic concerning its readiness, particularly in light of growing confidence in the national electrical supply grid.

The contingency plans noted above may, as appropriate, include the identification of alternate suppliers, vendors and service providers; accumulation of inventory; identification of manual alternatives; arrangement for rapid access to qualified vendor technical support; enhancement of operational communications; and limited configuration of manufacturing processes to prepare for the possibility of external power or communication failures.

Westvaco has contacted key vendors whose noncompliance, either individually or cumulatively, could materially impact the company's business. As of October 31, 1999, 86% of vendors contacted have responded, substantially all indicating they have addressed or expect to address their Year 2000 issues in a timely manner. The company continues to follow up with vendors yet to respond satisfactorily or at all to its inquiries. Fewer than 30 of these remaining vendors could individually be of such significance to the company or to a particular facility that such vendor's potential noncompliance could materially impact the company. Westvaco cannot provide assurance that the Year 2000 compliance plans of its vendors, particularly those providing broad infrastructural services or those in international markets, will be successfully completed in a timely manner.

The Year 2000 disclosures of major customers are reviewed on an ongoing basis. To date, Westvaco is not aware of any major customer failing to progress toward Year 2000 compliance. Although the company cannot predict the likelihood of disruption of its customers' businesses, Westvaco believes that its customer base is broad enough to minimize the impact of any single customer's disruption.

Estimated costs of the work necessary to address the company's Year 2000 issues are now between $7 million and $8 million. Previously estimated costs of $9 million to $12 million reflected initial uncertainty concerning the scope of the company's Year 2000 challenge. As before, the current estimate includes internal costs (e.g., related payroll and required downtime) and external costs (e.g., hiring consultants to assist in compliance efforts). Program costs do not include the cost of major new business system implementations scheduled prior to the company's specific Year 2000 compliance efforts described herein and completed during the last three years. Estimated costs would have been substantially greater but for the fact that recent modernization of many of the company's business systems involved the replacement of software with new software that is Year 2000 compliant at a cost of approximately $30 million. No significant technology projects have been deferred as a result of the company's Year 2000 compliance work.

As of October 31, 1999, approximately $7.1 million in costs incurred to date have been funded by operating cash

FINANCIAL REVIEW

flows and expensed as incurred except for newly installed systems which were capitalized in accordance with the company's accounting policies. Although such costs may be significant to the company's results of operations in one or more fiscal quarters, Westvaco does not expect a material adverse impact on its long-term results of operations, liquidity or financial position. Cost estimates may be further refined as technical assessment, remediation, testing and contingency planning continue and as compliance status information becomes available from third-party business partners.

If Westvaco were not taking any of the remedial steps detailed above, Year 2000 issues could possibly cause significant technological problems for the company, disrupting business and resulting in a decline in earnings. At this time, however, management does not believe this will happen.

The most reasonably likely worst case scenario should Westvaco, its customers or vendors be unable to adequately resolve Year 2000 issues would include reduced demand and a temporary slowdown or abrupt stoppage of operations at one or more of the company's facilities due to the failure of one or more critical process control elements or business systems. Such failures could result in interruptions in manufacturing, safety and/or environmental systems; and/or a temporary inability to receive raw materials, ship finished products and process orders and invoices. Although management does not believe that this will happen, if such or similar scenarios were to occur, they could, depending on their duration, have a material impact on the company's results of operations and financial position. Such theoretical consequences are of a kind and magnitude generally shared with other manufacturing companies. Assuming the successful completion of its Year 2000 efforts in a timely manner, the company expects any Year 2000 disruptions which occur, should there be any, will be minor and not material to its business.

The plans and actions described above do not include the Evadale bleached paperboard mill which Westvaco has agreed to purchase from Temple-Inland nor the seven packaging plants Westvaco has recently agreed to purchase from Mebane Packaging Group.

Temple-Inland has adopted and is implementing a companywide Year 2000 plan. On a corporate basis, most systems were reportedly compliant before the end of 1998. Westvaco has evaluated, to the extent feasible, the preparations and current status of Year 2000 readiness of the Evadale facility. This limited evaluation indicates that important remediation and testing remain to be completed in the process systems at Evadale. This work is expected to be accomplished during a previously planned ten-day shut down in mid-December 1999. Temple-Inland has represented to Westvaco that assuming the successful completion of Temple-Inland's Year 2000 plan in a timely manner that any Year 2000-related problems that occur, should there be any, will be minor and not material to the facility.

Mebane has also adopted and is implementing a companywide Year 2000 plan. Westvaco has not been able to ascertain the extent to which Mebane's program has been effectively executed. Given the company's recent agreement to acquire Mebane and its inability to review thoroughly Mebane's progress before the transition date, Westvaco has asked Mebane to focus on business contingency planning.

With respect to both the Evadale facility and the Mebane plants, Westvaco is currently unable to make a comprehensive assessment of their respective readiness or determine with certainty whether all necessary Year 2000 preparations will be complete by the acquisition dates.

Accounting changes

The company is required to adopt a new accounting standard issued by the Financial Accounting Standards Board, Statement of Financial Accounting Standards No. 133, *Accounting for Derivative Instruments and Hedging Activities,* in fiscal year 2001. The company does not believe that the adoption of this statement will have a material effect on the company's financial position or results of operations. For further discussion, see the "Summary of significant accounting policies" in the notes to the financial statements.

Forward-looking statements

Certain statements in this document and elsewhere by management of the company that are neither reported financial results nor other historical information are forward-looking statements within the meaning of the

FINANCIAL REVIEW

Private Securities Litigation Reform Act of 1995. Such information includes, without limitation, the business outlook, assessment of market conditions, anticipated financial and operating results, strategies, future plans, contingencies and contemplated transactions of the company. Such forward-looking statements are not guarantees of future performance and are subject to known and unknown risks, uncertainties and other factors which may cause or contribute to actual results of company operations, or the performance or achievements of the company, or industry results, to differ materially from those expressed in or implied by the forward-looking statements. In addition to any such risks, uncertainties and other factors discussed elsewhere herein, risks, uncertainties and other factors that could cause or contribute to actual results differing materially from those expressed in or implied by the forward-looking statements include, but are not limited to, competitive pricing for the company's products; the success of new initiatives, acquisitions and ongoing cost reduction efforts; changes in raw materials, energy and other costs; impact of Year 2000 issues; unanticipated manufacturing disruptions; fluctuations in demand and changes in production capacities; changes to economic growth in the U.S. and international economies, especially in Asia and Brazil; stability of financial markets; governmental policies and regulations, including but not limited to those affecting the environment and the tobacco industry; restrictions on trade; interest rates and currency movements.

Fourth quarter results

Sales were $771.5 million for the fourth quarter of 1999, compared to sales of $731.8 million for the fourth quarter of 1998. In the fourth quarter of 1999, the company recorded net income of $23.7 million, or $.24 per share, basic and diluted, compared to net income of $33.2 million, or $.33 per share, basic and diluted, for the prior year period.

During the fourth quarter of 1999, as a result of its recently completed strategic review process, the company adopted a plan to improve performance and established a related pretax restructuring charge of $80.5 million, or $.49 per share after-tax, basic and diluted. The restructuring charge is primarily a noncash writedown of assets, including underutilized production capacity in our packaging and bleached board operations and an older paper machine in our fine papers operations.

Net income for the fourth quarter also benefited from a decrease in the company's income tax expense, primarily attributable to a one-time $15 million, or $.15 per share after-tax, basic and diluted, reduction in the state deferred tax liability, resulting from a business reorganization.

Investor services plan

At year end, 14,890 shareholders, including members of the company's savings and investment plans for salaried and hourly employees, representing 14,886,201 shares of Westvaco common stock, were participants in the company's Investor Services Plan.

Number of shareholders

At year end, the number of individuals and institutions owning Westvaco common shares was about 19,070. This number includes 12,000 members of the company's salaried and hourly savings and investment plans. The plans, established in 1968 and 1995, respectively, hold 13,490,136 shares of Westvaco common stock for the accounts of participants. This represents 13% of the 100,292,843 shares of common stock outstanding at year end.

Payroll and benefit costs

The total cost of payroll and benefits was $623 million, compared with $671 million in 1998. This includes $44.7 million in Social Security taxes in 1999 and $47.4 million in 1998. Payroll and benefit costs were 22% of sales in 1999 and 23% in 1998. Sales per employee have increased 19% in the last five years. In 1994, they stood at $184,014, rising to $219,753 in 1999.

FINANCIAL STATEMENTS

CONSOLIDATED STATEMENT OF INCOME

In thousands, except per share Year ended October 31	1999	1998	1997
Sales	$2,801,849	$2,885,917	$2,982,288
Other income [expense]	29,384	18,747	28,743
	2,831,233	2,904,664	3,011,031
Cost of products sold [excludes depreciation shown separately below]	1,969,515	2,071,011	2,161,194
Selling, research and administrative expenses	230,963	238,097	240,814
Depreciation and amortization	280,470	280,981	269,151
Restructuring charge	78,771	–	–
Interest expense	123,538	110,162	93,272
	2,683,257	2,700,251	2,764,431
Income before taxes	147,976	204,413	246,600
Income taxes	36,800	72,400	83,900
Net income	$ 111,176	$ 132,013	$ 162,700
Net income per share:			
Basic	$1.11	$1.30	$1.60
Diluted	1.11	1.30	1.58
Shares used to compute net income per share:			
Basic	100,236	101,311	101,978
Diluted	100,495	101,788	102,704

The accompanying notes are an integral part of these financial statements.

FINANCIAL STATEMENTS

CONSOLIDATED BALANCE SHEET

In thousands At October 31	1999	1998
ASSETS		
Cash and marketable securities	$ 108,792	$ 105,050
Receivables	318,369	286,423
Inventories	248,963	285,783
Prepaid expenses and other current assets	61,884	61,936
Current assets	738,008	739,192
Plant and timberlands:		
Machinery	5,094,773	5,079,177
Buildings	672,744	655,020
Other property, including plant land	226,977	224,229
	5,994,494	5,958,426
Less: accumulated depreciation	2,779,199	2,634,702
	3,215,295	3,323,724
Timberlands–net	266,386	273,975
Construction in progress	99,702	204,732
	3,581,383	3,802,431
Other assets	577,301	467,045
	$4,896,692	$5,008,668
LIABILITIES AND SHAREHOLDERS' EQUITY		
Accounts payable and accrued expenses	$ 361,959	$ 346,552
Notes payable and current maturities of long-term obligations	50,200	99,072
Income taxes	12,955	21,501
Current liabilities	425,114	467,125
Long-term obligations	1,502,177	1,526,343
Deferred income taxes	798,113	768,752
Shareholders' equity:		
Common stock, $5 par, at stated value		
Shares authorized: 300,000,000		
Shares issued: 103,170,667 [1998–103,170,667]	765,810	764,574
Retained income	1,607,504	1,588,932
Accumulated other comprehensive income [loss]	[129,981]	[32,167]
Common stock in treasury, at cost		
Shares held: 2,877,824 [1998–2,844,300]	[72,045]	[74,891]
	2,171,288	2,246,448
	$4,896,692	$5,008,668

The accompanying notes are an integral part of these financial statements.

FINANCIAL STATEMENTS

CONSOLIDATED STATEMENT OF SHAREHOLDERS' EQUITY

In thousands

	Outstanding shares	Common stock	Common stock in treasury	Retained income	Accumulated other comprehensive income/[loss]	Total shareholders' equity
Balance at October 31, 1996	101,891	$750,457	$[19,745]	$1,479,025	$ –	$2,209,737
Net income	–	–	–	162,700	–	162,700
Cash dividends	–	–	–	[89,778]	–	[89,778]
Repurchases of common stock	[610]	–	[20,880]	–	–	[20,880]
Issuance	649	11,065	8,315	[2,591]	–	16,789
Balance at October 31, 1997	101,930	761,522	[32,310]	1,549,356	–	2,278,568
Comprehensive income						
Net income	–	–	–	132,013	–	132,013
Foreign currency translation	–	–	–	–	[32,167]	[32,167]
Comprehensive income						99,846
Cash dividends	–	–	–	[89,300]	–	[89,300]
Repurchases of common stock	[1,822]	–	[50,176]	–	–	[50,176]
Issuance	218	3,052	7,595	[3,137]	–	7,510
Balance at October 31, 1998	100,326	764,574	[74,891]	1,588,932	[32,167]	2,246,448
Comprehensive income						
Net income	–	–	–	111,176	–	111,176
Foreign currency translation	–	–	–	–	[97,814]	[97,814]
Comprehensive income						13,362
Cash dividends	–	–	–	[88,191]	–	[88,191]
Repurchases of common stock	[499]	–	[11,961]	–	–	[11,961]
Issuance	466	1,236	14,807	[4,413]	–	11,630
Balance at October 31, 1999	100,293	$765,810	$[72,045]	$1,607,504	$[129,981]	$2,171,288

The accompanying notes are an integral part of these financial statements.

FINANCIAL STATEMENTS

CONSOLIDATED STATEMENT OF CASH FLOWS

In thousands Year ended October 31	1999	1998	1997
CASH FLOWS FROM OPERATING ACTIVITIES:			
Net income	$111,176	$132,013	$162,700
Adjustments to reconcile net income to net cash provided by operating activities:			
Provision for depreciation and amortization	280,470	280,981	269,151
Provision for deferred income taxes	32,286	57,244	46,798
Restructuring charge	80,500	–	–
Pension credit and other employee benefits	[78,658]	[50,869]	[39,296]
[Gains] losses on sales of plant and timberlands	[17,891]	894	[10,537]
Foreign currency transaction [gains] losses	3,601	2,506	4,316
Net changes in assets and liabilities	[2,577]	[17,063]	[43,380]
Other, net	3,806	1,000	931
Net cash provided by operating activities	412,713	406,706	390,683
CASH FLOWS FROM INVESTING ACTIVITIES:			
Additions to plant and timberlands	[228,879]	[422,984]	[621,172]
Proceeds from sales of plant and timberlands	22,781	6,905	22,292
Other investments	[22,659]	–	–
Other, net	[1,135]	50	5,912
Net cash used in investing activities	[229,892]	[416,029]	[592,968]
CASH FLOWS FROM FINANCING ACTIVITIES:			
Proceeds from issuance of common stock	9,122	3,766	10,901
Proceeds from issuance of debt	881,518	548,194	649,186
Dividends paid	[88,191]	[89,300]	[89,778]
Treasury stock purchases	[10,792]	[49,484]	[17,374]
Repayment of notes payable and long-term obligations	[952,230]	[470,146]	[290,018]
Net cash [used in] provided by financing activities	[160,573]	[56,970]	262,917
Effect of exchange rate changes on cash	[18,506]	[4,011]	[646]
Increase [decrease] in cash and marketable securities	3,742	[70,304]	59,986
Cash and marketable securities:			
At beginning of period	105,050	175,354	115,368
At end of period	$108,792	$105,050	$175,354

The accompanying notes are an integral part of these financial statements.

NOTES TO FINANCIAL STATEMENTS

Summary of significant accounting policies

Basis of consolidation and preparation of financial statements: The consolidated financial statements include the accounts of all subsidiaries more than 50% owned. Investments in 20%- to 50%-owned companies are accounted for using the equity method. Accordingly, the company's share of the earnings of these companies is included in consolidated net income. In accordance with generally accepted accounting principles, the preparation of financial statements requires management to make estimates and assumptions that affect the reported amounts of some assets and liabilities and, in some instances, the reported amounts of revenues and expenses during the reporting period. Actual results could differ from these estimates. Certain prior years' amounts have been reclassified to conform with the current year's presentation.

Accounting standards changes: Effective November 1,1998, the company adopted Statement of Financial Accounting Standards (SFAS) No.130, *Reporting Comprehensive Income,* which establishes standards for the reporting and displaying of comprehensive income. During the fourth quarter of fiscal 1999, the company adopted SFAS No.132, *Employers' Disclosures about Pensions and Other Postretirement Benefits,* which standardizes the disclosure requirements for pensions and other postretirement benefits. These two standards do not affect the company's consolidated financial position or results of operations. The 1998 and 1997 comparative financial information has been restated to conform with the 1999 presentation.

In June 1998, the Financial Accounting Standards Board (FASB) issued SFAS No.133, *Accounting for Derivative Instruments and Hedging Activities,* which requires derivative instruments to be recorded in the balance sheet at their fair value, with changes in their fair value being recognized in earnings unless specific hedge accounting criteria are met. SFAS No.137, *Accounting for Derivative Instruments and Hedging Activities – Deferral of the Effective Date of SFAS No.133,* delayed the effective date of SFAS No.133 to the company's 2001 fiscal year. Given the current level of its derivative and hedging activities, the company believes the impact of this new standard will not be material.

Environmental matters: Environmental expenditures that increase useful lives are capitalized, while other environmental expenditures are expensed. Liabilities are recorded when remedial efforts are probable and the costs can be reasonably estimated. The estimated closure costs for existing landfills based on current environmental requirements and technologies are accrued over the expected useful lives of the landfills.

The company is currently named as a potentially responsible party with respect to the cleanup of a number of hazardous waste sites under the Comprehensive Environmental Response, Compensation, and Liability Act (CERCLA) and similar state laws. While joint and several liability is authorized under CERCLA, as a practical matter, remediation costs will be allocated among the waste generators and others involved. The company has accrued approximately $5 million for estimated potential cleanup costs based upon its close monitoring of ongoing activities and its past experience with these matters. In addition, the company is involved in the remediation of certain other than CERCLA sites for which the company has accrued approximately $10 million for remediation and closure costs.

Translation of foreign currencies: Due to the decline in the rate of inflation in Brazil in recent years, effective November 1,1997, the Brazilian real became the functional currency for the company's Brazilian operations. The assets and liabilities of the company's Brazilian subsidiary are translated into U.S. dollars using period-end exchange rates and adjustments resulting from financial statement translations are included in "Accumulated other comprehensive income [loss]" in the balance sheet.

Revenues and expenses are translated at average rates prevailing during the period.

Prior to November 1,1997, the functional currency for these operations was the U.S. dollar due to the high inflation rate which previously existed in that country. Foreign currency asset and liability accounts were remeasured into U.S. dollars at fiscal year-end rates except for inventories, properties and accumulated depreciation, which were translated at historical rates; revenues and expenses (other than those relating to assets translated at historical rates) were translated at average rates prevailing during the year. Translation gains and losses were included in "Other income [expense]."

Marketable securities: For financial statement purposes, highly liquid securities purchased three months or less from maturity are considered to be cash equivalents.

Inventories: Inventories are valued at the lower of cost or market. Cost is determined using the last-in, first-out (LIFO) method for raw materials, finished goods and certain production materials. Cost of all other inventories is determined by the first-in, first-out (FIFO) or average cost method.

Plant and timberlands: Owned assets are recorded at cost. Also included in the cost of these assets is interest on funds borrowed during the construction period. When assets are sold, retired or disposed of, their cost and related accumulated depreciation are removed from the accounts, and any resulting gain or loss is reflected in "Other income [expense]." Costs of renewals and betterments of properties are capitalized; costs of maintenance and repairs are charged to income. Costs of reforestation of timberlands are capitalized.

Depreciation and amortization: The cost of plant and equipment is depreciated, generally by the straight-line method, over the estimated useful lives of the respective assets, which range from 20 to 40 years for buildings and 5 to 30 years for machinery and equipment. The cost of standing timber is amortized as timber is cut, at rates determined annually based on the relationship of unamortized timber costs to the estimated volume of recoverable timber. The company periodically evaluates whether current events or circumstances warrant adjustments to the carrying value or estimated useful lives of its long-lived assets.

Other assets: Included in other assets are goodwill and other intangibles, which are amortized using the straight-line method over their estimated useful lives of 10 years. The company periodically reviews goodwill balances for impairment based on the expected future cash flows of the related businesses acquired.

Revenue recognition: The company recognizes revenues at the point of passage of title, which is at the time of shipment.

Income taxes: Deferred income taxes are recorded for temporary differences between financial statement carrying amounts and the tax basis of assets and liabilities. Deferred tax assets and liabilities reflect the enacted tax rates in effect for the years the differences are expected to reverse.

Income per share: Basic net income per share for all the periods presented has been calculated using the weighted average shares outstanding. In computing diluted net income per share, incremental shares issuable upon the assumed exercise of stock options have been added to the weighted average shares outstanding.

A. Provision for restructuring

During the fourth quarter of 1999, following completion of its strategic review process, the company adopted a plan to improve the company's performance, principally to enhance the strength and focus of its packaging-related businesses. Additionally, the company reviewed certain long-lived assets in its business for impairment. As a result of the above initiatives, a pretax charge of $80,500,000 was recorded in the fourth quarter of 1999. This charge is primarily due to the writedown of impaired long-lived assets, involuntary employee termination and other exit costs.

Production facilities were written down to their fair value using an assets-held-for-use model. An impairment of $67,430,000 was recorded as undiscounted cash flows were less than the carrying value of the assets prior to the impairment. Further, the company wrote off a paper machine and certain equipment with a total carrying value of $8,593,000 and abandoned the assets.

In addition to the asset impairments described above, the company also recognized inventory writedowns of $1,729,000 which have been included within the cost of products sold, employee termination costs of $1,508,000 and other exit costs of $1,240,000.

B. Other income [expense]

Components of other income [expense] are as follows:

In thousands	1999	1998	1997
Gains [losses] on sales of plant, equipment and timberlands	$17,891	$ [894]	$10,537
Interest income	15,115	18,010	15,089
Foreign currency transaction gains [losses]	[3,601]	[2,506]	[4,316]
Other, net	[21]	4,137	7,433
	$29,384	$18,747	$28,743

C. Research and development

Expenditures of $47,321,000 (1998 – $45,139,000, 1997 – $42,944,000) were expensed as incurred.

D. Income taxes

Income before provision for income taxes consisted of:

In thousands	1999	1998	1997
Domestic	$113,350	$157,075	$177,323
Foreign	34,626	47,338	69,277
	$147,976	$204,413	$246,600

The provision for income taxes is composed of:

In thousands	1999	1998	1997
Current:			
Federal	$ 4,430	$ 9,254	$23,982
State	[4,634]	[3,243]	3,503
Foreign	4,718	9,145	9,617
	4,514	15,156	37,102
Deferred:			
Federal	43,254	45,871	35,949
State	[15,366]	11,792	9,375
Foreign	4,398	[419]	1,474
	32,286	57,244	46,798
	$36,800	$72,400	$83,900

The net deferred income tax liability at October 31, 1999 and 1998 includes the following components:

In thousands	1999	1998
Current deferred tax assets:		
Employee benefits	$ 15,397	$ 15,430
Other	28,089	25,288
	43,486	40,718
Noncurrent deferred tax assets:		
Alternative minimum tax carryforward	143,802	143,581
Noncurrent deferred tax liabilities:		
Depreciation	654,604	643,834
Pension and other employee benefits	161,512	133,351
State and local taxes	91,662	99,487
Other	34,137	35,661
	941,915	912,333
Total net deferred tax liability	$754,627	$728,034

The differences (expressed as a percentage of pretax income) between the U.S. statutory federal income tax rate and the effective income tax rate as reflected in the accompanying consolidated statement of income are:

	1999	1998	1997
Statutory federal income tax rate	35.0%	35.0%	35.0%
State and local taxes	[8.8]	2.7	3.4
Foreign income at other than U.S. rates	[1.3]	[2.6]	[4.0]
Other, net	–	.3	[.4]
Effective tax rate	24.9%	35.4%	34.0%

The reduction in the company's fiscal 1999 income tax expense compared to fiscal 1998 is primarily attributable to a one-time $15 million reduction in the state deferred tax liability, resulting from a business reorganization completed during fiscal 1999. The reorganization lowered the state tax rates at which certain temporary differences, principally depreciation, are expected to reverse.

At October 31, 1999, for tax purposes, the company had available $144 million of alternative minimum tax credit carryforwards, which do not expire under current laws. At October 31, 1999, the company had available $4.9 million of foreign tax credit carryforwards, which, if unused, will expire in fiscal years 2000 to 2004.

Provision has not been made for income taxes which would become payable upon remittance of $167 million of the October 31, 1999 undistributed earnings of certain foreign subsidiaries representing that portion of such earnings which the company considers to have been indefinitely reinvested in the subsidiaries, principally in Brazil. Computation of the potential deferred tax liability associated with these undistributed earnings is not practicable.

E. Current assets

Marketable securities of $39,349,000 (1998 – $12,032,000) are valued at cost, which approximates market value. Receivables include $12,438,000 from sources other than trade (1998 – $5,731,000), and have been reduced by allowances for discounts and doubtful accounts of $12,828,000 (1998 – $12,748,000). Inventories at October 31 are composed of:

In thousands	1999	1998
Raw materials	$ 45,453	$ 55,580
Production materials, stores and supplies	66,191	74,338
Finished and in process goods	137,319	155,865
	$248,963	$285,783

If inventories had been valued at current cost, they would have been $368,105,000 in 1999 (1998 – $409,043,000).

F. Interest capitalization

In 1999, $132,428,000 of interest cost was incurred (1998 – $130,914,000, 1997 – $119,234,000) of which $8,890,000 was capitalized (1998 – $20,752,000, 1997 – $25,962,000).

G. Accounts payable and accrued expenses

Accounts payable and accrued expenses at October 31:

In thousands	1999	1998
Accounts payable:		
Trade	$118,413	$117,306
Other	18,812	24,258
Accrued expenses:		
Taxes, other than income	18,989	17,239
Interest	32,927	32,996
Payroll and employee benefit costs	85,179	83,652
Other	87,639	71,101
	$361,959	$346,552

H. Cash flows

Changes in assets and liabilities are as follows:

In thousands	1999	1998	1997
[Increase] decrease in:			
Receivables	$[41,054]	$ 12,765	$[23,674]
Inventories	24,545	[17,249]	[7,577]
Prepaid expenses and other current assets	[1,148]	[5,905]	1,633
Increase [decrease] in:			
Accounts payable and accrued expenses	24,766	[5,597]	[9,957]
Income taxes payable	[9,686]	[1,077]	[3,805]
	$ [2,577]	$[17,063]	$[43,380]

Reconciliation of capital expenditures on a cash basis:

In thousands	1999	1998	1997
New investment in plant and timberlands	$232,292	$419,705	$613,896
Less: debt assumed	[158]	[4]	[21]
net change in related current liabilities	[3,255]	3,283	7,297
Cash additions to plant and timberlands	$228,879	$422,984	$621,172

Cash payments for interest, excluding amounts capitalized, were $112,066,000 in 1999 (1998 – $108,082,000, 1997 – $84,503,000). Cash payments for income taxes were $12,108,000 in 1999 (1998 – $13,744,000, 1997 – $39,331,000).

I. Leasing activities and other commitments

The company leases a variety of assets for use in its operations. Leases for administrative offices, converting plants and storage facilities generally contain options which allow the company to extend lease terms for periods up to 25 years, or to purchase the properties. Certain leases provide for escalation of the lease payments as maintenance costs and taxes increase.

The company has no significant capital lease liabilities. Minimum rental payments under operating leases that have noncancellable lease terms in excess of 12 months are as follows:

In thousands	Operating leases
2000	$ 20,636
2001	17,829
2002	14,583
2003	11,438
2004	9,383
Later years	41,473
Minimum lease payments	$115,342

Rental expense under operating leases was $38,412,000 in 1999 (1998 – $40,179,000, 1997 – $38,031,000).

At October 31, 1999, commitments required to complete currently authorized capital projects are $147 million.

J. Notes payable and long-term obligations

Notes payable and long-term obligations at October 31, 1999:

In thousands	Current	Noncurrent
Debentures:		
9.65%, due 2002		$ 100,000
9¾%, due 2020		100,000
Sinking Fund Debentures:		
7%, due 2004-2023		150,000
7½%, due 2008-2027		150,000
7.65%, due 2008-2027		150,000
7.75%, due 2004-2023		150,000
8⅛%, due 2000-2007	$ 2,350	17,100
8.30%, due 2003-2022		125,000
10⅛%, due 2000-2019	5,000	95,000
10¼%, due 2000-2018	5,000	80,000
10.30%, due 2000-2019	5,000	95,000
Pollution Control Revenue Bonds:		
5.85-6.65%, due 2004-2018		26,620
5⅞-5.9%, due 2000-2003	1,865	6,740
5⅞-6.2%, due 2000-2007	550	11,480
5.9-6.2%, due 2004-2008		5,900
6⅜%, due 2026		5,740
7⅛-7½%, due 2000-2001	1,500	2,000
8¼%, due 2000-2010	105	3,995
9⅛-9.6%, due 2006-2015		10,100
10½%, due 2004		1,500
Industrial Revenue Bonds:		
7-7.67%, due 2000-2027	385	94,530
Economic Development Bonds:		
8¾%, due 2000-2010	110	4,190
Notes payable and other	28,335	117,282
	$50,200	$1,502,177

Outstanding noncurrent obligations maturing in the four years after 2000 are (in millions): 2001 – $37.1; 2002 – $133.3; 2003 – $36.1; 2004 – $56.6.

The company has a revolving credit agreement for $500 million which expires December 31, 2000. Borrowings under the agreement may be in unsecured domestic or Eurodollar notes and may be at rates approximating prime or the London Interbank Offered Rate, at the company's option. There is a nominal commitment fee on the unused funds. These facilities are used to support commercial paper borrowings. There were no borrowings under this facility during 1999 or 1998.

At October 31, 1999, the book value of financial instruments included in notes payable and long-term obligations was $1,477,162,000 (1998 – $1,557,477,000), and the fair value was estimated to be $1,495,290,000 (1998 – $1,636,093,000). The company has estimated the fair value of financial instruments based upon quoted market prices for the same or similar issues or on the current interest rates available to the company for debt of similar terms and maturities.

K. Shareholders' equity

During 1999, the company repurchased 460,000 shares (1998 – 1,800,000, 1997 – 500,000) of company stock under a repurchase program authorized in 1997 by the Board of Directors. The program was initiated to satisfy issuances under the company's stock option plans. There were no purchases in 1997, 1998 or 1999 under the stock repurchase program authorized in 1987 by the Board of Directors.

At October 31, 1999, there were 44,170 shares of nonvoting $100 par value cumulative preferred stock authorized and 10 million shares of preferred stock without par value authorized and available for issue.

Pursuant to a Rights Agreement approved by the company's Board of Directors in 1997, in the event a person or group were to acquire a 15% or greater position in Westvaco, each right would entitle its holder (other than the acquiror) to buy that number of shares of common stock of Westvaco which, at the time of the 15% acquisition, had a market value of two times the exercise price of the rights. If, after the rights have been triggered, an acquiring company were to merge or otherwise combine with Westvaco, or Westvaco were to sell 50% or more of its assets or earning power, each right would entitle its holder (other than the acquiror) to buy that number of shares of common stock of the acquiring company which, at the time of such transaction, would have a market value of two times the exercise price of the rights. The rights have no effect on earnings per share until they become exercisable. The rights expire in December 2007.

L. Stock option plans

At October 31, 1999, the company had five stock option plans. The 1983 and 1988 Stock Option and Stock Appreciation Rights Plans, 1995 Salaried Employee Stock Incentive Plan and the 1999

Salaried Employee Stock Incentive Plan provide for the granting of up to 4,725,000, 4,500,000, 4,837,500 and 5,000,000, respectively, of stock options and stock appreciation rights to key employees. The 1995 Non-Employee Director Stock Incentive Plan provides for the granting of up to 112,500 stock options and stock appreciation rights to outside directors. For the employee plans, stock options may be granted with or without stock appreciation rights and are granted at market value. They are exercisable after a period of six months to one year and expire not later than ten years from the date of grant. Under each employee plan, stock options may be granted with or without limited stock appreciation rights, which are exercisable upon the occurrence of certain events related to changes in corporate control. In 1999, nearly all outstanding limited stock appreciation rights, which had previously been granted to employees were cancelled or surrendered. In 1997, nearly all outstanding stock appreciation rights, which had previously been granted to employees and nonemployee directors, were cancelled or surrendered. Subject to limited exceptions, no new grants for stock appreciation rights were awarded during 1999.

The company applies APB Opinion 25, *Accounting for Stock Issued to Employees,* in accounting for its plans and, accordingly, no compensation cost has been recognized. If compensation cost for the company's stock options had been determined based on the fair value method of SFAS 123, *Accounting for Stock-Based Compensation,* the company's net income and net income per share would have been reduced to the pro forma amounts as follows:

In thousands, except per share	1999	1998	1997
Net income			
As reported	$111,176	$132,013	$162,700
Pro forma	107,924	127,470	159,089
Income per share–basic			
As reported	$1.11	$1.30	$1.60
Pro forma	1.08	1.26	1.56
Income per share–diluted			
As reported	$1.11	$1.30	$1.58
Pro forma	1.07	1.25	1.55

In determining the fair value of options for pro forma purposes, the company used the Black-Scholes option pricing model and assumed the following for options granted in 1999, 1998 and 1997, respectively: risk-free interest rate of 4.72%, 5.80% and 6.14%; dividend yield of 3.05%, 2.71% and 3.21%; an expected option life of six years for each year; and an expected volatility of 20% for each year. The weighted average fair values of the options granted during 1999, 1998 and 1997 were $5.34, $7.61 and $6.16 per share, respectively. The following table summarizes activity in the plans for 1999, 1998 and 1997:

	Options	Weighted average exercise price
Outstanding at October 31, 1996	4,438,224	$23.61
Granted	964,015	27.44
Exercised	[1,022,792]	21.92
Cancelled	[3,235]	24.55
Outstanding at October 31, 1997	4,376,212	24.84
Granted	981,780	32.53
Exercised	[218,159]	20.44
Cancelled	[992]	18.75
Outstanding at October 31, 1998	5,138,841	26.49
Granted	1,001,655	28.78
Exercised	[466,169]	22.31
Cancelled	[19,527]	26.71
Outstanding at October 31, 1999	5,654,800	27.24

The following table shows various information about stock options outstanding at October 31, 1999:

	Range of exercise prices			
	$18.29– $19.13	$23.08– $26.88	$27.44– $32.53	$18.29– $32.53
Number outstanding	128,322	2,639,003	2,887,475	5,654,800
Weighted average price	$18.52	$25.15	$29.63	$27.24
Weighted average remaining life (in years)	.85	4.84	8.10	6.41
Number exercisable	128,322	2,609,003	1,933,320	4,670,645
Weighted average price	$18.52	$25.16	$30.02	$26.92

There were 5,488,367 shares available for grant as of October 31, 1999 (1998–1,470,495, 1997–2,468,055). At October 31, 1999, 876,716 outstanding options had related limited stock appreciation rights.

M. Employee retirement, postretirement and postemployment benefits

Pension and retirement plans

The company provides retirement benefits for substantially all domestic employees under several noncontributory trusteed plans and also provides benefits to employees whose retirement benefits exceed maximum amounts permitted by current tax law under an unfunded benefit plan. Benefits are based on a final average pay formula for the salaried plans and a unit benefit formula for the hourly paid plans. Prior service costs are amortized on a straight-line basis over the average remaining service period for active employees. Contributions are made to the funded plans in accordance with ERISA requirements.

The 1999 net pension credit relating to employee pension and retirement benefits was $82,280,000 (1998 – $55,337,000, 1997– $42,058,000). The net pension credits reflect cumulative favorable investment returns on plan assets. The components of the net pension credit for 1999, 1998 and 1997 are as follows:

In thousands	1999	1998	1997
Service cost-benefits earned during the period	$ 28,966	$ 26,934	$ 23,369
Interest cost on projected benefit obligation	71,714	71,293	65,947
Expected return on plan assets	[171,223]	[148,042]	[126,808]
Net transition asset	[6,940]	[6,940]	[6,940]
Amortization of prior service cost	5,473	5,312	4,774
Net gain	[10,270]	[3,894]	[2,400]
Net pension credit	$[82,280]	$[55,337]	$[42,058]

Postretirement benefits

The company provides life insurance for substantially all retirees and medical benefits to certain retirees in the form of cost subsidies until medicare eligibility is reached and to certain other retirees, medical benefits up to a maximum lifetime amount. None of these benefits is funded. The components of net periodic postretirement benefits cost for the fiscal years ended October 31, 1999, 1998 and 1997 are as follows:

In thousands	1999	1998	1997
Service cost-benefits earned during the period	$1,200	$1,400	$1,300
Interest cost	1,200	1,500	1,500
Net amortization	[1,100]	[800]	[900]
Net periodic postretirement benefits cost	$1,300	$2,100	$1,900

The changes in the consolidated prepaid pension asset for defined benefit plans and the accrued postretirement benefit obligation are shown below. The net prepaid pension cost, from the following table, is included in other assets, except for an obligation of $24.1 million for an unfunded excess benefit plan which is recorded as a long-term liability.

The following table sets forth the funded status of the plans and amounts recognized in the consolidated balance sheet at October 31, based on a valuation date of July 31:

In thousands	Pension and retirement benefits		Postretirement benefits	
	1999	1998	1999	1998
Change in benefit obligation				
Benefit obligation at beginning of year	$1,084,468	$1,003,647	$ 23,200	$ 21,700
Service cost	28,966	26,934	1,200	1,400
Interest cost	71,714	71,293	1,200	1,500
Actuarial [gain] loss	[13,833]	24,205	[2,800]	1,100
Plan amendments	380	2,469	–	–
Termination benefits	1,491	–		
Benefits paid	[49,797]	[44,080]	[2,900]	[2,500]
Benefit obligation at end of year	$1,123,389	$1,084,468	$ 19,900	$ 23,200
Change in plan assets				
Fair value of plan assets at beginning of year	$2,337,713	$2,088,419	$ –	$ –
Actual return on plan assets	324,716	291,895	–	–
Company contributions	1,663	1,479	2,900	2,500
Benefits paid	[49,797]	[44,080]	[2,900]	[2,500]
Fair value of plan assets at end of year	$2,614,295	$2,337,713	$ –	$ –
Funded status of the plans	$1,490,906	$1,253,245	$[19,900]	$[23,200]
Unrecognized net actuarial [gain] loss	[1,017,279]	[860,223]	[7,100]	[5,300]
Unrecognized prior service cost [credit]	47,018	52,111	[100]	[200]
Unrecognized net transition obligation	[15,966]	[22,906]	–	–
Net prepaid [accrued] benefit cost included in the consolidated balance sheet	$ 504,679	$ 422,227	$[27,100]	$[28,700]
Prepaid benefit cost	$ 528,770	$ 444,075	$ –	$ –
Accrued benefit liability	[24,091]	[21,848]	[27,100]	[28,700]
Total recognized	$ 504,679	$ 422,227	$[27,100]	$[28,700]

Notes to Financial Statements

The assumptions used in the measurement of the company's benefit obligations are as follows:

	1999	1998	1997
Pension and retirement benefits			
Discount rate	6.75%	6.75%	7.25%
Expected return on plan assets	8.75%	9.50%	9.75%
Rate of compensation increase	5.00%	5.00%	5.50%
Postretirement benefits			
Discount rate	6.75%	6.75%	7.25%
Rate of compensation increase	5.00%	5.00%	5.50%

The annual rate of increase in health care costs was assumed at 6% for 1998, 5% for 1999 and remaining at that level thereafter. The effect of a 1% increase in the assumed health care cost trend rate would increase the July 31, 1999 accumulated postretirement benefit obligation by $288,000 and net postretirement benefits cost for 1999 by $70,000. The effect of a 1% decrease in the assumed health care cost trend rate would decrease the July 31, 1999 accumulated postretirement benefit obligation by $252,000 and the net postretirement benefits cost for 1999 by $63,000.

The company also has defined contribution plans that cover substantially all U.S. employees. Expense for company matching contributions under these plans was approximately $18.0 million in 1999, 1998 and 1997.

Postemployment benefits

The company provides limited postemployment benefits to former or inactive employees, including short-term disability, workers' compensation and severance.

N. Legal and environmental matters

The company is involved in various legal proceedings and environmental actions, generally arising in the normal course of its business. Although the ultimate outcome of such matters cannot be predicted with certainty, the company does not believe that the outcome of any proceeding, lawsuit or claim that is pending or threatened, or all of them combined, will have a material adverse effect on its consolidated financial position, liquidity or long-term results of operations. In any given quarter or quarters, however, it is possible such proceedings or matters could have a material effect on results of operations.

O. Business segment information

In 1997, the Financial Accounting Standards Board issued SFAS No. 131, *Disclosures about Segments of an Enterprise and Related Information,* which the company adopted at October 31, 1999. Adoption of the standard had no impact on our net income. Previously reported segment information has been restated to conform to the new standard.

Westvaco is a leading manufacturer of paper, packaging and chemicals serving both U.S. and international markets. The company's operating divisions have been classified into reportable segments based upon the nature of their products and services within these three major product categories, with separate disclosure of Rigesa, Ltda., our wholly owned Brazilian packaging subsidiary. Following is a description of our reportable business segments:

The paper segment is engaged in the manufacturing and marketing of printing grade papers and envelopes. All of this segment's operations are in the United States. It operates three mills in the eastern half of the country and manufactures envelopes at nine domestic plants.

The packaging segment manufactures, markets and distributes various bleached paperboard, kraft paper and board, corrugated shipping containers, food containers, folding cartons and cartons for liquid products. These products are manufactured at two domestic mills and two mills located in Brazil; paper and board are converted into packaging products at plants located in the eastern United States, Brazil and the Czech Republic. These products are sold primarily in the United States with additional markets located in Brazil, Europe, Asia and the Pacific Rim. In Brazil, Rigesa is a major producer of paperboard and corrugated packaging for the markets of that country. Operating results for Rigesa are subject to the economic conditions in Brazil, including its inflation and currency fluctuations.

The chemical segment manufactures products at four domestic locations. Major product groups are: activated carbon products and services; printing ink resins and lignin-based surfactants; tall oil fatty acid, rosin and derivative products.

The corporate and other segment includes the company's forestry operations and income and expense items and activities not directly associated with segment operations, including corporate support staff services and related assets and liabilities.

The segments are measured on operating profits before interest expense, income taxes, extraordinary items and cumulative effect of accounting changes, except for Rigesa in the packaging segment, whose operating profit includes interest income of $13.2 million in 1999 (1998–$14.6 million, 1997–$10.3 million) and interest expense of $4.6 million in 1999 (1998–$4.5 million, 1997–$6.1 million). The segments follow the same accounting principles described in the *Summary of Significant Accounting Policies*. Sales between the segments are recorded primarily at market prices. The restructuring charge following the completion of the company's strategic review related to paper, packaging and chemicals was $21.2 million, $57.7 million and $1.6 million, respectively.

No single customer accounts for 10% or more of consolidated trade sales in 1999. In 1998 and 1997, sales to a single customer accounted for approximately 11% of consolidated sales primarily from the company's packaging segment.

Total sales outside the United States, including sales of our foreign operating subsidiaries, accounted for approximately $663,483,000 in 1999 (1998–$709,567,000, 1997–$741,902,000). Export sales from the United States amounted to $504,480,000 in 1999 (1998–$499,792,000, 1997–$487,698,000).

Financial information by business segment follows:

In millions	Trade	Intersegment	Sales Total	Operating profit	Depreciation and amortization	Segment assets	Capital expenditures
Year ended October 31, 1999							
Paper	$1,005.1	$ 23.4	$1,028.5	$ 62.0	$100.6	$1,441.8	$ 60.0
Packaging	1,316.9	4.0	1,320.9	165.3	128.6	2,043.5	99.8
Rigesa	140.8	–	140.8	25.2	9.4	257.4	31.0
Packaging total	1,457.7	4.0	1,461.7	190.5	138.0	2,300.9	130.8
Chemical	293.9	20.6	314.5	52.5	23.8	314.7	18.1
Corporate and other	45.1	35.7	80.8	[157.0]	18.1	839.3	23.4
Total	2,801.8	83.7	2,885.5	148.0	280.5	4,896.7	232.3
Intersegment eliminations		[83.7]	[83.7]				
Consolidated totals	$2,801.8	$ –	$2,801.8	$148.0	$280.5	$4,896.7	$232.3
Year ended October 31, 1998							
Paper	$ 972.9	$ 52.7	$1,025.6	$ 84.8	$100.1	$1,497.2	$157.8
Packaging	1,380.2	4.0	1,384.2	172.3	128.1	2,146.6	158.6
Rigesa	184.0	–	184.0	35.2	12.4	322.4	41.1
Packaging total	1,564.2	4.0	1,568.2	207.5	140.5	2,469.0	199.7
Chemical	310.9	21.2	332.1	53.2	22.6	326.6	38.0
Corporate and other	37.9	34.8	72.7	[141.1]	17.8	715.9	24.2
Total	2,885.9	112.7	2,998.6	204.4	281.0	5,008.7	419.7
Intersegment eliminations		[112.7]	[112.7]				
Consolidated totals	$2,885.9	$ –	$2,885.9	$204.4	$281.0	$5,008.7	$419.7
Year ended October 31, 1997							
Paper	$1,003.3	$ 52.2	$1,055.5	$ 82.0	$ 96.2	$1,430.7	$236.7
Packaging	1,415.6	4.5	1,420.1	180.7	125.2	2,128.0	214.4
Rigesa	220.5	–	220.5	47.9	11.9	301.4	30.7
Packaging total	1,636.1	4.5	1,640.6	228.6	137.1	2,429.4	245.1
Chemical	304.5	19.3	323.8	49.1	17.1	304.6	97.6
Corporate and other	38.4	32.6	71.0	[113.1]	18.8	734.1	34.5
Total	2,982.3	108.6	3,090.9	246.6	269.2	4,898.8	613.9
Intersegment eliminations		[108.6]	[108.6]				
Consolidated totals	$2,982.3	$ –	$2,982.3	$246.6	$269.2	$4,898.8	$613.9

NOTES TO FINANCIAL STATEMENTS

P. Business combination

In October 1999, Westvaco signed a definitive agreement to acquire Temple-Inland's bleached paperboard mill in Evadale, TX. The company will pay $575 million for the mill's fixed assets and approximately $50 million for working capital. The acquisition will be accounted for as a purchase. The transaction is scheduled to close in December 1999. In connection with this pending acquisition, on November 5, 1999, the company issued $400,000,000 in notes comprised of $200,000,000 of 6.85% notes due November 15, 2004 and $200,000,000 of 7.10% notes due November 15, 2009.

Q. Subsequent event [unaudited]

On November 29, 1999, Westvaco signed a definitive agreement to acquire Mebane Packaging Group, a leading supplier of packaging for pharmaceutical products and personal care items. The sale is scheduled to close by the end of the first quarter of fiscal 2000.

R. Selected quarterly information [unaudited]

In thousands, except per share data

Quarter	1999	1998	1997
Sales			
First	$ 650,715	$ 702,113	$ 736,355
Second	679,481	724,187	724,593
Third	700,202	727,826	738,227
Fourth	771,451	731,791	783,113
Year	$2,801,849	$2,885,917	$2,982,288
Gross profit			
First	$ 119,239	$ 133,682	$ 131,145
Second	127,052	139,135	134,929
Third	139,515	130,835	137,467
Fourth	176,907	139,644	157,545
Year	$ 562,713	$ 543,296	$ 561,086
Net income			
First	$ 25,222	$ 32,516	$ 35,510
Second	27,295	34,606	37,940
Third	34,986	31,674	37,538
Fourth	23,673	33,217	51,712
Year	$ 111,176	$ 132,013	$ 162,700
Net income per common share – basic			
First	$ .25	$ .32	$ .35
Second	.27	.34	.37
Third	.35	.31	.37
Fourth	.24	.33	.51
Year	$1.11	$1.30	$1.60
Net income per common share – diluted			
First	$ .25	$ .32	$ .35
Second	.27	.34	.37
Third	.35	.31	.37
Fourth	.24	.33	.50
Year	$1.11	$1.30	$1.58

RESPONSIBILITY FOR FINANCIAL STATEMENTS

Management is responsible for the information and representations in the consolidated financial statements and related notes which appear on pages 21 through 33 as well as all other financial information contained in this report. These financial statements were prepared in accordance with generally accepted accounting principles and by necessity include some amounts determined using informed estimates and judgments.

Management is responsible for establishing and maintaining a system of internal control. The company's accounting systems include internal controls which management believes provide reasonable assurance of the reliability of its financial records and the proper safeguarding and use of its assets. In establishing the basis for reasonable assurance, management balances the cost of the internal controls with the benefits they provide. Additionally, it has long been the policy of the company to conduct its business affairs in accordance with high ethical standards, as set forth in the Westvaco Code of Conduct.

PricewaterhouseCoopers LLP, the company's independent accountants, were engaged to audit the consolidated financial statements and were responsible for conducting their audit in accordance with generally accepted auditing standards. The appointment of PricewaterhouseCoopers LLP as the company's independent accountants by the Board of Directors, on the recommendation of the Audit Committee, has been ratified each year by the shareholders. Their report immediately follows this statement.

The Audit Committee of the Board of Directors, composed solely of nonmanagement directors, meets regularly with the company's management, the internal audit manager and the independent accountants to discuss accounting and financial reporting matters and the nature, scope and results of audits. The Audit Committee meets with the independent accountants both with and without the presence of management. The committee also meets with the company's general counsel to review the company's legal compliance program as well as significant litigation issues. The independent accountants and the internal audit manager have full and free access to the Audit Committee.

John A. Luke, Jr.
Chairman, President and Chief Executive Officer

Karen R. Osar
Senior Vice President and Chief Financial Officer

November 17, 1999

REPORT OF INDEPENDENT ACCOUNTANTS

To the Board of Directors and Shareholders of Westvaco Corporation:

In our opinion, the consolidated financial statements appearing on pages 21 through 33 of this report present fairly, in all material respects, the financial position of Westvaco Corporation and its subsidiaries at October 31, 1999 and 1998, and the results of their operations and their cash flows for each of the three years in the period ended October 31, 1999, in conformity with generally accepted accounting principles. These financial statements are the responsibility of the company's management; our responsibility is to express an opinion on these financial statements based on our audits. We conducted our audits of these statements in accordance with generally accepted auditing standards which require that we plan and perform the

audit to obtain reasonable assurance about whether the financial statements are free of material misstatement. An audit includes examining, on a test basis, evidence supporting the amounts and disclosures in the financial statements, assessing the accounting principles used and significant estimates made by management and evaluating the overall financial statement presentation. We believe that our audits provide a reasonable basis for the opinion expressed above.

PricewaterhouseCoopers LLP

New York, New York
November 17, 1999

Year ended October 31	1999	1998	1997	1996	1995	1994	1993	1992	1991	1990	1989
EARNINGS In millions, except per share data											
Sales	$2,802	$2,886	$2,982	$3,045	$3,272	$2,607	$2,345	$2,336	$2,301	$2,411	$2,284
Net income before extraordinary charge and cumulative effect of accounting changes	111	132	163	212	283	104	57	136	137	188	223
Net income	111[1]	132[2]	163	212	281[3]	104	104[4]	136	137[5]	188	223
Net income per share – basic	1.11	1.30	1.60	2.09	2.78	1.03	1.04	1.37	1.40	1.93	2.30
Net income per share – diluted	1.11	1.30	1.58	2.07	2.76	1.03	1.04	1.36	1.39	1.92	2.28
Depreciation and amortization	280	281	269	240	230	219	195	183	179	169	156
COMMON STOCK											
Number of common shareholders	19,070	20,140	20,240	20,760	20,490	13,890	14,570	14,970	15,020	15,630	15,530
Weighted average number of shares outstanding [in millions]											
Basic	100	101	102	102	101	101	100	99	98	98	97
Diluted	100	102	103	102	102	101	101	100	99	98	98
Cash dividends [in millions]	$88	$89	$90	$90	$78	$74	$73	$73	$70	$66	$61
Per share:											
Dividends	.88	.88	.88	.88	.77	.73⅓	.73⅓	.73⅓	.70⅚	.67½	.62⅔
Book value	21.65	22.39	22.35	21.69	20.49	18.48	18.18	17.84	17.21	16.53	15.27
FINANCIAL POSITION In millions											
Working capital	$313	$272	$400	$297	$358	$269	$244	$319	$310	$370	$328
Current ratio	1.7	1.6	2.0	1.7	1.8	1.7	1.7	1.9	2.0	2.2	2.1
Plant and timberlands, net	$3,581	$3,802	$3,684	$3,354	$3,140	$3,063	$3,078	$2,838	$2,675	$2,539	$2,240
Total assets	4,897	5,009	4,899	4,437	4,253	3,983	3,928	3,704	3,462	3,332	2,961
Long-term obligations	1,502	1,526	1,513	1,153	1,147	1,234	1,258	1,055	970	961	768
Shareholders' equity	2,171	2,246	2,279	2,210	2,081	1,862	1,824	1,777	1,699	1,619	1,488
Debt to total capital	34%	34%	34%	29%	30%	34%	35%	31%	31%	32%	29%
OPERATIONS											
Primary production of paper, paperboard and market pulp [tons, in thousands]	2,992	3,028	3,058	3,001	3,105	2,848	2,626	2,595	2,587	2,512	2,499
New investment in plant and timberlands [in millions]	$232	$420	$614	$511	$309	$207	$442	$352	$322	$472	$537
Acres of timberlands owned [in thousands]	1,446	1,465	1,461	1,452	1,453	1,453	1,462	1,468	1,483	1,487	1,467
Employees	12,750	13,070	13,370	13,430	14,300	14,170	14,440	14,520	14,440	15,040	14,960

The following per share data is for basic and diluted:

1 1999 results include an after-tax charge for restructuring of $49 million, or $.49 per share, and a credit of $15 million, or $.15 per share, for a release of deferred taxes.

2 1998 results include an after-tax charge for restructuring of $3 million, or $.03 per share.

3 1995 results include an after-tax extraordinary charge of $2 million, or $.02 per share, for the extinguishment of debt.

4 1993 results include income of $55 million, or $.55 per share, from the cumulative effect of accounting changes, a provision of $12 million, or $.12 per share, for the impact of an increase in the federal income tax rate, an extraordinary charge of $8 million, or $.07 per share, for the extinguishment of high interest rate debt and a charge for restructuring of $26 million, or $.26 per share.

5 1991 results include an after-tax charge for restructuring of $15 million, or $.16 per share.